Dylan's Visions of Sin

Dylan's Visions of Sin

CHRISTOPHER RICKS

An Imprint of HarperCollins*Publishers*

HarperCollins books may be purchased for educational, business, or sales promotional use. For information, please write: Special Markets Department, HarperCollins Publishers Inc., 10 East 53rd Street, New York, NY 10022.

First published in 2003 by the Penguin Group, London, England

FIRST AMERICAN EDITION 2004

The acknowledgments on pp. 491–9 constitute an extension of this copyright page

Library of Congress Cataloging-in-Publication Data

Ricks, Christopher B.
Dylan's visions of sin / Christopher Ricks.
p. cm.
Includes bibliographical references.
ISBN 0-06-059923-5
1. Dylan, Bob, 1941—Criticism and interpretation. 2. Sin in music. I. Title
ML420.D98R53 2004
2004042056

04 05 06 07 08 QF 10 9 8 7 6 5 4

Contents

Sins, Virtues, Heavenly Graces

Of the seven deadly sins, Roger considered himself qualified in gluttony, sloth and lust but distinguished in anger.

Kingsley Amis, *One Fat Englishman*

Any qualified critic to any distinguished artist: All I really want to do is – what, exactly? Be friends with you? Assuredly, I don't want to do you in, or select you or dissect you or inspect you or reject you.

Maybe so. Anyway, Bob Dylan has made it clear that he is not favourably disposed towards critics in general (for all his being a favourite of so many of them), and – in particular – not favourably disposed towards critics who "dissect my songs like rabbits".[1]

Pulling rabbits out of hats, on the other hand, provided that he provides the hats: this may on occasion be something else.

As a student at Cambridge long ago (1928?), the young William Empson impressed his teacher, the not much older I. A. Richards, by his spirited dealings with a Shakespeare sonnet. "Taking the sonnet as a conjurer takes his hat, he produced an endless swarm of rabbits from it and ended by 'You could do that with any poetry, couldn't you?'" But only if the poetry truly teems, and only if the critic only *seems* to be a conjurer. What, then, is the critic's enterprise? To give grounds for the faith that is in him, in us, in those of us who are grateful. It is a privilege.

Dylan is not the first artist to clarify his responsibilities as he does: "I'm the first person who'll put it to you and the last person who'll explain it to you."[2] William Empson himself had a comically modest turn of phrase for the thing he needed first of all: *the right handle to take hold of the bundle.* Dylan handles sin. Manhandles it, sometimes, as burly burlesque.

> Jeremiah preached repentance
> To those who would turn from hell

---

[1] He says as much, and more, on *Biograph*, the anthology of his work that came with a commentary by him.

[2] Interview with Jonathan Cott, *Rolling Stone* (16 November 1978).

But the critics gave him bad reviews
Even threw him to the bottom of the well
(*Yonder Comes Sin*)

Jeremiah's in the well. "And they let down Jeremiah with cords. And in the dungeon there was no water, but mire: so Jeremiah sunk in the mire" (Jeremiah 38:6).

She opened up a book of poems and handed it to me, written by an English poet from the fourteenth century: *Handling Sin*.[1] Handling sin is for me the right handle to take hold of the bundle. My left hand waving free.

"Fools they made a mock of sin."[2] Dylan's is an art in which sins are laid bare (and resisted), virtues are valued (and manifested), and the graces brought home. The seven deadly sins, the four cardinal virtues (harder to remember?), and the three heavenly graces: these make up everybody's world – but Dylan's in particular. Or rather, his worlds, since human dealings of every kind are his for the artistic seizing. Pride is anatomized in *Like a Rolling Stone*, Envy in *Positively 4th Street*, Anger in *Only a Pawn in Their Game* . . . But Dylan creates Songs of Redemption (Allen Ginsberg's phrase), and so – hearteningly – Justice can reclaim *Hattie Carroll*, Fortitude *Blowin' in the Wind*, Faith *Precious Angel*, Hope *Forever Young*, and Charity *Watered-Down Love*.

What, in Dylan's eyes, are the words of his to which people have mostly turned a deaf ear? "The things I have to say about such things as ghetto bosses, salvation and sin, lust, murderers going free, and children without hope –"[3]

"The glamour and the bright lights and the politics of sin": this wide-sweeping fiercely lit line was held aloft by an interviewer. The line is from *Dead Man, Dead Man*. Interviews can be a form of living death, and Samuel Beckett once declined to be interviewed, saying to his friend: Not even for you, and in any case I have no views to inter. The politics of sin?

It just came to me when I was writing that's the way it is . . . the diplomacy of sin. The way they take sin, and put it in front of people . . . the way

---

[1] A verse translation, by Robert Mannyng, of a manual of the sins, by William of Wadington.

[2] *In the Summertime*. Proverbs 14:9: "Fools make a mock at sin."

[3] Interview with Scott Cohen, *Spin* (December 1985).

sin is taken and split up and categorised and put on different levels so that it becomes more of a structure of sin, or "These Sins are big ones, these are little ones, these can hurt this person, these can hurt you, this is bad for this reason and that is bad for another reason." The politics of sin; that's what I think of it.[1]

But it is in Dylan's music, not in his musings, that what he most deeply thinks of sin can be heard and felt. The word "sin" haunts the songs, with a range of insinuations such as should make us think.

People tell me it's a sin

Because he sinned I got no choice, it run in my vein

And there are no sins inside the Gates of Eden

That hollow place where martyrs weep and angels play with sin

Where charity is supposed to cover up a multitude of sins

To the sin of love's false security

I didn't commit no ugly sin

I'm gonna baptize you in fire so you can sin no more

They like to take all this money from sin, build big universities to study in

Well, if you can't quit your sinnin' . . .[2]

And if Dylan can't quit your sinnin'?

Desolation Row is a masque of the sins, worthy (in its pageant of unworthiness) of the Seven Deadly Sins who cavort in Marlowe's *Doctor Faustus* – Doctor Faustus, otherwise known as Doctor Filth, aided and abetted by his nurse:

> She's in charge of the cyanide hole
> And she also keeps the cards that read
> "Have Mercy on His Soul"

[1] Interview with Neil Spencer, *New Musical Express* (15 August 1981).
[2] *Simple Twist of Fate, Pressing On, Gates of Eden, Dirge, Something's Burning, Baby, Ballad in Plain D, Who Killed Davey Moore?, Bye and Bye, Foot of Pride,* and *Quit Your Low Down Ways.*

Her sin is her life-threatening officiousness. She has been preceded in the parade by Ophelia: "Her sin is her lifelessness."

Desolation Row sees and shows a Vision of Sin. Tennyson saw and showed *The Vision of Sin*:

> I had a vision when the night was late:
> A youth came riding toward a palace-gate.

The hour is getting late. One rider was approaching. The wind began to howl:

> Then the music touched the gates and died;
> Rose again from where it seemed to fail,
> Stormed in orbs of song, a growing gale.

There are seven deadly sins, but only four cardinal virtues (Justice, Prudence, Temperance, and Fortitude). Seven to four? But do not despair, for here come the three heavenly graces: Faith, Hope, and Charity. Seven-a-side, then. But there is imbalance still. The antonym of guilt is innocence, the antonym of a virtue is a vice – but what, pray, is the antonym of a sin?

Furthermore, isn't it rather bewildering that the sins, as they mount their masque, enjoy masquerading as one another? For lust can be seen as one form that may be taken by greed or gluttony, as can covetousness or avarice. "One sin very naturally leans on another": there is something appropriately creepy about this seventeenth-century description (by Thomas Wilson) of the pleasure that sins take in their leanings, in their *overlapping*.

A sin will have to be set, first and foremost, in opposition to the goodness that opposes it. Gratitude will have no truck with envy. Thomas Wilson again:

Every virtue consists in denying some corrupt inclination of our depraved nature; in opposing and resisting all temptations to the contrary vice; charity, in opposing continually self-love and envy; humility, in resisting all temptations to pride, etc.

But some of the discriminations that need to be made are more elusive. How confident can we be, for instance, in distinguishing a sin from the goodness to which it is immediately adjacent? Envy, bad: emulation of an honourable kind, good. Sloth, bad: relaxedness, good. Pride, bad: pride, good.

And then there are sins of omission. "Forgive me, baby, for what I didn't do" (*Maybe Someday*). *In the Summertime*, before it came to shake its head sorrowingly ("Fools they made a mock of sin"), had asked:

> Did you respect me for what I did
> Or for what I didn't do, or for keeping it hid?

Waltzing with Sin is not a Dylan song, but it danced along on *The Basement Tapes*. Dylan likes setting to music our besetting sins. He likes company in doing so, and he likes the comedy that company encourages. Which is one reason why *7 Deadly Sins* was issued by a joint stock company, the Traveling Wilburys.

> 7 deadly sins
> That's how the world begins
> Watch out when you step in
> For 7 deadly sins
> That's when the fun begins
> 7 deadly sins
>
> Sin number one was when you left me
> Sin number two you said goodbye
> Sin number three was when you told me a little white lie
>
> 7 deadly sins
> Once it starts it never ends
> Watch out around the bend
> For 7 deadly sins
>
> Sin number four was when you looked my way
> Sin number five was when you smiled
> Sin number six was when you let me stay
> Sin number seven was when you touched me and drove me wild
>
> 7 deadly sins
> So many rules to bend
> Time and time again
> 7 deadly sins

One of the endearing things about the song, tucked up in all innocence, is that there don't actually seem to be seven sins on the go at all. Just one good old one. Touching, really.

The claim in this book isn't that most of Dylan's songs, or even most of the best ones, are bent on sin. Simply that (for the present venture in criticism) handling sin may be the right way to take hold of the bundle. Dylan himself may make a mock of the idea that songs are *about* things, but he did speak of the "things I have to say about such things as ghetto bosses, salvation and sin". And even in his travesty of owlishness (the notes accompanying *World Gone Wrong*), he heads these comments of his on other men's songs with the words:

ABOUT THE SONGS
(what they're about)

Of *Broke Down Engine*, Dylan remarks (in a way that may freewheel, but is not out of control) that "it's about Ambiguity, the fortunes of the privileged elite, flood control – watching the red dawn not bothering to dress". So I shall take Ambiguity as an excuse for returning to the author of *Seven Types of Ambiguity*, William Empson.[1]

Empson explained why he came to do the explaining in which he took delight. His method, verbal analysis, started simply from the pleasure of his response to a poem.

I felt sure that the example was beautiful and that I had, broadly speaking, reacted to it correctly. But I did not at all know what had happened in this "reaction"; I did not know why the example was beautiful. And it seemed to me that I was able in some cases partly to explain my feelings to myself by teasing out the meanings of the text.[2]

Empson's example is crucial to me, not only in its happiness, but in his not being dead set upon convincing anybody else that a particular poem

---

[1] Coincidence is one of the few pleasures left in life. So: Dylan, "fortunes . . . the red dawn"/Empson, "for the Red Dawn" (*Note on Local Flora*). Dylan, "flood control"/Empson, "Glut me with floods" (*Aubade*). And Dylan, "the privileged elite . . . not bothering to dress"/Empson, "In evening dress in rafts upon the main" (*Your Teeth are Ivory Towers*). But it is time for flood control.

[2] *Seven Types of Ambiguity* (1930, second edition 1947), p. x.

is good. The idea was not so much to show someone that a poem is good, as to go some way towards showing how it comes to be good, so very good.

You think that the poem is worth the trouble before you choose to go into it carefully, and you know more about what it is worth when you have done so.[1]

In the same spirit, I think of what I am doing as prizing songs, not as prising-open minds. (Most people who are likely to read this book will already know what they feel about Dylan, though they may not always know quite why they feel it or what they think.)

I think that nowadays we can explain why Milton was right, but the explanations usually seem long and fanciful; they would only convince men who believed already that the line was beautiful, and wanted to know why.[2]

Literary criticism – unlike, say, music criticism or art criticism – enjoys the advantage of existing in the same medium (language) as the art that it explores and esteems. This can give to literary criticism a delicacy and an inwardness that are harder to achieve elsewhere. But, at the same time, this may be why literary critics are given to competitive envy: What I'd like to know, given that he and I are working in the same medium, in the same line of work, really, is why *I* am attending to *Tennyson*, instead of *his* attending to *me* . . .

And then there is the age-old difficulty and problem of *intention*. Briefly: I believe that an artist is someone more than usually blessed with a cooperative unconscious or subconscious, more than usually able to effect things with the help of instincts and intuitions of which he or she is not necessarily conscious. Like the great athlete, the great artist is at once highly trained and deeply instinctual. So if I am asked whether I believe that Dylan is *conscious* of all the subtle effects of wording and timing that I suggest, I am perfectly happy to say that he probably isn't. And if I am right, then in this he is not less the artist but more. There are such things as unconscious intentions (think of the unthinking Freudian slip). What matters is that Dylan is doing

---

[1] *Seven Types of Ambiguity*, p. xiii.

[2] Empson, *Obscurity and Annotation* (1930), in *Argufying*, ed. John Haffenden (1987), p. 78.

the imagining, not that he be fully deliberatedly conscious of the countless intimations that are in his art. As he put it:

As you get older, you get smarter and that can hinder you because you try to gain control over the creative impulse. Creativity is not like a freight train going down the tracks. It's something that has to be caressed and treated with a great deal of respect. If your mind is intellectually in the way, it will stop you. You've got to program your brain not to think too much.[1]

A shrewd turn, this, the contrariety of "You've got to program your brain" and the immediate "not to think too much".

T. S. Eliot, who knew that it "is not always true that a person who knows a good poem when he sees it can tell us why it is a good poem", knew as well that "the poet does many things upon instinct, for which he can give no better account than anybody else".[2]

Still, there are many admirers of Dylan who instinctively feel that adducing Mr Eliot when talking about Dylan is pretentious and portentous. So let me take an instance of a Dylan / Eliot intersection that is not of my finding (though I shall do a little developing). The *Telegraph* (Winter 1987) included a note:[3]

On a more literary level, had you noticed that *Maybe Someday* quotes from T. S. Eliot? In *Journey of the Magi*, Eliot has:

>   And the cities hostile and the towns unfriendly

Later in the same poem there's mention too of "pieces of silver". So in Dylan's lines:

>   Through hostile cities and unfriendly towns
>   Thirty pieces of silver, no money down

I remember the excitement I felt when I myself noticed Dylan's debt (*many* pieces of silver) – and then the unwarrantable disappointment I felt when I later discovered from the *Telegraph* that I was not the first to discover

---

[1] *USA Today* (15 February 1995).
[2] *The Use of Poetry and the Use of Criticism* (1933, second edition 1964), pp. 17, 129–30.
[3] By Graham Ashton and / or John Bauldie.

it. Mustn't be hostile or unfriendly about this not-being-the-first business. (The first shall be last.) But then the song is a tissue of memories of the poem. Here are a few more moments.

Eliot	*Dylan*
an open door	breakin' down no bedroom door
the voices singing in our ears	a voice from on high
it was (you may say) satisfactory	when I say / you'll be satisfied
I remember	you'll remember
all that way	every kind of way

Take what you have gathered from coincidence, yes, but these are not coincidences, once you concede that the likeness of Eliot's "And the cities hostile and the towns unfriendly" to Dylan's "Through hostile cities and unfriendly towns" goes beyond happenstance. Such a likeness, then, may give some warrant for taking literarily the art of the man who imagined Ezra Pound and T. S. Eliot fighting in the captain's tower.

Note

I wrote about Dylan in the *Listener* in 1972 (1 June); I gave a BBC talk, *Bob Dylan and the Language that He Used*, in 1976 (22 March); over the years there were talks, some of them again for the BBC, and one that was printed in the *Threepenny Review* in 1990.[1] Much of this, it's all been written in the book, but there are some further thoughts about Dylan not included here, to be found in my essay on *Clichés* and in the one on *American English and the inherently transitory*, both in *The Force of Poetry* (1984).

The words of the songs are quoted here in the form in which he sings them on the officially released albums on which they initially appeared. The Index of Dylan's Songs and Writings, at the back, is supplemented by a General Index and by a list, Which Album a Song is on.

The new edition of the lyrics, *Lyrics 1962–2002*, unlike the original *Writings and Drawings* and the later *Lyrics 1962–1985*, is apparently not going

[1] Later in *Hiding in Plain Sight*, ed. Wendy Lesser (1993).

to include Dylan's *Some Other Kinds of Songs* . . ., or his other poems and miscellaneous prose, so for these I give references to the earlier collections.

The discrepancies between the printed and the other versions (whether officially released, studio out-takes, or bootlegged from performances) are notable. Sometimes they are noted in the commentary here. Clearly they are of relevance to Dylan's intentions or changes of intention, and I have to admit that sometimes one performance decides to do without an effect that another has, and that I had thought and still think exquisite – for instance, the plaiting of the rhymes at the end of *If Not For You*. Oh well. I think of Shakespearean revision. Sometimes I read (or rather, listen) and sigh and wish.

Songs, Poems, Rhymes

Songs, Poems

Dylan has always had a way with words. He does not simply have his way with them, since a true comprehender of words is no more their master than he or she is their servant. The triangle of Dylan's music, his voices, and his unpropitiatory words: this is still his equilateral thinking.

One day a critic may do justice not just to all three of these independent powers, but to their interdependence in Dylan's art. The interdependence doesn't have to be a competition, it is a culmination – the word chosen by Allen Ginsberg, who could be an awe-inspiring poet and was an endearingly awful music-maker, for whom Dylan's songs were "the culmination of Poetry-music as dreamt of in the '50s & early '60s".[1] Dylan himself has answered when asked:

Why are you doing what you're doing?
[*Pause*] "Because I don't know anything else to do. I'm good at it."
How would you describe "it"?
"I'm an artist. I try to create art."[2]

What follows this clarity, or follows from it, has been differently put by him over the forty years, finding itself crediting the words and the music variously at various times. The point of juxtaposing his utterances isn't to catch him out, it is to see him catching different emphases in all this, undulating and diverse.

WORDS RULE, OKAY?

"I consider myself a poet first and a musician second."[3]

[1] Ginsberg's sleeve-notes to *Desire*.
[2] Interview with Ron Rosenbaum (November 1977), *Playboy* (March 1978).
[3] To Robert Shelton, *Melody Maker* (29 July 1978).

"It ain't the melodies that're important man, it's the words."[1]

MUSIC RULES, OKAY?

"Anyway it's the song itself that matters, not the sound of the song. I only look
at them musically. I only look at them as things to sing. It's the music that the
words are sung to that's important. I write the songs because I need something
to sing. It's the difference between the words on paper and the song. The song
disappears into the air, the paper stays."[2]

NEITHER ACOUSTIC NOR ELECTRIC RULES, OKAY?

Do you prefer playing acoustic over electric?
"They're pretty much equal to me. I try not to deface the song with electricity
or non-electricity. I'd rather get something out of the song verbally and phonetically
than depend on tonality of instruments."[3]

JOINT RULE, OKAY?

Would you say that the words are more important than the music?
"The words are just as important as the music. There would be no music without
the words."[4]

"It's not just pretty words to a tune or putting tunes to words, there's nothing
that's exploited. The words and the music, I can hear the sound of what I
want to say."[5]

"The lyrics to the songs . . . just so happens that it might be a little stranger than in
most songs. I find it easy to write songs. I have been writing songs for a long time
and the words to the songs aren't written out for just the paper, they're written
as you can read it, you dig? If you take whatever there is to the song away – the

---

[1] Anthony Scaduto, *Bob Dylan* (1971, revised edition 1973), p. 135.
[2] New York City (January 1968); *Newsweek* (February 1968); *Bob Dylan in His Own
Words*, compiled by Miles (1978), p. 90.
[3] *USA Today* (15 February 1995).
[4] Press conference / interview with Ralph J. Gleason (1965), *Rolling Stone* (14 December
1967, 20 January 1968).
[5] Probably Chicago (November 1965); *Bob Dylan in His Own Words*, p. 61.

beat, the melody – I could still recite it. I see nothing wrong with songs you can't do that with either – songs that, if you took the beat and melody away, they wouldn't stand up. Because they're not supposed to do that you know. Songs are songs."[1]

What's more important to you: the way that your music and words sound, or the content, the message?
"The whole thing while it's happening. The whole total sound of the words, what's really going down is –"[2]

– at which point Dylan cuts across himself, at a loss for words with which to speak of words in relation to the whole total: "it either happens or it doesn't happen, you know". At a loss, but finding the relation again and again in the very songs.

It ought to be possible, then, to attend to Dylan's words without forgetting that they are one element only, one medium, of his art. Songs are different from poems, and not only in that a song combines three media: words, music, voice. When Dylan offered as the jacket-notes for *Another Side of Bob Dylan* what mounted to a dozen pages of poems, he headed this *Some Other Kinds of Songs . . .* His ellipsis was to give you time to think. In our time, a dot dot dot communication.

Philip Larkin was to record his poems, so the publishers sent round an order form inviting you to hear the voice of the *Toads* bard. The form had a message from the poet, encouraging you – or was it discouraging you? For there on the form was Larkin insisting, with that ripe lugubrious relish of his, that the "proper place for my poems is the printed page", and warning you how much you would lose if you listened to the poems read aloud: "Think of all the mis-hearings, the *their / there* confusions, the submergence of rhyme, the disappearance of stanza shape, even the comfort of knowing how far you are from the end." Again, Larkin in an interview, lengthening the same lines:

I don't give readings, no, although I have recorded three of my collections, just to show how *I* should read them. Hearing a poem, as opposed to reading it on the page, means you miss so much – the shape, the punctuation, the italics, even

---

[1] Los Angeles (16 December 1965); *Bob Dylan in His Own Words*, p. 63.
[2] Press conference / interview with Ralph J. Gleason (1965), *Rolling Stone* (14 December 1967, 20 January 1968).

knowing how far you are from the end. Reading it on the page means you can go your own pace, take it in properly; hearing it means you're dragged along at the speaker's own rate, missing things, not taking it in, confusing "there" and "their" and things like that. And the speaker may interpose his own personality between you and the poem, for better or worse. For that matter, so may the audience. I don't like hearing things in public, even music. In fact, I think poetry readings grew up on a false analogy with music: the text is the "score" that doesn't "come to life" until it's "performed". It's false because people can read words, whereas they can't read music. When you write a poem, you put everything into it that is needed: the reader should "hear" it just as clearly as if you were in the room saying it to him. And of course this fashion for poetry readings has led to a kind of poetry that you can understand first go: easy rhythms, easy emotions, easy syntax. I don't think it stands up on the page.[1]

The human senses have different powers and limits, which is why it is good that we have five (or is it six?) of them. When you read a poem, when you see it on the page, you register – whether consciously or not – that this is a poem in, say, three stanzas: I've read one, I'm now reading the second, there's one to go. This is the feeling as you read a poem, and it's always a disconcerting collapse when (if your curiosity hasn't made you flick over the pages before starting the poem) you turn the page and find, "Oh, that was the end. How curious." Larkin's own endings are consummate. And what he knows is that your ear cannot hear the end approaching in the way in which your eye – the organ that allows you to read – sees the end of the poem approaching. You may, of course, know the music well, and so be well aware that the end is coming, but such awareness is a matter of familiarity and knowledge, whereas with a poem that you have never seen before, you yet can see perfectly well that this is the final stanza that you are now reading.

Of sonnet-writing, Gerard M. Hopkins wrote of both seeing and hearing "the emphasis which has been gathering through the sonnet and then delivers itself in those two lines seen by the eye to be final or read by the voice with a deepening of note and slowness of delivery".[2]

For the eye can always simply see more than it is reading, looking at; the ear cannot, in this sense (given what the sense of hearing is), hear a

---

[1] *Paris Review* interview (1982); *Required Writing* (1983), p. 61.
[2] *On the Origin of Beauty: A Platonic Dialogue* (1865); *The Note-Books and Papers of Gerard Manley Hopkins*, ed. Humphry House (1937), p. 71.

larger span than it is receiving. This makes the relation of an artist like Dylan to song and ending crucially different from the relation of an artist like Donne or Larkin to ending. The eye sees that it is approaching its ending, as Jane Austen can make jokes about your knowing that you're hastening towards perfect felicity because there are only a few pages left of the novel. A novel physically tells you that it is about to come to an end. *The French Lieutenant's Woman* in one sense didn't work, couldn't work, because you knew perfectly well that since it was by John Fowles and not by a post-modernist wag there was bound to be print on those pages still to come, the last hundred pages. So it couldn't be about to end, isn't that right?, because this chunk of it was still there, to come. But then John Fowles, like J. H. Froude, whose Victorian novel he was imitating in this matter of alternative endings, knows this and tries to build this, too, into the effect of his book.

Dylan has an ear for a tune, whether it's his, newly minted, or someone else's, newly mounted. He has a voice that can't be ignored and that ignores nothing, although it spurns a lot. Dylan when young did what only great artists do: define anew the art he practised. Marlon Brando made people understand something different by *acting*. He couldn't act? Very well, but he did something very well, and what else are you going to call it? Dylan can't sing?

Every song, by definition, is realized only in performance. True. A more elusive matter is whether every song is suited to re-performance. Could there be such a thing as a performance that you couldn't imagine being improved upon, even by a genius in performance? I can't imagine his doing better by *The Lonesome Death of Hattie Carroll*, for instance, than he does on *The Times They Are A-Changin'*. Of course I have to concede at once that my imagination is immensely smaller than his, and it would serve me right, as well as being wonderfully right, if he were to prove me wrong. But, as yet, what (for me) is gained in a particular re-performing of this particular song (and yes, there are indeed gains) has always fallen short of what had to be sacrificed. Any performance, like any translation, necessitates sacrifice, and I believe that it would be misguided, and even unwarrantably protective of Dylan, to suppose that his decisions as to what to sacrifice in performance could never be misguided. Does it not make sense, then, to believe, or to argue, that Dylan's realizing of *The Lonesome Death of Hattie Carroll* was perfect, a perfect song perfectly rendered, once and for all?

Clearly Dylan doesn't believe so, or he wouldn't re-perform it. He makes judgements as to what to perform again, and he assuredly does not re-perform every great song (you don't hear *Oxford Town* or *Sad-Eyed Lady of the Lowlands* in concert). Admittedly there are a good many good reasons why a song might not be re-performed, matters of quality newly judged, or aptness to an occasion or to a time, or a change of conviction, all of which means that the entire rightness of a previous performance wouldn't have to be what was at issue. Still, Dylan takes bold imaginative decisions as to what songs to re-perform, so can we really not ask whether there are occasions on which a particular decision, though entirely within his rights and doing credit to his renovations and aspirations and audacities, is one for which the song has been asked to pay too high a price? "Those songs have a life of their own."[1]

I waver about this when it comes to this song, one of Dylan's greatest, *The Lonesome Death of Hattie Carroll*, even while I maintain that the historical songs, the songs of conscience, can't be re-created in the same way as the more personal (not more personally felt) songs of consciousness, with the same *kind* of freedom. "The chimes of freedom" sometimes have to be in tune with different responsibilities. Dylan can't, I believe, command a new vantage-point (as he might in looking back upon a failed love or a successful one) from which to see the senseless killing of Hattie Carroll. Or, at least, the question can legitimately come up as to whether he can command a new vantage-point without commanding her and even perhaps wronging her.

He makes the song new, yes, but in the mid 1970s, for example, he sometimes did so by sounding too close for comfort to the tone of William Zanzinger's tongue ("and sneering, and his tongue it was snarling"). "Doomed and determined to destroy all the gentle": the song is rightly siding with the gentle, and it asks (asks this of its creator, too) that it be sounded gently. But then the song can be sung too gently, with not enough sharp-edged dismay.

I used to put this too categorically, and therefore wrongly:

He cannot re-perform the song. He unfortunately still does. There is no other way of singing this song than the way in which he realizes it on *The Times They Are A-Changin'*. If he sings it any more gently, he sentimentalizes it. If he sings it any more ungently, he allies himself with Zanzinger.[2]

---

[1] Interview with Robert Shelton, *Melody Maker* (29 July 1978).

[2] A talk published in the *Threepenny Review* (1990) and then in *Hiding in Plain Sight*, ed. Wendy Lesser (1993).

Alex Ross, of the *New Yorker*, who is generous towards my appreciation of Dylan, thinks any such reservation narrow-minded of me:

Ricks went on to criticize some of Dylan's more recent performances of *Hattie Carroll*, in which he pushes the last line a little: "He doesn't let it speak for itself. He sentimentalizes it, I'm afraid." Here I began to wonder whether the close reader had zoomed in too close. Ricks seemed to be fetishizing the details of a recording, and denying the musician license to expand his songs in performance.[1]

I bridle slightly at that *fetishizing-a-recording* bit. (What, me? All the world knows that it is women's shoes that I am into.) Nor do I think of myself as at all denying Dylan licence to expand his songs. (Who's going to take away his licence to expand?) I'm only proposing that, although he has entire licence in any such matter, freedom is different from (in one sense) licence, and it must be that on occasion an artist who is on a scale to take immense risks will fall short of his newest highest hopes. Samuel Beckett has the courage to fail, and he urges *fail better*. He knows there's no success like failure. And that it is not clear what success would mean if failure were not exactly rare but simply unknown. Dylan in 1965:

I know some of the things I do wrong. I do a couple of things wrong. Once in a while I do something really wrong, y' know, which I really can't see when I'm involved in it; and after a while I look at it later, I know it's wrong. I don't say nothin' about it.[2]

It is the greatest artists who have taken the greatest risks, and it is impossible to see what it would mean to respect the artists for this if on every single occasion you were to find that the risks that were run simply ran away. Doesn't it then start to look as though the risks were only "risks"? If you were, for instance, to think of revision as a form that re-performing may take when it comes to the written word, it is William Wordsworth and Henry James, the most imaginative and unremitting of revisers, who on occasion get it wrong and who lose more than they gain when it comes to some of their audacious post-publication revisions.

Hattie Carroll is a special, though not a unique, case. "License to expand

[1] *New Yorker* (10 May 1999).
[2] *Whaaat?* (the 1965 interview with Nat Hentoff, in full, differing from *Playboy*, March 1966), p. 17.

his songs"? But strait is the gate, and narrow is the way, which leadeth unto life, and few there be that find it. It must at least be possible that the gains of re-performing this particular song could fall short of the losses.

Alex Ross went on at once to evoke beautifully the beauty of a particular re-performing:

I had just seen Dylan sing *Hattie Carroll*, in Portland, and it was the best performance that I heard him give. He turned the accompaniment into a steady, sad acoustic waltz, and he played a lullabylike solo at the center. You were reminded that the "hotel society gathering" was a Spinsters' Ball, whose dance went on before, during, and after the fatal attack on Hattie Carroll. This was an eerie twist on the meaning of the song, and not a sentimental one.

Why am I, though touched by this, not persuaded by it? Because when Ross says "You were reminded that the 'hotel society gathering' was a Spinsters' Ball", his word "reminded" is specious. At no point in *Hattie Carroll* is there any allusion to this. You can have heard the song a thousand times and not call this to mind, since Dylan does not call it into play. Is Ross really maintaining that the performance alluded to a detail of the newspaper story that never made it into the song, which doesn't say anything about a Ball, Spinsters' or Bachelors'? And that such an allusion would then simply validate a thoroughgoing waltz?

Dylan must be honoured for honouring his responsibilities towards Hattie Carroll, and this partly because of what it may entail in the way of sacrifice by him. His art, in such a dedication to historical facts that are not of his making, needs to set limits (not *too* expanded) to its own rights in honouring hers. This, too, is a matter of justice.

Wordsworth famously recorded that "every author, as far as he is great and at the same time *original*, has had the task of *creating* the taste by which he is to be enjoyed: so it has been, so will it continue to be".[1] T. S. Eliot, sceptical of romanticism, offered a reminder, that "to be original with the *minimum* of alteration, is sometimes more distinguished than to be original with the *maximum* of alteration".[2]

But is Dylan a poet? For him, no problem.

---

[1] *Essay, Supplementary to the Preface* (1815).
[2] Introduction to Samuel Johnson's *London* and *The Vanity of Human Wishes* (1930).

Yippee! I'm a poet, and I know it
Hope I don't blow it
(*I Shall Be Free No. 10*)

Is he a poet? And is this a question about his achievement, and how highly to value it, or about his choice of medium or rather media, and what to value this as?

The poetry magazine *Agenda* had a questionnaire bent upon rhyme. Since Dylan is one of the great rhymesters of all time, I hoped that there might be something about him. There was: a grudge against "the accepted badness of rhyme in popular verse, popular music, etc. A climate in which, say, Bob Dylan is given a moment's respect as a poet is a climate in which anything goes." (To give him but a moment's respect would indeed be ill judged.) This is snobbery – I know, I know, there is such a thing as inverted snobbery – and it's ill written.[1] ("A climate in which anything goes"? Climate? Goes?)

The case for denying Dylan the title of poet could not summarily, if at all, be made good by any open-minded close attention to the words and his ways with them. The case would need to begin with his medium, or rather with the mixed-media nature of song, as of drama. On the page, a poem controls its timing there and then.

Dylan is a performer of genius. So he is necessarily in the business (and the game) of playing his timing against his rhyming. The cadences, the voicing, the rhythmical draping and shaping don't (needless to sing) make a song superior to a poem, but they do change the hiding-places of its power. T. S. Eliot showed great savvy in maintaining that "Verse, whatever else it may or may not be, is itself a system of *punctuation*; the usual marks of punctuation themselves are differently employed."[2] A song is a different system of punctuation again. Dylan himself used the word "punctuate" in a quiet insistence during an interview in 1978. Ron Rosenbaum made his pitch – "It's the sound that you want" – and Dylan agreed and then didn't: "Yeah, it's the sound and the words. Words don't interfere with it. They – they – punctuate it. You know, they give it purpose. [*Pause*]."

"They – they – punctuate it": this is itself dramatic punctuation, though perfectly colloquial (and Dylan went on to say "Chekhov is my favorite

---

[1] Alan Brownjohn, in *Agenda* (Winter 1991), p. 11.
[2] *TLS* (27 September 1928).

writer"). [1] Words: "they give it purpose. [*Pause*]", the train of thought being
that punctuation, a system of pointing, gives point.

Not just the beauty but the force will be necessarily in the details,
incarnate in a way of putting it. So that any general praises of Dylan's
art are sure to miss what matters most about it: that it is not general,
but highly and deeply individual, particular. This, while valuing human
commonalty – "Of joy in widest commonalty spread", in Wordsworth's
line. Joy, and grief, too.

Larkin, reviewing jazz in 1965, took it on himself to nick a Dylan album.
(Hope I'm not out of line.)

I'm afraid I poached Bob Dylan's "Highway 61 Revisited" (CBS) out of curiosity
and found myself well rewarded. Dylan's cawing, derisive voice is probably well
suited to his material – I say probably because much of it was unintelligible to
me – and his guitar adapts itself to rock ("Highway 61") and ballad ("Queen Jane")
admirably. There is a marathon "Desolation Row" which has an enchanting tune
and mysterious, possibly half-baked words. [2]

"Half-baked" is overdone. But "well rewarded" pays some dues.

A poem of Larkin's has the phrase "Love Songs" in its title and is about
songs, while itself proceeding not as a song but as a poem. For when you
see the poem on the page, you can see that it is in three stanzas, and you
could not at once hear – though you might know – such a thing when
in the presence of a song. Larkin, we have already heard, thought that
"poetry readings grew up on a false analogy with music": "false because
people can read words, whereas they can't read music". But this poem of
his contemplates someone who used to be able to read music and play it
on the piano, and who can still, in age, look at the sheet music and re-learn
how it is done.

LOVE SONGS IN AGE

She kept her songs, they took so little space,
    The covers pleased her:
One bleached from lying in a sunny place,
One marked in circles by a vase of water,

---

[1] *Playboy* (March 1978).
[2] *All What Jazz* (1970, 1985), p. 151.

One mended, when a tidy fit had seized her,
   And coloured, by her daughter –
So they had waited, till in widowhood
She found them, looking for something else, and stood

Relearning how each frank submissive chord
   Had ushered in
Word after sprawling hyphenated word,
And the unfailing sense of being young
Spread out like a spring-woken tree, wherein
   That hidden freshness sung,
That certainty of time laid up in store
As when she played them first. But, even more,

The glare of that much-mentioned brilliance, love,
   Broke out, to show
Its bright incipience sailing above,
Still promising to solve, and satisfy,
And set unchangeably in order. So
   To pile them back, to cry,
Was hard, without lamely admitting how
It had not done so then, and could not now.

A widow comes across the love songs that she had played on the piano when she was young; how painfully they remind her of the large promises once made by time and even more by love.[1]

That sentence exercises a summary injustice. It is not much more than perfunctory gossip, whereas Larkin's three sentences are a poem. The poet makes these dry bones live – or rather, since he is not a witch-doctor and the poem is not a zombie, he makes us care that these bones lived. "An ordinary sorrow of man's life": that is how Wordsworth spoke of his lonely sufferer (in widowhood, likewise?) in her ruined cottage. Larkin, too, redeems the ordinary.

His is not a poem simply about life's disappointments, but about realizing these disappointments. He reminds us that to realize is to make real. Here are three sentences that shrink as life cannot but shrink. From 106 words to 30 to 23. The first sentence has all the amplitude of the remembered past into

[1] I draw here on a piece I wrote for the *Sunday Times* (7 January 1968).

which it moves. It has world enough and time, with lovingly remembered details calmly patterned ("One bleached . . . One marked . . . One mended"), a world "set in order". It flows on, and its own words remark on what they are re-living – they "spread out", they manifest a sense of "time laid up in store". The first sentence can take its time – time is not doing the taking.

But from this leisure the second sentence dwindles. It begins with "But", unlikely to be a reassuring start here, and instead of what is lovingly recalled, we have love itself. Instead of the actually loved, in its inevitable imperfection (the unmentioned husband, the mentioned daughter), there is the daunting abstraction, love. Its brilliance is a "glare", too bright to be ignored, somehow pitiless in its "sailing above". And if love "broke out" in those songs, here, too, there is something of an ominous suggestion. Light breaks out, but so do wars and plagues. Love, too, can break hearts, or cannot but break hearts if we think of all that the abstraction love promised.

Then the further shrinkage into the last sentence, briefer, bleaker. Instead of the abstraction of the middle sentence, which was large and metaphorical and aerial, we reach a stony abstraction – no metaphors, no details, no grand words like "incipience". Simply pain generalized, compacted into the plainest words in the language. Earlier the poem had opened its mouth and sung; in the end it bites its lip.

From copious memories recalling what promised to be a copious future, through high hopes, down to severe humbling. From a romantic compound, "spring-woken", through a laconically dry one, "much-mentioned", down to uncompounded plainness. From "a tidy fit", through the promise to "set unchangeably in order", down to "pile them back".

Yet this is poetry, not prose, so it exists not only as sentences but as lines and stanzas. Larkin is a master of all such patterning. The pattern does not impose itself upon the sense, it releases and enforces the sense. See how he uses line-endings and stanza-endings – "see how", because this is much more possible than "hear how". Larkin's point about "the disappearance of stanza shape" when you hear a poem read aloud can be extended to include our being able to see the valuable counterpointing of stanza shape and, say, sentence shape. A song's stanzas are less concerned to stand, more to move.

Love Songs in Age has no stanza that is self-contained. There is a marked visual pause in passing from the first to the second stanza:

> So they had waited, till in widowhood
> She found them, looking for something else, and stood

> Relearning how each frank submissive chord
> > Had ushered in
> Word after sprawling hyphenated word,

("Sprawling hyphenated", because the sheet-music sets the words, sub-divided and stretched out, below the musical notes, so Larkin can remind us of the different systems of punctuation that are poetical and sheet-musical.) The visual pause after "stood" is all the more effective because in the first six lines of the poem the lines have been placidly end-stopped, tidily congruous, the units of sense at one with (rather than played against) the units of rhythm and rhyme.

Then, with "stood", a powerful pause enforces itself – the poem pauses, rapt, just as the widow pauses here, rapt into memory. Swelling in the second stanza is a change from the equable line-endings of the first. Instead of such a complete unit as "The covers pleased her", there is the line "Had ushered in", which has to move on from its predecessor and to *usher in* its successor. The ebullience of this middle stanza spreads out over its line-endings, the clauses proliferate and spill over (". . . in / . . . wherein"). And then, at the very end of the stanza, a sudden drastic check:

> That certainty of time laid up in store
> As when she played them first. But, even more,
>
> The glare of that much-mentioned brilliance, love,

With a harsh gracelessness, the second sentence is imperatively beginning, tugging across the cadences (and, duly, demanding a pause). If the opening of this second sentence, "But", is threateningly ungraceful, how much more is the third: "So" thrust out with grim emphasis, cutting across the order that immediately precedes it, insisting doggedly on the truth:

> Still promising to solve, and satisfy,
> And set unchangeably in order. So
> > To pile them back, to cry,
> Was hard, without lamely admitting how
> It had not done so then, and could not now.

The point of running one stanza into the next is more than to create pregnant pauses, more even than to imitate the musical interweaving of love songs. It is to create the austere finality of the conclusion. Only once in this poem does a full stop coincide with the end of a line or with the end of a stanza. This establishes the fullness of this stop, the assurance that Larkin has concluded his poem and not just run out of things to say. The same authoritative finality is alive in the rhyme scheme. Larkin's pattern (*abacbdcdd*) allows of a clinching couplet only at the end of a stanza. He then prevents any such clinching at the end of the first two stanzas by having very strong enjambment, spilling across the line-endings. The result is that the very last couplet is the first in the poem to release what we have been waiting for, the decisive authority of a couplet, rhyme sealing rhyme in a final settlement. But also with a rhythmical catch in the throat, a brief stumble before "lamely": "Was hard, without lamely admitting how" is a line that cannot move briskly, has to feel lamed, because of the speed-bump between "without" and "lamely". And then an inexorable ending, here and now: "and could not now". The poem focuses time, much as time focuses itself for us in the dentist's chair into a concentrated "now".

The conclusive couplet isn't the only subtly meaningful rhyming. The gentle disyllabic, or double, rhymes of the first stanza (*pleased her* / *seized her*, *water* / *daughter*) create softer cadences, all the more so because of the *-er* association among themselves. It is against this softer light that the glare of the last stanza stands out, its rhymes bleak. Only one rhyme in the poem is inexact, and with good reason: *chord* / *word*. That the words of life do not quite fit its music is one of the things that the poem knows.

Love Songs in Age is far more than a five-finger exercise in the manner of the poet whom Larkin most admired, Thomas Hardy. Like the best of Hardy, the best of Larkin lives in the context of an imagined life. The widow's story is there, between the poem's lines, treated obliquely and unsentimentally. The appeal is to experiences already understood ("That hidden freshness", "That certainty", "That much-mentioned brilliance"). "She kept her songs, they took so little space" – how much of an everyday sadness is here, of possessions sold off, a home relinquished, the life lived in what Larkin elsewhere calls (in *Mr Bleaney*) a "hired box". The songs, she kept – the piano, she could not (though this, too, has to be glimpsed between the lines, especially in "*stood* / / *Relearning* . . ."). Self-possession is bound to be so much involved with possessions.

Yet the end of the poem makes a point rather different from the expected. It doesn't say that she cried or wanted to cry, but that it was hard to cry without admitting how huge the failure of love had been in comparison with any triumphs of love. Not hard to cry, heaven knows, but hard to cry without dissolving, hard to admit any cause for grief without admitting too shatteringly much. "Admitting": in its unostentatious truth-telling, it is a perfect Larkin word. Not that memory is merely unkind. When we look back across the whole poem, we realize that it was not only in the literal physical sense that "She kept her songs". Meantime, the poem at least has set something unchangeably in order.

Such, at any rate, is my reading of the poem. To hear the poem read aloud, even by the poet himself, is a different story. Yet the story turns upon the same sad pertinent fact: that the only rhyme that is not a true rhyme, the only one that is a rhyme only to the eye and not to the ear, is *chord / word*. For ever refusing to fit, to be set perfectly in order. There on the page, like sheet-music that both is and is not the real thing.

Dylan said of *Lay, Lady, Lay*: "The song came out of those first four chords. I filled it up with the lyrics then." And elsewhere he said something that suggests the economy that characterizes such a poem as *Love Songs in Age*: "Every time I write a song, it's like writing a novel. Just takes me a lot less time, and I can get it down . . . down to where I can re-read it in my head a lot."[1]

Love Songs in Age is a poem that imagines songs within it, and shows us what this might mean, humanly. I don't know of a counterpart to this in Dylan: that is, a song that imagines poems within it, as against bearing them in mind. Poets like Verlaine and Rimbaud, Dylan is happy to acknowledge. But when it comes to Dylan and the sister-arts, it is, naturally, the traditional sister-art of butter sculpture that most engages his interest, as does the traditional relation between the artist and his brother, the critic.

> look you asshole – tho i might be nothing but
> a butter sculptor, i refuse to go on working
> with the idea of your praising as my reward –
> like what are your credentials anyway? excpt for
> talking about all us butter sculptors, what else
> do you do? do you know what it feels like to
> make some butter sculpture? do you know what
> it feels like to actually ooze that butter around
> & create something of fantastic worth? you said
> that my last year's work "The King's Odor" was
> great & then you say i havent done anything as

[1] *Whaaat?*, p. 6.

great since — just who the hell are you talking to
anyway? you must have something to do in your
real life — i understand that you praised the piece
you saw yesterday entitled "The Monkey Taster"
about which you said meant "a nice work of butter
carved into the shape of a young man who likes
only african women" you are an idiot — it doesnt
mean that at all . . . i hereby want nothing to do
with your hangups — i really dont care what you think
of my work as i now know you dont understand it
anyway . . . i must go now — i hve this new hunk of
margarine waiting in the bathtub — yes i said
MARGARINE & next week i just might decide to use
cream cheese —[1]

But, butter sculpture apart, it is famously the art of film that Dylan most likes to stage or to screen within his songs. And the greatest of such is *Brownsville Girl*.[2] It starts Well.

Well, there was this movie I seen one time
About a man riding 'cross the desert and it starred Gregory Peck
He was shot down by a hungry kid trying to make a name for himself
The townspeople wanted to crush that kid down and string him up by the neck

I once tried to sum up why it earned its place among his Greatest Hits, third time around:

The end of an age, an age ago, ending "long before the stars were torn down". At 11 minutes, it has world enough and time to be a love story, a trek, a brief epic . . . Patience, it urges. We wait for eager ages for his voice to introduce us to the Brownsville Girl herself. Great rolling stanzas ("and it just comes a-rolling in"), and memories of the Rolling Thunder Revue, especially since Sam Shepard plays his part. About films, it has the filmic flair of Dylan's underrated masterpiece, *Renaldo and Clara*. Delicious yelps from the back-up women, who sometimes comically refuse to back him up. He: "They can talk about me plenty when I'm gone." They: "Oh yeah?" It moves, and yet stays put, circling back round. One of those great *still* songs.[3]

[1] *Tarantula* (1966, 1971), pp. 93–4.
[2] With Sam Shepard, of stage and screen.
[3] *The Liner Notes that Sank*, in the *Telegraph* (Winter 1994).

What particularly takes Dylan about films, I take it, is that they move – why else would they be movies? – while at the same time or in a different sense they don't. Don't thereafter move from what they once were. For to film it is to fix it. And a re-make of a film is not the same thing as re-performing a song. Like *Brownsville Girl*, a film – including this one within the song that someone remembers or kinda remembers – moves and yet stays still. It stays more than just stills, that is true, but to see it again is to see it exactly as it was, for all time. (Eternity is a different story.) There is comedy in *Brownsville Girl*'s beginning "Well, there was this movie I seen one time", for although "one time" makes perfectly good sense and we know what he means, it is going to be many more than one time that we shall hear tell of his seeing it. The second time it goes, or rather, arrives, like this:

> Something about that movie though, well I just can't get it out of my head
> But I can't remember why I was in it or what part I was supposed to play
> All I remember about it was Gregory Peck and the way people moved
> And a lot of them seemed to be lookin' my way

The way people moved, and meanwhile the film moved, and how they looked out my way from the screen as though I were the performer (no longer "a hungry kid trying to make a name for himself"), not – on this relief of an occasion – the performee. And yet the film, once and for all, is not going to move, or move out of my head. Even when an actor returns in the re-make of a film, as did Robert Mitchum for the second *Cape Fear*, he is not himself or is not his previous self. One man in his time plays many parts. And so the song muses on the Muse of Film:

> Well, I'm standing in line in the rain to see a movie starring Gregory Peck
> Yeah, but you know it's not the one that I had in mind
> He's got a new one out now, I don't even know what it's about
> But I'll see him in anything so I'll stand in line

A new one out now, the old one being in then, preserving its people, just as they were, for ever and a day. "Welcome to the land of the living dead." Not just *The Night of the Living Dead*, which is one particular film, but the land of the living dead, filmland. "I'll stand in line": much is made of lines in this song, the medium of song being lines and it's not being only Dylan's audience that has to be willing to stand in line. Any song must. And Dylan reels out the lines themselves, one of the furthest extended being a line that does indeed find itself over the line (we forgive it its trespasses):

> Now I've always been the kind of person that doesn't like to trespass but
>   sometimes you just find yourself over the line

And then, as the song winds to a conclusion, it winds back to the beginning, this time underlining "one time" with "twice":

There was a movie I seen one time, I think I sat through it twice
I don't remember who I was or where I was bound
All I remember about it was it starred Gregory Peck, he wore a gun and he was
    shot in the back
Seems like a long time ago, long before the stars were torn down

And so – in this requiem for the stars, the living dead – on to the refrain for the last time, a refrain that is a showing, or a plea for a showing:

> Brownsville girl with your Brownsville curls
> Teeth like pearls shining like the moon above
> Brownsville girl, show me all around the world
> Brownsville girl, you're my honey love

Show me all around the world: that is all that any film asks.

There is in Dylan's songs a sense that competition between sister-arts is as inevitable and (mostly) as unproductive as any other sibling rivalry, but that only a very touchy visual artist would object to a singer's envisaging the day *When I Paint My Masterpiece*. But there is (praise be) such a thing as stealthy competition.

> Praise be to Nero's Neptune
> The Titanic sails at dawn
> And everybody's shouting
> "Which Side Are You On?"
> And Ezra Pound and T. S. Eliot
> Fighting in the captain's tower
> While calypso singers laugh at them
> And fishermen hold flowers
> Between the windows of the sea

Where lovely mermaids flow
And nobody has to think too much
About Desolation Row

There is some pitching of poems against songs here. The question "Which
Side Are You On?" can be approached from many sides, one being the
premiss that these words will strike slightly differently upon the ear. For it
is the case that not even Dylan can unmistakably sing the difference between
upper and lower case (not "Which side are you on?"), whereas to the eye
the distinction is a Piece of Cake. It's just that there is something that you
need to know. The capital title of that unmisgiving political song.

So the central contention turns out not to be between those two
heavyweight modernists, or between their high art and that of the lowly
calypso, or between poems and songs, or even between the *Titanic* and
the iceberg,[1] but between two deeply different apprehensions of what it

---

[1] The excellent mock-raking magazine the *Onion*, in its collection *Our Dumb Century*
("100 Years of Headlines from America's Finest News Source"), excelled itself with
its front page for the *Titanic*:

WORLD'S LARGEST METAPHOR HITS ICE-BERG

TITANIC, REPRESENTATION OF MAN'S HUBRIS, SINKS IN NORTH ATLANTIC

1,500 DEAD IN SYMBOLIC TRAGEDY

TITANIC STRUCK BY ICY REPRESENTATION OF NATURE'S SUPREMACY STOP INSUFFICIENT LIFEBOATS DUE TO POMPOUS CERTAINTY IN MAN'S INFALLIBILITY STOP MICROCOSM OF LARGER SOCIETY STOP

The *Onion* reproduces the memorable message
received at 4.23 a.m. Greenwich Standard
Time from the rescue ship:

is that songs can most responsibly be. And of what the world truly is, as
against the simplicities of Once upon a time. "An I see two sides man" –

> It was that easy –
> "Which Side're You On" aint phony words
> An' they aint from a phony song[1]

Dylan didn't like to bad-mouth a song that was in a good cause. But he
knew, even back then in 1963, that this "two sides" business was averting its
eyes and its ears from too much. So before long he was hardening his art.
"Songs like 'Which Side Are You On?' . . . they're not folk-music songs;
they're political songs. They're *already* dead."[2]

What does the word protest mean to you?
"To me? Means uh . . . singing when I don't really wanna sing."
What?
"It means singing against your wishes to sing."
Do you sing against your wishes to sing?
"No, no."
*Do you sing protest *songs*?*
"No."
What do you sing?
"I sing love songs."[3]

Love songs in age, as in youth.

Rhymes

"What is rhyme?" said the Professor. "Is it not an agreement of sound –?"

"With a slight disagreement, yes" broke in Hanbury. "I give up rhyme too."

"Let me however" said the Professor "in the moment of triumph insist on rhyme,
which is a short and valuable instance of my principle. Rhyme is useful not only
as shewing the proportion of disagreement joined with agreement which the ear

[1] *For Dave Glover*, programme for Newport Folk Festival (July 1963); bootleg reprinting
in *Bob Dylan in His Own Write*, compiled by John Tuttle, p. 6.
[2] *Playboy* (March 1966).
[3] Los Angeles (16 December 1965); *Bob Dylan in His Own Words*, p. 53.

finds most pleasurable, but also as marking the points in a work of art (each stanza being considered as a work of art) where the principle of beauty is to be strongly marked, the intervals at which a combination of regularity with disagreement so very pronounced as rhyme may be well asserted, the proportions which may be well borne by the more markedly, to the less markedly, structural. Do you understand?"

"Yes" said Middleton. "In fact it seems to me rhyme is the epitome of your principle. All beauty may by a metaphor be called rhyme, may it not?"

Gerard M. Hopkins (*On the Origin of Beauty: A Platonic Dialogue*)[1]

Rhyme, in the words of *The Oxford English Dictionary*, is "Agreement in the terminal sounds of two or more words or metrical lines, such that (in English prosody) the last stressed vowel and any sounds following it are the same, while the sound or sounds preceding are different. Examples: *which*, *rich*; *grew*, *too* . . .*"

A device, a matter of technique, then, but always seeking a relation of rhyme to reason (without reason or rhyme?), so that "technique" ought to come to seem too small a word and we will find ourselves thinking rather of a resource. Rhymes and rhythms and cadences will be what brings a poem home to us.

People have always complained that rhyme puts pressure on poets to say something other than what they really mean to say, and people have objected to Bob Dylan's rhyming. Ellen Willis told him off: "He relies too much on rhyme."[2] It's like some awful school report: you're allowed to rely on rhyme 78 per cent, but Master Dylan relies on rhyme 81 per cent. Anyway, you can't rely too much on rhyme, though you can mistake unreliable rhymes for reliable ones.

For success, there is the simple (not easy) stroke that has the line, "Oh, Mama, can this really be the end?", *not* as the end, but as nearing the end of each verse of *Stuck Inside of Mobile with the Memphis Blues Again*. And the rhyme in this refrain is beautifully metaphorical, because it's a rhyme of the word "end" with the word "again":

> Oh, Mama, can this really be the end
> To be stuck inside of Mobile
> With the Memphis Blues again?

[1] *The Note-Books and Papers of Gerard Manley Hopkins*, pp. 74–5.
[2] *Cheetah* (1967).

"End" and "again" are metaphorically a rhyme because every rhyme is both an endness and an againness. That's what a rhyme is, intrinsically, a form of again (a gain, too), and a form of an ending.

In *Death is Not the End*, each verse ends:

> Just remember that death is not the end
> Not the end, not the end
> Just remember that death is not the end

And the four verses at first maintain the tolling of this severe rhyme: *friend / mend, comprehend / bend, descend / lend*, and then at last soften it, though not much, from an *end* rhyme into the assonance *men / citizen*. (Assonance differs from rhyme in not having the same *end*.) But just remember that the song has not only four verses but a bridge, and that the bridge (a bridge to the next world) is variously at a great remove from the sound of that particular rhyming or assonance on *end*, having instead the sound-sequence that springs from *life*: *dies / bright light / shines / skies*:

> Oh, the tree of life is growing
> Where the spirit never dies
> And the bright light of salvation shines
> In dark and empty skies

The rhyme *dies / skies* depends upon its distance from the *end* sound, just as it depends upon "dies" being, in full, "never dies". The bridge is, then, at a great remove. And yet it is not complacently or utterly removed from the end-world, given the sound in "empty".

"All beauty may by a metaphor be called rhyme, may it not?" asked a speaker in Hopkins's imaginary conversation. Moreover, rhyme is itself one of the forms that metaphor may take, since rhyme is a perception of agreement and disagreement, of similitude and dissimilitude. Simultaneously, a spark. Long, long ago, Aristotle said in the *Poetics* that the greatest thing by far is to be a master of metaphor, for it is upon our being able to learn from the perception of similitude and dissimilitude that human learning of all kinds depends. One form that mastery of metaphor may take is mastery of rhyme.

Ian Hamilton said of "Dylan's blatant, unworried way with rhyme" in *All I Really Want to Do* that it *is* irritating on the page, but sung by him it very often becomes part of the song's point, part of its drama of aggression. Many of Dylan's love songs are a kind of verbal wife-battering: she will be *rhymed* into submission – but to see them this way you have to have Bob's barbed wire tonsils in support.[1]

I think it's true that women in Dylan's vicinity sometimes have as their mission being rhymed into submission, but that isn't battering, it's bantering.

Still, the rhyming can be fierce. Take the force of the couplet in *Idiot Wind*,

> Blowing like a circle round my skull
> From the Grand Coulee Dam to the Capitol

Rolling Stone reported: "It's an amazing rhyme, Ginsberg writes, an amazing image, a national image like in Hart Crane's unfinished epic of America, *The Bridge*. The other poet is delighted to get the letter. No one else, Dylan writes Ginsberg, had noticed that rhyme, a rhyme which is very dear to Dylan. Ginsberg's tribute to that rhyme is one of the reasons he is here":[2] that is, on the Rolling Thunder Review and then in Dylan's vast film *Renaldo and Clara*.

And it's a true rhyme because of the metaphorical relation, because of what a head of state is, and the body politic, and because of the relation of the Capitol to the skull (another of those white domes), with which it disconcertingly rhymes. An imperfect rhyme, perfectly judged.

Dylan: "But then again, people have taken rhyming now, it doesn't have to be exact anymore. Nobody's gonna care if you rhyme 'represent' with 'ferment', you know. Nobody's gonna care."[3] Not going to care as not going to object, agreed; but someone as imaginative about rhymes as Dylan must care, since always aware of, and doing something with, imperfect rhymes, or awry rhymes, or rhymes that go off at half-cock, so that their nature is to the point. The same goes for having assonance instead of rhyme: entirely acceptable but not identical with the effect of rhyme, and creatively available as just that bit different. The rhyme *skull / Capitol* is a capital one.

---

[1] *Observer* (11 June 1978).

[2] 15 January 1976. Ginsberg wrote in his sleeve-notes for *Desire*: "By the time Dylan made the great disillusioned national rhyme *Idiot Wind* – '. . . Blowing like a circle round your skull / From the Grand Coulee Dam to the Capitol . . .' – he must've been ready for another great surge of unafraid prophetic feeling."

[3] Dylan in 1991; Paul Zollo, *Songwriters on Songwriting* (1997), p. 81.

Dylan adapts the skull of the Capitol to the White House elsewhere, in *11 Outlined Epitaphs*:

> how many votes will it take
> for a new set of teeth
> in the congress mouths?
> how many hands have t' be raised
> before hair will grow back
> on the white house head?

But can it be that Dylan was guilty of baldism? A bad hair day. Time to soothe and smoothe: *A Message from Bob Dylan to the Emergency Civil Liberties Committee* (13 December 1963) assured those of us who are bald oldsters or baldsters that "when I speak of bald heads, I mean bald minds". You meant bald heads, and it was a justified generational counter-attack, given how the young (back then) were rebuked for their hair.

A rhyme may be a transplant.

> The highway is for gamblers, better use your sense
> Take what you have gathered from coincidence
> (*It's All Over Now, Baby Blue*)

One of the best rhymes, that. For all rhymes are a coincidence issuing in a new sense. It is a pure coincidence that *sense* rhymes with *coincidence*, and from this you *gather* something. Every rhyme issues a bet, and is a risk, something for gamblers – and a gambler *is* a better ("for gamblers, better use . . .").

Granted, it is possible that all this is a mere coincidence, and that I am imagining things, rather than noticing how Dylan imagined things. We often have a simple test as to whether critical suggestions are far-fetched. If they hadn't occurred to *us*, they are probably strained, silly-clever . . . So although for my part I believe that the immediate succession "gamblers, better . . ." is Dylan's crisp playing with words, not my doing so, and although I like the idea that there may be some faint play in the word "sense", which in the American voicing is indistinguishable from the small-scale financial sense "cents",[1] I didn't find myself persuaded when a friend suggested that all this money rolls and flows into "coincidence",

---

[1] Dylan rhymes *cents / fence* in *Sitting on a Barbed Wire Fence*.

which does after all start with *c o i n*, coin. Not persuaded partly, I admit, because I hadn't thought of it myself, but mostly because this is a song, not a poem on the page. On the page, you might see before your very eyes that coincidence spins a coin, but the sound of a song, the voicing of the word "coincidence", can't gather coin up into itself. Anyway Dylan *uses* his sense.

"One of the very nice things about working with Bob is that he loves rhyme, he loves to play with it, and he loves the complication of it."[1] A quick canter round the course of his rhyming. There is the comedy: it is weird to rhyme *weird / disappeared*, reckless to rhyme *reckless / necklace*, and outrageous to rhyme *outrageous / contagious*.[2] And in *Goin' to Acapulco* the rhyme *what the hell / Taj Mahal* mutters "what the hell". There is the tension, for instance that of a duel in the world of the Western:

> But then the crowd began to stamp their feet and the house lights did dim
> And in the darkness of the room, there was only Jim and him
>> (*Lily, Rosemary and the Jack of Hearts*)

Once "did dim" has set the scene, the two of them stand there: Jim and him, simplicity themselves. And there is the satire: Dylan can sketch a patriotic posturing simply by thrusting forth the jaw of a rhyme with a challenge.

> Now Eisenhower, he's a Russian spy
> Lincoln, Jefferson, and that Roosevelt guy
> To my knowledge there's just one man
> That's really a true American:
> George Lincoln Rockwell

A true American will pronounce the proud word, juttingly, *Americán*. You got a problem with that?

Clearly, rhyme is not exactly the same phenomenon on the page as it is when voiced (on stage or on album). On the page, "good" at the line-ending in *One Too Many Mornings* is likely to be broadly the same in its pronunciation (though not necessarily in its tone, and this affects

[1] *A Chat with Jacques Levy* (*Isis*, April / May 2000). And Ginsberg, sleeve-notes to *Desire*: "Half-month was spent solitary on Long Island with theatrist Jacques Levy working on song facts phrases & rhymes."

[2] Jacques Levy: "We had a great time coming up with ideas though; we were laughing a lot and we were enjoying coming up with these rhymes like '*contagious*' and '*outrageous*'."

pronunciation) as the same word, "good", at the line-ending two lines later. But in singing, Dylan can play what his voice may do (treat them very differently) against their staying the same: the word both is and is not the one that you heard a moment earlier. Or take "I don't want to be hers, I want to be yours" (*I Wanna Be Your Lover*). On the page, no rhyme; in the song, "yers", which both is and is not a persuasive retort to, or equivalent of, "hers", both does and does not enjoy the same rights. The first rhyme in *Got My Mind Made Up*, *long* / *wrong*, has an effect that it could never have on the page, since Dylan sings "wrong" so differently from how he sang "long". There is something very right about this, which depends upon comprehending the way in which the multimedia art of song differs from the page's poetry.

Other favourites. The rhyme in *Talkin' World War III Blues*, "ouch" up against "psychiatric couch".

> I said, "Hold it, Doc, a World War passed through my brain"
> He said, "Nurse, get your pad, the boy's insane"
> He grabbed my arm, I said "Ouch!"
> As I landed on the psychiatric couch
> He said, "Tell me about it"

Ouch: no amount of plump cushioning can remove the pain that psychiatry exists to deal with – and that psychiatry in due course has its own inflictions of. (There's a moment in the film *Panic* when the doleful hit-man played by William H. Macy is asked by the shrink as he leaves – after paying $125 for not many minutes – how he is feeling now? "Poor.") Dylan's word "pad" plays its small comic part; to *write* on, not like the padded couch (not padded enough: Ouch!) or the padded cell. *Ouch / couch* is a rhyme that is itself out to grab you, and that knows the difference between "Tell me about it" as a soothing professional solicitation and as a cynical boredom. Moreover, rhyme is a to-and-fro, an exchange, itself a form of this "I said" / "He said" business or routine.

Another rhyme that has spirit: "nonchalant" against "It's your mind that I want" in *Rita May*:

> Rita May, Rita May
> You got your body in the way
> You're so damned nonchalant
> It's your mind that I want

You don't have to *believe* him (I wouldn't, if I were you, Rita May), but "nonchalant" arriving at "want" is delicious, because nonchalant is so undesiring of her, so cool, so not in heat.

Or there's the rhyme in *Mozambique* of "Mozambique" with "cheek to cheek" (along with "cheek" cheekily rhyming with "cheek" there, a perfect fit). There's always something strange about place names, or persons' names, rhyming, for they don't seem to be words exactly, or at any rate are very different kinds of word from your usual word.[1]

My favourite of all Dylan's rhymes is another that turns upon a place name, the rhyme of "Utah" with "me 'Pa'", as if "U–" in Utah were spelt *y o u*:

> Build me a cabin in Utah
> Marry me a wife, catch rainbow trout
> Have a bunch of kids who call me "Pa"
> That must be what it's all about
> (*Sign on the Window*)

That's not a rhyme of "tah" and "pa", it's a rhyme of "Utah" and "me 'Pa'" – like "Me Tarzan, You Jane". And it has a further dimension of sharp comedy in that Dylan has taken over for his peaceful pastoral purposes a military drill, words to march by – you can hear them being chanted in Frederick Wiseman's documentary *Basic Training* (1971):

> And now I've got
> A mother-in-law
> And fourteen kids
> That call me "Pa"

Yet there is pathos as well as comedy in *Sign on the Window*, for the Utah stanza is the closing one of a song of loss that begins "Sign on the window says 'Lonely'". But then "lonely" is perhaps the loneliest word in the language. For the only rhyme for "lonely" is "only". Compounding the lonely, Dylan sings it so that it finds its direction home:

---

[1] For instance, in *Day of the Locusts* there is *diploma / Dakota*, and in *When I Paint My Masterpiece*, *Brussels / muscles*. In *Union Sundown* there is a bravura performance: "El Salvador" rhyming with "dinosaur", "raw", and "law", but with a line tucked in among them: "They used to grow food in Kansas". Now if it had been *Arkansas* . . .

> You've gone to the finest school all right, Miss Lonely
> But you know you only used to get juiced in it
> > (*Like a Rolling Stone*)

Dylan knows the strain that has to be felt if you want even to be in the vicinity of finding another rhyme for "lonely":

> Sign on the window says "Lonely"
> Sign on the door said "No Company Allowed"
> Sign on the street says "Y' Don't Own Me"
> Sign on the porch says "Three's A Crowd"
> Sign on the porch says "Three's A Crowd"
> > (*Sign on the Window*)

Lonely / Y' Don't Own Me. No Company Allowed? Company is inherent in rhyming, where one word keeps company with another. And rhyme, like any metaphor, is itself a threesome, though not a crowd: tenor, vehicle, and the union of the two that constitutes the third thing, metaphor.

Arthur Hallam, Tennyson's friend in whose memory *In Memoriam* was written, referred to rhyme as "the recurrence of termination". A fine paradox, for how can termination recur? Can this really be the end when there is a rhyme to come?

Rhyme has been said to contain in itself a constant appeal to Memory and Hope. This is true of all verse, of all harmonized sound; but it is certainly made more palpable by the recurrence of termination. The dullest senses can perceive an identity in that, and be pleased with it; but the partial identity, latent in more diffused resemblances, requires, in order to be appreciated, a soul susceptible of musical impression. The ancients disdained a mode of pleasure, in appearance so little elevated, so ill adapted for effects of art; but they knew not, and with their metrical harmonies, perfectly suited, as these were, to their habitual moods of feeling, they were not likely to know the real capacities of this apparently simple and vulgar combination.[1]

Rhyme contains this appeal to Memory and Hope (is a container for it, and contains it as you might contain your anger, your laughter, or your

[1] *The Influence of Italian Upon English Literature*; *The Writings of Arthur Hallam*, ed. T. H. Vail Motter (1943), p. 222.

drink) because when you have the first rhyme-word you are hoping for the later one, and when you have the later one, you remember the promise that was given earlier and is now fulfilled. Responsibilities on both sides, responsively granted.

So rhyme is intimately involved with lyric – Swinburne insisted on this, back in 1867: "Rhyme is the native condition of lyric verse in English: a rhymeless lyric is a maimed thing." There are few good unrhymed lyrics of any kind because of the strong filament between lyricism, hope, and memory.[1]

Dylan loves rhyming on the word "memory" (and rhyme is one of the best aids to memory, is *the* mnemonic device: "Thirty days hath September, / April, June, and November . . ."). The line in *Sad-Eyed Lady of the Lowlands*, "With your sheet-metal memory of Cannery Row", rings true because of the memory within this song that takes you back to the phrase "your sheets like metal", and because of the curious undulation that can be heard, and is memorable, in "memory" and "Cannery". And Cannery Row is itself a memory, since the allusion to John Steinbeck's novel has to be a memory that the singer shares with his listeners, or else it couldn't work as an allusion.

As for rhyming on "forget": *True Love Tends to Forget*, aware that rhyming depends on memory, has "forget" begin in the arms of "regret", and end, far out, in "Tibet". The Dylai Lama. And *True Love Tends to Forget* rhymes "again" and "when", enacting what the song is talking about, for rhyme is an *again / when*. And rhyme may be a kind of loving, two things becoming one, yet not losing their own identity.

Or there is Dylan's loving to rhyme, as all the poets have loved to do, on the word "free". *If Dogs Run Free* does little else than gambol with the rhyme (but what a good deal that proves to be). Or there are "free" and "memory" in *Mr. Tambourine Man*.

> Yes, to dance beneath the diamond sky with one hand waving free
> Silhouetted by the sea, circled by the circus sands
> With all memory and fate driven deep beneath the waves
> Let me forget about today until tomorrow

There the word "free" can conjure up a freedom that is not irresponsible,

---

[1] Few, not none. Thomas Campion, Dylan's great predecessor as the creator of the music and the words, has some exquisite instances. Pre-eminent is *Rose-cheekt Laura, come.*

and "memory" asks you *not* to forget, but to have in mind – whether consciously or not – another element of the rhyme: trustworthy memory.

Dylan wouldn't have had to learn these stops and steps of the mind from previous poets, since the effect would be the same whether the parallel is a source or an analogue.[1] But Dylan is drawing on the same sources of power, when he sings in *Abandoned Love*:

> I march in the parade of liberty
> But as long as I love you, I'm not free

– as was John Milton when he protested against irresponsible protesters:

> That bawl for freedom in their senseless mood,
>   And still revolt when truth would set them free.
>   Licence they mean when they cry liberty.
>
>   (Sonnet XII)

Licence is different from liberty, don't forget – and Milton makes this real to us, by rhyming "free" with "liberty". Licence is not rhymed by Milton (though it grates against "senseless"), and is sullen about rhyming at all. *Does* it rhyme? In a word, no? But whatever Milton's sense of the matter, *my* sense is that he would never have sunk to poetic licence, though Dylan could well have risen to it.

What did Milton himself mean by "Licence they mean when they cry liberty"? That true freedom acknowledges responsibility. The choice is always between the good kind of bonds and the bad kind, not the choice of some chimerical world that is without bonds. That would be licence. D. H. Lawrence warned against idolizing freedom, happily alive to rhyming in his prose even as poetry is: "Thank God I'm not free, any more than a rooted tree is free."

---

[1] As a brief reminder of the variety that the rhyme on "free" may manifest: Donne, *The Apparition*: "When by thy scorn, O murderess, I am dead / And that thou think'st thee free / From all solicitation from me, / Then shall my ghost come to thy bed . . .". Crabbe, *The Hall*: "Those who believed they never could be free, / Except when fighting for their liberty." Edward Thomas, *Words*: "Let me sometimes dance / With you, / Or climb / Or stand perchance / In ecstasy, / Fixed and free / In a rhyme, / As poets do." Rhyming on "rhyme", too.

Milton described his choice of blank verse for his epic as "an example set, the first in English, of ancient liberty recovered to heroic poem from the troublesome and modern bondage of rhyming". But he knew that there are such things as good bonds, and he valued rhymes all the more because he knew that their effect could be all the greater if not every single line had to rhyme. T. S. Eliot began the final paragraph of his *Reflections on "Vers Libre"* (1917): "And this liberation from rhyme might be as well a liberation of rhyme. Freed from its exacting task of supporting lame verse, it could be applied with greater effect where it is most needed."[1]

A particular pleasure attaches to rhyming on the word "rhyme".[2] Keats:

> Just like that bird am I in loss of time
> Whene'er I venture on the stream of rhyme
> (*To Charles Cowden Clarke*)[3]

The beginning of *Sad-Eyed Lady of the Lowlands* is superb in what it does with its first three rhyme-words, as simple as can be in the mystery of such spells, three by three, with the triple rhymes interlacing assonantally with the triple "like" (*eyes like / like rhymes / like chimes*):

> With your mercury mouth in the missionary times
> And your eyes like smoke and your prayers like rhymes
> And your silver cross, and your voice like chimes
> Oh, who among them do they think could bury you?

"Times", "rhymes", and "chimes" are rhymes because they are chimes that come several times. ("And your eyes like smoke": a chime from *Smoke Gets in Your Eyes*.) "Your prayers like rhymes": rhymes being like prayers because of what it is to trust in an answer to one's prayer. With his voicing, Dylan does what the seventeenth-century poet Abraham Cowley did with

[1] *To Criticize the Critic* (1965), p. 189.
[2] Here are some more words that in various ways relate metaphorically to the nature of rhyme, and that occur in Dylan as rhymes: "again", "chains", "coincidence", "complete", "control", "correct", "cure", "empty", "escape", "fit", "follow", "happen", "knot", "loyalty", "next", "place", "plenty", "reach", "reflection", "relief", "remain", "revealed", "reward", "same", "satellite", "satisfied", "timed", "tomorrow", "unresolved".
[3] Is Keats to be heard in Dylan's "And I'm just like that bird"? Keats's "stream" might enter "in midstream", later in *You're a Big Girl Now*.

different rhythmical weightings for this same triplet of rhymes in his *Ode: Upon Liberty*. "If life should a well-ordered poem be", then it should avoid monotony:

> The matter shall be grave, the numbers loose and free.
> It shall not keep one setled pace of time,
> In the same tune it shall not always chime,
> Nor shall each day just to his neighbour rhime.

Sad-Eyed Lady of the Lowlands uses the rhyme on rhyme poignantly. *You're Gonna Make Me Lonesome When You Go* uses it ruefully, in singing of "Crickets talking back and forth in rhyme". For all rhyme is a form of talking back and forth, something that crickets are in a particularly good position to understand, rubbing back and forth, stridulating away. "I could stay with you forever and never realize the time": that is Dylan's rhyming line upon rhyme, and this is the way in which the loving thought is realized. "Forever" is so entirely positive, but then so, on this occasion, is the negative word with which it rhymes, "never".

Even as a yearning is realized – which is not the same as a hope being realized in actuality – in *Highlands*:

> Well my heart's in the Highlands wherever I roam
> That's where I'll be when I get called home
> The wind, it whispers to the buckeyed trees in rhyme
> Well my heart's in the Highlands
> I can only get there one step at a time

The whisper here rises to a determination when "time" comes, in due time, to consummate the rhyme with "rhyme"; and furthermore when "roam" finds itself not only rhyming with "home" ("roam" takes you away – "wherever I roam" – but "home" calls you home again) but when "roam" is rotated into "rhyme", a tender turn. But then rhyme, too, works "one step at a time", the feet being metrical. Hopkins:

> His sheep seem'd to come from it as they stept,
> One and then one, along their walks, and kept
> Their changing feet in flicker all the time
> And to their feet the narrow bells gave rhyme.
>
> (*Richard*)

Like Hopkins, Dylan fits together rhymes in favour of rhyme. In the seventeenth century Ben Jonson notoriously, in mock self-contradiction, gave the world *A Fit of Rhyme against Rhyme*. Dylan is well aware of the hostility that rhymes can evoke, in readers (or listeners), and between the rhymes themselves. For although there is a place where rhymes can whisper (think of it as the Highlands), there are ugly places where rhyme needs to grate hideously, to make you yearn to break free, to change:

> You've had enough hatred
> Your bones are breaking, can't find nothing sacred
> > (*Ye Shall Be Changed*)

Dylan can be a master of war. The friction of "hatred" against "sacred" sets your teeth on edge, or makes you grit them. "You know Satan sometimes comes as a man of peace."

Rhyme can give shape to individual lines and to a song or poem as a whole, which is where rhyme-schemes come in. A change in the rhyming pattern can intimate that the song or the poem is having to draw to a close, is fulfilling its arc. Life is short, art is long: true, but art is not interminable. Think back to early days with Dylan's endings, and to how he chose to end *Just Like Tom Thumb's Blues*. The last two lines:

> I'm going back to New York City
> I do believe I've had enough

End of song. And it feels like a due ending for the perfectly simple reason that, in this final verse (one that, in closing, starts out "I started out"), all the lines (odd and even) rhyme – something that is not true of any previous verses.

> I started out on burgundy
> But soon hit the harder stuff
> Everybody said they'd stand behind me
> When the game got rough
> But the joke was on me
> There was nobody even there to call my bluff
> I'm going back to New York City
> I do believe I've had enough

The other verses rhyme only the even lines. You don't have to be conscious of it, but it works on your ear to tell you that there's something different about this final verse: all its lines are rhyming away. Whether or not you consciously record this, you register it. An ending, not a stopping. And ("I'm going back to New York City") it has an allusive comic relation to his first album, where the first of his own two songs, *Talking New York*, has as its ending:

> So long, New York
> Howdy, East Orange

Why was that such a wittily wry ending? First, because of the Orange as against an apple. New York is the Big Apple, so there's a subterranean semantic rhyming going on, sense rather than sound, Big Apple versus East Orange. But the ending depends, too, upon the fact that "orange" famously is a word that does not have a rhyme in English. Dylan was asked once about this:

Do you have a rhyme for "orange"?
"What, I didn't hear that."
A rhyme for "orange".
"A-ha . . . just a rhyme for 'orange'?"
It is true you were censored for singing on the "Ed Sullivan Show"?
"I'll tell you the rhyme in a minute."[1]

Apple, on the other hand, is easy as pie. Dylan uses the awry feeling at the particular part of such a blues song, where the last throw-away moment throws away rhyme, and goes in instead for a sloping-off movement. "Howdy, East Orange". So long, rhyme.

The reason that Andrew Marvell's lines about the orange are so delectable is that the poetical inversion is not lapsed into, but called for:

> He hangs in shades the orange bright,
> Like golden lamps in a green night.
>
> (*Bermudas*)

[1] Press conference / interview with Ralph J. Gleason (1965), *Rolling Stone* (14 December 1967, 20 January 1968).

The inversion of "the orange bright" is justified by there not being a rhyme for orange anyway, and if Marvell had said, "He hangs in shades the bright orange", he'd have had to set out for a mountain range a long way from Bermuda. (That's right, Blorenge, in Wales.) Even the great rhymester Robert Browning never ventured to end a line of verse with the word "orange".

There's a deft comedy that Dylan avails himself of here, in making something from the simple fact that some words do and other words don't rhyme. True, the voice that exults in forcing "hers" into rhyming rapport with "yours" ("I don't wanna be hers, I wanna be yers") is one that never rests when it comes to wresting and wrestling, but there are limits . . .

Emotionally Yours: the phrase signs off, the usual formula unusually worded and unusually used. The song takes the great commonplaces of rhyme and makes them not quite what you would have expected. But then love is like that in its comings and goings. The first rhyme in *Emotionally Yours* is *find me / remind me* – itself a reminder that every rhyme is an act of finding and of reminding (that's what a rhyme is, after all). Later there is *rock me / lock me*, this *not* locked into position (no feeling of being trapped), and with "rock me" – "Come baby, rock me" – having the lilt of a lullaby, not the drive of rock. It's a song about how someone can be indeed "emotionally yours" but not yours in every way (not domestically, for instance – not available for marriage, for who knows what reasons?). Every verse signs off, as if in a letter at once intimate, cunning, and formal, "be emotionally yours". Dylan sings it with a full sense that it is a deep pastiche of a good old old-time song, with stately exaggerated movements of his voice, especially at the rhymes – and he makes it new.

And how does this song, *A Valediction: forbidding Mourning*, like John Donne's great poem about absence, end so that we are "satisfied"? Satisfied that though the song ends, the gratitude doesn't. Again it's the rhyming that realizes the song's story. After a clear pattern:

> *find me / remind me*
> *show me / know me*
> *rock me / lock me*
> *teach me / reach me*

– after these:

> Come baby, shake me, come baby, take me, I would be satisfied
> Come baby, hold me, come baby, help me, my arms are open wide
> I could be unraveling wherever I'm traveling, even to foreign shores
> But I will always be emotionally yours

Shake me / take me: this is unexpected only in the benign impulse recognized in "shake" there. And *unraveling / traveling*: this is unexpected only in its sudden twinge of darkness. "As he lay unravelling in the agony of death, the standers-by could hear him say softly, 'I have seen the glories of the world.'"[1] But *hold me / help me*? How easily "Come baby, hold me" could have slid equably into "come baby, fold me", with "my arms are open wide" simply waiting there to do the folding. But "Come baby, hold me, come baby, help me": the rotating of "hold me" into that unexpected calm plea, at once central and at a tangent, "help me". The turn has the poignancy of Christina Rossetti, who thanks the Lord *For a Mercy Received*:

> Till now thy hand hath held me fast
> Lord, help me, hold me, to the last.[2]

To the last. Will always be more-than-emotionally Yours. The thought lightens her darkness and ours.

In the lightness of a *Doonesbury* strip there was an exchange that enjoyed its comedy not exactly at Dylan's expense (Jimmy Carter is the one who is quoted) but on his account:

– "An authentic American voice!" Can you beat that, Jim? I mean, I just want it to rhyme, man.
– Now he tells us.

Not so much "Now he tells us" as How he tells us, or rather How he does more than just *tell* us. Show and Tell. Anyway, Dylan himself has been happy to convey the ways in which rhyme, among the many things that it can be, can be fun.

Is rhyming fun for you?
"Well, it can be, but you know, it's a game. You know, you sit around . . . It

---

[1] Isaac Barrow at the foreign shores of death in 1670. John Aubrey (1626–97) began to compile his *Brief Lives* in 1680.
[2] Jim McCue gave me this.

gives you a thrill. It gives you a thrill to rhyme something you might think, well, that's never been rhymed before."[1]

> an' new ideas that haven't been wrote
> an' new words t' fit into rhyme
> (if it rhymes, it rhymes
> if it don't, it don't
> if it comes, it comes
> if it won't, it won't)[2]

Robert Shelton had recourse to a rhyme of a sort when he put it that "Dylan pretends to know more about freight trains than quatrains." Dylan, years later, spoke of what he knows:

"As you get older, you get smarter and that can hinder you because you try to gain control over the creative impulse. Creativity is not like a freight train going down the tracks. It's something that has to be caressed and treated with a great deal of respect. If your mind is intellectually in the way, it will stop you. You've got to program your brain not to think too much."
And how do you do that?
"Go out with the bird dogs."[3]

What is at issue is not pretence but premeditation. Dylan is conscious of how much needs to be done by the unconscious or subconscious.

Still staying in the unconscious frame of mind, you can pull yourself out and throw up two rhymes first and work it back. You get the rhymes first and work it back and then see if you make it make sense in another kind of way. You can still stay in the unconscious frame of mind to pull it off, which is the state of mind you have to be in anyway.[4]

Georg Christoph Lichtenberg, the aphorist and sage, believed that artists both do and do not know what they are doing, and that their works are

---

[1] Zollo, *Songwriters on Songwriting*, p. 81.
[2] *11 Outlined Epitaphs*, in *Lyrics 1962–1985* (1985), p. 112.
[3] Interview, *USA Today* (15 February 1995). See also p. 8.
[4] Zollo, *Songwriters on Songwriting*, p. 81.

even wiser than they are. "The metaphor is much more subtle than its inventor."[1]

There's a lyric in "License to Kill": "Man has invented his doom / First step was touching the moon". Do you really believe that?
"Yeah, I do. I have no idea why I wrote that line, but on some level, it's just like a door into the unknown."[2]

---

[1] *Aphorisms*, tr. R. J. Hollingdale (1990), p. 87.
[2] *Rolling Stone* (21 June 1984).

The Sins

Envy

Song to Woody

It would have been only too human for Bob Dylan at nineteen to envy Woody Guthrie. His fame, for a start, and (not the same) the sheer respect in which Guthrie was held, his staunch stamina, his being an icon who wouldn't have had any truck with such a self-conscious word and who had not let himself become an idol. Enviable. Inevitably open, therefore, on a bad day, to competitive petulance.

> For 'tis all one to courage high,
> The emulous or enemy.[1]

And yet not so. Truly high courage knows the difference between emulation and its enemy, envy. Dylan was sufficiently secure of his genius, even at the very start, to be able to rise above envy, rising to the occasion that was so much more than an occasion only.

Song to Woody is one of only two songs written by Dylan himself on his first album. (If the song had been called *Song for Woody*, it would not be the same, would be in danger of mildly conceited cadging as against a tribute at a respectful distance.) The other song by Dylan on the album, *Talking New York*, also paid tribute to "a very great man",[2] and didn't even need to tell you that it was again Woody Guthrie to whom Dylan was showing gratitude. *Talking New York* brings home that there was not all that much to be grateful for, back then, when it was early days:

> Well, I got a harmonica job, begun to play
> Blowin' my lungs out for a dollar a day
> I blowed inside out and upside down
> The man there said he loved m' sound
> He was ravin' about he loved m' sound
> Dollar a day's worth

[1] Andrew Marvell, *An Horatian Ode upon Cromwell's Return from Ireland*.
[2] "Now a very great man once said / That some people rob you with a fountain pen".

But *Song to Woody* appreciates a life's worth, and it knows about gratitude: that, for a start, gratitude is the due of Woody Guthrie, and not of him alone. That to give gratitude is to be the richer, not the poorer, for the giving. And that it is gratitude that sees through and sees off envy. Gratitude is the sublime sublimation of envy. Meanwhile, all this is of course easier said than done. Or, if your doing takes the form of the art of song, easier said than sung.

For there is, from the very start, a challenge about how you are going to end any expression of gratitude. The expression of it has to end without ever suggesting for a final moment that the feeling itself has come to an end. The song, like everything human, will have to end, but not because gratitude has ceased.

SONG TO WOODY

I'm out here a thousand miles from my home
Walkin' a road other men have gone down
I'm seein' your world of people and things
Your paupers and peasants and princes and kings

Hey, hey, Woody Guthrie, I wrote you a song
'Bout a funny ol' world that's a-comin' along
Seems sick an' it's hungry, it's tired and it's torn
It looks like it's a–dyin' an' it's hardly been born

Hey, Woody Guthrie, but I know that you know
All the things that I'm a-sayin' an' a-many times more
I'm a-singin' you the song, but I can't sing enough
'Cause there's not many men 've done the things that you've done

Here's to Cisco an' Sonny an' Leadbelly too
An' to all the good people that traveled with you
Here's to the hearts and the hands of the men
That come with the dust and are gone with the wind

I'm a-leavin' tomorrow, but I could leave today
Somewhere down the road someday
The very last thing that I'd want to do
Is to say I've been hittin' some hard travelin' too

How do we sense that the final verse of this simple (far from easy) song is to be the final verse, without there being a cadging nudge? Things would be different on the printed page, because your eye can see that you're reading the last lines, whereas your ear can't in the same way hear that it is hearing them.[1]

You sense that the end is imminent because the song turns back to the beginning (gratitude is a virtuous circle, not a vicious one): the opening words of the final verse, "I'm a-leavin'", recall the opening of the first verse, "I'm out here", passing back through – though not passing over – the hailing that heartens the three central verses of the song: "Hey, hey, Woody Guthrie", "Hey, Woody Guthrie", "Here's to Cisco ... Here's to the hearts and the hands ...".

And there are other intimations that the song, which is not going to quit, is about to leave. For instance, the second line of the first verse, "Walkin' a road other men have gone down", is glimpsed in the vista of the second line of this final verse, "Somewhere down the road someday". Again, this feels like the final verse because of the announcement "I'm a-leavin' tomorrow" – and yet not obdurately the last verse since it does go on immediately "but I could leave today", so there may or may not be a little time in hand. The rhyme *today / someday* has a stranded feeling, reluctant to leave (-*day* after -*day*), especially when combined with the wistful effect in the move from the beginning to the end of the line: "Somewhere down the road someday".

Added to all of which, it feels truly like the last verse, because in the sentence that makes up these two lines (the penultimate line and then the last line) the song concedes what it needs to:

> The very last thing that I'd want to do
> Is to say I've been hittin' some hard travelin' too

The singer (the young Dylan, yes, but the point is art, not autobiographical application) is truthful and rueful: I wouldn't want even to seem to upstage you or pretend that I've had your life's experiences, including the hard travelling of the hard old days. Hard, though, my disclaimer, for I do have some claim to share things with you, don't I? And then "The very last thing" turns out to be *almost* the very last thing in the song: that is, it opens the very last sentence of the song but it does not close the song. For the very last line of the song is not where those words occur.

This is an arc completed, not a feeling vacated. Our mind is tipped off – through Dylan's play with the phrase "The very last thing" – and so is our ear: for this is the first time, the only time, then, that a rhyme has returned

[1] See p. 14.

in the song: *too/you* in the one but last verse, and then *do/too* in these very last lines. ("Travelin' too": the word has itself travelled on from the previous stanza: "that traveled with you".)

> I'm a-singin' you the song, but I can't sing enough
> 'Cause there's not many men 've done the things that you've done

– so Dylan sings, finding a way of making this truth of gratitude's benign insatiability ring true. Some of the tribute's authenticity, and its being so entirely an envy-free zone, must come from the reluctance to make an inordinate claim even for the singer whom you are honouring, audible in "not many men". Any men, really, when it comes to the world that Dylan is evoking? Let us leave it at not many men.

"Walkin' a road other men have gone down": and other men than both Guthrie and Dylan are to be the beneficiaries of the song's gratitude. Not only as being thanked both personally and on behalf of us all, but because of the nature of gratitude itself, which appreciates – even in the moment when it is grateful to genius – that genius is not solitary and can thrive only because of all the others that keep it company, "all the good people" that travel with it – and with the rest of us.

> Here's to Cisco an' Sonny an' Leadbelly too
> An' to all the good people that traveled with you

This is full of respect, even while the names themselves are duly differentiated: Cisco Houston, Sonny Terry, and Leadbelly are spoken of famously and familiarly, though not impudently. Woody Guthrie is Woody in the title, *Song to Woody*, but in the song proper he is treated with a propriety that is saved from being too deferential by the affectionately chaffing lead-in: "Hey, hey, Woody Guthrie, I wrote you a song" (that might seem cheeky of young me, but honestly it isn't), and

> Hey, Woody Guthrie, but I know that you know
> All the things that I'm a-sayin' an' a-many times more

That is quite something to say, and to sing, and it asks – as art, I mean, not as a personal plea – a substantiated trust that we will take it in the spirit in which it is offered: not as false modesty but as true tribute. For the song has not moved, as it so easily might have done, from the words of the first verse, "I'm seein' your world", to something along the lines of "Now I'm goin' to show you *my* world", but to a world that is neither yours, Woody Guthrie, nor mine (as yet . . .), "a funny ol' world that's a-comin' along". And "I know that you know" can, on this happy unenvious occasion, have nothing of the icy negation of *Positively 4th Street* with its soured repetition of the word "know". No?

Positively 4th Street

If you want your good book to get a bad review, have a friend review it. Envy has a way, regrettably and even regretfully, of rearing its sore head. Of course friendship thinks of itself as the enemy of envy, but then there is nothing more embitteredly envious than a friendship betrayed.

> You got a lotta nerve
> To say you are my friend
> When I was down
> You just stood there grinning
>
> You got a lotta nerve
> To say you got a helping hand to lend
> You just want to be on
> The side that's winning

But if there had always been positively no two-way street, they wouldn't now be standing in this acid rain.

For friendship (and *Positively 4th Street* has to be a song about a friendship that went wrong, that soured) differs most of all from love in this: that friendship has to be reciprocal, reciprocated. I can love you without your loving me, but I can't be your friend without your being my friend. (My befriending you is something quite other.) "You just want to be on / The side that's winning"? Careering into envy, are you? The song itself is concentratedly one-sided, and from the very beginning it makes clear that it is going to strike unrelentingly the same note and the same target.

This starts with the immediately metallic rhyme within "You got a lotta nerve". (Nerve as impudence, but with nerves tautly a-quiver in every arrow-strung line.) Then there's the re-insistence, promptly, of the entire line repeated, "You got a lotta nerve", same timing, same placing, pounding with the same instrument – and this with the very next line then saying yet once more "you got a". (Helping hand to lend? You must be joking.) At once obsessedly repetitive and laconically flat-tongued, the song is a masterpiece of regulated hatred – the great phrase for the key-cold clarity (not charity) of Jane Austen.[1] The fire next time, maybe, but the ice this time. Anyway, revenge is a dishing-it-out that is best eaten cold.[2]

Impact impinges. Repeatedly. The song exercises its sway while swaying (like a boxer), for it has an extraordinary sense of powerfully moving while threateningly not moving.[3] "You just stood there grinning": the song just stands there, not grinning, but grinding. Might it even be said to just stomp there? No, because it bobs a bout. So when we suddenly find (it is a surprise) "surprised" precipitating "paralyzed" –

> You see me on the street
> You always act surprised
> You say, "How are you?" "Good luck"
> But you don't mean it

> When you know as well as me
> You'd rather see me paralyzed
> Why don't you just come out once
> And scream it

[1] D. W. Harding: "Her books are, as she meant them to be, read and enjoyed by precisely the sort of people whom she disliked; she is a literary classic of the society which attitudes like hers, held widely enough, would undermine." Some of this would go for Dylan and his subterranean underminings, of glassy self-confidence, for instance, in *Like a Rolling Stone*, or of sales-talk in *Clean-Cut Kid*. Likewise, perhaps, with Harding's closing words in 1939: "I have tried to underline one or two features of her work that claim the sort of readers who sometimes miss her – those who would turn to her not for relief and escape but as a formidable ally against things and people which were to her, and still are, hateful." (*Regulated Hatred and Other Essays on Jane Austen*, ed. Monica Lawlor, 1998, pp. 6, 25.)

[2] As against the affable warmth, the forget-it extravagance, in *I Shall Be Free No. 10*:

> Now I gotta friend who spends his life
> Stabbing my picture with a bowie-knife
> Dreams of strangling me with a scarf
> When my name comes up he pretends to barf
> I've got a million friends!

[3] *Not Dark Yet*: "I know it looks like I'm movin' but I'm standin' still". This, as contemplation, not as confrontation.

– it is that the song has realized its power, tonic and toxic, to paralyze its opponent.

"You say, 'How are you?' 'Good luck'". Disarming? No, and Dylan declines to lower his guard. For luck invites envy, as is understood in *Idiot Wind*:

> She inherited a million bucks and when she died it came to me
> I can't help it if I'm lucky

You can't be blamed for being lucky – but you can be disliked for it, and you are likely to be envied for it. All you can do is shrug and propitiate ("I can't help it if I'm lucky"). It was good of Dylan to wish us well at the end of an interview in 1965:

Is there anything in addition to your songs that you want to say to people?
"Good luck!"
You don't say that in your songs.
"Oh, yes I do; every song tails off with, 'Good Luck – I hope you make it.'"[1]

It is a nice thought that every Dylan song tails off with "Good Luck" to those of us who are listening to it, but what about those whom the song addresses as *you*?[2] *Positively 4th Street* does not tail off, it heads off, and in any case it does not tail off with "Good Luck" to its interluckitor. Dylan's farewell in the interview has a cadence that is illuminatingly close to the wording of the cited farewell in this song from the very same year.

"Good Luck – I hope you make it"

"Good luck"
But you don't mean it

The feeling of paralysis (the root notion of *fascination*[3]) is a consequence

[1] Press conference / interview with Ralph J. Gleason, *Rolling Stone* (14 December 1967, 20 January 1968).

[2] Paul Zollo, *Songwriters on Songwriting* (1997), p. 79. Zollo: "In your songs, like his [Guthrie's], we know a real person is talking, with lines like, 'You've got a lot of nerve to say you are my friend'." Dylan: "That's another way of writing a song, of course. Just talking to somebody that ain't there. That's the best way. That's the truest way."

[3] *OED*, 2b: "To deprive of the power of escape or resistance, as serpents are said to do through the terror produced by their look or merely by their perceived presence."

of the counterpointing – or counterpunching – of the units musical and verbal. Musically, the unit is of four lines, but verbally (as lyrics) the unit has a rhyme scheme that extends over eight lines. Positively 4th and 8th. The effect is of a sequence that both is and is not intensely repetitive. So while musically the song is in twelve verses, rhymingly it is in six. The armour-plated template in each set is simply the rhyming of lines two and six, and of lines four and eight. But Dylan, as so often, loves not only to attend but to bend his attention, and so to intensify, and what we hear within those first eight lines is the not-letting-go of any of the first four lines: "nerve" is repeated in the fifth line, the whole line back again as though in a lethal litany; "lend" takes up "friend"; "on" off-rhymes with "down"; and "winning" is in a clinch with "grinning". (All the more a clinch in that the final rhyme, here as throughout, is a disyllabic rhyme, all the way from this *grinning / winning* to the final *be you / see you*.) As though on probation, not one line of the first four is let off its obligation to report back during the ensuing four.

Whereupon the next set can afford to relax, as though the template should be enough for now (*that / at*, and *show it / know it*), yet not quite enough, since Dylan threateningly dandles a rhyme-line from the first verse, whose "When I was down" immediately gets re-charged here:

> You say I let you down
> You know it's not like that
> If you're so hurt
> Why then don't you show it

> You say you lost your faith
> But that's not where it's at
> You had no faith to lose
> And you know it[1]

The accuser is the one who had faith to lose. The music and the voice combine to create a chilling thrilling pause after that word "lose", so that "And you know it", pouncing, brooks no resistance.

Such an evocation of faith negated is a positive achievement, because

---

[1] On a different occasion this would be a charge more likely to be pressed against another than against oneself. "I hurt easy, I just don't show it / You can hurt someone and not even know it" (*Things Have Changed*). The rhyme reasons differently.

it makes sense only as founded upon faith in the possibility of something better. For every *Positively 4th Street* about faith misplaced in friendship, there is a *Bob Dylan's Dream* about friendship's solid solidarity for all its pains and losses. And in any case the vibrant anger in *Positively 4th Street* does itself directly convey what friendship ought to be and can be. For how could there be a true indictment of false friends that didn't call upon and call up true friends?

But now it settles into third, fourth, and fifth sets of verses, all in the sedate template. First, *my back / contact*, and *in with / begin with*:

> I know the reason
> That you talk behind my back
> I used to be among the crowd
> You're in with
>
> Do you take me for such a fool
> To think I'd make contact
> With the one who tries to hide
> What he don't know to begin with

Then, *embrace / place*, and *rob them / problem*:

> No, I do not feel that good
> When I see the heartbreaks you embrace
> If I was a master thief
> Perhaps I'd rob them
>
> And now I know you're dissatisfied
> With your position and your place
> Don't you understand
> It's not my problem

"Understand" is irresistible ("Don't you understand"), an unobtrusive triumph, mindful both of "You just stood there" at the beginning and of the undeviating repetition of "You could stand inside my shoes" at the end.

But the *problem / rob them* rhyme is something of a problem. The rhyme is a touch far-fetched, and is it worth the carriage? Perhaps, but that would have to be the point, for the other rhymes are living near at hand, and are simply telling: *friend / lend, grinning / winning* . . . The rhyme *problem / rob them* precipitates a different world or mood, suggesting the uneasy bravura of *half sick / traffic* in *Absolutely Sweet Marie* (absolutely sweet there). Nothing wrong with one pair of rhymes asking a different kind of attention (not more attention, really) than do the other rhyme-pairs in a song, and this would be congruent with the perplexity of the syntax in this verse. For whereas elsewhere in *Positively 4th Street* the syntax is positively forthright, advancing straight forward, here it is circuitous, and it pauses for a moment upon "Perhaps":

> No, I do not feel that good
> When I see the heartbreaks you embrace
> If I was a master thief
> Perhaps I'd rob them

What is it (the phrase is cryptic) to embrace heartbreaks? To enjoy one's own sufferings? To be sicklily solicitous of other people's suffering, creepily commiserating away? And do these tangents amount to one of those mysterious triumphs of phrasing that exquisitely elude paraphrase (like "One too many mornings / And a thousand miles behind"), or is this one of those occasions when something eludes not us but the artist? Dylan is a master of living derangements of syntax[1] but even he must sometimes let things slip. Dr Johnson ventured to characterize as an imperfectionist that Dylanesque writer William Shakespeare:[2]

---

[1] See p. 227 on the simply knotty lines in *Hattie Carroll*: "And handed out strongly, for penalty and repentance / William Zanzinger with a six-month sentence."

[2] William James on the artist-entertainer Shakespeare:

He seems to me to have been a professional *amuser*, in the first instance, with a productivity like that of a Dumas, or a Scribe; but possessing what no other amuser has possessed, a lyric splendor added to his rhetorical fluency, which has made people take him for a more essentially serious human being than he was. Neurotically and erotically, he was hyperaesthetic, with a playful graciousness of character never surpassed. He could be profoundly melancholy; but even then was controlled by his audience's needs . . . Was there ever an author of such emotional importance whose reaction against false conventions of life was such an absolute zero as his?

(To T. S. Perry, 22 May 1910, *The Letters of William James*, 1920, vol. II, p. 336)

William James's love of Shakespeare: love minus "an absolute zero". An interviewer asked Dylan: "Are you trying to say something when you write or are you just entertaining?" And he: "I'm just an entertainer, that's all." Sure. Los Angeles (16 December 1965); *Bob Dylan in His Own Words*, compiled by Miles (1978), p. 77.

It is incident to him to be now and then entangled with an unwieldy sentiment, which he cannot well express, and will not reject; he struggles with it a while, and if it continues stubborn, comprises it in words such as occur, and leaves it to be disentangled and evolved by those who have more leisure to bestow upon it.[1]

> No, I do not feel that good
> When I see the heartbreaks you embrace
> If I was a master thief
> Perhaps I'd rob them

It must be granted that if these lines induce queasiness, they do make a point of saying "No, I do not feel that good". So an unsettling rhyme such as *problem / rob them* might rightly be hard to stomach, especially given the tilting "Perhaps". And given what a *problem* is: not just "a difficult or puzzling question proposed for solution; a riddle; an enigmatic statement" (the song takes care to couch these "problem"-lines enigmatically, riddlingly), but a forcible projectile, "lit. a thing thrown or put forward". The song throws out and puts forward its weaponry.

But again, "Perhaps I'd rob them": what does this enigmatic phrase mean? "I'd steal them" (these heartbreaks)? Then what would you do with them? And wouldn't that have to be "I'd rob *you of* them"? Rid you of them? Not rob them, the heartbreaks, presumably – except that *rob* is sometimes used to mean "to carry off as plunder; to steal" (*The Oxford English Dictionary*, 5, "Now rare"), as in "rob his treasure from him", or "Passion robs my peace no more",[2] so Dylan wouldn't have to be taking or stealing much of a liberty. Especially as there may be a suggestion of heart-breaking and heart-entering (or exiting). And yet the lines, like nothing else in the song, continue to rob my peace. Not that the song offers itself as a peace-maker. A truce at most.

On and on and on and on the song weaves, and yet with a left and a right or a shifting of weight all the time pugnaciously, combatively. But we can sense that the round must be drawing to an end, or may be nearing a knock-out, when the pattern of the opening re-emerges. There, the line "You got a lotta nerve" had opened two successive quatrains, and now the reminder that even this vituperation must come to an end is brought home

[1] *Preface to Shakespeare* (1765).
[2] Thomas Campbell, *Farewell to Love* (1830).

to us when we hear, as we have not heard along the way, such a repetition again at the head of two successive quatrains: "I wish that for just one time" / "Yes, I wish that for just one time". (Relentless, this pressing home twice the words "just one time".) But then there is a further compounding of the shape in which the tireless tirade had been launched, for back then it had been only a matter of repeating the first line, whereas now that there is to be a complete dismissal of the ex-friend, it is not one but two lines that will be repeated to begin the excommunication:

> I wish that for just one time
> You could stand inside my shoes
> And just for that one moment
> I could be you

> Yes, I wish that for just one time
> You could stand inside my shoes
> You'd know what a drag it is
> To see you

Usually the idiom about wishing that someone could stand inside your shoes is a movement inviting sympathy (see it my way, please); here it swings round into antipathy. And Dylan gives voices to these feelings so that at the end of each verse – and consummately at this very end – the few syllables are held, stretched on a rack all the more frighteningly for there being nothing of a scream at this end.

Until this unpalliated ending you feel that Dylan could have gone on pounding for ever (*Eternal Circle* of hell), so that the challenge was to arrive at a conclusion that could bring proof and reproof to an end. And then, for the only time in the song (truly "for just one time"), there is a shrewd little tilting of the stress within the disyllabic rhyme, with "be you" not having exactly the same measured pressure as "see you", the first asking slightly more emphasis upon "you" than does the second:

> And just for that one moment
> I could be yóu

> You'd know what a drag it is
> To sée you

There is a famous poignancy in Hardy's poem *The Voice*:

Can it be you that I hear? Let me view you, then,
Standing as when I drew near to the town
Where you would wait for me; yes, as I knew you then,
Even to the original air-blue gown!

F. R. Leavis brought out how Hardy's rhythms escape the "crude popular lilt" that might endanger the poem: "you that I *hear*" is set in contrast with the hope "Let me *view* you then", asking that there be some emphasis on "view", whereas in the line that rhymes with this, the antithesis is of "now" as against "then", so that there has to be a touch tilting it away from a lilt. As Leavis saw and heard, "The shift of stress ('víew you then', 'knew you thén') has banished the jingle from it."[1]

Positively 4th Street was never going to succumb to a jingle, or even to a jingle jangle, but it is the deadly precision of the emphasis that consummates the act of banishment, giving the unanswerable last word to this song that is not *I and I* but You and I.

It has the hammering away at words, and with words, that characterizes a quarrel, and one word above all others: *know*. About this friend or "friend" we know nothing except what the song declares through and through. If I now quote something that Dylan himself said, it is not in order to invoke whatever biographical facts might exist outside the song, or to adduce Dylan's own character − it is the character of his songs that matters to me. But *Positively 4th Street* is an act of retaliation, and it gives some warrant for stressing *know* in the song that Dylan makes much of the word in this context. "I'm known to retaliate you know; you should know I'm known to *retaliate*."[2] You know; you should know I'm known . . .

You say I let you down
You know it's not like that

You had no faith to lose
And you know it

I know the reason
That you talk behind my back

[1] *New Bearings in English Poetry* (1932), p. 54.
[2] In reply to Anthony Scaduto: "I told him once more that I would not delete the references to his family and Bob replied . . ." *Bob Dylan* (1971, revised edition 1973), p. 293.

> With the one who tries to hide
> What he don't know to begin with
>
> When you know as well as me
> You'd rather see me paralyzed
>
> And now I know you're dissatisfied
> With your position and your place
>
> You'd know what a drag it is
> To see you[1]

It's all over, then. Envy has shown itself to be one of the corrosive agents (but only one, for this is a song that compacts a good many bad impulses).

> And now I know you're dissatisfied
> With your position and your place
> Don't you understand
> It's not my problem

Your envy (of what you seem to imagine my position and my place to be) is your problem. Sorry about your dissatisfaction with your position and your place (your standing), but it's not my problem, "Don't you understand". You don't understand (and that's your problem).

The song is sharply shaped when it comes to questions. The first two quatrains don't have any questions in them and the last two don't have any either. But the middle of the song is a quartet of questions, most of them such as are not really questions at all, any more than is "Who do you think you are" or "Can I help you". Dylan doesn't print them with question-marks or sing them very interrogatively:

---

[1] See what a difference it makes when Scaduto, variously misquoting *Positively 4th Street*, does without "You'd know": "There is no line in all pop music filled with more hate than the last line of the song, which sums it up: *If you could stand in my shoes you'd see what a drag it is to be you.*" Not "in my shoes", but "inside". Not "you'd see what a drag it is to be you", but "You'd know what a drag it is / To see you" (Scaduto, *Bob Dylan*, p. 230).

Why then don't you show it

Do you take me for such a fool

Why don't you just come out once
And scream it

Don't you understand

The only question in the song that is manifestly sung (and printed in *Lyrics 1962–1985*) with a question-mark is the one that is treacherously considerate, the inquiry in the street from the friend: "How are you?" Not "You ask, 'How are you?'", but "You say, 'How are you?'"

It may seem a bit late for this commentary to raise the question of whether the friend is a man or a woman. Not to be raised as a biographical or historical matter – it's clear that the friend could be a compound ghost, and many candidates have been proposed over the years, with Joan Baez appearing in the company of half a dozen men in David Hajdu's annals *Positively 4th Street* (2001). Who, except an uncouth sleuth-hound, cares? But much of the song's power may lurk in its decision not to decide this for us. In a Dylan song it is usually clear whether a man or a woman is being addressed. This time, not so. "Just talking to somebody that ain't there." What matters is that a friend has let you down. Badly. Because of envy and rivalry and . . . And is still capable of unctuating ("Good luck") unconvincingly.

A question at a press conference in 1965:

In a lot of your songs you are hard on people – in *Like a Rolling Stone* you're hard on the girls and in *Positively 4th Street* you're hard on a friend. Do you do this because you want to change their lives, or do you want to point out to them the error of their ways?

Answer: "I want to needle them."[1]

It was a needle that injected the songs back then; now it is more likely to be a laser beam.

For my part, I have always taken the no-friend-of-his to be a man. Friends of mine, it seems, have taken a woman. At one point, the force of the lines would have to be taken differently if the irritant were not a he but a she.

[1] Press conference/interview with Ralph J. Gleason, *Rolling Stone* (14 December 1967, 20 January 1968).

> I know the reason
> That you talk behind my back
> I used to be among the crowd
> You're in with
>
> Do you take me for such a fool
> To think I'd make contact
> With the one who tries to hide
> What he don't know to begin with

I envisage the friend himself as despised here, to his face, as "the one who tries to hide / What he don't know to begin with". And I take this to be the formally aggressive mock-incredulity or distancing ("one who . . .") that says "he" even while speaking to "you": "Now he tells me!" This, with "know" as yet another of the occurrences of a word angrily bandied between the two of them throughout the song. I get more from this than from the other interpretation, the one that travels out, via the third-person pronoun, to a third party who forms part of an obscure narrative that ripples into further rivalries. For I have always thrilled to the immitigably binary set-up for the song. You and I, not You and I and He.

Oh, there is a crowd you're in with, but for the duration of the song the crowd is outside the ring, and inside the ring there are just the two of us, with no referee to boot. So I'd like to continue to hear "one who tries to hide / What he don't know to begin with" as contemptuously third person – especially if "third" be pronounced in the Irish fashion. But I can understand the feeling (and I value the reminder) that a woman could well have proved to be just such a friend.[1] And I'd grant that the word "heartbreaks" ("the heartbreaks you embrace") might consort better, albeit prejudicially, with a woman. Not that heartbreak need be sexual or amatory – there is no end to the things that break hearts. (In *Among School Children*, Yeats saw how

---

[1] Those for whom the friend sounds just like a woman could find support, albeit jokey, in the fact that the next song in *Lyrics 1962–1985* (the previous one on *Biograph*), *Can You Please Crawl Out Your Window?* (where "You" is assuredly a woman), can be heard to end, in the only released performance, with four lines not printed in *Lyrics*: "You got a lotta nerve / To say you are my friend / If you won't come out your window / Yes come out your window". Dylan is fooling around, but the guest-appearance of the first two lines there may say something about how to envisage the friend. Michael Gray mentions "the 'Good Luck!' that the woman is permitted to actually say", following this with "she . . . her . . . her . . . her", but a footnote now says: "I no longer assume the 'you' to be a woman" (*Song and Dance Man III*, 2000, pp. 68–9).

different are the images that nuns, as against mothers, worship: "And yet they too break hearts".) Heartbreak, like so much else in the song, could have a root in envy. Bursting with envy. Jealousy is not the same, but bear in mind the words set down in 1586: "Shun jealousy, that heartbreak love".

It may be a valuably unsettling thing about the song that the sex or gender of the friend is not settled. In an interview in *Spin*, Dylan said:

Outside of a song like *Positively 4th Street*, which is extremely one-dimensional, which I like, I don't usually purge myself by writing anything about any type of quote, so-called, relationships. I don't have the kinds of relationships that are built on any kind of false pretense, not to say that I haven't.[1]

Two-dimensional, not one-dimensional, this 4th Street, and although one-sided, it is two-edged, a two-handed engine that stands ready to smite more than once and smite some more. As to sex or gender: the canting word "relationships" ("quote, so-called"), though these days it does suggest lovees and lovers more than friends, can't be denied its applicability to friendship, or to ex-friendship. Catharsis, the ancient critical metaphor in Dylan's phrase "purge myself", would be one way of getting rid of the catharsole and of the waste matter that is pretense.[2] The metaphor in "purge myself" is critical, but Dylan's target isn't formally a critic. "Some would later think the vitriolic lyrics were addressed to the critics of his new style. Dylan denies it. 'I couldn't write a song about something like that,' he said, 'I don't write songs to critics.'"[3]

I don't envy the imagined or imaginary "friend" in this song. One other candidate as the sin of the song would be anger. But the power and the threat are felt in the very restraint: there is no yielding of any kind in the song, and that includes yielding to anger (as against understanding what anger might yield). Anger is a sin resisted or at least curbed by the song. But if I ask what sin might have tempted the artist himself here, the answer isn't going to be envy. When it comes to sin, the song is all the more ample in that its position and its place are not circumscribed by envy. The song looks searchingly into those who, having opted for emptinesses, now want to co-opt someone back into their misvalued ethos and pathos. Pity for the infected, as Pound said, but preserve antisepsis.

[1] Interview with Scott Cohen, *Spin* (December 1985).
[2] A student essay (*not* from the university where I teach): "Tragedy makes you cathart."
[3] Note to *Positively 4th Street* in *Biograph*.

They tell me to be discreet for all intended purposes
They tell me revenge is sweet and from where they stand, I'm sure it is

(*Dark Eyes*)

What sin, come to think of it, might envy incite? Why, pride. *My* position
and *my* place. Pride in being envied, even sometimes (and this is the very
bad bit) if it is being envied by creeps. And then pride's further pleasure:
contempt for the envious flatterers. But Dylan does not flatter himself –
again, not a biographical point but an artistic accomplishment. He can be
proud of the song, not least because he is not proud in it.

Blind Willie McTell

Gratitude to a fellow-singer, no less than in *Song to Woody* (1962), is the
life of *Blind Willie McTell* (1983), of which the burden is both a happy
refrain and the possibility of an unhappy weight, the burden that would
be envy, were it not that the song goes free from it.

Song to Woody had acknowledged something without sounding as though
this were only conceding or admitting, let alone grudgingly admitting:

> Hey, Woody Guthrie, but I know that you know
> All the things that I'm a-sayin' an' a-many times more

That I'm saying and that I'm singing. It may cost a singer a good deal to
say this unenviously about another singer, but the cost is gladly paid by a
solvent artist, for it is not so much paid as repaid, and is a debt of honour.
And gratitude doesn't run to ingratiation. The refrain of *Blind Willie McTell*
is likewise happy to do some acknowledging. The earlier "I know that you
know" becomes this:

> And I know no one can sing the blues
> Like Blind Willie McTell

This might sound negative, *know no* (no, no), but then that is how to convey
that nothing could be more positive. Or more compacted (I know that no
one can, and I know no one who can). Gratitude is called upon and called
for, as it is in the warning voice (O . . . no . . . know . . . know . . . no)
above Adam and Eve in *Paradise Lost*:

Sleep on,
Blest pair; and O yet happiest if ye seek
No happier state, and know to know no more.

(IV, 773–5)

After Guthrie in Dylan's creative life, though before Guthrie historically, there comes – welcomed – a new arrival who is a newer rival. The rivalry has its chivalry.

BLIND WILLIE McTELL

Seen the arrow on the doorpost
Saying, this land is condemned
All the way from New Orleans
To Jerusalem
I traveled through East Texas
Where many martyrs fell
And I know no one can sing the blues
Like Blind Willie McTell

Well, I heard that hoot owl singing
As they were taking down the tents
The stars above the barren trees
Was his only audience
Them charcoal gypsy maidens
Can strut their feathers well
But nobody can sing the blues
Like Blind Willie McTell

See them big plantations burning
Hear the cracking of the whips
Smell that sweet magnolia blooming
See the ghosts of slavery ships
I can hear them tribes a–moaning
Hear the undertaker's bell
Nobody can sing the blues
Like Blind Willie McTell

There's a woman by the river
With some fine young handsome man

He's dressed up like a squire
Bootlegged whiskey in his hand
There's a chain gang on the highway
I can hear them rebels yell
And I know no one can sing the blues
Like Blind Willie McTell

Well, God is in his heaven
And we all want what's his
But power and greed and corruptible seed
Seem to be all that there is
I'm gazing out the window
Of the St. James Hotel
And I know no one can sing the blues
Like Blind Willie McTell

There is a road that runs for twenty years from the one travelling song, *Song to Woody*, to the other, *Blind Willie McTell*. Take, for instance, Dylan's sequence "This land is", moving on to "from New Orleans / To Jerusalem". Guthrie didn't own the franchise on this sequence of words, but it has a way of summoning him. *This Land is Your Land* was his.[1]

The land is your land, this land is my land
From California to the New York island

Dylan puts his own grim spin on this by having the phrase "This land is" be consummated not by "your land" but by "condemned". It is a withering word, once you think of how much it might compact: "condemned" as blamed, censured, judicially sentenced, doomed by fate to some condition, pronounced officially to be unfit for use (we often hear of a house as being condemned, but a *land*?), or – and this is an odd twist – just the opposite, not unfit for use but so fit for use that the government claims the right to take it over: to pronounce judicially (land etc.) as converted or convertible to public use. ("The condemnation of private lands for a highway, a railroad, a public park, etc.") All these might be seething in the word "condemned", and so perhaps – since the train of thought is "Seen the arrow on the

[1] "this land is your land & this land is my land – sure – but the world is run by those that never listen to music anyway" (*Tarantula*, 1966, 1971, p. 88).

doorpost / Saying, this land is condemned" – might be the application to "a door or window: to close or block up". Henry James, *Portrait of a Lady*: "the door that had been condemned, and that was fastened by bolts".

"This land" was all the more Woody Guthrie's because not his alone. Behind it there is an inheritance that is respected in *Blind Willie McTell*, too. The phrase "this land" has its own substantial entry in *Cruden's Concordance to the Bible*, and the phrase's being more than a casual pointer in Dylan's song will be clear if we recall the word in whose company "this land" repeatedly appears in the Bible: "Unto thy seed will I give this land" (Genesis 12:7, repeated in 24:7); "Unto thy seed have I given this land" (Genesis 15:18); "I will multiply your seed as the stars of heaven, and all this land that I have spoken of I will give unto your seed" (Exodus 32:13). "The stars" rise in Dylan's second verse, but the song then bides its time, and it is not until the final verse that "this land" meets the word that is sown so often in its vicinity: "seed".

> But power and greed and corruptible seed
> Seem to be all that there is

The indeflectible internal rhyme *greed / seed* then has "seed" succeeded immediately by "Seem" rounding the corner of the line, and this with a two-edged effect, compounding the insistence (clinched by this assonance and consonance) and yet at the same time mitigating it. For to give emphasis to "Seem" must be to hold open some hope. This final verse does not say that power and greed and corruptible seed are all that there is. Only (only!) that they seem to be all that there is. At which point one realizes the conjunction of the Old Testament's "this land" and "seed" with the New Testament's offering its hope: "being born again, not of corruptible seed, but of incorruptible, by the word of God, which liveth and abideth for ever" (the First Epistle of Peter 1:23). So the song's "corruptible seed" cannot but call up the affirmation that makes divine sense of it by antithesis: "not of corruptible seed, but of incorruptible, by the word of God".

This final verse of Dylan's has begun with a repudiation of hopefulness, for the line "Well, God is in his heaven" does not follow through to the naivety of the famous moment in Victorian poetry (dramatized naivety, there, for Browning's poem *Pippa Passes* is darkened by the larger older sadder story within which it has its young hopes):

> God's in his heaven –
> All's right with the world!

When Dylan moves from "Well, God is in his heaven" to "And we all want what's his", he ignites a flash of doubt. We want to seize what is not ours but his? Or we do want what he wants, want what is his wish? It is an equivocal line to take, and furthermore the benign reading is itself equivocal, since not necessarily to be taken straight. Do we genuinely pray, "Thy will be done"? Or is our prayer lip-service? (We kid others and ourselves that we all want what's His.) But Dylan's run of lines does keep open the respectful colouring of "And we all want what's his", since he moves at once to a chastening "But", where otherwise the rotation of "But" wouldn't fit:

> Well, God is in his heaven
> And we all want what's his
> But power and greed and corruptible seed
> Seem to be all that there is

Dylan does not go along with the blitheness of "God's in his heaven – / All's right with the world!" But his song does not rebound into *All's wrong with the world*, it proceeds as "power and greed and corruptible seed / Seem to be all that there is". *Blind Willie McTell*, which contemplates cruel injustice ("Hear the cracking of the whips", cracking its rhyme with "the ghosts of slavery ships"), does not succumb either to hopefulness or to hopelessness. Try hope. (And while you're at it, try faith and charity.) Remember that those verses of the Epistle of Peter proclaim "the word of God, which liveth and abideth for ever", and remember that this hope is immediately reasserted there in the face of mortality and loss:

For all flesh is as grass, and all the glory of man as the flower of grass. The grass withereth, and the flower thereof falleth away: but the word of the Lord endureth for ever.

Yet not only the word and the voice of the Lord, but the words and the voice of a great singer.

> Well, God is in his heaven
> And we all want what's his
> But power and greed and corruptible seed
> Seem to be all that there is

> I'm gazing out the window
> Of the St. James Hotel
> And I know no one can sing the blues
> Like Blind Willie McTell

What kind of answer can those last two lines of this final verse, the enduring refrain, be to its first four lines? Only an answer at once partial and heartening; McTell's singing is one of the things that there is. And we arrive at this conclusion, at art's being a glory of man that does not wither, via the two lines about the singer of this song itself: "I'm gazing out the window / Of the St. James Hotel". I admire and love the way in which this claims so little, even perhaps claims nothing, does no more than report one of those moments when, abstracted from evil, you gaze out of a window in contemplative regard that is not self-regard.[1]

It is as if the question of envy doesn't even arise. And yet it is knowing this, knowing that envy does not even arise, that plays so generous a part throughout this lucid mysterious song.

> And I know no one can sing the blues
> Like Blind Willie McTell

If Dylan were someone who never sang the blues (someone who limited

---

[1] There is poignancy in the contrast of the hotels (the Chelsea Hotel, recalled two thirds of the way through *Sara*, the St. James Hotel as the penultimate moment of *Blind Willie McTell*). *Sara* is a song that asked of Dylan not that he be himself (a true thing to be) but that he be autobiographically himself (which is less true to his genius and how it sees truths). This meant claims and disclaimers ("Sara, Sara, / You must forgive me my unworthiness"):

> I can still hear the sound of those Methodist bells
> I'd taken the cure and had just gotten through
> Stayin' up for days in the Chelsea Hotel
> Writin' "Sad-Eyed Lady of the Lowlands" for you

Granted, "Those Methodist bells" are other than "the undertaker's bell"; Sara's "arrow and bow", two lines after "your door", other than "the arrow on the doorpost"; "Wherever we travel", other than "I traveled"; and "an old ship", other than "slavery ships". Nevertheless, "I'm gazing out the window / Of the St. James Hotel", writing *Blind Willie McTell* for Blind Willie McTell. On Dylan, McTell, and the blues song *St. James Infirmary* and what it meant to McTell and others, see Michael Gray, *Song and Dance Man III*, chapter 15.

himself to *Living the Blues*), then this might be a comparatively easy
generosity, rather as someone who is a tennis champion might have
little difficulty in granting that no one can play table tennis like A. N.
Other. And if Dylan were someone who sang only the blues, then this
might be demanding too much of him – or of us when it came to trusting
his self-abnegation. The refrain is perfectly pitched and poised. And even
the form that the magnanimous praise takes –

> And I know no one can sing the blues
> Like Blind Willie McTell

– is one that very humanly and decently combines the utmost praise with
a somewhat different inflection, one that emphasizes McTell's uniqueness,
not simply or solely his superiority. That no one can sing the blues like
him: this endearingly combines the superlative and the highly individual,
without having to enter competitively into the proportions of the one to
the other. Perfectly judged, and determined to do justice to McTell. More,
determined to see and hear justice done at last to him.

After the final refrain, there is no more to be said. Or sung. But there
is more to hear, the fully instrumental that is yet an end in itself.

It was the repudiation of envy that brought the hoot owl into the picture
or into the soundtrack. This, with a courteous comedy. Keats had assured
his nightingale that the poet's heartache was not caused by envy: "'Tis not
through envy of thy happy lot". Dylan's night bird sings beautifully in its
way, and its way is one with which neither Blind Willie McTell nor Dylan
is in any way in competition. The owl doesn't fuss about how big or how
enthusiastic his audience is:

> Well, I heard that hoot owl singing
> As they were taking down the tents
> The stars above the barren trees
> Was his only audience

Like the rain in *Lay Down Your Weary Tune*, the hoot owl "asked for no
applause". Hooting, the opposite of applause, is how they drive you off the
stage. The hoot owl could well be – though it is happily not – pleased with
itself. But then so could the others who are good at what they do, whom
we now meet:

> Them charcoal gypsy maidens
> Can strut their feathers well

Well, "well" is a word that had opened this verse (as it will again the final verse), and that chimes with Blind Willie McTell. The owl does well, as others do, too – but, come on, admit it,

> Them charcoal gypsy maidens
> Can strut their feathers well
> But nobody can sing the blues
> Like Blind Willie McTell

Those others have their accomplishments – to wit the owl, and the maidens to woo – but when it comes to the blues . . . And what an accomplishment is the placing of the phrase "Can strut their feathers well". It doesn't forget the owl and his feathers (which it is important not to ruffle), and it brings together so much that makes up what it is to strut. There is "to brace or support by a strut or struts; to be fixed diagonally or slantwise". (I used to hear "Construct their feathers well".) But plainly this should then be puffed out with "to puff out" (*The Oxford English Dictionary* quotes "His lady looked like a frightened owl, with her locks strutted out"). Moreover, there is "to walk with an air of dignity" (this, particularly "of a peacock or other fowl"). And given Dylan's full phrase, "Can strut their feathers well", there is the performing art: to strut one's stuff = to display one's ability.[1]

The young Dylan strutted his stuff as Blind Boy Grunt.[2] I don't know whether there enters into this tribute to Blind Willie McTell any shade of Dylan's ruefully remembering this. It is sure, though, that the song takes blindness seriously, tragically. The first word of *Blind Willie McTell*, inviting

---

[1] Those of us who wonder about Dylan the ten-o'-clock-scholar may recall Milton, *L'Allegro*, 49–52:

> While the cock with lively din,
> Scatters the rear of darkness thin,
> And to the stack, or the barn door,
> Stoutly struts his dames before

This, three lines after Milton's "at my window". McTell sang of the Atlanta Strut, and in *Sugar Baby* Dylan sings of "the Darktown Strut".

[2] His pseudonym when recording in January 1963 with Richard Fariña and Eric von Schmidt.

us to trust that it is not being insensitive, is "Seen". There is a shape given to
the senses throughout the song. The first verse's opening, "Seen", moves to
the third verse's opening, "See" – and then to the last verse as it nears its
ending: "I'm gazing out the window". The second verse brings us to our
sense, the one that brings us Willie McTell and which brought him, in his
blindness, so much of what fostered him: "Well, I heard". And this is the
sense of which we hear tell in the fourth verse: "I can hear them rebels
yell". The word "yell" is in a different register from the other words in the
song (even from "bootlegged whiskey"), and, like a sudden yell, it bursts in
on us like Tennyson's use of the down-to-earth word "scare" in the high
heavenly world of his classical poem *Tithonus*: "Why wilt thou ever scare
me with thy tears?"

But it is the third verse, there at the centre of the song, that is moved to
a celebration of the senses' riches, even while almost all of what the senses
yield is a sad business, the wages of sin, the South's sin, though not the
South's alone:[1]

> See them big plantations burning
> Hear the cracking of the whips
> Smell that sweet magnolia blooming
> See the ghosts of slavery ships
> I can hear them tribes a-moaning
> Hear the undertaker's bell
> Nobody can sing the blues
> Like Blind Willie McTell

In this verse, the movement *See / Hear* is extended into *See / hear / Hear*,
hearing being of its very nature the sense that matters most to song and
to Blind Willie McTell. The stroke of genius, it strikes me, is the sudden
arrival, wafting in along the way, of "Smell that sweet magnolia blooming".
The eye and the ear have been known to put on airs, too confident that
they are the two senses that rule; how good that the sense of smell puts
in its unexpected claim. Good, too, that the smell of burning does not
overpower the sweet magnolia. It is a rich moment, snuffing the air. As
Dylan put it in 2001, "There's a secret sanctity of nature."[2] Even within

---

[1] In performance he sometimes abbreviates, combining lines from the third and fourth
verses into one verse. I wish that he didn't exercise his prerogative just here.
[2] *Rolling Stone* (22 November 2001).

tragedy the life that is nature may reassert itself. The tragedy could be that of *Strange Fruit*.[1] Smell the sweet magnolia after the lynching:

> Pastoral scene of the gallant South, the bulging eyes and the twisted mouth,
> Scent of magnolia sweet and fresh, and the sudden smell of burning flesh!

Strange Fruit invokes the magnolia to point a moral; Dylan, to adorn a tale, hauntingly. "See them big plantations burning".

The fresh flesh of the magnolia, which incited the poet William Empson,[2] anticipates the sudden arrival of the four lines about the "woman by the river" and "some fine young handsome man", no tragedy now but a pastoral moment that thankfully gratifies the remaining two senses (touch and taste, the bodies and the whiskey) that we had not been sure of – a moment that is not rescinded, though it is changed, by what immediately follows, the return of tragedy: "There's a chain gang on the highway".

The tragedy of blindness is not lessened, it is widened, in the tradition that sees the blind poets as inspired by their suffering. There is Homer. There is Milton, who calls up as his inspiration not only Homer but three other poet-prophets, and who prays that through his blindness he may "see and tell / Of things invisible to mortal sight". And, perhaps even more darkly, there is the cruelty that inflicts blindness upon birds in the belief that they will sing the better. A hideous castration for the caged bird-chorister. This is the suffering behind the lines that open a poem by Dylan Thomas:

> Because the pleasure-bird whistles after the hot wires,
> Shall the blind horse sing sweeter?

---

[1] Words and music by Abel Meeropol ("Lewis Allan"). See Nancy Kovaleff Baker, *American Music*, vol. 20 (Spring 2002).

[2] In his poem *Doctrinal Point*:

> Magnolias, for instance, when in bud,
> Are right in doing anything they can think of;
> . . .
> Whether they burgeon, massed wax flames, or flare
> Plump spaced-out saints, in their gross prime, at prayer,
> Or leave the sooted branches bare
> To sag at tip from a sole blossom there
> They know no act that will not make them fair.

They know no act that . . . I know no one can . . .

– a question that may have combined with a nursery rhyme[1] to prompt two moments in Dylan:

> This is the blind horse that leads you around
> Let the bird sing, let the bird fly
>   (*Under the Red Sky*)

> The Cuckoo is a pretty bird, she warbles as she flies
> I'm preachin' the Word of God
> I'm puttin' out your eyes
>
>   (*High Water*)

Our pity for the blind horse and for the blinded bird might serve to remind us how free of self-pity is the art of Blind Willie McTell. Dylan:

What made the real blues singers so great is that they were able to state all the problems they had; but at the same time, they were standing outside of them and could look at them. And in that way, they had them beat. What's depressing today is that many young singers are trying to get *inside* the blues, forgetting that those older singers used them to get *outside* their troubles.[2]

They could look at them: true of Blind Willie McTell.

Ballads love myth, including the myth of love, the blindfolded archer Cupid. Ballads respect legends, including those of the master-bowman: Robin Hood, or (on *Desolation Row*) "Einstein, disguised as Robin Hood", Einstein who had no time for Time's Arrow. Eddington: "I shall use the phrase 'time's arrow' to express this one-way property of time which has no analogue in space."[3] The maidens have their feathers; style in literature has been characterized as the feather in the arrow, not the feather in the hat.

The first words of *Blind Willie McTell* are "Seen the arrow". Does this arrow point to the man who gave the world the most famous of all arrow anecdotes? William Tell's arrow hit the apple on the head of the apple of

---

[1] "I paid ten shillings for a blind white horse" (or "for an old blind horse"), from "My mother said that I never should / Play with the gypsies in the wood" (*The Oxford Dictionary of Nursery Rhymes*, ed. Iona and Peter Opie, 1951, pp. 315–16).

[2] Quoted in the sleeve-notes to *The Freewheelin' Bob Dylan*. These were not included in the collected lyrics.

[3] Arthur Eddington, *The Nature of the Physical World* (1928).

his eye, his son. Since *Mc* means "son of", the son of William Tell may be living in another country under another name: William, or Willie, McTell. There are filaments, strings.

The story of William Tell's skill in shooting at and striking the apple which had been placed on the head of his little son by order of Gessler, the tyrannical Austrian bailiff of Uri, is so closely bound up with the legendary history of the origin of the Swiss Federation that they must be considered together.[1]

It seems that the Tell story is first found in a ballad written before 1474, within an oral ballad tradition apt enough to the world of Blind Willie McTell. And "legendary history", like tyranny, ripples out, too. Not just to McTell himself as legend and as history, but to the cruelly unjust world of the song, tyranny, and dismay at power and greed.

> Seen the arrow on the doorpost
> Saying, this land is condemned

Psalms 11:2: "For, lo, the wicked bend their bow, they make ready their arrow upon the string". The bow is a stringed instrument, like the guitar that looses its arrow.

> I glanced at my guitar
> And played it pretendin'
> That of all the eyes out there
> I could see none
> As her thoughts pounded hard
> Like the pierce of an arrow
> But the song it was long
> And it had to get done
> (*Eternal Circle*)

Blind Willie McTell had no eyes with which to see that of all the eyes out there he could see none.

> But the song it was long
> And it had to get done

---

[1] *Encyclopaedia Britannica*, eleventh edition.

But nobody can sing the blues
Like Blind Willie McTell

Handy Dandy

On *Positively 4th Street*, envy was what was coming off the person who had it in for the person who was telling us about it. The retaliation was armed with the word "got", but not the "got" of possessions that we might envy, and certainly not of an enviable self-possession.

You got a lotta nerve
To say you are my friend

You got a lotta nerve
To say you got a helping hand to lend

Handy Dandy, on the other hand, does have a helping hand to lend, or even to give with, but a sinister hand:

He'll say, "Ya want a gun? I'll give you one". She'll say, "Boy, you talking crazy"

And the world of the scoundrel Handy Dandy is full of things that invite and excite envy, most of them got hold of with the little envy-catcher "got":

He got an all girl orchestra and when he says "Strike up the band", they hit it
Handy dandy, he got a stick in his hand and a pocket full of money
He'll say, "Oh darling, tell me the truth, how much time I got?"
She'll say, "You got all the time in the world, honey".

He got that clear crystal fountain
He got that soft silky skin
He got that fortress on the mountain

Handy dandy, he got a basket of flowers and a bag full of sorrow

– at which, at last, we might be tempted to thank our lucky stars that we haven't got what he's got, for who would want a bag full of sorrow? Except that the person who's got a bag full of sorrow isn't likely to be someone who has a heart full of it, and he's probably carrying it around in a bag after collecting it or so that he can give it to other people. We might want to think again about all these things that he has got.

Handy Dandy is a sequence of filmy moments, or photo importunities, about the life-and-death styles of the rich and famous. Or infamous. The first thing that we learn about him? "Controversy surrounds him". The song summons the celebrities (the lavish people before whom we are slavish) about whom we yearn to learn the worst so that we will not be eaten up with envy about their having on the face of it the best, the best of all impossible worlds.

The sin of envy, along with its sibling sin covetousness, is gleefully activated by the gossipy glossies such as *People* or *Hello!*, while at the same time these glamorous journalistic evokers know that they would do well to bring home to all us ordinary readers that these extraordinarily affluent famosities are gratifyingly in trouble, in danger, and even, with any luck, in despair. Do you *really* want to be them? No, or Nope. But the envy is still there all right, skilfully played upon, and the form of lust that is envy may often enjoy itself most as prurience, all prying and clucking.

> Handy dandy, controversy surrounds him
> He been around the world and back again
> Something in the moonlight still hounds him
> Handy dandy, just like sugar and candy

The words, the melody, the voicing, all have a swagger to them, an exultation that is partly that of Handy Dandy himself and partly his infecting us with the wish to go along with it. But concessions to us are proffered straightaway, so that we may enjoy safe sexploitation, flirting with the thought of being him in his world, or being with him there, without actually wanting to be. Controversy, eh. Lucky dog, though: "He been around the world and back again". There's luxury for you, sheer needlessness, since unless the guy got back again, he wouldn't have been around the world. An odd way of putting it (unlike, say, He been to the ends of the earth and back again), but having a strong appropriate whiff of redundancy, of extravagance, of a menacing over-insistence: "around the world *and back again*". (The world comes back around in "You got all the time in the world, honey".) But then "around" itself had arrived in the second line of the song by courtesy of "surrounds" four words earlier, and "around" will come back around again in the sound of "hounds him". (There had been a hint of danger: surrounds him as though cornered.) "Something in the moonlight still hounds him". That's nice to know. We wouldn't want our celebrities to be unhounded. For one thing, this lends them an air of mystery (*Something in the moonlight?*). For another, it reconciles us to our position and our place (at least we aren't hounded).

Mystery and detection (and violence) are in the air of the song, so perhaps it isn't a vacant coincidence that the celebrity hound from the world of mystery and detection did his hounding by moonlight. Within a page and a half of *The Hound of the Baskervilles* (chapter 2), we meet, first, the hounds "in the moonlight", and then the "hound of hell". We hear about the revellers, "some calling for their pistols . . . and some for another flask of wine". (*Handy Dandy*: "Ya want a gun?"; "Pour him another brandy".) We hear of "their crazed minds", "so crazed with fear". (*Handy Dandy*: "you talking crazy".) "The moon shone clear above them", "The moon was shining bright" above the "hound of hell", "shaped like a hound, yet larger than any hound", "the hound which is said to have plagued the family so sorely ever since". Plagued the family, and perhaps – since Handy Dandy is something of a gangster (crook? rogue? thug?) – plagued The Family. "Something in the moonlight still hounds him".

It is his scene. *Him he him he he he*: so it goes, with other people at his beck-and-call or part of the decor. Handy Dandy is at once so cool and so hot. A shady character. But he has more than a touch of insolent charm, so he may be (in Beckett's weird phrase) a well-to-do ne'er-do-well. He swaggers well, but he wouldn't have to be doing this genuinely brave thing if his were not a dangerous world. So, given the incipient violence that is strong in the song, the word "if" has a way of suggesting "when": "Handy dandy, if every bone in his body was a-broken he would never admit it". Phrases that might be innocent in a way, albeit sexually suggestive ("He'll say, 'Oh darling, tell me the truth, how much time I got?'"), get darkened as though by dramatic irony: how much time *has* he got? (Before someone from this sleazy world puts paid to him.) "Okay, boys, I'll see you tomorrow". Maybe. They are his last words in the song. Might be his last words.

> You'll say, "What are you afraid of?"
> He'll say, "Nothing neither 'live nor dead".

There is in all this an affinity with T. S. Eliot: "I was neither / Living nor dead, and I knew nothing",[1] and with his poem about killings, paranoia, danger, and finishing drinks, *Sweeney Among the Nightingales*.

Heated and poisonous, the atmosphere. The erotic surroundings and glamour are agog at the easy brutality with which girls and music may be made: "He got an all girl orchestra and when he says 'Strike up the band', they hit it". There is an air of purchasable sexual favours ("a stick in his hand and a pocket full of money"), and of diffused lust, "soft silky skin", that sort of thing. It comes as something of a surprise, though a fair cop, when, after his fountain and his soft silky skin, there immediately comes, not "He got that mistress", but "He got that fortress". Sensible man.

There is instilling and distilling of fear in this gangsterish world. Question and answer can mount to interrogation or inquisition. A question is countered not with an answer but with a question.

> You'll say, "What are ya made of?"
> He'll say, "Can you repeat what you said?"
> You'll say, "What are you afraid of?"
> He'll say, "Nothing neither 'live nor dead"

That whole *You'll say / He'll say* routine is as if someone is being instructed in a code of behaviour, or coached not to blow it, some meeting with someone scary. And when you are asked to repeat your question ("Can you repeat what you said?"), perhaps asked threateningly, you will wisely substitute, thanks to the rhyme (*made of / afraid of*), words that just might make your listener think that he misheard you the first time. "What are ya made of?" might have been asking about the human qualities of which a man is made, compacted. (Chaucer: "A man maked all of sapience and virtue" – not our Handy Dandy, clearly.) But "What are you afraid of?" is a set-up, a silver salver with a brandy on it, an ingratiation pretending to be a challenge, perfectly happy with the answer that it knew it would precipitate: "Nothing neither 'live nor dead".

But say we stay a moment with that first question: "What are ya made of?" One answer is as plain as the hard nose on Handy Dandy's face: he

---

[1] *The Waste Land*. Eliot's preceding line has "Your arms full"; Dylan's succeeding line has "a stick in his hand and a pocket full of money". Michael Gray is good on the cherry riddle that supplies both "a stick in his hand" and the money (a groat in the riddle), though I wish that he didn't call the line from the riddle "this obscure, innocuous quotation" (*Song and Dance Man III*, p. 670).

is made of money. And sure enough, in no time at all the word can be heard to clink and to clinch. "Handy dandy, he got a stick in his hand and a pocket full of money". The line takes much weight in the song, partly because this is the moment when the *hand* of Handy Dandy extends itself – and is immediately underlined by *and*.

"What are ya made of?" Well, this is a song that includes an all-girl orchestra and a girl named Nancy and "Boy, you talking crazy" and "Okay, boys", so why not summon the traditional question and answer?

> What are little boys made of?
> What are little boys made of?
>> Frogs and snails
>> And puppy-dogs' tails,
> That's what little boys are made of.

> What are little girls made of?
> What are little girls made of?
>> Sugar and spice
>> And all that's nice,
> That's what little girls are made of.

Handy Dandy chimes all through the song with "sugar and candy". This may suggest that he is sexually ambiguous, in with the sugar and spice girls. For there is a whole underworld or undergrowth of sexual equivocation here. The man who "got an all girl orchestra" and who "got that soft silky skin" may or may not be made of sugar and spice. A candy-bar punk is "a convict who has become a passive homosexual in prison".[1] "A girl named Nancy" might make us think of what a nancy boy would be ("an effeminate male homosexual"). "'Anybody plays a guitar's a goddamned nancy,' said Lensky" (Sheldon, 1951). "He got a basket": "Esp. *Homosex.* the scrotum and penis, esp. as outlined by the trousers". And as for that "bag of sorrow": notum the scrotum, an item there in Evan Hunter (1956), who, like Sheldon, shows us Handy Dandy types: "I was hooked clean through the bag and back again" – which just happens to chime with "around the world and back again". Whereupon I call to mind that "around the world" is "to kiss or lick the entire body of one's lover".

[1] These are all from *The Random House Historical Dictionary of American Slang* (1994, 1997–).

Okay, boys, I'll pull myself together. But *Handy Dandy* is an itchy scratchy raunchy song that does have affinities with an earlier world of Dylan's, that of *The Basement Tapes*, of *Million Dollar Bash* and *Please Mrs. Henry* and *Tiny Montgomery*. The linguistic underworld may further remind us that the world of Handy Dandy might have a soft spot for hard drugs. Candy all around my brain. Sugar and candy are drug words, and so is crystal ("*Narc.* methamphetamine in powdered form"), and a stick, and a bag: "*Narc.* a small packet, typically an envelope or folded paper, containing heroin, marijuana, or the like". He got "a bag full of sorrow". Sorrow, not the ecstasy that you were hoping for.

But then candy is wonderfully capacious, happy not to exclude anything whatsoever that is "excellent, easy": "Fine and dandy. You're all the candy".[1] A candy kid is "a fellow who is lucky, successful, or held in high favor, esp. with women", and a candy-leg "a wealthy fellow who is attractive to women".

The point of all this rooting around in suspect words is not that *Handy Dandy* tells a clear story about the drug world or the gangster world or the polymorphous perverse world. An unclear story is the point, with sharp vignettes glimpsed within the murk. There is a multitude of sins swilling around in the song: envy and covetousness, plus greed – "sugar and candy", "Pour him another brandy"[2] – and a touch of sloth: "Handy dandy, sitting with a girl named Nancy in a garden feelin' kind of lazy". That undulating line is long and languorous, with all the time in the world, honey, and with the participles "sitting" and "feelin'" stretching their legs, and with the rhymes stretching themselves too: *Handy dandy . . . Nancy . . . lazy . . . crazy*. Many sins, and some guilt perhaps, and all this then set against a disconcerting reminder of innocence. For nursery rhymes – "What are little boys made of?" – recall innocence, even if it is innocence lost. And *Under the Red Sky*, the album that houses *Handy Dandy*, is a combination of ancient nursery rhymes and of modern malaise: cursery rhymes (not cursory ones). Such

---

[1] *The Random House Historical Dictionary of American Slang.*

[2] For brandy / sugar candy, see *The Oxford Dictionary of Nursery Rhymes*, pp. 115–16:

> Over the water and over the lea,
> And over the water to Charley.
> Charley loves good ale and wine,
> And Charley loves good brandy,
> And Charley loves a pretty girl
> As sweet as sugar candy

is the title song itself, *Under the Red Sky*, and such is *10,000 Men*, and *2 x 2*. Ding Dong Bell: *Cat's in the Well*.[1]

Handy Dandy is a game, one that Handy Dandy is happy to play rough.

A person conceals an object in one of his two closed hands, and invites his companion to tell which hand contains the object in the following words: Handy-Bandy, sugar-candy, Which hand wun yo have?[2]

Often the game has a further act of hiding in it, hiding the hands behind one's back before offering them. One oddity is that the figurative application of "handy dandy" gets an earlier citation in *The Oxford English Dictionary* than does the game itself (1579 as against 1585). Sugar-candy has long been the due rhyme ("Handy pandy, Sugary candy,/Which will you have?"), but other jinglings like "prickly prandy" have found themselves called on.[3] "Handy-spandy, Jack-a-dandy,/Which good hand will you have?" The conjunction of this question – "Which hand?" – with that other nursery-rhyme question, "What are little boys made of?", underlies the run of four questions in the song's bridge, beginning "What are ya made of?" And it is apt to the atmosphere of the song that "handy dandy" came to have the meaning "Something held or offered in the closed hand; a covert bribe or present." He got "a pocket full of money". In his poem *The Quip*, George Herbert heard this cunning clinking of a bribe:

> Then Money came, and chinking still,
> What tune is this, poor man? said he:
> I heard in Music you had skill.
> *But thou shalt answer, Lord, for me.*

Money and music and the music of money: Handy Dandy has an ear for all this.

One variant of the game's jingle goes:

---

[1] *The Oxford Dictionary of Nursery Rhymes*, p. 149: "The cat's in the well".
[2] *OED*, a quotation from 1887, *Handy-Bandy*.
[3] *The Oxford Dictionary of Nursery Rhymes*, pp. 232–3:

> Handy spandy, Jack-a-Dandy,
> Loves plum cake and sugar candy;
> He bought some at a grocer's shop,
> And out he came, hop, hop, hop, hop

Handy dandy, riddledy ro,
Which hand will you have, high or low?

"Riddledy ro" might remind us that Handy Dandy is himself something of a riddle.

Michael Gray saw what Dylan had got in his hand and up his sleeve.[1]

He got that clear crystal fountain
He got that soft silky skin
He got that fortress on the mountain
With no doors or windows, so no thieves can break in

Riddledy ro:

In marble halls as white as milk,
Lined with a skin as soft as silk,
Within a fountain crystal-clear,
A golden apple doth appear.
No doors there are to this stronghold,
Yet thieves break in and steal the gold.

The answer to the good riddle is an egg.[2] Handy Dandy is a bad egg. And Handy Dandy might be an alias for Humpty Dumpty. I wouldn't envy him, or them, if I were you. Easy to fall into, though . . .

There is comedy in what Dylan makes of the world of the nursery rhyme. But there is danger, too, and tragedy. For the celebrated instance of "handy dandy" is the one from *King Lear*. Justice, the cardinal virtue, is everywhere vitiated by corrupt justices. The mad King interrogates the blinded Earl.

---

[1] *Song and Dance Man III*, pp. 668–9. Furthermore, in *The Oxford Dictionary of Nursery Rhymes* this riddle is on the page facing "Handy dandy, riddledy ro" (pp. 196–7), because of the alphabetical sequence "halls", "handy".

[2] Michael Gray, hard-boiled as ever, says "the solution is merely 'an egg'" (*merely*, eh), and goes on to speak ill of the riddle and its "earthbound explanation for the break-in": Dylan, praise be, "strips away the old Classical Greekery", the "florid or portentous Victorian formalism", the "vicarishly nineteenth-century versifying tone" and the "purring poesy". Like Gray, I think *Handy Dandy* is terrific (though I find it scary, not "good-natured" or full of "refreshing sunlit glimpses"), but do we have to bad-mouth the egg riddle in order to good-mouth the song?

LEAR: No eyes in your head, nor no money in your purse? Your eyes are in a heavy case, your purse in a light, yet you see how this world goes.

GLOUCESTER: I see it feelingly.

LEAR: What, art mad? A man may see how this world goes, with no eyes. Look with thine ears. See how yond Justice rails upon yond simple thief. Hark in thine ear: change places, and handy-dandy, which is the Justice, which is the thief.

(IV, vi)

If I were a writer of songs, I would prick up my ears at "Look with thine ears". The merciless indifference of "handy dandy" is set within an exchange that speaks of the world ("how this world goes", in tune with "all the time in the world" and "around the world"), and of madness ("What, art mad?" – "you talking crazy"), and of money ("There's money for thee", "no money in your purse"), and even of "O let me kiss that hand". All of these might be felt to figure within *Handy Dandy*, as do both the sin of envy and the sin of lust, which Lear excoriates in this scene. And as does the vision that Lear has of sin and of its wealthy imperviousness to the virtue that is justice:

> Plate sin with gold,
> And the strong lance of justice hurtless breaks;
> Arm it in rags, a pygmy's straw does pierce it.

Covetousness

Gotta Serve Somebody

There is a story of a country squire who, leaving church after having heard tell (once more) of the Ten Commandments, took some comfort to himself: "Well, anyhow I haven't made a graven image."[1]

Only one of the seven deadly sins is granted one of the Ten Commandments to itself. For although anger may lurk within "Thou shalt do no murder", and lust within "Thou shalt not commit adultery", these Commandments neither identify nor identify with one particular sin. But the sin of covetousness has its very own Commandment, the Tenth, no less. "Thou shalt not covet thy neighbour's wife, nor his servant, nor his maid, nor his ox, nor his ass, nor any thing that is his." Do not covet his wife or his maid, even though you may happen to find your pleasure in somebody's mistress or in having women in a cage. Do not covet his servant, and do remember that you yourself are going to have to serve somebody. You may be this, that, or the other,

> But you're gonna have to serve somebody, yes indeed
> You're gonna have to serve somebody
> Well, it may be the devil, or it may be the Lord
> But you're gonna have to serve somebody

The Old Testament concurs with the New Testament in the warning against covetousness that is *Gotta Serve Somebody*. "Lay not up for yourself treasures upon earth," Christ urges in the Sermon on the Mount.[2]

No man can serve two masters: for either he will hate the one, and love the other, or else he will hold to the one, and despise the other. Ye cannot serve God and mammon. Therefore I say unto you, Take no thought for your life,

---

[1] *Geoffrey Madan's Notebooks*, eds. J. A. Gere and John Sparrow (1981), p. 94.
[2] Matthew 6.

what ye shall eat, or what ye shall drink; nor yet for your body, what ye shall put on. Is not the life more than meat, and the body than raiment?

> Might like to wear cotton, might like to wear silk
> Might like to drink whiskey, might like to drink milk
> Might like to eat caviar, you might like to eat bread
> May be sleeping on the floor, sleeping in a king-sized bed

> But you're gonna have to serve somebody

The Victorian provocateur Samuel Butler put in a word against the word of the Lord, that we cannot serve God and Mammon.

Granted that it is not easy, but nothing that is worth doing ever is easy. Easy or not easy, not have only we got to do it, but it is exactly in this that the whole duty of man consists.

If there are two worlds at all (and about this I have no doubt) it stands to reason that we ought to make the best of both of them, and more particularly of the one with which we are most immediately concerned.[1]

Gotta Serve Somebody is unrelenting, and this in itself presented its creator with a challenge. How do you vary the unrelenting? And how, once you have started on the infinite possibilities of *You may be* anything-you-care-to-name *but you're gonna have to etc.*, will you ever be through with instances and remonstrances? You are assuredly characterizing all these people most vividly, with no end of styptic scepticism, but you're gonna have to serve notice on the song sometime.

But the first thing of which to take the force is the combination of the song's inexorable speed with its radiating deftness of sidelong glances, sly touches and chances. Take the opening verse, which opens, very diplomatically, on to the summit of the social world:

> You may be an ambassador to England or France
> You may like to gamble, you might like to dance
> You may be the heavyweight champion of the world
> You might be a socialite with a long string of pearls

[1] *Samuel Butler's Notebooks*, eds. Geoffrey Keynes and Brian Hill (1951), p. 276. Butler, in passing, tilts at *The Whole Duty of Man*, a devotional work from 1658.

What's going on here? Everything.

"An ambassador is an honest man sent to lie abroad for the good of his country." Such was the straightfaced definition given by the seventeenth-century ambassador Sir Henry Wotton. An ambassador is a servant of his country (as a minister is supposed to be), and the word "ambassador" is from *ambactus*, a servant. To England or France: old sparring partners, and – in their European culture – constituting a rival to the United States of America as to who should be the heavyweight champion of the world.

So to the second line, where at once we can't help wondering whether the move has immediately been to two other very different worlds and *You*s, or whether there aren't mischievous intimations that the second line has not lost touch with the first.

> You may be an ambassador to England or France
> You may like to gamble, you might like to dance

Being an ambassador is a bit of a gamble, for you and for your country, and it often asks a poker face. Moreover, you had better like to dance all right, not just because of all those social occasions at the Embassy but because the diplomatic soft-shoe shuffle is one name of the game. Anyway, "gamble" makes its way smilingly across to "dance" on the arm of *gambol*. "You may like to gamble, you might like to dance": one "You" after another, presumably, and yet the two halves of the line are perfectly happy either to be dancing partners or to form a onesome. The world of the song is socially gathering:

> You may be an ambassador to England or France
> You may like to gamble, you might like to dance
> You may be the heavyweight champion of the world
> You might be a socialite with a long string of pearls

England and France have become the world – but then these are the two countries that were (formerly) the ones most in danger of supposing that they *were* the world. Not just the social world, although the social world is there as the string that connects the ambassador and the long string of pearls. The heavyweight with a long string of successes[1] turns into the socialite with a long string of pearls, lite on her feet. The long string of

---

[1] *OED*, 16e, "string: a continuous series of successes or of failures". (A long string particularly proffers this, and Dylan sings the word "long" with relish.)

pearls helps to reinforce, with a glint, the point that she is a socialite, not a socialist.[1] She is a lightweight champion of her world, not with a towel but with pearls around her neck.

Dancing, whether on the international ambassadorial stage or in the ring, turns now to prancing, bringing on some more of the worldly successes who keep forgetting something:

> May be a rock 'n' roll addict prancing on the stage
> Money, drugs at your command, women in a cage

The initiating ambassador has given way to a rock 'n' roll performer, but then a performer – like a heavyweight champion – is often presented as an ambassador of a kind. (Never forget that you are an ambassador for our way of life, representing your country abroad . . .) The "rock 'n' roll addict" is apparently addicted to his own rock 'n' roll (the fans are another story), though not only to rock 'n' roll: "Money, drugs at your command". Is it truly the case that, thanks to money, the drugs are at his command, or is he at theirs? As printed in *Lyrics 1962–1985*, the next line was straightforward, "You may be a business man or some high degree thief", but I hear what he sings as askew and buttonholing: "You may be in business, man", with a sudden addressing of "You", and with the further suggestion that things are proceeding apace, you're in business, that's for sure, man, you're not just some business man.

> You may be in business, man, or some high degree thief
> They may call you Doctor or they may call you Chief

The high degree is wittily succeeded by "They may call you Doctor" – now, *there's* a higher degree for you, not just a high degree (of whatever). "If I were a master thief", Dylan had sung in *Positively 4th Street*. But even a Master thief would have to yield to a Doctor thief.

> You may be a state trooper, you might be a young Turk
> May be the head of some big TV network
> You may be rich or poor, you may be blind or lame
> May be living in another country under another name

---

[1] "Socialism, hypnotism, patriotism, materialism", he sings in *No Time to Think*, immediately following this with "Fools making laws for the breaking of jaws". The Queensberry Rules in boxing, for the heavyweight champion?

From England or France, things have dwindled (or not, given states' rights) to a state trooper, with the geographical allocations then receiving a comic twist from "a young Turk". (You might be an ambassador to Turkey or France? Or even to "another country"?) Meanwhile, the state trooper is keeping communications open with both the ambassador and the rock 'n' roller addict prancing on a stage, each of whom is a trouper in his way.

> May be a construction worker working on a home
> Might be living in a mansion, you might live in a dome
> You may own guns and you may even own tanks
> You may be somebody's landlord, you may even own banks

This starts by coming a long way down the social ladder from that ambassador (slumming?), with the two successive work-words here establishing the daily grind: "May be a construction worker working on a home". "Worker working": that is what it feels like (work, work, work), with the redundancy not being of the luxurious kind, simply repetitive and a bit blank. But up the scale again, at once, into that "mansion" and into "you might live in a dome". Living *in* a dome is a combination of the grand and the offhand. The usual thought is that it is very nice to have a dome over one's head again.

Perhaps this verse seems for a moment tamed, compared with its predecessors, but not for long, for it swings into a different kind of action as it makes a place for the word that until now has exerted its energies only within the refrain, the word "somebody". The power here is felt in the momentum from the verse into the refrain:

> You may own guns and you may even own tanks
> You may be somebody's landlord, you may even own banks
>
> But you're gonna have to serve somebody, yes you are
> You're gonna have to serve somebody
> Well, it may be the devil, or it may be the Lord
> But you're gonna have to serve somebody

Every somebody is a nobody in the eyes of the Lord, or of the devil, come to that.

You may be a preacher, Mr Dylan, and it may be necessary to take this bull, whether papal or not, by the horns.

> You may be a preacher preaching spiritual pride
> May be a city councilman taking bribes on the side
> May be working in a barbershop, you may know how to cut hair
> You may be somebody's mistress, may be somebody's heir

As printed in *Lyrics 1962–1985*, it was "You may be a preacher with your spiritual pride", but what Dylan sings, "a preacher preaching", is much more telling, as adopting – and adapting – "a construction worker working", and as suggesting that the preacher not only has spiritual pride but preaches it. He may think that he is preaching against pride, but this is not what actually happens as soon as he opens his ripe and fruity mouth.

And then there is scattered another flurry of darts. Preacher is in touch with councilman, because of what council is. Taking bribes is in touch with cut, because of what it is to take a cut (my usual percentage, I trust?). Taking bribes on the side is in touch with somebody's mistress, because of what *The Oxford English Dictionary* knows carnally about *on the side*: "surreptitiously, without acknowledgement. (Freq. with connotation of dishonesty: illicitly; outside wedlock.)". "What would some of you say if I told you that I, as a married man, have had three women on the side?" (1968). In the momentum from this verse into the refrain (a mounting momentum now), there is twice a "somebody" before hitting the refrain:

> You may be somebody's mistress, may be somebody's heir
>
> But you're gonna have to serve somebody, yes
> You're gonna have to serve somebody
> Well, it may be the devil, or it may be the Lord
> But you're gonna have to serve somebody

The verse that follows is both the seed of the song and – because of the Sermon on the Mount – its flower.

And why take ye thought for raiment? Consider the lilies of the field, how they grow; they toil not, neither do they spin: and yet I say unto you, that even Solomon in all his glory was not arrayed like one of these.

"Might like to wear cotton, might like to wear silk": Dylan sings this quatrain most elegantly, with an equable commitment to its being so pat, rhythmically and vocally and syntactically, so symmetrical. The bed may be king-sized but it is a perfect fit. The danger of the fit and of the pat could not be better intimated (complacency completely self-satisfied), intimated delicately to the point of daintiness, but without palliation. For the "But" is biding its time.

> Might like to wear cotton, might like to wear silk
> Might like to drink whiskey, might like to drink milk
> Might like to eat caviar, you might like to eat bread
> May be sleeping on the floor, sleeping in a king-sized bed

> But you're gonna have to serve somebody . . .

And so the song moves to its moving on. The turn that finally releases it from its perpetual motion is its decision to switch from what you may be, and what they may call you, to what you may call me – and thence to what little difference this could ever make, given the inescapable truth of our all having to serve somebody. Earlier the song had dangled titles and entitlements: "They may call you Doctor or they may call you Chief". They may call you these things servilely, but don't forget that you, too, are gonna have to serve somebody. "They may call you . . ." now returns, from the opposite direction, as "You may call me . . ."

> You may call me Terry, you may call me Timmy
> You may call me Bobby, or you may call me Zimmy
> You may call me R. J., you may call me Ray
> You may call me anything, no matter what you say

> You're still gonna have to serve somebody, yes
> You're gonna have to serve somebody
> Well, it may be the devil, or it may be the Lord
> But you're gonna have to serve somebody

On every previous occasion, not only the last line of the refrain but its first line had crystallized in an opening obdurate "But". Dylan has always respected the patient power of life's most important little insister, "But", which will not be cheated or defeated. To bring the song to an end, while urging us not to forget the unending truth of its asseveration, there is this time no opening "But", only the conclusive one.[1]

You're gonna have to serve somebody. You may not like the thought, but there are forms of the thought that ought to do more than reconcile you to it. At Morning Prayer, the Second Collect, for Peace:

> O God, who art the author of peace and lover of concord, in knowledge of whom standeth our eternal life, whose service is perfect freedom; Defend us thy humble servants in all assaults of our enemies.

Thy humble servants, thou whose service is perfect freedom. It is perfectly paradoxical, like so much else.

Meanwhile, the crasser forms of covetousness keep up their assaults. The artist seeks to defend us against them.

> You can't take it with you and you know that it's too worthless to be sold
> They tell you, "Time is money" as if your life was worth its weight in gold
> > (*When You Gonna Wake Up?*)

It is one of the most enduring of proverbial reminders, *You can't take it with you*. In the different accents of St Paul:

> For we brought nothing into this world, and it is certain we can carry nothing out. And having food and raiment let us be therewith content. But they that will be rich fall into temptation and a snare, and into many foolish and hurtful lusts, which drown men in destruction and perdition. For the love of money is the root of all evil: which while some coveted after, they have erred from the faith, and pierced themselves through with many sorrows.
> > (1 Timothy 6:7–10)

> They tell you, "Time is money" as if your life was worth its weight in gold

Not that any of these matters are as simple as the confident repudiation of covetousness would like to believe. The realist Samuel Butler would again like to say a word:

---

[1] As printed in *Lyrics 1962–1985*, the last line of the penultimate verse had accommodated a "but" ("You may call me anything, but no matter what you say"), in anticipation of, and instead of, the start of the final refrain, but this is not what he sings.

It is only very fortunate people whose time is money. My time is not money. I wish it was. It is not even somebody else's money. If it was he would give me some of it. I am a miserable, unmarketable sinner, and there is no money in me.[1]

Sad-Eyed Lady of the Lowlands

Sad to say, there has been many a sad-eyed lady. One of the most haunting, and haunted, is Dolores, she whose very name means sadness.[2] Swinburne's *Dolores* (1866) opens with her hidden eyes, and soon moves to her flagrant mouth, all this then issuing in a question:

> Cold eyelids that hide like a jewel
>> Hard eyes that grow soft for an hour;
> The heavy white limbs, and the cruel
>> Red mouth like a venomous flower;
> When these are gone by with their glories,
>> What shall rest of thee then, what remain,
> O mystic and sombre Dolores,
>> Our Lady of Pain?

He covets her, even as she covets so much.

Sad-Eyed Lady of the Lowlands opens with the mouth of our lady of pain, and soon moves to her eyes, all this then issuing in a question, one that is on its way to further questions:

> With your mercury mouth in the missionary times
> And your eyes like smoke and your prayers like rhymes
> And your silver cross, and your voice like chimes
> Oh, who among them do they think could bury you?
> With your pockets well protected at last
> And your streetcar visions which you place on the grass
> And your flesh like silk, and your face like glass
> Who among them do they think could carry you?

---

[1] *Samuel Butler's Notebooks*, p. 277.
[2] In his edition of *Poems and Ballads & Atalanta in Calydon* (2000), Kenneth Haynes notes: "Dolores is Swinburne's anti-madonna; her name derives from the phrase 'Our Lady of the Seven Sorrows'." The subtitle of *Dolores* is NOTRE-DAME DES SEPT DOULEURS.

Sad-eyed lady of the lowlands
Where the sad-eyed prophet says that no man comes
My warehouse eyes, my Arabian drums
Should I leave them by your gate
Or, sad-eyed lady, should I wait?

He covets her, even as she covets so much. The seductive "mercury mouth" may be a death-dealing poison (thanks to a particular plant), or it may be a health-dealing antidote (thanks to a compound of the metal).[1] Swinburne has "Red mouth like a venomous flower" (and "eyelids that hide like a jewel"); Dylan has "eyes like smoke", and then "like rhymes", "like chimes".[2] The first question (within a song that puts so many searching questions), "Oh, who among them do they think could bury you?", might summon the goddess who is summoned in *Dolores*, "Libitina thy mother". For she is the Roman goddess of burials, who since ancient times has been identified – in a sad misguidance – with the goddess of love, Venus herself.

Dolores moves in time to that of which it speaks, "To a tune that enthralls and entices", as does *Sad-Eyed Lady of the Lowlands*. Throughout, *Dolores* sings of sins. Like *Sad-Eyed Lady of the Lowlands*, it insists upon listing – sometimes directly, sometimes to one side. It retails all of her energies, her incitements and excitements, her accoutrements, her weapons, her pockets of resistance well protected at last, moving inclusively through all these with an indeflectibility that runs parallel to Dylan's "With your . . .", the obdurate formula of his that sets itself, all through the song, to contain her and her properties, her wares. "With your sheets like metal and your belt like lace", "With your childhood flames on your midnight rug", "With your holy medallion which your fingertips fold" . . . Part inventory, part arsenal, these returns of phrase are bound by awe of her and by suspicion of her, alive not only with animation but with animus. The more times the initiatory "*With* your . . ." recurs, the more pressure it incurs, both as threat and as counter-threat.

Swinburne's "thy", in comparison, loses terror in archaism, and it lacks the pointed needling of "With your . . .". The run within *Dolores*, 205–67, soon starts to feel of the mill: thy serpents, thy voice, thy life, thy will, thy passion, thy lips, thy rods, thy foemen, thy servant, thy paces, thy pleasure, thy gardens, thy rein, thy porches, thy bosom, thy garments, thy body . . .

---

[1] *OED*, 7b (a preparation of the metal, used in medicine), to be kept carefully separate from *OED*, 10b (the euphorbiaceous poisonous plant *Mercurialis perennis*).
[2] On the rhyme on "rhymes", see p. 41.

But again like the song, Swinburne's poem has recourse to questions that are stingingly unanswerable:

> Who gave thee thy wisdom? what stories
>   That stung thee, what visions that smote?
> Wert thou pure and a maiden, Dolores,
>   When desire took thee first by the throat?
> What bud was the shell of a blossom
>   That all men may smell to and pluck?
> What milk fed thee first at what bosom?
>   What sins gave thee suck?[1]

These are no streetcar visions, but they, too, take flesh. Dylan's song, for its part, is given form by its questions and by their specific shape.

> Oh, who among them do they think could bury you?

> Who among them do they think could carry you?

* * *

> Who among them can think he could outguess you?

> Who among them would try to impress you?

* * *

> But who among them really wants just to kiss you?

> Who among them do you think could resist you?[2]

* * *

---

[1] There are, for instance, four questions in lines 73–80, one of them tilting at credulous presumption: "What spells that they know not a word of". Later (lines 393–6): "Who are we that embalm and embrace thee / With spices and savours of song? / What is time that his children should face thee? / What am I, that my lips do thee wrong?" *Who among them . . .*

[2] A unique colouring is given to this rhyme, since alone of these insistences that shape the song, this one picks up a preceding rhyming (with the word "kiss", and its likeness to rhyming itself) from earlier in the verse: "The kings of Tyrus with their convict list / Are waiting in line for their geranium kiss / And you wouldn't know it would happen like this / But who among them really wants just to kiss you?", into "Who among them do you think could resist you?"

> Oh, how could they ever mistake you?
>
> How could they ever, ever persuade you?

– through to the end:

> Who among them do you think would employ you?
>
> Oh, who among them do you think could destroy you?

Their credulity is matched only by yours, my dear. (From "do they think" to "do you think".) "And you wouldn't know it would happen like this". Our Lady of Pain, wide-eyed as being credulous for all her worldliness, will meet her match in our gentlemen of pained surprise. "Oh, how could they ever mistake you?"

Dolores would not have to be a source for *Sad-Eyed Lady of the Low-lands* (leave alone an act of allusion by Dylan) for it to illuminate the song's art. More than decor is a tissue. Overlappings include (in the order within Dylan's song, though neglecting singular/plural differences): "mouth", "times", "eyes", "like", "prayers", "voice", "visions", "flesh", "face", "lady", "prophet", "man", "comes", "[ware]house", "the sun", "light", "moon", "songs", "kings", "kiss", "know", "flames", "midnight", "mother", "mouth", "the dead", "hide", "feet", "child", "go", "thief", "holy", "finger[tip]s", "face", and "soul". And Dylan's "outguess" ("Who among them can think he could outguess you?") is in tune with Swinburne's "outsing", "outlove", "outface and outlive us".

What may be revelatory is that these apprehensions of languor and danger so often coincide in their cadences and decadences. Swinburne's anti-prayer to his anti-madonna, an interrogation that hears no need why it should ever end, may be heard as a prophecy of the Dylan song, a song that has been sensed, in its turn, as blandishingly hypnotic.[1] Hypnotic, or even (in the

---

[1] Wilfred Mellers:

Sad-Eyed Lady of the Lowlands stands with *Mr. Tambourine Man* as perhaps the most insidiously haunting pop song of our time. It's impossible to tell from the verses whether the Lady is a creature of dream or nightmare; but she's beyond good and evil, as the cant phrase has it, only in the sense that the simple, hypnotic, even corny waltz tune contains, in its unexpected elongations of line, both fulfilment and regret. Mysteriously, the song also effaces Time. Though chronometrically it lasts nearly 20 minutes, it enters a mythological once-upon-a-time where the clock doesn't tick.

(*Bob Dylan: A Retrospective*, ed. Craig McGregor, p. 165)

unlovely form of the word that F. R. Leavis liked when disliking Swinburne) *hypnoidal*.

T. S. Eliot – slightly to his surprise – found himself having to put in a word for Swinburne's ways with words, his ways with all those words. (Surprise, because Eliot said of his own choice of creative direction, as "a beginner in 1908": "The question was still: where do we go from Swinburne? and the answer appeared to be, nowhere."[1]) Eliot retained his sense of humour within his puzzled respect for Swinburne. I cannot imagine a better evocation than Eliot's of the kind of art that Dylan exercises in this song (itself unmistakably his and yet nothing like any other achievement of his), a kind that has moved some people to condemnation, Michael Gray for more than one. Gray brands the song "a failure".

The camera shots, the perspectives: do they create more than wistful but nebulous fragments? Do they add up to any kind of vision, as the whole presentation, duration and solemnity of the song imply that they should? No. Dylan is resting, and cooing nonsense in our ears (very beguilingly, of course).

The only thing that unites the fragments is the mechanical device of the return to the chorus and thus to the title . . . It is, in the end, not a whole song at all but unconnected chippings, and only the poor cement of an empty chorus and a regularity of tune give the illusion that things are otherwise.

In the end, whatever the song's attractions and clever touches, they have been bundled together, and perhaps a bit complacently, without the unity either of a clear and real theme or of cohesive artistic discipline.

In a footnote added later, Gray tried to square the circle, tried to square his readers by rounding on himself:

When I read this assessment now, I simply feel embarrassed at what a little snob I was when I wrote it. In contrast (and paradoxically), when I go back and listen, after a long gap, to Dylan's recording, every ardent, true feeling I ever had comes back to me. Decades of detritus drop away and I feel back in communion with my best self and my soul. Whatever the shortcomings of the lyric, the recording itself, capturing at its absolute peak Dylan's incomparable capacity for intensity of communication, is a masterpiece if ever there was one.[2]

---

[1] *Poetry* (September 1946); reprinted with a postscript, 1950, in *Ezra Pound*, ed. Peter Russell (1950).

[2] *Song and Dance Man III*, pp. 155–8.

No one would begrudge Gray his feeling back in communion with his best self and his soul, or want him to be crippled by detritus, but there is something hollow about this claim that an ill-worded song prompted a masterpiece of voicing. For it is only at a very low level of craft that any such distinction – between what the words can do and what the singer can do with them – could operate. A *masterpiece* of singing needs to be precipitated by an answering masterliness or masterfulness in what is sung. Matthew Arnold repudiated, unanswerably, an inordinate praise of Joseph Addison:

> to say of Addison's style, that "in its varied cadence and subtle ease it has never been surpassed", seems to me to be going a little too far. One could not say more of Plato's. Whatever his services to his time, Addison is for us now a writer whose range and force of thought are not considerable enough to make him interesting; and his style cannot equal in varied cadence and subtle ease the style of a man like Plato, because without range and force of thought all the resources of style, whether in cadence or in subtlety, are not and cannot be brought out.
>
> (*A Guide to English Literature*)

By the same token, all the resources of Dylan's voice, in varied cadence and subtle ease and much else, are not and cannot be brought out except by (say) range and force of thought – and it is such qualities that are, in Gray's judgement, missing from a song that shows such "shortcomings" in the writing. I don't believe that the recording *could* be "capturing at its absolute peak Dylan's incomparable capacity for intensity of communication" if what were communicated were compounded of "nonsense" and of "fragments" held together by "the mechanical device of the return to the chorus", and if "only the poor cement of an empty chorus and a regularity of tune give the illusion that things are otherwise". If *Sad-Eyed Lady of the Lowlands* really is "not a whole song at all but unconnected chippings", then it could never have been the occasion for an absolute peak of Dylan's intensity of communication, any more than an ill-written speech in a play could be the occasion for an absolute peak (as against, at best, quite a tour de force) of an actor's genius.

For it cannot be just a matter of *how* Dylan sings such a moment as this, however exquisite its timing –

> With your silhouette when the sunlight dims
> Into your eyes where the moonlight swims

– but of *what* had swum into his mind and his eyes and his ears by way of wording, wording of an inspiration that is commensurate with the voice.

Sad-Eyed Lady of the Lowlands is a masterpiece, but of a kind that Gray – trained as a literary critic in the bracing but narrow convictions of Dr Leavis – was sure to disparage: the Swinburnean. Eliot knew better:

The words of condemnation are words which express his qualities. You may say "diffuse". But the diffuseness is essential; had Swinburne practised greater concentration his verse would be, not better in the same kind, but a different thing. His diffuseness is one of his glories. That so little material as appears to be employed in *The Triumph of Time* should release such an amazing number of words, requires what there is no reason to call anything but genius.

What he gives is not images and ideas and music, it is one thing with a curious mixture of suggestions of all three.[1]

> Thy life shall not cease though thou doff it;
> Thou shalt live until evil be slain,
> And good shall die first, said thy prophet,
> Our Lady of Pain.
>
> Did he lie? did he laugh? does he know it,
> Now he lies out of reach, out of breath,
> Thy prophet, thy preacher, thy poet,
> Sin's child by incestuous Death?

> Sad-eyed lady of the lowlands
> Where the sad-eyed prophet says that no man comes
> My warehouse eyes, my Arabian drums
> Should I leave them by your gate
> Or, sad-eyed lady, should I wait?

The possessions of the song, irrespective of where exactly they should be left, were retrieved from the warehouse that stores all such evocations – whether by Swinburne or by Keats – of *La Belle Dame sans Merci*:

> I saw pale kings and princes too,
> Pale warriors, death-pale were they all;
> They cried – "La Belle Dame sans Merci
> Thee hath in thrall!"

[1] *Swinburne* (1920); *Selected Essays* (1932, 1951 edition), p. 324.

To a tune that enthrals and entices.

Keats does not tell you where his "pale kings" reigned. Dylan does: "The kings of Tyrus". Why that particular city? But this can be answered only by first identifying "the sad-eyed prophet" who is held in a dance of tension, throughout the song, with the sad-eyed lady of the lowlands.

And the word of the Lord came unto me, saying Son of man, prophesy against the prophets of Israel that prophesy.

(Ezekiel 13:1)

Sad-Eyed Lady of the Lowlands prophesies against the prophets that prophesy. Ezekiel is sad at what he sees before his eyes:

Because with lies ye have made the heart of the righteous sad, whom I have not made sad; and strengthened the hands of the wicked . . . therefore ye shall see no more vanity.

(Ezekiel 13:22)

Ezekiel is sad-eyed, and the more so because of being forbidden to weep:

And the word of the Lord came unto me, saying, Son of man, behold, I take away from thee the desire of thine eyes with a stroke: yet neither shalt thou mourn nor weep, neither shall thy tears run down. Forbear to cry.

(Ezekiel 24:16)

Moved by a poem of mourning and forbearance, Thomas Carlyle said of Tennyson's *Ulysses*: "These lines do not make me weep, but there is in me what would fill whole lachrymatories as I read."[1] A lachrymatory is a "vase intended to hold tears; applied by archaeologists to those small phials of glass, alabaster, etc., which are found in ancient Roman tombs" (*The Oxford English Dictionary*). "Oh, who among them do they think could bury you?"

"Where the sad-eyed prophet says that no man comes": the phrase "no man" comes more than once in the Book of Ezekiel, and there is a gate nearby. Ezekiel 44:2: "This gate shall be shut, it shall not be opened, and no man shall enter in by it." (Similarly, 14:15: "that no man may pass through".) "No man" is heard again and again in the Bible. Isaiah 24:10: "Every house

---

[1] Hallam Tennyson, *Alfred Lord Tennyson: A Memoir* (1897), vol. I, p. 214.

is shut up, that no man may come in. There is a crying for wine in the streets; all joy is darkened, the mirth of the land is gone. In the city is left desolation, and the gate is smitten with destruction." Isaiah is another of the prophets who toll the words "no man". As printed in *Lyrics 1962–1985*, the refrain is always "the sad-eyed prophet says"; in singing, Dylan moves from this to "the sad-eyed prophets say".

"The Prophets Isaiah and Ezekiel dined with me," William Blake recorded, straightforwardly, "and I asked them how they dared so roundly to assert that God spoke to them; and whether they did not think at the time that they would be misunderstood, & so be the cause of imposition" (*The Marriage of Heaven and Hell*).

"Moreover the word of the Lord came unto me, saying, Son of man, take up a lamentation upon the king of Tyrus" (Ezekiel 28:12). In chapter 26 of Ezekiel, the pride of Tyrus is brought low, for Tyrus will be set "in the low parts of the earth" (26:20), the low lands. A king of kings "shall enter into thy gates" (26:10). And the city's music will have a dying fall. "I will cause the noise of thy songs to cease; and the sound of thy harps shall be no more heard" (26:13).

> Sad-eyed lady of the lowlands
> Where the sad-eyed prophets say that no man comes
> My warehouse eyes, my Arabian drums
> Should I leave them by your gate
> Or, sad-eyed lady, should I wait?

– and then, scarcely waiting:

> The kings of Tyrus with their convict list
> Are waiting in line for their geranium kiss

Should I wait? At which point we wait only a moment to hear (two lines later) that they are waiting in line, "The kings of Tyrus with their convict list" – Tyrus, the city of Tyre, having been found guilty by the judgement of the Lord (*convict*: proved or pronounced guilty, as in "convict to eternal damnation").[1]

Guilty of what? Of being not only covetous but the cause of covetousness in others, of gratifying the covetous and of profiting from their covetousness.

---

[1] *OED*, 1b, Tindale's New Testament, 1525.

"With your pockets well protected at last": glad to hear it, but their pockets are in need of protection.

Guilty of what would now be called conspicuous consumption or consumerism, a fast-fed greed that supposes that it can float free of the terrible ancient verb "consume", a verb that utters its fierce condemnation throughout Ezekiel.

Guilty of such a commodification as exults in its wealth of modifications. Tyrus is "a merchant of the people for many isles" (27:3). This one chapter includes among Tyrus's world trade splendours its shipboards of fir trees of Senir; cedars of Lebanon to make masts; oaks of Bashan for oars; ivory from Chittim for benches; and fine linen from Egypt for sails. (Where are the Arabian drums?) It deals in silver, iron, tin, lead, and brass; ivory and ebony; emeralds, and fine linen, and coral, and agate; honey, and oil, and balm; wine and wool; iron, cassia, and calamus; precious clothes; lambs, and rams, and goats; all spices, and all precious stones, and gold; blue clothes, and broidered work, and chests of rich apparel. (Rich apparel, precious clothes, blue clothes, a cut above our modern world and "your basement clothes".) The recurrent tribute in this chapter of Ezekiel, a tribute full of peril, is ". . . were thy merchants". All this, with a sense that we haven't even started yet. *With your,* and *with your,* and *with your.*

These chapters of Ezekiel, with an unmisgiving redundancy that apes the extravagance that it sets down, marvel repeatedly at the city's "merchandise" and its "merchants". Tyrus is "thy merchant by reason of the multitude of all kind of riches; with silver, iron, tin, and lead, they traded in thy fairs" (27:12). But wait, there is a force that can outwait the kings of Tyrus: the Lord, he who speaks, through his prophet Ezekiel, of the doom to come: "And they shall make a spoil of thy riches, and make a prey of thy merchandise" (26:12). The prophet speaks unto the prince of Tyrus, a warning delivered (should I leave it by your gate?) against covetousness and this sin's compact with its fellow-sin, pride:

with thy wisdom and with thine understanding hast thou gotten thee riches, and hast gotten gold and silver into thy treasures: by thy great wisdom and by thy traffick hast thou increased thy riches, and thine heart is lifted up because of thy riches: therefore thus saith the Lord God; Because thou hast set thine heart as the heart of God; behold, therefore will I bring strangers upon thee, the terrible of the nations. (28:4–7)

With thy wisdom and with thine understanding were these riches gained,

whereupon wisdom and understanding forgot the Lord God, and so pre-
cipitated their own folly and destruction.

What is Tyrus but one huge warehouse of hubris? Its wares are of every
kind. Tyrus is "thy merchant by reason of the multitude of the wares of thy
making" (27:16), a lavish phrase that is repeated two verses later, as though
itself a gesture of conspicuously luxurious consumption. Thy wares, and the
multitude of the wares of thy making: where better to see them all than by
looking deep in my eyes, "My warehouse eyes"? Warehouse eyes, taking
a turn for the worse, can become whorehouse eyes. "Thou hast opened
thy feet to every one that passed by, and multiplied thy whoredoms"
(Ezekiel 16:25).

> My warehouse eyes, my Arabian drums
> Should I leave them by your gate

I can see how someone can leave his drums by your gate, and I can
sense the pulse that throbs from "eyes" to "drums" via the disconcertingly
different drums that are eardrums.[1] But his *eyes*? Forget about *should* he
leave them by your gate, how *could* he? The surrealistic glimpse is of
body-parts and parcels.

If we try to understand the way in which the phrase "my warehouse eyes"
may be not only a riddle but a mystery, we are likely to ask ourselves in
what circumstances of language a noun (rather than an adjective) may be
found preceding the noun that is "eyes". Say, a noun with a sense, perhaps,
of an occupied space, something that pertains to a house?

Ah, I guess I know with what eyes he gazes upon the sad-eyed lady,
even as her eyes look alive with what Ezekiel calls "the desire of thine
eyes": his bedroom eyes. See *The Oxford English Dictionary*, 3b, from
W. H. Auden (1947), "Making bedroom eyes at a beef steak", flanked
by "Italians are bedroom-eyed gigolos" (1959), and by "George's wife had
bedroom eyes" (1967).

The song engages with what it is to be queasily grateful for yet more gifts
than wise men bring – or have brought to them. If there is one invitation
even more covetable than the glad eye, it is what the lady gives him: the
sad eye. As for him:

---

[1] The not-at-all ghostlike soul in Andrew Marvell's *A Dialogue between the Soul and
Body* complains of the bodily senses and of how they thwart it, poor soul: "Here
blinded with an eye; and there / Deaf with the drumming of an ear, / A soul hung
up, as 'twere, in chains / Of nerves, and arteries, and veins".

My warehouse eyes, my Arabian drums
Should I leave them by your gate
Or, sad-eyed lady, should I wait?

You think he's just an errand boy to satisfy your wandering desires.

Greed

The Natural History of Iceland (1758) is known as an icon of the laconic.

Chapter LXXII
Concerning snakes

No snakes of any kind are to be met with throughout the whole island.

The notoriety of this chapter, like a lot of notoriety, is unjust, since the Danish traveller Niels Horrebow had merely undertaken to rebut an inaccurate history of Iceland, and since in any case this superbly succinct chapter (would that more works of history were this brisk and frank) was a liberty taken by the English translator.[1]

DYLAN'S VISIONS OF SIN
Chapter XYZ
Concerning greed

No songs of any kind about greed are to be met with throughout the whole Dyland.[2]

A Latin tag, risking self-righteousness, avers that Plato is my friend, and Socrates is my friend, but Truth is my best friend. True, the sins are sometimes my low companions, and my scheme for this book is proving to be my friend (no?), but the truth about – and within – Dylan's songs is or ought to be my best friend. And the truth about greed as a nub in Dylan's songs is that where you might have expected conspicuous consumption there is conspicuous absence. Greed simply isn't (even though the reasons for such things could never be simple) a sin that either sufficiently attracts him (his art) or sufficiently repels. So let me come clean and not fudge.

[1] See *Boswell's Life of Johnson*, ed. G. Birkbeck Hill, rev. L. F. Powell, vol. III, p. 279 and note; 13 April 1778.
[2] The snake is seen but not heard ("snake" goes unsung) in *Man Gave Names to All the Animals*.

Oh, my divine scheme – the sins, the virtues, and the heavenly graces – may suffer, but just think how my reputation for critical probity, far from suffering, is sure to wax.

That said, the insistence that *No songs of any kind about greed etc.* might seem rather to misdo things. Are there not, for instance, several songs that flirt or cavort with greed as their need? But they turn out to be about sensual exuberance rather than greed, and insofar as what feels like greed does course through their vinous veins, it is high-spirited appetite as corporeal capering, not any slumped lumpish piggishness in clover.

Have a *Million Dollar Bash*.

> Well that big dumb blonde
> With her wheel gorged
> And Turtle, that friend of theirs
> With his checks all forged
> And his cheeks in a chunk
> With his cheese in the cash
> They're all gonna be there
> At that million dollar bash
> Ooh, baby, ooh-ee
> Ooh, baby, ooh-ee
> It's that million dollar bash

Printed in *Lyrics 1962–1985* "With her wheel in the gorge", but he sings "With her wheel gorged". The gorging or engorging, which takes a loud pleasure in all this, has to do with more than one appetite, and with one appetite more than others, the cheese being far from cheddar and the Cheddar Gorge. Churning, yearning. "Come now, sweet cream / Don't forget to flash". "I took my potatoes / Down to be mashed". But to be having in mind a meal would be square, the voracious teenage feelings in the song being what they are, all spilt aggression and argot and gossip and chaos and sexual comings and goings and goings-on. "Ooh, baby, ooh-ee". Just so. But *greed*? Not really.

Just like *Country Pie*.

> Just like old Saxophone Joe
> When he's got the hogshead up on his toe
> Oh me, oh my
> Love that country pie

Dylan never confuses one exultant cry with another, so "Oh me, oh my" is a far cry from "Ooh, baby, ooh-ee". And yet of course they do overlap one another all up.

> Listen to the fiddler play
> When he's playin' 'til the break of day
> Oh me, oh my
> Love that country pie

Greed? Fiddlesticks. Cornucopious fruits may come tumbling in, and the lines, happy to be mouthed, may be watery and wet:

> Raspberry, strawberry, lemon and lime
> What do I care?
> Blueberry, apple, cherry, pumpkin and plum
> Call me for dinner, honey, I'll be there

"Just you comin' and spillin' juice over me" (*Odds and Ends*). But "What do I care?" means what it sings, and the tastiest word of them all is "honey". "Saddle me up my big white goose", don't carve her up. With both the singer and the goose turned loose in this peasant dance of a song, realism in the Dutch manner calls for some reminder of what can follow these throaty excitements, so the possibility of vomiting does get thrown up at one point:

> Give to me my country pie
> I won't throw it up in anybody's face

This slides "throw up" into "throw it in anybody's face", while exploiting a small brassy hinge when the last word of that first line, "pie", becomes immediately the first word of the next, "I". Pie-eyed?

> Shake me up that old peach tree
> Little Jack Horner's got nothin' on me
> Oh me, oh my
> Love that country pie
>
> Little Jack Horner
> Sat in the corner,
> Eating a Christmas pie;

> He put in his thumb,
> And pulled out a plum,
> And said, What a good boy am I!

Little Jack Horner, eh, putting in his thumb and pulling out blueberry, apple, cherry, pumpkin, *and* plum. You can't beat Christmas pie. (Oh yes you can. You'd love that country pie.) There is a sudden flash or streak ("Little Jack Horner's got nothin' on"!), but no, 's got nothin' on *me* (you dirty minder). "And said, What a good boy am I!" No, and said "Oh me, oh my".

As with *Million Dollar Bash*, there is a bosom companion that you need for this song, *The Random House Historical Dictionary of American Slang*. But the sexual suggestiveness of the words that are bouncing about in *Country Pie* is hardly likely to escape any right-minded listener, and would certainly have been altogether clear to the man – step forward, Dr Thomas Bowdler – who gave to the language the verb to "bowdlerize", to cut out the dirty bits, flashing an edition of Shakespeare (1818) "in which those words and expressions are omitted which cannot with propriety be read aloud in a family". As for that country pie itself: when Hamlet speaks meaningly to Ophelia ('neath her window of opportunity), he offers Dr Bowdler an opportunity to cut to the chaste: "Do you think I meant country matters?"

The Basement is the place for furnishing the right tapes when it comes to these rough-riding energies.[1] The raucous raunchy world comes alive, all right, and only a prig – such as Dr Bowdler – would fail to feel his spirits rise, even if then a bit shamefaced about it, to the hollering and the squalor.

> Well, I've already had two beers
> I'm ready for the broom
> Please, Missus Henry won't you
> Take me to my room?
> I'm a good ol' boy
> But I've been sniffin' too many eggs
> Talkin' to too many people
> Drinking too many kegs

[1] *Odds and Ends, Million Dollar Bash, Goin' to Acapulco, Lo and Behold!, Apple Suckling Tree, Please, Mrs. Henry, Yea! Heavy and a Bottle of Bread, Tiny Montgomery.*

> Please, Missus Henry, Missus Henry, please!
> Please, Missus Henry, Missus Henry, please!
> I'm down on my knees
> An' I ain't got a dime

Gross, as the young say with palpable furtive pleasure, but not greedy, neither exploring nor deploring greed. Out of control, and yet struggling to maintain control, the drunken speaker has all these emotions knocking about and lashing out: the obscenely obscure, the aggressive ("Now, don't crowd me, lady"), the maudlin ("I'm a good ol' boy"), the concessive ("I've been sniffin' too many eggs"), the seething yet oddly self-knowing ("*Pretty soon* I'll be mad" – and is this angry or insane?), and the precariously steady ("I've been known to be calm"). There is the open indecorum of "My stool's gonna squeak" up against the strained propriety of the title "Please, Mrs. Henry".

It is rightly in the last verse of *Please, Mrs. Henry* that he issues the pleading admission, "There's only so much I can do". Same here. When it comes to greed and Dylan, there's only so much I can do. He does a great deal with it, in a way, but the way is not direct, is not a matter of having greed ever be the pith or gist or nub of a song. Rather, greed will be found – with grim likelihood – doing its dirty business all over the place, this worldly place.

> Well, God is in his heaven
> And we all want what's his
> But power and greed and corruptible seed
> Seem to be all that there is

Blind Willie McTell on blind greed. *Union Sundown* on greed as in your line of vision:

> Sure was a good idea
> 'Til greed got in the way

Sloth

If some particular sin – sloth, say (no longer sayable, "sloth", too old-world a word) – isn't for you, good for you. But this may not be good for you. You may be a prig about it, self-righteous. (Ain't no man righteous, no, not oneself.) Human beings, all too human, have long found it convenient to

> Compound for sins they are inclined to,
> By damning those they have no mind to.[1]

And for the artist, the imaginer, this not-being-tempted may turn out to be a mixed blessing, a bit of a curse. For temptation is a profound form that imagination may take. Is it possible to imagine deeply a sin that tempts you not a whit? The greatest artists have always been those who take the full force of temptation, and who know what they – not just *we* or *you guys* – are in for and are up against. So it is not surprising that on occasion these will be the very artists who lapse. The profoundest comprehension of snobbery, for instance, has come from writers who are not simply and unwaveringly impervious to it: Henry James, Marcel Proust, T. S. Eliot, F. Scott Fitzgerald, Ivy Compton-Burnett . . . True, they don't invariably get it right, but this is inseparable from their getting it.

Certain of the seven sins engage Dylan more rewardingly, and more often, than others, because he knows full well where he is susceptible. It can be salutary to be prone to these things, as against being either supine under them or superior to them. From this admission or admittance, there can rise the achievement of an art free from condescension and smugness.

When it comes to the sins of anger and pride, there is many a Dylan song that comes to mind. You might, though, find yourself having to cast about a bit before seizing upon a Dylan song that settles upon – or into – *sloth* as the sin that challenges. Anger, yes; languor (sloth's cousin), scarcely.

"Energy is eternal delight". Hear the voice of the bard, William Blake, in whom Dylan has often delighted. And Dylan is energy incarnate. Energy is

[1] Samuel Butler, *Hudibras*, since you ask.

Activity. Sloth finds its place in *Roget's Thesaurus* under "Inactivity". But does sloth – could it – find a place in Dylan's art, given his indefatigable energy? It asks of us a positive effort even to imagine Dylan's being lazy, slothful, idle, slack, inert, sluggish, languid, or lethargic (to pick up sticks from the thesaurus). The opposite of slothful? "Diligent" is the opposing term that is everywhere in the Book of Proverbs (which Dylan knows like the back of God's hand). O O O O that Dylanesque rag. It's so elegant. So intelligent. So Dyligent. Never negligent.

But Dylan, as an heir of Romanticism (Blake's and Keats's, for a start), was sure to be drawn to imagine in depth those slothful-looking moods or modes that smilingly put it to us that we might put in a good word for them. Sloth is bad, but "wise passiveness" (Wordsworth) is the condition of many a good thing, including the contemplative arts in both their creation and reception. Sloth is bad, but leisure may be an amiably ambling ambience that should not be mistaken for, or misrepresented as, sloth. British English rhymes "pleasure" with "leisure", relaxed about it, but perhaps in danger of complacency; American English combines "seizure" and "lesion" for its "leisure", uneasy about it, but perhaps in danger of morbidity. And then again we differ about sloth. The American pronunciation, with a short *o* (sloppy, sloshy, this sloth, for slobs who haven't even the energy for a long *o*), is differently evocative from the long *o* of British English, which assimilates the slow to sloth.[1] "Blue river running slow and lazy". Sloth drags its eels.

There is an undulating hammock of a word from the good old days: "indolence". Keats, who had more energy than others would have known what to do with, valued indolence very highly, and devoted an Ode to it, to "The blissful cloud of summer-indolence", such a relaxation as makes poetry seem hardly worth the effort. But then is poetry perhaps just a relaxation anyway?

> For Poesy! – no, she has not a joy –
>> At least for me – so sweet as drowsy noons,
> And evenings steeped in honeyed indolence.

It is characteristic of true art to be willing to acknowledge such feelings about art, feelings that pass for truth, but will pass.

[1] When Theodore Roethke reads his poem *The Sloth* (1972), he hesitates as to the long or the short *o*.

William Empson once invoked *The Pilgrim's Progress* in a poem:

> Muchafraid went over the river singing
>
> Though none knew what she sang. Usual for a man
> Of Bunyan's courage to respect fear.
>
> (Courage means Running)

Usual for a man of Keats's energy to respect indolence. Or for a man of Dylan's energy, he who goes over the river singing. ("I'll take you 'cross the river, dear / You've no need to linger here": *Moonlight.*) *No need to linger here?* Oh, reason not the need, for it may be the fact that there is no *need* to do something that makes it so tempting, needless, and heedless, so innocently remiss. Dylan can sit by the river while never forgetting the claims of the activities that will sometime have to be resumed. He is not brushing them off, he is sitting them aside:

> Wish I was back in the city
> Instead of this old bank of sand
> With the sun beating down over the chimney tops
> And the one I love so close at hand
> If I had wings and I could fly
> I know where I would go
> But right now I'll just sit here so contentedly
> And watch the river flow
>
> (Watching the River Flow)

What brings this to a very different life in the singing is an unexpected cross-current or counter-current. You would never guess from the words alone that the phrasing and the arrangement would be so choppy, so bent on disrupting any easy flowing. Stroppy stomping is the note from the very start, before Dylan even hits the words – and hit them is what he does, not mollify them or play along with their sentiments or go with their flow. The third and then the last verse both kick off with "People disagreeing" – "People disagreeing on all just about everything, yeah", "People disagreeing everywhere you look" – but then the song is thrillingly disagreeing with itself. Its rhythmical and vocal raucousness is far from flowing. More like shooting a few rapids. Bracing, really, because braced. In the singing, *Watching the River Flow* turns out not to be one of your usual floatings downstream. "Sweet Thames run softly, till I end my song": this was sheer fluency in Spenser, but when T. S. Eliot incorporated the line as part of his own song, he did not leave it at that. Later in this same section of *The Waste Land*, his river is an old man, back in the city, who works for his living and who sweats at it.

> The river sweats
> Oil and tar
> The barges drift
> With the turning tide

Watching the River Flow is tarred with a realism that qualifies and complicates the lure of the lazy, though never to the point of abolishing what the words express a hope for: some relaxing, please, if at all possible. For, whatever the abrupt music may say, the unruffled words have a right to be heard. Independence, yes, but interdependence, too, some balance and sustenance of alternate tones and claims.

> right now I'll just sit here so contentedly
> And watch the river flow.

Right now this is the right thing, young man Dylan sitting by old man river. ("But this ol' river keeps on rollin', though".) No hurry. It's got to be done sometime, why not do it then . . . You can muse as long as you like, for now at least, murmurously imagining (that, at least) that you might repeat yourself as a river contentedly does. To the unbitter end.

> Watch the river flow
> Watchin' the river flow
> Watchin' the river flow
> But I'll just sit down on this bank of sand
> And watch the river flow

The right kind of sloth, a good-natured indolence that acknowledges a realistic feeling for what life is like, had better be no more than a mood, something that must not harden into habit or addiction. So *Baby, I'm in the Mood for You* understands the link between being in the mood for you and being, sometimes, in the mood for vacancy:

> Sometimes I'm in the mood, I ain't gonna do nothin' at all
> But then again, but then again, I said oh, I said oh, I said
> Oh babe, I'm in the mood for you

As printed in *Lyrics 1962–1985*, eighteen lines of the song each begin with "Sometimes I'm in the mood", but this one, "Sometimes I'm in the mood, I ain't gonna do nothin' at all", is the only one repeated. Very apt, too. "I ain't gonna do nothin' at all" – except just maybe say this again before long. This doesn't happen as released on *Biograph*, where there are only four verses (plus an elaborated refrain at the end), in a different order and with different wording but with one excellent stroke, I must say: "Sometimes I'm in the mood, I'm goin' to give away all my sins". The innocent exuberance of the song ought to warn us against taking any of these moods other than lightly. Scarcely any sloth to give away, that's for sure, despite "Sometimes I'm in the mood, I ain't gonna do nothin' at all".

How light at heart the song is, to be sure, and what a contrast to the context within which A. E. Housman once imagined what a relief it might be to do (and perhaps feel) nothing at all. His characteristic letter is dated Boxing Day, 1930:

Between a Feast last night and a dinner-party this evening, I sit me down to thank you and your wife and family for their Christmas greetings and wish you all a happy New Year. Rutherford's daughter, married to another Fellow of Trinity, died suddenly a day or two ago; the wife of the Emeritus Professor of Greek, who himself is paralysed, has cut her throat with a razor which she had bought to give her son-in-law; I have a brother and a brother-in-law both seriously ill and liable to drop dead any moment; and in short Providence has given itself up to the festivities of the season. A more cheerful piece of news is that I have just published the last book I shall ever write, and that I now mean to do nothing for ever and ever. It is one of my more serious works, so you will not read it.[1]

Housman's is a stoically doleful challenge. The playful challenge is to convey a pleasure in leisure without being too too leisurely about it all. The word "lazy" – the only everyday term hereabouts – agrees to make light of the matter, easy-coming and easy-going. (*Sin?* "I say, 'Aw come on now'".)

[1] To Percy Withers; *The Letters of A. E. Housman*, ed. Henry Maas (1971), pp. 306–7.

Flowers on the hillside, blooming crazy
Crickets talkin' back and forth in rhyme
Blue river running slow and lazy
I could stay with you forever
And never realize the time
(*You're Gonna Make Me Lonesome When You Go*)

"Running slow": it is good of "slow" to be both an adjective and an adverb
(*The Oxford English Dictionary* is no slouch in these matters), for this means
that "slow" can preserve the proprieties and at the same time can keep
the adjective "lazy" company. Not itself lazy, this, for all the predictable
casualness by which "crazy" ushers in "lazy". For there is plenty quietly
going on: in the invoking of rhyme itself,[1] and of the crickets working
their little legs or wings off (for nature is not slothful, nor is the sloth);
in the equable paradox of "running slow" (how slow would it have to
be to no longer be running?); and in the assonance that is itself a form
of staying, when "lazy" finds itself talking, three words later, with "stay
with". Laziness is prudently acknowledged and very prudently shifted:
you're not to think, my dear, that I'm the one that's lazy, it's the river
that's lazy. "And never realize the time"? But always realize the art, with
honestly deceptive ease.

Winterlude, waltzing along on its skating rink, likewise takes its ease, but
again not selfishly, since the song is in the unbusied business of giving
ease, too, not just taking it. "My little daisy" effortlessly rhymes with
"Winterlude, it's makin' me lazy", and the ludic trick upon which the whole
song turns – the telescoping of "winter" into "interlude" – depends on the
mixed feelings that we have about such compactings. Lewis Carroll took
out the patent on portmanteau words: "'*slithy*' means 'lithe and slimy' . . .
You see, it's like a portmanteau – there are two meanings packed up into
one word."[2] On the one (iron) hand, you might be sliding one word into
another because you're a busy man, packing for your business trip, in haste
and under pressure, no time for both the words in full, economy of effort
in the interests of economics (Federal Express takes too long, so FedEx
it) . . . Or, on the other (velvet) hand, you might be smoothly idly sliding
one word into another in quite the opposite spirit, not seeing why you

[1] On rhymes on rhyme, see p. 41. For an edgy frictive rhyme of "lazy" with "crazy",
not relaxed at all this time around, see *Handy Dandy*, p. 85.
[2] *Through the Looking Glass*, chapter VI.

should be expected to go through the effort of saying both "winter" and "interlude", given that there is an overlap of the words, one word in the other word's lap, *relax*, okay?

Either way, Dylan has a feeling for how laziness – which is how we prefer to think of sloth these days, making it lighter, less sodden – can be unlazily evoked:

> And yer train engine fire needs a new spark to catch it
> And the wood's easy findin' but yer lazy to fetch it
> *(Last Thoughts on Woody Guthrie)*

Off-hand, the off-rhyme of *catch it / fetch it*; you catch it, even if he couldn't quite bring himself to fetch it. "And the wood's easy findin'" – no excuse, really – "but yer lazy to fetch it". Two ways of putting it, collapsed into one: You're disinclined to fetch it / You're too lazy to fetch it. Then we can hear the reducing of the effort down to the minimum. *But you are too lazy to fetch it.* Reduced to *But you're too lazy to fetch it.* Further reduced, not just *you're* to *yer* but *too lazy* to *lazy.* Can't be bothered to say *too* right now, since I'm going to have to say *to* in just a moment. "But yer lazy to fetch it".

All the Tired Horses

There is comedy in the thought that someone as up and about as Dylan might settle for what Keats called "summer-indolence". Such comedy is in the air, even if the air is thick and heavy, in the first song on *Self Portrait*: *All the Tired Horses*. The wish to take the day off, surlily glad of the excuse of the heat (which even gets to the animals, you know), comes up against the faintly guilty acknowledgement that some activity or other does have a claim on you. The song consists of two lines of words, followed by a musing hmm sound that might be one line or two:

> All the tired horses in the sun
> How'm I s'posed to get any ridin' done
> Hmm[1]

[1] Not included in *Lyrics 1962–1985* (1985), but in *The Songs of Bob Dylan: from 1966 through 1975* (1976), sheet-music. The song-book for *Self Portrait* has at the end "Repeat 6 times and fade." The women are not satisfied with a mere six.

– or rather

hmmmmmmmm hmmmm hmm hmm-hmm

This sequence arrives gradually from silence, and departs gradually into silence, and you hear it fourteen times. It's that and that only. Oh, the orchestration of it varies and does some mock-pompous clowning around, but nothing changes, it's just a matter of shifting weight while having to rest rather restlessly.

Dylan, who believes every word of it, doesn't sing a word of it. With endearing effrontery, he leaves it to the back-up singers – except that it doesn't make sense to call them back-up singers in the absence of any full frontal voice of his. Dylan has not backed down exactly or backed out, but he has backed away – from the very first song on an album called, of all things, *Self Portrait*. Where is Dylan's self now that we need it? But then you don't need it. The song gets on very beautifully without him, thank you. A good Self Portrait may begin with Self Abnegation. Of a kind. Or, if you think putting it like that is too grand, the man is still on holiday – not back for this opener of a song, one that turns upon mildly cursing that the day isn't sheer holiday.

Not away for long, though: in the two songs that follow, *Alberta* and *I Forgot More than You'll Ever Know*, Dylan gets some writing done (as he had hinted he would like to), though not all that much, since *Alberta* is a traditional song slightly adapted by him.[1] Some writing done, and some singing, too, with backing from the serene women. After that, he is on his own, in *Days of '49*. The women will never again on the album find themselves left frontless. Our man wouldn't want to make a habit of such amicable sloth.

Genial relaxation hangs about *All the Tired Horses*, this plain-spun plaint, in some other respects, too. Attributed to Dylan on the album, the song doesn't make it into the *Lyrics 1962–1985*. Someone couldn't be bothered, was slothered?

And then again, with that receptiveness of leisure that may amount to

---

[1] Roger Ford points out to me that the songwriting credits in the *Self Portrait* song-book are more explicit than those on the LP. *Alberta #1*: Revised Melody and Arrangement by Bob Dylan. *Days of '49*: Revised Melody and New Music by Bob Dylan. *All the Tired Horses*: Words and Music by Bob Dylan. I learn, again from Roger Ford, that Donovan, Dylan's imitator, had written and recorded (three years earlier) *Writer in the Sun*, with its "And here I sit, the retired writer in the sun" (*Sunshine Superman*).

creative sloth, the song cocks an ear for coincidences, or at any rate might not resent our wondering (mustn't be *heavy*) about a possible coincidence or two. That word "tired", for instance. It just happens that this is the word crucial to the musical drowsiness of *The Lotos-Eaters*:

> Music that gentlier on the spirit lies,
> Than tir'd eyelids upon tir'd eyes.

Tennyson on how to pronounce "tir'd" there: "making the word neither monosyllabic nor disyllabic, but a dreamy child of the two".[1] This dreaminess in *The Lotos-Eaters* is from within the "Choric Song", and there is something about song that often finds itself drawn to such relaxation in the sun. Dylan, dawdling drawlingly into "All the tired horses in the sun", wouldn't have to have known this; all he would have needed was to be in sympathy with its sympathies. *The Oxford English Dictionary*'s first definition of "in the sun" is "free from care or sorrow". The phrase "in the sun" likes to close the line when figuring in a song. In *The Pirates of Penzance*, there is an instance within a song that finds pleasure in contemplating the leisure of another: "He loves to lie a-basking in the sun". A good old tradition, this, for in *As You Like It* the three-word phrase (likewise in conclusion) had been at play in a song that happily invoked the person "Who doth ambition shun / And loves to live i' the sun". In *Twelfth Night* there is a song of which we hear before we actually hear the song itself, one woven by those who weave, "The spinsters and the knitters in the sun". Dylan's "All the tired horses in the sun" is interknitted with such a feeling for it all, placing and timing. A very different feeling from the energetic aggression that can be felt in *It's All Over Now, Baby Blue*:

> Yonder stands your orphan with his gun
> Crying like a fire in the sun

Marlowe staged a parade of the Seven Deadly Sins in his *Doctor Faustus*. And what is the first thing that Sloth wants to tell you? "I am Sloth. I was begotten on a sunny bank, where I have lain ever since." And the last thing he wants to say? "I'll not speak a word more for a king's ransom."

A word more: perhaps in the recesses of the song's few words there is something else that is worth a king's ransom. Or am I alone in flirting

---

[1] See p. 156, on *Lay, Lady, Lay*.

with the thought that if we had a crossword clue, *All the —— horses* (5), the word we might wish we could ink in would be *King's?*[1] Dylan, who loves to make play with nursery rhymes, might enjoy playing the energetic pointlessness of "All the King's horses and all the King's men" (pointless because *How were they s'posed to get any repairs done?* whereas the Dylan women are all getting the singing done) against the unenergetic pointedness of

> All the tired horses in the sun
> How'm I s'posed to get any riding done

A good question (with no question-mark), though not exactly a question, really. A quasi-querulousness, rather, the weary aggrievance of someone who can't muster the energy to mount an argument, let alone a horse. *How'm I s'posed . . .*: So you creak it, and I want the heart to scold. (To invoke the music of Browning's *A Toccata of Galuppi's*.) "How'm I s'posed . . .": with, perhaps again, some pleasure derivable from this striking a chord, if we happen to know that "supposed" was for ages a helpful musical term, as *The Oxford English Dictionary* records:

Mus. Applied to a note added or introduced below the notes of a chord, or to an upper note of a chord when used as the lower note (*supposed bars*) etc.

Passivity rules? But Dylan's words have their unobtrusive activity, as does his syntax, his articulate energy. There is no verb in the first line, as if unable to bring itself to do more than just point to, point out: "All the tired horses in the sun". Blankly, as though a verb (for the verb is the activating part of speech) would be too much of a bustle or hassle. And then no syntactical relation between the first line, which just adduces those horses, and the second line, which is nothing but a fatigued remonstration. "How'm I s'posed to get any riding done". I ask you. Not that you need take the trouble to answer. It is in vain for any of us to kick against the pricks – and anyway kicking would be more of an effort than I'm prepared to make, I don't mind telling you. Forget it. But don't forget the song, even though *Lyrics 1962–1985* does.

Self Portrait doesn't leave it at that. For there are other occasions when

[1] Not that a responsible crossword would permit *King's*, with its apostrophe, to count as a five-letter word.

the album puts us in mind of the lure of sloth, easy though queasy. *Wigwam* is happy to undertake its instrumental operations, its ineffable wordlessness, for three minutes, just singing over and over again "la" and "da". If you were to complain about this, you would only come across as la-di-da. And there is *Copper Kettle* (attributed on the album to A. F. Beddoe), which Dylan sings with an exquisite slowness that languorously lingers in the knowledge that "sloth" is a noun from the adjective "slow". So easy and so slow.

> Get you a copper kettle
> Get you a copper coil
> Fill it with new-made corn mash
> And never more you'll toil
> You'll just lay there by the juniper
> While the moon is bright
> Watch them jugs a-filling
> In the pale moonlight

"And never more you'll toil". Dylan, working against the grain of his own character and disposition, has found a way of imagining this with affection – thanks to another. (Maybe Beddoe didn't have to toil at it, but he must have had to work at it, which is how it manages to sound so effortless.) "They toil not, neither do they spin": those are the gospel words that Keats chose as epigraph for his *Ode on Indolence*. Dylan isn't the type to envy the lilies of the field, but he knows why you and I might.

Time Passes Slowly

Whereas the cadences of *All the Tired Horses* are entirely at one (vocally, musically, verbally), *Time Passes Slowly* sets itself to set your teeth on edge. On the page, it looks at first entirely equable in its setting, at its setting out:

> Time passes slowly up here in the mountains
> We sit beside bridges and walk beside fountains
> Catch the wild fishes that float through the stream
> Time passes slowly when you're lost in a dream

It never becomes a nightmare exactly, but it assuredly isn't voiced as happily idle, a happy idyll. From the start, the song evinces the kind of contrariety that characterizes *Watching the River Flow*; *Time Passes Slowly*, too, is rhythmically and vocally bumpy, jagged, pot-holed, unsettled and unsettling, straining its musical strains, not soporific at all, at all. And more and more the song commits itself to the implications of the words that follow that first verse. "Once I had a sweetheart, she was fine and good-lookin'". Time passes slowly; this love has passed but not the wrenched and wrenching memory of it. The rhymes refuse to stay right, and the voicing then does nothing to ameliorate this (the way of Dylan's comedy, but then this is tragedy), rather it skewers the rhymes askew:

> Time passes slowly up here in the daylight
> We stare straight ahead and try so hard to stay right

On the page, you are likely to glimpse the having to try so hard; in performance, you are sure to hear it, compounded vocally and musically so that it really won't stay right. "Up here in the mountains", from the opening, has become, here at the closing, "up here in the daylight", which is perfectly calm, but the rhyme of "daylight" with "stay right" is tense: you have to stay cautiously with "stay" for a moment, and you have to make sure that you get "right" right when it comes to the run of the words or rather to their halting.

> Time passes slowly up here in the daylight
> We stare straight ahead and try so hard to stay right
> Like the red rose of summer that blooms in the day
> Time passes slowly and fades away

This final verse plaits its rhymes as no previous verse had done: "daylight" → "stay right" → "the day" → "away". But this conclusiveness is not that of a love-knot.

This is no love song, a no-love song. It would all feel less hopeless if things were over and done with. But. "Time passes slowly when you're searching for love". This entailing some sour soul-searching.

Those three words, "Time passes slowly", open the song, open it up. They open the first and last lines of the first and last verses, and of the second (the remaining) verse they open the last line. They are perspicuously absent from the song's bridge. Five lines of the verses' twelve begin with "Time passes slowly", five times the bridge rings no changes on a different tedium of words, five of them:

> Ain't no reason to go in a wagon to town
> Ain't no reason to go to the fair
> Ain't no reason to go up, ain't no reason to go down
> Ain't no reason to go anywhere

This is obdurate, blockish, an evocation of a dangerous state of mind. Indifference can harden, before long, into something damnable: "accidie", sloth, torpor. *The Oxford English Dictionary* says that this is "the proper term for the 4th cardinal sin, *sloth, sluggishness*", and that when its Greek origin (= non-caring-state, heedlessness) was forgotten, the Latin *acidum*, sour, lent its harsh flavour to the word. Not-caring: or, Ain't no reason to go in a wagon to town, or to go to the fair, or to go up, or to go down, or to go anywhere. No go. You name it, I'll disclaim it. Can you reason with someone who just keeps saying *Ain't no reason to*? It might even vie with the vista of the child's *Why?*

   "Apathy' is a word that drifts to mind, but apathy doesn't carry the bone-deep surrender that is the accent of accidie. "Her sin is her lifelessness".[1] Beckett could joke about "a new lease of apathy"; you can't pull that off with accidie, the extremity of not-caring that has been characterized as "an acquiescence in discouragement which reaches the utmost of sadness when it ceases to be regretful".[2]

   The lines of the song's bridge do have their equanimity all right, but it is an emptied equanimity that has persuaded itself (as Satan did) that it will be able to say farewell to despair if it says farewell to hope. It acquiesces, yes, but so grimly as to bring home that it constitutes no bridge from this not-caring to any other state of mind. Thank Somebody that there is, elsewhere in Dylan, a world elsewhere:

---

[1] *Desolation Row.*

[2] Francis Paget on Accidie, quoted in *George Lyttelton's Commonplace Book*, ed. James Ramsden (2002), p. 105. For an analysis of accidie, or acedia, its relations to sloth, and its refusal of God's "gift of laughter", see F. H. Buckley, *The Morality of Laughter* (2003), pp. 169–70. *Clothes Line Saga* both accepts and transmits the gift of comedy. Buckley: "The acedic may indeed be listless, for they lack a motive for action. With Kierkegaard, they simply can't be bothered." Dylan can be bothered, even as to those who can't be.

> Happiness is but a state of mind
> Anytime you want to you can cross the state line

So sings *Waitin' for You*,[1] and very happily, too. But unhappiness is convicted, convinced that there is nothing, nobody, to wait for. And it has long ceased to see any point in making an effort. "Ain't no reason to go anywhere" – and that includes going across the state line into the state of mind that is happiness.

"Time passes slowly and fades away" – this, too, is an estranging thing to say. There is a glimpse of the lethal state of mind that asks only to kill time. But old Father Time never dies, he only fades away, or rather fades from our fading sight.

Clothes Line Saga

The not-caring, the nothingness, the depths beyond apathy even, at the heartland of *Time Passes Slowly* is as nothing compared to the vacuity of *Clothes Line Saga*, which raises small talkative mindlessness and affectlessness from down there in the Basement. Family values, of a sort, flat, faithful, not careless, just not caring. The two things that make it possible for us not to scream ("Why aren't they screaming?", in the words of Philip Larkin, *The Old Fools*) are that the song is stringently straight-faced and that it does give an adolescent's-eye-view. The adolescent, after all (it may be a long time after – the song begins with the words "After a while"), usually turns out to be a worm that turns. ("Well, I just do what I'm told" – Do you now . . .) Time passes slowly, and so does adolescence but it does pass. Teenagers age. Meanwhile here is a vinegary vignette, the vinaigrette dressing that is *Clothes Line Saga*. It is sung levelly at a steady sturdy rhythm of monumental unconcern.

CLOTHES LINE SAGA

> After a while we took in the clothes
> Nobody said very much
> Just some old wild shirts and a couple pairs of pants
> Which nobody really wanted to touch

---

[1] Released in 2002 on *Divine Secrets of the Ya-Ya Sisterhood*.

Mama come in and picked up a book
An' Papa asked her what it was
Someone else asked, "What do you care?"
Papa said, "Well, just because"
Then they started to take back their clothes
Hang 'em on the line
It was January the thirtieth
And everybody was feelin' fine

The next day everybody got up
Seein' if the clothes were dry
The dogs were barking, a neighbor passed
Mama, of course, she said, "Hi!"
"Have you heard the news?" he said, with a grin
"The Vice-President's gone mad!"
"Where?" "Downtown." "When?" "Last night"
"Hmm, say, that's too bad!"
"Well, there's nothin' we can do about it," said the neighbor
"Just somethin' we're gonna have to forget"
"Yes, I guess so," said Ma
Then she asked me if the clothes was still wet

I reached up, touched my shirt
And the neighbor said, "Are those clothes yours?"
I said, "Some of 'em, not all of 'em"
He said, "Ya always help out around here with the chores?"
I said, "Sometime, not all the time"
Then my neighbor, he blew his nose
Just as papa yelled outside
"Mama wants you t' come back in the house and bring them clothes"
Well, I just do what I'm told
So, I did it, of course
I went back in the house and Mama met me
And then I shut all the doors

The song makes its point about pointlessness, and the title as given in *Lyrics 1962–1985*, *Clothes Line*, was the better for not letting sarcasm have the last word, as against *Clothes Line Saga*.

It feels like a parody of a way of lifelessness. And so it is, while taking a shot at a previous shot at this: Bobbie Gentry's *Ode to Billie Joe*, which had been a hit with its doggèd tedium, its *Papa said*, and *Mama said*, and *Brother said*. Hard to get flatter-footed than the *Ode*.[1] Hard, but not impossible. For along came Dylan and levelled it some more, the flatly faithful flat-liner. Full of mindless questions, the song is an answer of a sort, and something of a parody.

As so often in Dylan, there may be a touch of the nursery rhyme (and nursery rhymes like to accommodate parodies).

> The maid was in the garden hanging out the clothes,
> When down came a blackbird and pecked off her nose.

The song avails itself of this in its *nose / clothes* lines, but its social setting doesn't have any maids to help out around here with the chores. And there will be nothing as penetrating as a peck, although there is a pecking order: "Papa yelled outside 'Mama wants you t' come back in the house and bring them clothes.'"

It starts bored, and it stays that way.

> After a while we took in the clothes
> Nobody said very much

To put it mildly. This is classic boredom, the more so because not really admitted to, with not just the vacancy but the vacuum of smalltown smalltalk. Why are you telling me all this? "Well, just because".

> Just some old wild shirts and a couple pairs of pants
> Which nobody really wanted to touch

Really? And they are bleached of any real wildness, those "old wild shirts". *The Oxford English Dictionary* has, under "wild":

U.S. *slang*. Remarkable, unusual, exciting. Used as a general term of approbation . . . "amazing range of colours (including some wild marble-like effects)".

Exciting? Amazing? Forget it. "It was January the thirtieth / And everybody was feelin' fine". ("Feelin' fine" has never been so evacuated in the delivery.

[1] On *The Basement Tapes* box, Dylan's song was listed as *Answer to Ode*, not as *Clothes Line* or *Clothes Line Saga*. I learn all this from Roger Ford.

Not tonic, catatonic.) January the thirtieth, eh. Why that day? (King Charles I's deathday? The birthday of President Franklin Delano Roosevelt, who had run for Vice-President but had not "gone mad"?) Who knows? Who cares? Just being retentive as to the annals, that's all. "Hmm, say, that's too bad". Sloth, which shoulders nothing, shrugs its shoulders, shrugs everything off. "Well, there's nothin' we can do about it". Or can do about anything, come to that. Or can do, period.

The conversation from the start has proceeded apace. A sluggish pace.

> Mama come in and picked up a book
> An' Papa asked her what it was
> Someone else asked, "What do you care?"
> Papa said, "Well, just because"

The boredom is always edgy, on the brink of bad temper (you might think of the opening scenes of the film *Badlands*, with its smalltown voice-over of incipient family violence). Everything is a matter of course: "Mama, of course, she said, 'Hi!'" – the voice flattening the exclamation mark, since not-caring is never marked by exclamations. "Well, I just do what I'm told / So, I did it, of course". Everything just takes its course. And nothing courses, least of all through anybody's veins.

"The next day everybody got up" – No!! ?*!?!* You gotta be kidding.

If people ask you pointless questions, you do well to stick to your rights, and to answer with matching pointlessness:

> I reached up, touched my shirt
> And the neighbor said, "Are those clothes yours?"
> I said, "Some of 'em, not all of 'em"
> He said, "Ya always help out around here with the chores?"
> I said, "Sometime, not all the time"

The empty questions, the cagey answers, let nothing out, give nothing away. (Here's some nothing for you, says the song all the way through.) Nothing to give, nothing gives. Or rather, not quite nothing, for there is that one surprising yelp or yodel from Dylan, exultation even, of "Yoo ooh" in the last verse just before the end, as though signalling a way out, an end, an escape from a world in which when "my neighbor, he blew his nose", that just might be the most interesting thing that you'll ever hear from him.

Hold on to that little yelp, for it is just about all that might give you a glimpse of hope. For the end of the song doesn't sound as though it can imagine much of a way out:

> Well, I just do what I'm told
> So, I did it, of course
> I went back in the house and Mama met me
> And then I shut all the doors

Faintly sinister? Or would that be paranoid? Just nothing? Yet I'm reminded of the disconcerting close of another parodic piece that achieves more than it bargained for: A. E. Housman's *Fragment of an English Opera* ("designed as a model for young librettists").[1] Reminded, not just because of words for music, and not just because of the family: Father (bass), Mother (contralto), Daughter (soprano).

DAUGHTER: I am their daughter;
> If not, I oughter:
>> Prayers have been said.
> This is my mother;
> I have no other:
>> Would I were dead!
> That is my father;
> He thinks so, rather:
>> Oh dear, oh dear!
> I take my candle;
> *This* is the handle:
>> I disappear.

FATHER & MOTHER: The coast is clear.

I beg your pardon? Is it curtains for the primal scene?

    And then I shut all the doors. Which shuts the song. And shuts the rhyme-scheme, too, as no previous verse had done. The first verse: *much / touch; was / because; line / fine*. The second verse: *dry / Hi; mad / bad; forget / wet*. But the last verse: *yours / chores; nose / clothes; course / doors*. Of course.

    Among the undertakings of an artist, there may be the wish "To ease the

---

[1] Parodying Thomas Hood, *The Bridge of Sighs*, as Archie Burnett notes in *The Poems of A. E. Housman* (1997), p. 544.

pain of idleness and the memory of decay" (*Every Grain of Sand*). Idleness may be all the worse when it doesn't rise to pain but sinks into numbness. In British English, *couldn't care less*, but in American English, oddly, *could care less*. (A sarcasm? See if I care?) Why? "Well, just because". Anyway, "What do you care?"

Artists care. And share. This entails their not talking glibly, as institutions like to, about the caring and the sharing. The line about sharing –

> We've been through too much tough times that they never shared

– may find itself sardonically paired:

> Now all of a sudden it's as if they've always cared
> (*Let's Keep It Between Us*)

Artists will on occasion have to give voice to unsentimentalities: "I used to care but things have changed" (*Things Have Changed*).

Lay Down Your Weary Tune

Nobody in the world of *Clothes Line Saga* would know the word "accidie", but that is what they are suffering from – or perhaps not *suffering* from, just sick with: a spiritual malaise. Such sloth is a malign growth. Cut it out.

Fortunately, blessedly, there are the other (benign) forms that stretched-out leisureliness may take, with no need for all of us to be at full stretch every waking minute of every day. (Even January the thirtieth.) We owe it to ourselves sometimes to heed the gentle admonition, *Rest yourself.* And music, given how often it takes a musical rest, is in its element in such a fluent urging.

> Lay down your weary tune, lay down
> Lay down the song you strum
> And rest yourself 'neath the strength of strings
> No voice can hope to hum

So it opens, this tender pitying admonition that is sung with sweet solemnity and yet has its own implicit comedy. For there must be something rueful about starting a tune by saying that it is time to stop it. Andrew Marvell began his great poem about war and peace, *An Horatian Ode upon Cromwell's Return from Ireland*, with the paradox that this is no time to be writing poems or even reading them:

> The forward youth that would appear
> Must now forsake his muses dear,
>   Nor in the shadows sing
>   His numbers languishing.
> 'Tis time to leave the books in dust,
> And oil the unusèd armour's rust . . .

Dylan sings that 'tis time to sing his numbers languishing no longer. But his strings weave so many exquisite variations on this that we find ourselves wanting the song to go on for ever saying that it should not go on. For ever? So it has seemed to some.

Joan Baez: "He could never resist singing what he had just written, and he had just written *Lay Down Your Weary Tune*, it was 45 minutes long."[1]
Scaduto: "The one that somebody called '*War and Peace*'?"
Baez: "Right, it was just endless. Of course, I was perfectly happy, except I was concerned. I've always had an audience conscience. I've always worried about making them tired or whatever, and he wasn't."[2]

Or whatever.

Dylan has a note on *Biograph*: "I had heard a Scottish ballad on an old 78 record that I was trying to really capture the feeling of, that was haunting me. I couldn't get it out of my head." Not only could he not get it out of his head, he could not get it out of our heads once he had started to put it into them.

The song both begins and ends with its refrain or chorus, and is describing an eternal circle – as does another of his songs about singing, *Eternal Circle*. An eternal circle not infernal but paradisal.

> Lay down your weary tune, lay down
> Lay down the song you strum
> And rest yourself 'neath the strength of strings
> No voice can hope to hum

---

[1] On *Biograph*, it is 4′ 32″.
[2] Anthony Scaduto, *Bob Dylan* (1971, revised edition 1973), p. 194.

The refrain or chorus is at once utterly simple and unobtrusively intricate in its utterance. The modulation quietly changes what it urges: "Lay down your weary tune" is one thing, and the immediately ensuing "lay down" both is and is not the same thing. Is, in that it may simply urge again that you lay down your weary tune; is not, in that as a unit on its own it may be – in American English, in *Lay, Lady, Lay* – an intransitive verb: not lay down your tune, just lay down. The next one, "Lay down the song you strum", is transitive again all right, but then "And rest yourself" not only calls back to "lay down" (lay down and rest), but gives us something that ought sometimes to trump both a transitive and an intransitive verb: a reflexive verb, "rest yourself", five times in the song. Fifteen times there comes the injunction "lay down", which mostly means "relinquish" but is alive to the wish still to *play*, since – in the usual weird way that language has – "lay down" can mean "set up": *The Oxford English Dictionary*, 51, "To set up or establish (a certain beat)." The dictionary lays down "beat", "stomp", "rhythm", and this: "The soloist can play anything he chooses to play on the time that I lay down for him" (from *Melody Maker*, 6 April 1968). The song lays down a tune, unwearyingly.

Dylan's voice swells and elongates the word "weary" with what feels like stoical resilience. The schoolbook would tell you that in the phrase "your weary tune" the word "weary" is a transferred epithet – you are the weary one, not the tune. (You are thirsty for blood, not your sword.) Poetic licence, but we need to ask what the poet does once he has gained his licence, and what he does here could not be more apt. Weariness is just the right thing to transfer, a musical burden to lift from your own shoulders and transfer to the tune. This, in the confidence that the tune will not grow weary really, and that the listeners will not weary of it.

As often in Dylan's songs about singing, he is sensitive to the need to acknowledge gratefully such powers as are not his own (whether a person's, say, Woody Guthrie's or Blind Willie McTell's, or a creature's, say, birdsong), and so to rise above envy or the wrong kind of competitiveness. This is effected here by means of the telling words "no voice can hope to hum". Not even my voice, gentle listener. For the natural kingdom is a divine orchestra, and Dylan's strings evoke the other instruments and their indispensability: the breeze like a bugle, the drums of dawn, the ocean like an organ, the waves like cymbals, the rain like a trumpet, the branches like a banjo (an instrument that puts on no airs), the water like a harp. (Like both kinds of harp perhaps, living from hand to mouth, and with such different class associations.) And "like a hymn", since there are not only kinds of musical instrument, there are other kinds of musical and poetical form. *Lay Down Your Weary Tune* itself both is and is not a hymn.

It plays its own sounds with unostentatious dexterity. Oh, "strum" into "strength" into "strings" – and then into "Struck by the sounds before the sun". No hiding of the alliterative litheness, and no brandishing of it, either. No competitiveness, for the preposition "against" is not in opposition when it sets the breeze "Against the drums of dawn" (sets musically, not combatively), or the waves "Against the rocks and sands". And no vanity: "The cryin' rain" – which was not in tears, though raindrops may look like teardrops – "sang / And asked for no applause". A lesson to us all, the singer included. But not *too* saintly, for there is a little room for manoeuvre: "And asked for no applause" might mean *asked positively that there be none*, or might mean *did not ask that there be any*. Anyway "The water smooth ran like a hymn": no applause in church, please. Meanwhile, when it comes to an audience, you can't better the winds:

> The branches bare like a banjo moaned
> To the winds that listened the best[1]

Come gather round, winds . . . Not just the best of them all, the best of us all.

Baez: "Right, it was just endless." Such was indeed the impression that the song meant to give (to give, rather than to make, since it is not in the making-an-impression game). So how does Dylan bring it to an end without stopping it in its track? With some movements of mind. First:

> The last of leaves fell from the trees
> And clung to a new love's breast
> The branches bare like a banjo moaned
> To the winds that listened the best

"The last of . . ." is an intimation of an ending, and Dylan then tips us a wink of his hat by doing what he has not once hitherto done in the song: *not* following the four-line verse with the four-line refrain. Instead, and trusting that this registers upon us, he moves at once to another four-line verse, and then – with great imaginative coherence in the substitution –

[1] Dylan sings "moaned" and "the best" on *Biograph*; as printed in *Lyrics 1962–1985*, "played" and "best".

he has this verse be fully reminiscent of the refrain, of which it offers a variant along the same rhymes. So that the end runs like this:

> The last of leaves fell from the trees
> And clung to a new love's breast
> The branches bare like a banjo moaned
> To the winds that listened the best
>
> I gazed down in the river's mirror
> And watched its winding strum
> The water smooth ran like a hymn
> And like a harp did hum
> Lay down your weary tune, lay down
> Lay down the song you strum
> And rest yourself 'neath the strength of strings
> No voice can hope to hum

The turn at the successive endings, from "hymn" to "hum", is finely judged, a rotation of the sound (in the benign spirit of the Dorset poet William Barnes, who uses such para-rhymes happily,[1] not ominously as Wilfred Owen does in his pangs from the Great War) that asks for no applause but deserves it. The strength of strings is all in such interlacing, a relaxation that is altogether other than lax.

Mr. Tambourine Man

So lithe is the movement of *Mr. Tambourine Man* that to number it among the songs of sloth might seem perverse or even counter-intuitive. The song may talk of being "too numb to step", but that is not the way it walks.

> My senses have been stripped, my hands can't feel to grip
> My toes too numb to step, wait only for my boot heels
> To be wanderin'

I don't believe you, one is happy to report, since the gait of the song is quite other. "My weariness amazes me"? Weariness, my foot. An amazing thing for the song to maintain. Refreshing and refreshed is how it sounds.

Would not sloth be sluggish? Yet there are affinities between *Mr. Tambourine Man* and some other songs engaging with sloth, those that breathe

[1] See the lines from Barnes on p. 399, delighting in such rhymes.

relaxation and escape, relief and release.[1] For instance, *Lay Down Your Weary Tune*, which started with its refrain, as though it had already arrived – in good time and with all effort over – where it was hoping to come to rest:

> Lay down your weary tune, lay down
> Lay down the song you strum
> And rest yourself 'neath the strength of strings
> No voice can hope to hum

His weary tune amazes him? No matter, the time has come to lay it down. *Mr. Tambourine Man* opens, likewise, with a refrain that is an injunction, yet not this time to himself, to lay down a tune, but to someone else, to take up a tune, to play a song.

> Hey! Mr. Tambourine Man, play a song for me
> I'm not sleepy and there is no place I'm going to
> Hey! Mr. Tambourine Man, play a song for me
> In the jingle jangle morning I'll come followin' you

A singer will sometimes wish to sing his refrain no more. "Sometimes my burden is more than I can bear" (*Not Dark Yet*). So a singer may wish that, for just one time, another would sing to him, sing for him. The first line of *Mr. Tambourine Man* takes us back to Dylan's first album, but with a difference. "Hey, hey, Woody Guthrie, I wrote you a song". And so he did, but right now he may not feel too good, and would appreciate it if someone would write a song for him. Or play a song for him. So "Hey, hey, Woody Guthrie, I wrote you a song" becomes "Hey! Mr. Tambourine Man, play a song for me", with a heart-lifting lilt when this "Hey!" modulates into "play". And *for me*, instead of my always having to be the one, always having to do it (I know, I know, and I'm not complaining exactly) for other people. What in *Lay Down Your Weary Tune* had been "And rest yourself 'neath the strength of strings" has become a promise to stir myself if you will just be so kind as to stir me:

> play a song for me
> In the jingle jangle morning I'll come followin' you

---

[1] The setting of *Time Passes Slowly*, where time "fades away", might suggest "ready for to fade", "there is no place I'm going to", and "no one to meet" in *Mr. Tambourine Man*.

"I'm not sleepy", but this does not mean that what I stand in need of is a lullaby. *Mr. Tambourine Man* is not out to lullify.

Lay Down Your Weary Tune had delighted in the music of the rain, because such a music-maker "asked for no applause". *Mr. Tambourine Man* asks for little or no applause, for it wants to keep up the playful subterfuge that the song that it really values is not the one it is singing but the one that it is requesting, asking another to sing. "Yes, to dance beneath the diamond sky with one hand waving free". Free, among other things, of any obligation either to offer or to ask for applause (even while the waving does look like encouragement). What is the sound of one hand clapping? Quite something, as when an audience is asked – even before anything has been performed tonight – to give the performer a big hand. Big-hearted. An advance.

"Yes, to dance . . .": the affirmative energy of this is partly a matter of its finally fulfilling the promise that had been given earlier:

> cast your dancing spell my way
> I promise to go under it

In fairy stories, the dancing spell is not something that you would like to have cast on you (unable to stop dancing, your weariness will amaze you, and as for the spell, there will be no escaping it on the run), yet Dylan has put this in such a way as to escape any thought of the curse of exhaustion. Instead the murmur is *relax*. For the spell is not being cast on you, it is being cast your way.

"Yes, to dance . . .": the "Yes" is able to work wonders, for it comes after a succession of negative formations throughout the song. The refrain: "I'm not sleepy and there is no place I'm going to". The first verse: "not sleeping", "no one to meet". The second verse: "can't feel". The third verse: "not aimed at anyone", "no fences". The final verse is the only one that is a negative-free zone, and this despite all the dark things in it.

> Down the foggy ruins of time, far past the frozen leaves
> The haunted, frightened trees, out to the windy beach
> Far from the twisted reach of crazy sorrow

– whereupon, the word "Yes" is a sudden exultant freedom:

> Yes, to dance beneath the diamond sky with one hand waving free

True, a negative formation can carry a positive message ("there are no fences facin'"), but there is no substitute for a cry of "Yes".

The comedy of the song is a matter of its criss-cross. It is marked not by mock-modesty, but by a mocking modesty, by bantering and antics. Take "the jingle jangle morning". Jingle-jangle is a characteristic creation of the English language, and *The Oxford English Dictionary* lists its low companions: "dilly-dally, dingle-dangle, ding-dong, clink-clank, etc."

An alternating jingle of sounds; a sentence or verse characterized by this. Something that makes a continuous and alternating jingle; a jingling ornament or trinket.

But although the compound "jingle-jangle" is admirable, it is not admiring. "Such a paltry collection of commonplace tunes, handled clumsily" . . . "jingle-jangles its way through the piece" (1899). The same goes for "jingle":

The affected repetition of the same sound or of a similar series of sounds, as in alliteration, rime, or assonance; any arrangement of words intended to have a pleasing or striking sound without regard to the sense; a catching array of words, whether in prose or verse.

At which point, the dictionary reaches its verdict and its sentence: "Chiefly contemptuous". "Frivolous hearers, who are more pleased with little jingles, and tinkling of words than with the most persuasive arguments" (1663). The comical audacity of the song makes sure that it, too, is among Dylan's Songs of Redemption: jingle and jingle jangle are redeemed from the contempt that has been visited upon them. "Commonplace tunes"? "Without regard to the sense"? "The affected repetition"? No, the effective repetition. I had not known the terminology of the tambourine until *The Oxford English Dictionary* evoked the "pairs of small cymbals, called jingles, placed in slots round the circumference".[1]

Alliteration, rhyme, or assonance: it would not be true to say that *Mr. Tambourine Man* consists of nothing else, but it is true that the song – like all such lyrical creations – is fascinated by the relations between these resources of sound and everything else that is the case, all those things in life that

[1] The *OED* includes a reminder of the tambourine's "use as a collecting dish": "Will you kindly drop a shilling in my little tambourine". Kipling's *Absent-Minded Beggar* in hope of a shilling, Dylan's "ragged clown behind / I wouldn't pay it any mind".

are not words but that we often need the life of words to help us catch. There is, for instance, the indefatigable standby, a rhyme on "rhyme", "And if you hear vague traces of skippin' reels of rhyme", where the vague traces of skipping ropes and of spinning wheels swirl exuberantly along with those skippin' reels.

The furthest reach of rhyme in every verse of the song is the one that has the eighth line hearken back to the fourth line. In the final verse, this is "tomorrow" completing the thought of "sorrow", a rhyme that Dylan often uses and never fails to vary.[1]

> Then take me disappearin' through the smoke rings of my mind
> Down the foggy ruins of time, far past the frozen leaves
> The haunted, frightened trees, out to the windy beach
> Far from the twisted reach of crazy sorrow
> Yes, to dance beneath the diamond sky with one hand waving free
> Silhouetted by the sea, circled by the circus sands
> With all memory and fate driven deep beneath the waves
> Let me forget about today until tomorrow

The rhyme *sorrow / tomorrow* is the song's final rhyme except for the return to the final refrain, and the sense of this rhyme's simple predictability is perfectly right. Relax, again; forget about it. But there is, over and above and below this, the vocal timing of the words across and against the musical cadence. Don't forget about this voicing, his stationing of "until tomorrow" so that it is both gingerly and gingered up: "Let me forget about today until tomorrow". "Far from the twisted reach of crazy sorrow": yet not so far as to be beyond reach of the rhyme, the longest stretch that a rhyme is here called on to make.

"Let me forget about today until tomorrow": simple, but cryptic. This is not your usual reminder that procrastination is the thief of time. It may want us to hear the Sermon on the Mount, but not along the established lines:

Take therefore no thought for the morrow: for the morrow shall take thought for the things of itself. Sufficient unto the day is the evil thereof.

(Matthew 6:34)

Rather the reverse. Let me forget about tomorrow today.

A song that delights in what might be deplored as "jingle jangle" is

---

[1] See *Boots of Spanish Leather* and *Mama, You Been on My Mind.*

likely to intensify its rhyming. The first triplet of rhymes in the first verse, *sand / hand / stand*, moves then to "sleeping", which will in the end be consummated by the off-rhyme, "dreaming" – but only after crossing the stepping stones of the next triplet of rhymes, with their assonantal bridge to *sleeping / dreaming: feet / meet / street*. And then as the song nears and then reaches its ending, with the third and fourth verses, we hear the conclusiveness realized. For the last verse inaugurates itself with a sound that is far from having disappeared:

> Then take me disappearin' through the smoke rings of my mind
> Down the foggy ruins of time,

– a sound that rings from the previous verse:

> And if you hear vague traces of skippin' reels of rhyme
> To your tambourine in time, it's just a ragged clown behind
> I wouldn't pay it any mind,

Whereupon the rhymes and assonances find themselves at once free and driven (driven deep in memory), with *leaves / trees / beach / reach* mounting to this climax:

> Yes, to dance beneath the diamond sky with one hand waving free
> Silhouetted by the sea, circled by the circus sands
> With all memory and fate driven deep beneath the waves
> Let me forget about today until tomorrow

Free / sea / memory / deep / me: this presses forward while never forgetting the first verse of the song with its *sleeping / feet / meet / street / dreaming*. But then it doesn't forget an earlier rhyme (*sand / hand*), either. For when the "one hand" picks up, a moment later, "the circus sands", it circles back to the beginning:

> Though I know that evenin's empire has returned into sand
> Vanished from my hand

Nothing simply vanishes, and the circus sands return to sand.

Sloth is a form of escape, but not "escaping on the run" since that would ask too much energy. Dylan has said: "I don't write songs for escape",[1] but that isn't the same as not writing songs that comprehend the yearning to escape, and respect it and suspect it. Wilfrid Mellers gave us the dope:

Far from being socially committed, it looks as though it might be an escape song, and is so, in that a tambourine man is a peddler of pot. Yet Dylan says he's "not sleepy", even though there ain't no place he's going to; and his pied piper myth encourages us to follow the unconscious where spontaneously it may lead us. This is subtly suggested by the wavery refrain and by the irregularity of both verbal and musical clauses, which pile or float up like smoke rings. As the rings unfurl, we are liberated.[2]

Dylan himself has not felt liberated by any such readings of *Mr. Tambourine Man*: "Drugs never played a part in that song" (*Biograph*).

What clearly did play a part is Dylan's sense of how precariously thrilling the whole matter of *following* may be. The Pied Piper is there all right, but with all the mixed feelings that we ought to feel about the story of someone who was cheated by "the city fathers" and who took his revenge by making off with the city children, "the sweet pretty things", as they are called in *Tombstone Blues*. "The town has no need to be nervous"? Rather the reverse, as is clear when *Tombstone Blues* goes on to imagine a king who "Puts the pied pipers in prison".

The Pied Piper has a dancing spell that he casts their way. The Pied Piper was wronged, and then was the wronger. "And Piper and dancers were gone forever": those words are Robert Browning's, in *The Pied Piper of Hamelin*. For words of Dylan's:

> Farewell Angelina
> The bells of the crown
> Are being stolen by bandits
> I must follow the sound
> The triangle tingles
> And the trumpets play slow
> Farewell Angelina
> The sky is on fire
> And I must go

---

[1] *New York Times* (8 January 1978).
[2] *Bob Dylan: Freedom and Responsibility*, in *Bob Dylan: A Retrospective*, ed. Craig McGregor (1972), p. 164.

If you really must follow the sound, then better the jingle jangle than the triangle tingle.

"Don't follow leaders". Might it be safe to follow the children that follow the Piper? "Wherever the children go I'll follow them".[1] No, on further thought, don't follow anything. Even an enthusiasm.

Jazz is hard to follow; I mean, you actually have to *like* jazz to follow it; and my motto is, never follow *anything*. I don't know what the motto of the younger generation is, but I would think they'd have to follow their parents. I mean, what would some parent say to his kid if the kid came home with a glass eye, a Charlie Mingus record and a pocketful of feathers? He'd say: "Who are you following?" And the poor kid would have to stand there with water in his shoes, a bow tie on his ear and soot pouring out of his belly button and say: "Jazz, Father, I've been following jazz."[2]

So is it folly to follow? "& he say 'just you folly me baby snooks! jus you folly me & you feel fine!'"[3] Cock some snooks at him, that's my advice. And yet perhaps just this once, it would truly be fine: "Yes, to dance . . ." In the jingle jangle morning, who knows what music might be made, and how? Not "swingin' madly across the sun", but by courtesy of it.

The Ethiopians, over whom Memnon reigned, erected a celebrated statue to the honour of their monarch. This statue had the wonderful property of uttering a melodious sound every day, at sun-rising, like that which is heard at the breaking of the string of a harp when it is wound up. This was effected by the rays of the sun when they fell upon it.

(John Lemprière, *Classical Dictionary*)[4]

> Struck by the sounds before the sun
> I knew the night had gone
> (*Lay Down Your Weary Tune*)

---

[1] *Abandoned Love*, which mounts, like *Mr. Tambourine Man*, a parade. "I march in the parade of liberty".

[2] *Playboy* (March 1966).

[3] *Tarantula* (1966, 1971), p. 32.

[4] Ed. F. A. Wright (1948). It was first published in 1788, and Keats learnt much from it.

Struck by the sounds that were struck by the sun, I knew the night had gone.

But not for good. Immediately following (on *Bringing It All Back Home*) the melodious sound of the words "I'll come followin' you", there is heard a different evocation of light and darkness:

> Of war and peace the truth just twists
> Its curfew gull just glides
> Upon four-legged forest clouds
> The cowboy angel rides
> With his candle lit into the sun
> Though its glow is waxed in black
> All except when 'neath the trees of Eden
>   (*Gates of Eden*)

The trees of Eden are haunting frightening trees, true. In the fullness of time, the dawn will be back: "At dawn my lover comes to me". But evening's empire will return, likewise. To return to Lemprière and "the foreign sun": "At the setting of the sun, and in the night, the sound was lugubrious."

Lust

A note in *Biograph* says unassumingly of *Lay, Lady, Lay*: "It became one of Dylan's best-known love songs, almost by accident." "Almost by accident" is good, like love and its felicities.

> Somebody got lucky
> But it was an accident
> Now I'm pledging my time to you
> Hopin' you'll come through, too
> (*Pledging My Time*)

A best-known love song, *Lay, Lady, Lay* is all the better for knowing about carnal knowledge. Love, good. Lust, bad? Meanwhile *Desire*, Dylan's inspired title for an album, is a word that knows too much to argue or to judge: its lips are sealed, for the moment. Then there is concupiscence, a lasciviously lissom word that stands in need of banter if it is not to come on too strong: James Joyce having fun with *The Old Curiosity Shop* as the old concupiosity shape, or Wallace Stevens opening with rounded imperiousness a severely sad poem, *The Emperor of Ice-Cream*:

> Call the roller of big cigars,
> The muscular one, and bid him whip
> In kitchen cups concupiscent curds.

"Call the roller": an injunction ("Listen to me, baby") is likewise the launching of *If You Gotta Go, Go Now*, a song that consists not of taking out an injunction, but of making one out, not an injunction to stop someone from entering but to discourage someone from leaving.

> Listen to me, baby
> There's something you must see
> I want to be with you, gal
> If you want to be with me
>
> But if you got to go
> It's all right

>   But if you got to go, go now
>   Or else you gotta stay all night

One happy effect of this regular conclusion, "Or else you gotta stay all night", is that it does have the decency not to contract itself into the warning or threat that would be the two opening words alone: *or else*. ("The alternative to be imagined", as *The Oxford English Dictionary* explains the menace.[1]) Another other happy effect is the song's giving of patently bogus grounds. Don't misunderstand me, it pleads – or better still, I know I can count on you to understand that I am laying myself open. (How about you?) A girl with a sense of humour (and why else would I want to be with you, gal? . . .) is sure to get it.

>   It's just that I ain't got no watch
>   And you keep askin' me what time it is

Does that do the trick, make you tick? Not really? Then try this:

>   It's just that I'll be sleepin' soon
>   An' it'll be too dark for you to find the door

Deft, the move from the opening "There's something you must see" to the closing, "It'll be too dark for you to find the door". Canny, the respect for her sense of humour, her seeing through the tomcatfoolery, that is implied by the obligatory invoking of *respect*:[2]

---

[1] W. K. Wimsatt used to give a lecture entitled *Aristotle or Else*. The scholar Gerald Else declined to be warned off.

[2] Gary Gilmore, a brutal murderer, is allowed by Norman Mailer the right to tell brutal truths:

When a girl finally decided to let you fuck her she'd always put on this act like she was being taken advantage of and 9 times outa 10 the girl would say "Well, will you still respect me?" Some goof-ball shit like that. Well the cat was always so hot and ready to go by then that he was ready to promise anything, even respect. That always seemed so silly, but it was just the way the game was played. I had a chick ask me that once, a real pretty little blond girl, everybody really was hot for her ass and I had her alone one nite in her house. We were both about 15 and necking pretty heavy both getting worked up and I was in and I knew it and then she came up with that cornball line: "Gary, if I let you do it would you still respect me?" Well, I blew it, I started laffing and I told her: "Respect you? For what? I just wanta fuck and so do you, what the fuck am I sposed to respect you for? You just won a first place trophy in the Indianapolis 500 or something?" Well, like I said I blew that one.

(*The Executioner's Song*, 1980, p. 410)

> I am just a poor boy, baby
> Lookin' to connect
> But I certainly don't want you thinkin'
> That I ain't got any respect

"A guilty conscience, too"? No, because you and I both know that in this particular gamble I am parlaying the innocent. There is no sarcasm in the song, only witty panache (as in Marvell's complicated compliment *To His Coy Mistress*), and no self-respecting girl would ever leave a room that housed such self-knowledgeable effrontery. Stay, lady, stay? Stay, baby, stay.

There is comparable comedy in *All I Really Want to Do*, another desirous song of seducing or inducing (or educing – let me call out of you an admission of what you too want to do):

> I ain't lookin' to compete with you
> Beat or cheat or mistreat you
> Simplify you, classify you
> Deny, defy or crucify you
> All I really want to do
> Is, baby, be friends with you

Sometimes the question to ask in life is *Is this true?* Sometimes (again) it should be *What truth is there in this?* Irony, which disagrees with its single-minded brother sarcasm, enjoys the flesh-brush friction that comes of there being an element of truth in what the other person is maintaining, even when what is said is self-serving and is not simply to be credited. (When it is simply to be discredited, the effect is usually cheap.) The vivacity of the song, which is on the side of life, comes from its meaning what it says, or at any rate kinda meaning it, meaning it in its way. Desire likes the thought of liking those whom it desires. Love and friendship love to curl up. Strictly speaking (but do you really want to speak strictly?), it is not true that *All* I really want to do is, baby, be friends with you. But nor is score the *only* thing I really want to do. Far more than the protest song, it is the protestation song that Dylan has always loved. And there is always not only play, but a play within the play, something dramatized. "The lady doth protest too much, methinks." The gentleman, on this occasion, not so?

> And I ain't lookin' for you to feel like me
> See like me, or be like me

True, and standing there as the very last thing said in the song before its final assurance,

> All I really want to do
> Is, baby, be friends with you

"Feel like me / See like me, or be like me"? No. To *like* me, now that is certainly hoped for, but not those three hopes, "Feel like me / See like me, or be like me", for the song does not identify with the self-absorption that postulates something called "identifying with". That is not how the song is voiced on *Another Side of Bob Dylan*, what with the vocal ogling and the yodelled "do". There is a counterpointing of the torrential rhyming against the evenness of rhythm and of delivery, the voice throughout self-possessing a sheer comic persistence (I shall no more weary of assuring you than I shall of you, I assure you), heard in his tender laugh at "Frighten you or uptighten you". Living seems a laugh, and so does loving, especially at – of all places – "uptighten you". Only someone uptight would object to the slangy creation "uptight". (From 1934, "in a state of nervous tension or anxiety"; from 1969, "strait-laced", *The Oxford English Dictionary*.) But you will look in vain in the dictionary for a verb, to uptighten. This is a turn of the screw, and apparently one that Dylan turned to along the way, for the printed lyrics have "or tighten you". Relax. You have my word.

Sometimes the comedy takes a melodramatic turn:

> I don't want to meet your kin
> Make you spin or do you in

– with "do you in' then giving to what could be an abstract word, "dissect", a cutting edge:

> Make you spin or do you in
> Or select you or dissect you

The song constitutes an extraordinary list of all the ways in which you can mistreat somebody: are there *any* that don't figure somewhere in it? And yet how benign the whole exhibition is.

> I ain't lookin' to block you up
> Shock or knock or lock you up
> Analyze you, categorize you

Finalize you, or advertise you
All I really want to do
Is, baby, be friends with you

There "Finalize" gets its pouncing power from a sense of how finality fleets away, like an advertisement ("Finalize you, or advertise you") – from its being such a shrug of a word. And one might, in making a passing, notice Dylan's dexterity with "knock you up":

I ain't lookin' to block you up
Shock or knock or lock you up

The cunning propriety tactfully, pregnantly, separates "knock" from "you up" for a couple of words; after all, the preceding "shock" would more suggest "shock you" than "shock you *up*" – though one of the things that Dylan is doing is giving a shake to the phrase "shake you up".[1]

New Pony shook people up in the 1970s. No way to treat a lady.

Come over here pony, I, I wanna climb up one time on you
Come over here pony, I, I wanna climb up one time on you
Well, you're so bad and nasty
But I love you, yes I do

Oats, wild and there for the having, and animal spirits: these often animated the young Dylan, or (more precisely) his songs. (His life is *his* business; his art is something else, not being business but a vocation, even while – like Shakespeare's – it earns his living.) Fun and games, much of this. Not all of it, for there are occasions when the devil and sin have their insinuations.

Satan whispers to ya, "Well, I don't want to bore ya
But when ya get tired of the Miss So-and-so I got another woman for ya"

That is *Trouble in Mind* and in body, but only a prig or prurient prude would hiss "the sin of lust" when hearing the knowing words

[1] I draw on an essay of mine on *American English and the inherently transitory* (*The Force of Poetry*, 1984).

> I know of a woman
> That can fix you up fast
> (*Bob Dylan's New Orleans Rag*)

– or when hearing of a triste tryst with a good time who has been had by all:

> Well, I took me a woman late last night,
> I's three-fourths drunk, she looked alright
> Till she started peelin' off her onion gook
> An' took off her wig, said, "How do I look?"
> I was high-flyin' . . . bare-naked . . .
> Out the window!
> (*I Shall Be Free*)[1]

A Beautiful Young Nymph Going to Bed: Jonathan Swift's poem, "Written for the Honour of the Fair Sex", reveals how Corinna, back at midnight from the streets, "Takes off her artificial hair" and her eyebrows, takes out her falsies and her false teeth . . . A strip-tease? Jeeze. *She* can't find her knees. Don't even think of what she will look – and worse than look – like in the morning. "Who sees, will spew; who smells, be poisoned". After Swift's savage sewerage, *I Shall Be Free* smells pretty sweet-natured. And that is because, unlike in Swift, there is a man in the song who shall not be free from bodily ridicule: hot-footed perhaps, bare-naked for sure (a compound epithet that, far from being stripped, is tautological . . .). She took off her this, and her that, and her other. And me? "I took me a woman". And then I took off. ("Out the window!") "She looked alright"? Serves him right.

The real right thing, after the while, is (*of course*) not lust but desire. No question. Blake posed the question, and poised it with perfect justice.

THE QUESTION ANSWERED

> What is it men in women do require?
> The lineaments of gratified desire.
> What is it women do in men require?
> The lineaments of gratified desire.

[1] As sung; as printed in *Lyrics 1962–1985* (1985), "She took off her wheel, took off her bell, / Took off her wig, said, 'How do I smell?' / I hot-footed it . . ."

I Want You gives voice to a yearning for this reciprocated requirement, this double desirement. Poignant and pained (all the more pained because there is such a prospect of pleasure if only she will want him back), the voice repeats – with patience and with passion – "I want you", four times in each of four verses, the third time in each verse succeeding the three words with the plea "so bad", and the last time preceding them with the pleasing "Honey".

In the world of *Handy Dandy* the easy woman can assure him: "She says, 'You got all the time in the world, honey'". But not here. There is an aching wait just after we pass the last "because", for all the world as if there soon will not be all the time in the world.

> And because I   want you[1]

And in any case time is on someone else's side.

For there is a rival, and he sounds too cutely and flutily pleased with his own suitability, and the rhymes get cutting:

> Now your dancing child with his Chinese suit
> He spoke to me, I took his flute
> No, I wasn't very cute to him
> Was I?

In due course, "Was I?" will be clinched as a rhyme, a rhyme with a cause ("Because I") and with a pause:

> But I did it because he lied
> Because he took you for a ride
> And because time was on his side
> And because I . . .
> Want you, I want you
> I want you so bad
> Honey, I want you

The heartfelt inconsequentiality of this love song (what a game, Truths and Inconsequences) has always made it especially teasing and pleasing. There is a magnanimity evoked in the person of the other woman, the less loved one –

[1] *Lyrics 1962–1985* prints an ellipsis. Dylan doesn't sing dot dot dot, he sings a void.

> She knows where I'd like to be
> But it doesn't matter

– and magnanimity is in the body of the song, too, when it turns back from the competitive to the appetitive. "I want you". And I feel the want of you. But a tricky preposition, "of". If only I could feel the want of you as a wanting that emanates from you. Not that I'd order you around, even if love could be ordered. There are no imperatives in the song. Many declaratives, and one reiterated declaration, a declaration of love. And of desire.

I Want You opens with the rhyme of "sighs" and "cries". It closes with a sigh and a cry still, with "I" audible on its way to "you": *Was I → Because I → lied → ride → side → I want you.*

> The guilty undertaker sighs
> The lonesome organ grinder cries

Touching, and the more so for the hint of touching oneself. "I want you so bad". Blake again:

> The moment of desire! the moment of desire! The virgin
> That pines for man shall awaken her womb to enormous joys
> In the secret shadows of her chamber; the youth shut up from
> The lustful joy shall forget to generate and create an amorous image
> In the shadows of his curtains and in the folds of his silent pillow.
>
> (*Visions of the Daughters of Albion*)

To Blake might be added Ecclesiastes, chapter 12, on the time "when desire shall fail".

Ecclesiastes	*Dylan*
and the grinders cease	organ grinder
the silver cord	The silver saxophone
in the streets	Upon the street
the golden bowl be broken, or the pitcher be broken	my broken cup
all the daughters of music shall be brought low	all their daughters put me down

"True love they've been without it": not only fathers but sons and daughters. But it is not necessarily too late, which means that it is necessarily not too late.

Lay, Lady, Lay

> The cracked bells and washed-out horns
> Blow into my face with scorn
> > (*I Want You*)

Scorn and discomfiture and discomfort have their burlesque part to play. But, in some other room, so do corporeal confidence and the peace of mind that it alone can bring. Such is *Lay, Lady, Lay*, a comedy of command and demand.

LAY, LADY, LAY

> Lay, lady, lay, lay across my big brass bed
> Lay, lady, lay, lay across my big brass bed
> Whatever colors you have in your mind
> I'll show them to you and you'll see them shine
>
> Lay, lady, lay, lay across my big brass bed
> Stay, lady, stay, stay with your man awhile
> Until the break of day, let me see you make him smile
> His clothes are dirty but his hands are clean
> And you're the best thing that he's ever seen
>
> Stay, lady, stay, stay with your man awhile
> Why wait any longer for the world to begin
> You can have your cake and eat it too
> Why wait any longer for the one you love
> When he's standing in front of you
>
> Lay, lady, lay, lay across my big brass bed
> Stay, lady, stay, stay while the night is still ahead
> I long to see you in the morning light
> I long to reach for you in the night
> Stay, lady, stay, stay while the night is still ahead

How much longer? The old question in many a Dylan song is how long you can go on urging.[1] *Don't Think Twice, It's All Right*. Here it's how long you can go on asking somebody to lay across your big brass bed. Or, *Anglicè*, lie across it. Everyday American English, with its established divergences from the old-country matters, is what enforces this way of putting it to her. Still, *lay* across my bed? Yet if you were to say, with Queen's English correctitude, "Lie, lady, lie", this would open up an ungentlemanly possibility: "Lie, lady, lie – you usually do on these occasions". And so on. Men accusing of mendacity the fair sex. It is true that the American usage might permit of its own ludicrous train of thought ("Lady, lady, lay the table – or, if you prefer, an egg"), but at least there wouldn't be the casting of aspersions. Remember another opening of Dylan's, the first words of *Fourth Time Around*, positively fourth:

> When she said
> "Don't waste your words, they're just lies"
> I cried she was deaf

She was deaf, or – in the case of *Lay, Lady, Lay* – will she be deaf to his importunate cries? There's a certain point at which she either does lie across your big brass bed or she does not. You would sound fatuous if into the small hours you continued to urge "Lay, lady, lay". The repetition is there, very strongly, from the beginning, but there's a real question about how, with dignity, you extricate yourself once you've issued this injunction. So rhyming (which can be a way of effecting release or relief) becomes a distinctive part of the story. Added to which, rhyming is sure to be crucial to any song that begins with words such as "Lay, lady, lay . . .", where "lady" feels like or feels for a relaxedly languorous and open and welcoming expansion of "lay". Expansion and contraction constitute the movement of the phrase "Lay, lady, lay" and of the song that bears those words as its title. Less common than you might think, in Dylan, to have the words of the title be absolutely identical with the opening words of the song. A perfect congruity is intimated, as it is in one of the other instances, *If Not For You*, which begins, yes, with the words "If not for you".

The expansion and contraction are simply evoked in the relation of two words: "long" and "longer". Ah, but the first is a verb, not an adjective. Exactly.

---

[1] See p. 439.

> I long to see you in the morning light
> I long to reach for you in the night

– where there are not only the parallel syntax and the rhyme but the internal assonance (*see / reach*), with "I long to see you" reaching across to "I long to reach for you".[1] The couplet is for a couple and a coupling, and it reaches back (we should see and hear) to two earlier parallel lines:

> Why wait any longer for the world to begin

> Why wait any longer for the one you love

It is as though "longer" were a longer form of the word "long", and so it is, but not of this yearning meaning of the word. The feeling of longing is evoked, of longing and waiting. But how much longer?

That phrase might float in from a burlier song, *New Pony*, where the women's voices interject "How much longer?" – how much longer would your new pony satisfy you before she, too, needed shooting? The blunter-spoken world of *New Pony* might accommodate the embittered dismay of the ageing man (imagined by the man Hilary Corke) who looks at himself physically and emotionally: "My lust grows longer and my lunger shorter".[2] The line is a lunge, with the word "lunger" inviting the thought that, gee, that's a soft *g* that you have there. But in *Lay, Lady, Lay* the continuing question is: How much longer can you continue to invite or solicit or plead?

Dylan has spoken of how *Lay, Lady, Lay* came, came to him:

The song came out of those first four chords. I filled it up with the lyrics then, the la la la type thing, well that turned into Lay Lady Lay, it's the same thing with the tongue, that's all it was really.

"The la la la type thing" is a nice way of putting it because so indifferent to the niceties; the phrase has the casualness of just a way of getting amiably or amatorily started on a song. But the bit about its being "the same

---

[1] As performed on *Before the Flood* (1974), the song ends: "I long to reach out for you in the dead of the night / Stay, lady, stay, stay while the night is still ahead". This chooses the different pattern of chiasmus, *abba: dead . . . night . . . night . . . ahead.*

[2] *A Man's Song*, which begins "In deeper fat the sense of sin retires"; *New Poems 1963*, ed. Lawrence Durrell (1963).

thing with the tongue" might remind us that the occasion for the song is immediately erotic. Erotolalia: sexual excitement that is intimate with the linguistic tongue's taking things into its head: "*lalia*: terminal element representing Greek [λαλιά] speech, chatter, used in forming words denoting various disorders or unusual faculties of speech".[1] Try erotolayladylaylia. The chatter might be just the thing for a chatter-up of someone. There's a song on *New Morning* in which Dylan has a blithe delight in making a prompt start, not in words but through la la la: *The Man in Me* opens with la la la accompanying a whole verse of the tune, more than forty of them, before he gets over his sheer exuberance and into the words "The man in me", and the song ends with the return of this glee that finds and expresses its pleasure in the mouth but not in words exactly.

And what an innocent childlike pleasure alliteration may be, with "Lay, lady, lay" only too happy to move across to "big brass bed". Among the games that the song plays, there is a number game: playing twos (two couplets as the first verse) against threes (*lay lay lay / stay stay stay*, plus *big brass bed*) against an opening alliterative foursome: *lay lady lay lay*. It is with the phrase "until the break of day" that something new breaks through, in that the internal rhyme is continued into this third line of the second verse:

> Lay, lady, lay, lay across my big brass bed
> Stay, lady, stay, stay with your man awhile
> Until the break of day, let me see you make him smile

With "day", something should dawn upon us.

"Lay, lady, lay, lay across my big brass bed": he sings the word "bed" king-sizedly. It's not a monosyllable when he sings it, something happens to it by which it becomes extraordinarily wide. Yet it isn't quite a disyllable. What he does with it is like the way Tennyson says you should register the word "tired" in *The Lotos-Eaters*: "making the word neither monosyllabic nor disyllabic, but a dreamy child of the two".[2] (Or a child of the two that are the one and the two.) You are to hear in your mind's ear something that isn't as monosyllabic as, say, *tied*, and isn't as disyllabic as "tie-erd", but is just hovering, vacillating, between the contracted and the expanded. That's

---

[1] The *OED* includes this suffix and various words such as "glossolalia", but it neglects erotolalia, though sexologists have murmured the word.

[2] See p. 122, on *All the Tired Horses*.

how the song makes its word "bed", one that it likes the luxurious thought of lying across.

Jonathan Swift had let his unhappy imagination play over *A Beautiful Young Nymph Going to Bed*. More than a century earlier, John Donne had let his happy imagination play over his hope, *To His Mistress Going to Bed*. She is to disrobe for him: "Off with" this, and off with that. And so to "This love's hallowed temple, this soft bed". The poem's opening lines are instinct with the powers that alliteration and rhyme can call upon, in touch with the same thing with the tongue:

> Come, Madam, come, all rest my powers defy,
> Until I labour, I in labour lie.

Come, Madam, come: or Lay, lady, lay. Donne's second line is alive not only with the insinuating word "lie" (chiming with "I", twice) but with the rotation of this sound ("lie" into "labour"): "labour . . . labour". Donne's poem might be a source but what matters is that it is an analogue. Great minds feel and think alike.

Donne	*Dylan*
laymen	lay, lady
bed	bed
show	show
seen	see
one man	your man
unclothed	clothes
my . . . hands	his hands
world	world
standing	standing
still	still
lighteth	light

Alliteration and rhyme are ways of having one thing lead to another. An opening injunction or plea, in both Donne and Dylan, makes play with all these devices of the tongue, so that there is a real likeness between the age-old urging and the long-standing urgencies of the body. Love, not lust, but physically candid. Give him an inch, and he'll take an ell. There is many an ell in the Dylan lines, as in the Donne lines. And when Wallace Stevens in *The Plot Against the Giant* imagined what would really capture "this yokel", he gave the climactic temptation to the "Heavenly labials" of the Third Girl. The First Girl was planning "the civilest odors", and the Second Girl was planning "cloths besprinkled with colors" –

> Whatever colors you have in your mind
> I'll show them to you and you'll see them shine
> (*Lay, Lady, Lay*)

– but it is the Third Girl on whom we should put our money:

> Oh, la . . . le pauvre!
> I shall run before him,
> With a curious puffing.
> He will bend his ear then.
> I shall whisper
> Heavenly labials in a world of gutturals.
> It will undo him.

La . . . le -ly labials: Dylan, who knows how to bend people's ears, knows all about heavenly labials. Good on gutturals, too:

> He got a sweet gift of gab, he got harmonious tongue
> He knows every song of love that ever has been sung
> Good intentions can be evil
> Both hands can be full of grease
> (*Man of Peace*)

Lay, Lady, Lay is itself a lay, "a short lyric or narrative poem intended to be sung" (a Lay of our First Minstrel), even apart from all the other puns that stretch themselves provocatively. "Lay, lady, lay": at once, and at once an imperative. No pretence at a question, nothing along the lines of *Do you come here often?* or *Where did you get those cute beads?* or *Didn't we meet at a Ralph Nader rally?* No messing.

There are twenty-four imperatives in the song, but they amount to there being one imperative. And the power of the song as sung is a matter of its not being imperious in its imperatives. When Donne begins his poem with "Come, Madam, come", we enjoy the privilege of deciding for ourselves just what tone those words are uttered in: wheedling? pleading? urging? enjoining? dictating? But *Lay, Lady, Lay* is a song, and one that is sung by its creator with his sense not only of its sense but of the senses. And from the very first chords and words, it is clear that the woman addressed is not being dressed down. She is being invited. Invited to swoon, as the music with its voice swoons and croons or even cwoons.

It is this patience that is the calmly reassuring air of the song. No hurry. No flurry. No need to scurry. True, he has an end in view. But then, as John Donne put it in the very first words of another of his Elegies,

> Whoever loves, if he do not propose
> The right true end of love, he's one that goes
> To sea for nothing but to make him sick.
>
> (*Love's Progress*)

Choppy, the waters there, unlike the leisurely sway of *Lay, Lady, Lay* (which has more the feeling of a hammock than of a brass bed).

There are other ways in which the song does not allow impatience to raise its butting head.[1] For instance, the promise that is made is not the self-assertive one that would say that if we make love, you will find out what is within me. Or, come to that, that I shall find out what is within you. Rather, I shall show you what is yours already (in the unspoken hope that you will be doing the same for me):

> Whatever colors you have in your mind
> I'll show them to you and you'll see them shine

It is by courtesy of others that we get to see – are shown – what is in our minds. What on earth is in your mind? Colours that we are shown by our bodies, with the help of another's body.

These interanimations are intimate with the song's play with pronouns,

---

[1]   He'll say, "Oh darling, tell me the truth, how much time I got?"
        She'll say, "You got all the time in the world, honey"
        (*Handy Dandy*)

pronouns that have the singer – in a spirit altogether different from the relationship in *Positively 4th Street* – stand outside his shoes.

> Lay, lady, lay, lay across my big brass bed
> Stay, lady, stay, stay with your man awhile
> Until the break of day, let me see you make him smile
> His clothes are dirty but his hands are clean
> And you're the best thing that he's ever seen

My bed, but *your man* – who is me, you know. You can rest assured on my big brass bed. Then, as the hinge, there is the comedy that has him be both first person and third person in the run of a few words: "let me see you make him smile". Split personality, but splitting into a grin. And then there is the confident standing back from himself, to see ourselves as others see us (or as we ask that they should, or hope that they may). "His clothes are dirty but his hands are clean". Casting himself in the third person is a way of making sure that the person addressed, the second-person *you*, gets to feel unquestionably the first person in the eyes of the pleading lover:

> His clothes are dirty but his hands are clean
> And you're the best thing that he's ever seen

His hands are clean because he is innocent, free of sin: no lust, for all the honest desire, and no guile.[1] And this is the moment when Dylan in singing does not abide exactly by the words as printed, for he sings, not "His clothes are dirty but his hands are clean", but "His clothes are dirty but his – his hands are clean". It is a lovely catch in the line, though there is no catch to it.

One central effect in the song's rhyming is that there are – and you are likely to have registered this whether consciously or not – two lines that *don't* rhyme. This matters very much in a love song, particularly since one of these two lines ends in "love". Dylan pairs the unrhymed lines structurally, syntactically, changing only their final three words, so that you will pick up on them:

---

[1] As sung on *Hard Rain*, the song lets things rip, an invitation to what Dylan in *Tarantula* (1966, 1971, p. 53) dubs "humanity in the gang bang mood". So there need to be some new words in the new swing of things: "Forget this dance, let's go upstairs", rhyming with "Who really cares?"

Why wait any longer for the world to begin

Why wait any longer for the one you love

The paired lines don't rhyme, but the first one has some relation, in the sound of "begin", to the rhyme *clean / seen* in the previous verse, particularly given how Dylan sounds those words. Nevertheless there isn't a word that completes or ends the rhyme begun with the word "begin' – that is, "begin" doesn't fully rhyme with anything and doesn't lead to, lead into, anything. And nor does "love". The song intimates – urges – that the rhyme upon "love" would not be any word or any sound: it would be an action. That is, the act of love, if she will lie across his big brass bed. (A plea, without a *please*.) That would be the answer to the question "Why wait any longer for the one you love", which isn't really a question after all (Dylan doesn't sing it or print it with a question-mark), but an invitation. "Love" doesn't rhyme there. Yet it is comical and affectionate, and perfectly happy, because it trusts that the rhyme will be consummated by behaviour – by trust and love and acquiescence. With time to acquiesce, since the song is patient; no need for the *ahquickyes* of James Joyce.

Meanwhile "the one you love" comes to more than "the man you love", since "the one" keeps the love singular, and doubly singular: "the", not "a", and "one" as not just a formal or objective way of speaking but as one and only. For Donne, the mistress going to bed is "My kingdom, safeliest when with one man manned".

Just how warm Dylan's song is can be brought out by comparing it with a poem by Thomas Hardy that leaves the word "love" unrhymed, a deeply chilling poem. Likewise leaves it unrhymed, but how unlike.

SHUT OUT THAT MOON

Close up the casement, draw the blind,
    Shut out that stealing moon,
She wears too much the guise she wore
    Before our lutes were strewn
With years-deep dust, and names we read
    On a white stone were hewn.

Step not out on the dew-dashed lawn
    To view the Lady's Chair,

Immense Orion's glittering form,
   The Less and Greater Bear:
Stay in; to such sights we were drawn
   When faded ones were fair.

Brush not the bough for midnight scents
   That come forth lingeringly,
And wake the same sweet sentiments
   They breathed to you and me
When living seemed a laugh, and love
   All it was said to be.

Within the common lamp-lit room
   Prison my eyes and thought;
Let dingy details crudely loom,
   Mechanic speech be wrought:
Too fragrant was Life's early bloom,
   Too tart the fruit it brought!

Hardy in the first stanza rhymes only the even lines: *moon / strewn / hewn*.[1] In the second stanza, he rhymes all the lines, alternately (with assonance at one point instead of rhyme, *lawn / form / drawn*). In the final stanza, he rhymes all the lines, perfectly: *room / loom / bloom*, and *thought / wrought / brought*. But in the penultimate stanza he has hauntingly violated this progression: the even lines rhyme perfectly: *lingeringly / me / be*, but the odd lines have an oddity: *scents / sentiments / love*. Love unrhymed, never to be fully rhymed (ah . . .), all the more poignantly because within the line there is that other feature of language that so often cooperates with rhyme, alliteration: "When living

---

[1] There is a question as to the pronunciation of one line's end-word (not that this would affect the rhyming). Is "read" present tense [*reed*]: that we now read? Or is it past tense [*red*]: that we used to read? The former, I take it (reading the inscription on the commemoration stone); but one thing that the word on the page can do is leave us insecure. (Are these things present or past? That is a question on which Hardy often declines to rule.) Geoffrey Hill begins a poem: "Rilke could ['riːd] Bible in bad light / or shaky script. Most of what I claim / can be so ['rɛd]" (*Scenes from Comus*, 2002, section III, 16). But in a song the voicing may leave us in no doubt (which can be a differently good thing). Dylan: "It's been nice seeing you, you read me like a book" – past tense [*red*], no longer the case (you flatter yourself). *Under Your Spell* has this serious joke about spelling.

seemed a laugh, and love / All it was said to be". (Dylan, likewise, on the sounds of *w* and *l*: "Why wait any longer for the one you love / When . . ."[1]) Just listen to, and feel acidly, acerbically, on your tongue the terrible taste of the terminations in Hardy's final stanza, the dental dismay in those *t*'s, always terminating the lines, their rhymes, but appearing not only there:

> Within the common lamp-lit room
> Prison my eyes and thought;
> Let dingy details crudely loom,
> Mechanic speech be wrought:
> Too fragrant was Life's early bloom,
> Too tart the fruit it brought!

The sharpness of the Hardy poem makes it very unlike a few songs by Dylan that might otherwise be its kin.

> Close up the casement, draw the blind,
> Shut out that stealing moon,

– "Shut the light, shut the shade . . ." But then *I'll Be Your Baby Tonight* moves on to a less bitter injunction, "Bring that bottle over here". Yet Hardy's title, *Shut Out That Moon*, might open into Dylan's way with titles. Hardy's title derives not from the opening or shutting line of his poem, but from that second line: "Shut out that stealing moon". But *Shut Out That Moon*: the word "stealing" has been stolen. Hardy is a hard man. Dylan's title is harsher than the song that is *Baby, Stop Crying*: those words never exactly come in the song, where it is always "Baby, please stop crying". The discrepancy is pleasingly teasing. What happened to the magic word?

Love is a gamble, and so is inviting someone to make love. This sense of a responsible risk is playfully there in the phrase "while the night is still ahead". This endearingly turns the tables on the phrase. Quit while you are still ahead? No, stay, you can go on winning, the night – our night of love – is still ahead.[2]

William Empson memorably insisted that "the pleasure in style is continually to be explained by just such a releasing and knotted duality, where

---

[1] Weird, on the face of it, that "one" alliterates with "why", but what do you know.
[2] "I'm stayin' ahead of the game", Dylan sings in *Waitin' for You* (released on the soundtrack of *Divine Secrets of the Ya-Ya Sisterhood*, 2002), where the opening verse includes the rhymes *way / say / day* and *head / spread / dead*. (*Lay, lady, lay* and *bed / ahead*.)

those who have been wedded in the argument are bedded together in the phrase".[1] But "wedded", they wouldn't have to be. The phrase and the argument might be living in sin. Which would not have to mean falling into the sin of lust.

On a Night Like This

In *The Merchant of Venice* the young lovers thrill one another (and themselves) by bandying, in loving rivalry of to and fro, a little run of words that they love: "In such a night as this". These words are always the completion of a line and of a cadence. Or more than a completion, a consummation, and yet one that does not cease there but immediately opens into further worlds of love and lovers, worlds to which these young lovers, Lorenzo and Jessica, lay claim with all the innocently insolent rights that young love takes to itself. The opening of the scene (V, i) immediately intimates that "In such a night as this" is set to be the conclusive charm, first by at once proffering a line in two reciprocal parts, and next by having these two embrace one another in an internal rhyme: *bright / night.* He:

> The moon shines bright. In such a night as this,
> When the sweet wind did gently kiss the trees,
> And they did make no noise, in such a night
> Troilus methinks mounted the Trojan walls,
> And sighed his soul toward the Grecian tents
> Where Cressid lay that night.

And she at once picks up his triple "night", completing his half-line, "Where Cressid lay that night", with the fondled word, rhyming with itself and yet happily. (Throughout the exchanges, all the classical lovers who are invoked are famous for being unhappy, and how warmly happy this makes our young couple feel, and so secure.) She:

> In such a night
> Did Thisbe fearfully o'ertrip the dew,
> And saw the lion's shadow ere himself,
> And ran dismayed away.

[1] *Seven Types of Ambiguity* (1930, second edition 1947), p. 132.

Whereupon he (trumping pathos with tragedy):

> In such a night
> Stood Dido with a willow in her hand
> Upon the wild sea-banks, and waft her love
> To come again to Carthage.

And she, not to be outdone (a perfectly natural inclination that will have recourse to the supernatural):

> In such a night
> Medea gathered the enchanted herbs
> That did renew old Æson.

Not romancy,[1] necromancy! Young Lorenzo had better remember that one day he may be as old as Æson. He (thinking to win the game by having the night be this very night, and by speaking not only to her but of her, stealing a pun on her):

> In such a night
> Did Jessica steal from the wealthy Jew,
> And with an unthrift love did run from Venice,
> As far as Belmont.

But she has no intention of being beguiled by his sly self-deprecation – "an unthrift love", indeed. She (if stealing is what is at issue . . .):

> In such a night
> Did young Lorenzo swear he loved her well,
> Stealing her soul with many vows of faith,
> And ne'er a true one.

Her soul, not her body, he is mock-sternly reminded. At which point his dignity requires that he retort with mock-indignation. Time to tame his shrew. He:

---

[1] There is such a word ("Associated with, or redolent of, romance"), and it likes nights as well as knights: "Where others' lamps have burnt long Attick nights, / With rank romancie oil to grease their knights" (*OED*).

> In such a night
> Did pretty Jessica (like a little shrew)
> Slander her love, and he forgave it her.

The condescension of the man! Forgive her, forsooth. She is all set for another round of wrestling ("I would out-night you"), but the game has to be called off, and neither they nor we will ever know who would have won. Not (and this is the sweet thought) that it matters in the slightest, for no one has been slighted. She:

> I would out-night you, did nobody come:
> But hark, I hear the footing of a man.

There is no reason to think that Dylan set himself to out-night "In such a night", and probably, for all its currency, it wasn't in his mind. Yet there are overlaps beyond the refrain: "kiss" taking up "this", "wind" / "winds", "run", "away", "old", "far", "pretty", "like", plus the relation of "hand" to "fingers", and of "hark" to "listen". The opening in Shakespeare, "The moon shines *bright*. In such a *night* as this", has an affinity with Dylan's prompt move from "On a *night* like this" to "Hold on to me so *tight*". Anyway, whether source or analogue, to have the one love scene keep the other company may cast some light (or is it moonshine?) on why *On a Night Like This* sure feels right.

ON A NIGHT LIKE THIS

> On a night like this
> So glad you came around
> Hold on to me so tight
> And heat up some coffee grounds
> We got much to talk about
> And much to reminisce
> It sure is right
> On a night like this
>
> On a night like this
> So glad you're here to stay
> Hold on to me, pretty miss
> Say you'll never go away to stray

Run your fingers down my spine
And bring me a touch of bliss
It sure feels right
On a night like this

On a night like this
I can't get any sleep
The air is so cold outside
And the snow's so deep
Build a fire, throw on logs
And listen to it hiss
And let it burn, burn, burn, burn
On a night like this

Put your body next to mine
And keep me company
There is plenty a room for all
So please don't elbow me

Let the four winds blow
Around this old cabin door
If I'm not too far off
I think we did this once before
There's more frost on the window glass
With each new tender kiss
But it sure feels right
On a night like this

The song is not at all cryptic, which makes Dylan's comment on it doubly so: "I think this comes off as sort of like a drunk man who's temporarily sober. This is not my type of song. I think I just did it to do it" (*Biograph*). Assuredly tentative, this, with "I think" and "I think" and "as sort of like".

> If I'm not too far off
> I think we did this once before

But maybe I am too far off. Anyway (since I just did it to do it) I think I'll not do this again. Not my type? Not my type of song.

Is he questioning the song, to take part in some kind of quiz? He clearly catches the heady unclear mixture of inebriation and sobriety that is in the vinous air of *On a Night Like This*, as well as what this does to one's sense of time ("temporarily"?). What we wait for all through the song is the rhyme for which the opening line yearns, "On a night like this", this line that both opens and closes the first three verses, though not the last verse, which, throwing open a window, throws the refrain-line to the winds (instead: "Let the four winds blow"). "On a night like this" can't wait – except that it can, since it just has to – for the word "kiss", the rhyme that is then enfolded within all the playful foreplay ("Run your fingers down my spine/And bring me a touch of bliss": a nice touch, that) rising to the last verse:

> Let the four winds blow
> Around this old cabin door
> If I'm not too far off
> I think we did this once before
> There's more frost on the window glass
> With each new tender kiss
> But it sure feels right
> On a night like this

At the start it looked likely that the rhyming would establish the title-refrain within a particular setting. "On a night like this" opens and closes the first verse, where it rhymes with the sixth line, "And much to reminisce". (Entirely at ease, this use of "reminisce", not as an intransitive verb – which is how it operates these days – but as transitive, as in the old days that we now reminisce, or reminisce about.) The rhyme-pattern, though, then comes to enjoy its freedom, especially when it comes to expanding and contracting. The triple rhyme of the first verse, *this / reminisce / this*, is followed by an expansion as though to the four winds: *this / miss / bliss / this*, a pretty stroke that is the consequence of the newly arrived further rhyme, "Hold on to me, pretty miss". The third verse reverts to the triple rhyme (*this / hiss / this*), only to be followed again by a change, though this time in the opposite direction: not an expansion but a contraction in the last verse, twofold only, *kiss / this*. Finis. A contraction, were it not that "kiss" is a consummation devoutly to be wished, and the more so as one fertile figure of speech for a rhyme is a kiss.[1] Furthermore, like expansion, contraction is of

---

[1] See p. 430. The scene from *The Merchant of Venice* makes its opening move: "The moon shines bright. In such a night as *this*, / When the sweet wind did gently *kiss* the trees".

the nature of love and of this song. Take, for instance, the penultimate line of the refrain. In the first verse, "It sure is right". In the second verse, "It sure feels right", which both expands (feeling right is a larger truth than being right, right?) and contracts (come on, being right is a larger truth than feeling right – am I right or am I right?). The song stands by the claim for feelings, and then has – in the final verse – one word to add: "But it sure feels right". Intriguing, this final "But", in the lover's train of thought or rather of feeling:

> There's more frost on the window glass
> With each new tender kiss
> But it sure feels right
> On a night like this

"But", not "So" it sure feels right? Anyway, we are yielding to our passions all right, but that feels right. Just this once? "I think we did this once before": a jovial insult (can you really not remember *that*, reminisce *that*?) that reminds me of how Shakespeare's lovers ribbed one another. Lorenzo and Jessica not only have much to talk about, they talk to one another. The song, though, is the sound of one man clapping ("So glad you came around", in both senses of *came around*), and it needed to do what it very well does: that is, build in a good many recognitions of the person spoken to, the person he's grateful to, the person who will not take amiss the jaunty joshing. The warmth within the room is thanks to all the logs but also thanks to our heat in love – yet nothing steamy or misty. (There is pure heat playing against the crisp clarity of the frost on the panes.) And why is there no "It sure feels right" in the third verse? Because what takes its place is such a solid core of heat, such delight as stands in need of no validation or certification:

> On a night like this
> I can't get any sleep
> The air is so cold outside
> And the snow's so deep
> Build a fire, throw on logs
> And listen to it hiss
> And let it burn, burn, burn, burn
> On a night like this

"I can't get any sleep": we quite understand, and yet the claim is up to the same tricks as the one in *If You Gotta Go, Go Now*, opposite direction though it might seem to suggest:

> It's just that I'll be sleepin' soon
> An' it'll be too dark for you to find the door

But then one of the qualities that may distinguish desire from lust is that lust has no time for humour, whereas *On a Night Like This* likes fooling around, whether it be "heat up some coffee *grounds*", or

> There is plenty a room for *all*
> So please don't elbow me

"Don't crowd me, lady" (*Please, Mrs. Henry*), but don't misunderstand me, pretty miss:

> Put your body next to mine
> And keep me company
> There is plenty a room for all
> So please don't elbow me

Good company, he is, well worth keeping. And the humour is the vivacious evidence that there is someone else in the room, someone who is complimented by the spirited jokes and complemented by the trustworthy body.

Anger

Only a Pawn in Their Game

It need not take much courage to take a life. "A bullet from the back of a bush took Medgar Evers' blood". That the killer was a skulker is enough to make your blood boil.

Medgar Evers (1925–63) was Mississippi's first African-American field secretary of the National Association for the Advancement of Colored People (NAACP). He was an active organizer of voter-registration drives until he was murdered by a sniper.[1]

But the word "sniper", with its possibility of solitary courage in military combat,[2] is in danger of flattering the lurker. Evers' killer was no soldier. A pawn is a foot-soldier (this is what the word means), but a foot-soldier might find himself called upon to show courage in open warfare.

It took courage in Dylan, back in the summer of 1963 only a month after the murder of Medgar Evers, to say of the white killer – to sing of the white killer, there in front of a Mississippi audience that was mostly black – "But he can't be blamed". Dylan understood the anger that he might invite by not sounding angry enough. He was aware of how he might himself be blamed for not blaming. A society is indicted, and with an anger that is all the more forcefully contained, because the killer, "he can't be blamed". And then this is averred again, in the second, third, and fourth verses; in these, the wording changes to something that is in its way uneducated and so might be heard as sympathizing with the poor white (not condescending, because elsewhere in quite different Dylan songs there are similar moments when the demotic meets the democratic): "But it ain't him to blame". It is

---

[1] *The American Spectrum Encyclopedia* (1991).
[2] The original military application ("a sharp-shooter", *OED*) dates from 1824. "Several sepoys were killed and wounded by the enemy's snipers." 1897: "It is impossible to see the snipers, who generally stalk the sentries from behind stones." 1900: "The artillery keep the Boer snipers down."

not until the final verse that there is no longer any talk of blaming or of not blaming. But then at this conclusive stage the scene is set in the imagined future, with the killer himself duly in his grave, and with the words that have constituted the climax of every verse becoming – in the final end – not only his epitome but his epitaph:

> His epitaph plain:
> Only a pawn in their game

A pawn is pressed to believe that the game is his, too, not just their game, and in a way he is right since it isn't for him to pretend that a pawn is no piece of the action. But it may be for someone else – in the spirit of Robert Lowell's cry "Pity the monsters!"[1] – to grant him the chilling charity "But it ain't him to blame". He being a dupe an' all.

> A bullet from the back of a bush took Medgar Evers' blood
> A finger fired the trigger to his name
> A handle hid out in the dark
> A hand set the spark
> Two eyes took the aim
> Behind a man's brain
> But he can't be blamed
> He's only a pawn in their game

"A bullet from the back of a bush took Medgar Evers' blood". The act is furtive but the line's arc is direct. Yet the force is forked, two turns of phrase at once doubly dealing death.

> – *A bullet took Medgar Evers' life*

> – *A bullet shed Medgar Evers' blood*

"A bullet from the back of a bush took Medgar Evers' blood": this compounds the guilt. And the sequence looks to the tracks that are traces of blood: *bullet . . . back . . . bush . . . blood*. Of these four words that alliterate, it is the first that fells: "bullet", with its two syllables (as though double-barrelled) as against the others' one.

[1] *Florence* in *For the Union Dead* (1965).

Anonymity is furtive, and the killer is reduced to body-parts as indifferently as a bullet reduces a body: a finger, a handle, a hand, two eyes, a man's brain. Dashed out, these.

From the back of a bush. From behind his back. The words "back" and "behind" can be heard to pound in the song, compounding the disease that rages in the killer – and that the song itself will need vigilant prophylaxis to escape infection from.[1] This first verse, a moment later, eyes the murderous moment:

> Two eyes took the aim
> Behind a man's brain

– the back of his head, behind a man's back. The more forceful, these lines, because they are unobtrusively paradoxical: the brain is behind the eyes, not the other way round – except that the eyes are behind the brain in the grim sense that they carry out the brain's decision, they back the brain: *behind*, "supporting, backing up", "at the back of (any one) as a support; backing (one up)", with the earliest *Oxford English Dictionary* citation being honourably military, "The remainder of the regiment . . . being behind Captain Lucy".

> From the poverty shacks, he looks from the cracks to the tracks
> And the hoof beats pound in his brain

This seethes. A bloodshot gaze can be felt to tack from "shacks" ("the poverty shacks", a stricken phrase) to "cracks" to "tracks", joining the "pack" en route to the word that comes back from the back of a bush: "back".

> From the poverty shacks, he looks from the cracks to the tracks
> And the hoof beats pound in his brain
> And he's taught how to walk in a pack
> Shoot in the back
> With his fist in a clinch
> To hang and to lynch
> To hide 'neath the hood

[1] For a different infection, see Michael Gray, who believes that Medgar Evers and his killer are "a device for strengthening an essentially political and social polemic": "the two men are just pawns in Dylan's 'game'" (*Song and Dance Man III*, 2000, p. 24). For me, either this judgement is crassly "a handle" (for the critic) or the song is.

> To kill with no pain
> Like a dog on a chain
> He ain't got no name
> But it ain't him to blame
> He's only a pawn in their game

Poverty . . . pound . . . pack / beats . . . brain . . . back: the persistent insistence might remind us what kind of consonant a *p* or a *b* is. A plosive. Plosion and explosion. His head was exploding.

Dylan's head knows how to contain such explosions. His exposure of them makes us hear what it is for something to pound in a brain. The throbbing pounding rhythms of the song are in time with its alliterations, rhymes, and assonances, so as to make audible the insanity of a raging obsession, an insanity that is cause and consequence of killing. A hundred and fifty years ago, Tennyson took the sick pulsations of a man who had killed and who was now in the living death that is madness:

> Dead, long dead,
> Long dead!
> And my heart is a handful of dust,
> And the wheels go over my head,
> And my bones are shaken with pain,
> For into a shallow grave they are thrust,
> Only a yard beneath the street,
> And the hoofs of the horses beat, beat,
> The hoofs of the horses beat,
> Beat into my scalp and my brain,
> With never an end to the stream of passing feet[1]

"A bullet from the back of a bush took Medgar Evers' blood": this opening shot is taken up, caught up, in the opening line of the final verse: "Today, Medgar Evers was buried from the bullet he caught". Here is the return not only to the name that is to be honoured but to the dishonour of the bullet (which now alliterates anew). The first line of the song had the death-scene in its sights. The second line sounded the unrelenting note that commands the song, there in "name" as it will be in "game".

---

[1] *Maud*, II, v, 1. Tennyson and Dylan: "beat", "brain", "grave", "hoof(s)", "never", "pain". Tennyson, "handful"; Dylan, "handle" and "hand".

> A bullet from the back of a bush took Medgar Evers' blood
> A finger fired the trigger to his name

His name: Medgar Evers. A bullet had his name on it – but not because of divine destiny, only because of human hatred. As to the killer's name: it means nothing, it means nothingness.[1] "There be of them that have left a name behind them, that their praises might be reported. And some there be, which have no memorial" (Ecclesiasticus 44: 8–9). Medgar Evers left a name behind him. His praises are reported. He has a memorial. His name is there in the first line of the first verse (as it will be in the first line of the last verse), and it remains the only name in the fifty-two lines of the song, a song in which the word "name" is sounded four times. In another Dylan song about the brutal killing of someone black by someone white (*The Lonesome Death of Hattie Carroll*), the killer enjoys a certain infamy: William Zanzinger, immortalized for that mortal blow of his. But *Only a Pawn in Their Game* accords its killer no name. "He ain't got no name". The last words of the song, the killer's laconic epitaph, get their dour force from the vacuity of "Carved next to his name":

> He'll see by his grave
> On the stone that remains
> Carved next to his name
> His epitaph plain:
> Only a pawn in their game

Medgar Evers is named. Twice. As for the rest of those who are set upon by – and are set against – the poor whites, back in the sixties there was the word that had not yet become opprobrious to those who have since chosen to be known as African-Americans: the word "negro", or rather (in this song) "Negro". The n-word that is not Negro is never heard in this song, but you are incited to imagine it, to acknowledge that it, not "Negro", is the word that "the South politician" (not quite the same, darkly, as a Southern politician or even a politician from the South), the marshals, the cops, and the poor whites will all be most pleased to use most unpleasantly. Dylan doesn't flinch from using the word, dramatized, in *Hurricane*:

[1] In 1994 Byron de la Beckwith was found guilty of Evers' murder. This matters, but not to the conscience of the song.

> And to the black folks he was just a crazy nigger
> No one doubted that he pulled the trigger[1]

Those two lines (a dozen years later, admittedly, and in collaboration with
Jacques Levy) make me wonder whether I am imagining things – as against
Dylan's imagining how to get us to do so – when I sense that the word
"nigger" lurks or skulks in the vicinity. Juxtapose with that couplet from
Hurricane these two evocations in *Only a Pawn in Their Game*:

> A finger fired the trigger to his name[2]

> And the Negro's name
> Is used it is plain
> For the politician's gain

The word "name" links these two moments in the song, and the alliter-
ation in "finger fired" plays along with the off-rhyme of *finger/trigger*, an
off-rhyme (*Medgar . . . finger . . . trigger*) that was to become the true rhyme
– truly dramatized and dismaying ("the black folks" use the word themselves) –
in *Hurricane*: *nigger/trigger*. For there should be no ducking the fact that, whereas
Only a Pawn in Their Game rightly observes the decencies, it manages to intimate
to us that the racists in the South didn't observe them. It is not "the Negro's
name" that "Is used it is plain/For the politician's gain", but the slur-name,
contemptuous and contemptible. The song doesn't utter the word, doesn't
even mutter the word, but does not let us forget it.

> A South politician preaches to the poor white man
> "You got more than the blacks, don't complain
> You're better than them, you been born with white skin" they explain
> And the Negro's name
> Is used it is plain
> For the politician's gain
> As he rises to fame
> And the poor white remains

[1] *Only a Pawn in Their Game*: "the one/That fired the gun". *Hurricane*: "And though
they could not produce the gun/The D.A. said he was the one".
[2] A disconcertingly deranged and unforgettable way of putting it. "A finger fired the
trigger to his name"? Pulled the trigger that put an end to his name? (Not that it
succeeded in doing that.) To? *To*?

> On the caboose of the train
> But it ain't him to blame
> He's only a pawn in their game

For the poor white, the caboose of the train. For the black, whether poor or not, the back of the bus. And the name of the game that realizes in art this refusal to blame the poor white? The game is play that is in earnest: assonance laced with rhyme – *complain . . . explain . . . name . . . plain . . . gain . . . fame . . . remains . . . train . . . blame . . . game.*

The first line of the song ends in "blood". No rhyme is ever forthcoming, though off in the distance there is to be a glimpse of the hood that masks the Ku Klux Klan. "To hide 'neath the hood": "hide" rotating menacingly into "hood".

The second line of the song, "A finger fired the trigger to his name", establishes as the song's finger the rhyme-word "name", triggering the cumulative obduracy of the sequence *aim . . . brain . . . blamed . . . game.* This same sound is then pressed to the point of explosion in the second verse (ten of these assonances running). Then, still unignorable, it is the sound that opens and closes the third verse, from the opening "paid" and "same" to the pinioning at the end: *hate . . . straight . . . blame . . . game.* And it is the assonance that then does almost the same for the fourth verse, "brain" into the closing accumulation: *pain . . . chain . . . name . . . blame . . . game.* And that then, in the final verse, after first of all allowing a few lines to be released from the pain of this assonance, has the duty of reverting at the end – from the word "grave" – to this tolling insistence again:

> Today, Medgar Evers was buried from the bullet he caught
> They lowered him down as a king
> But when the shadowy sun sets on the one
> That fired the gun
> He'll see by his grave
> On the stone that remains
> Carved next to his name
> His epitaph plain:
> Only a pawn in their game

See it, he won't. "Two eyes took the aim": but now death has taken aim and taken their life. "He'll see by his grave . . .": the shadowy sun may see the scene, but he the killer will not. He will no longer be in a position to see anything. Unless, of course, death is not the end. "But he can't be blamed"? He shall see. God only knows.

There is, as there should be in the whereabouts of these hatreds, a great deal that we shall never know. "Is there any cause in nature that makes these hard hearts?" The question is a king's, King Lear's.

> Today, Medgar Evers was buried from the bullet he caught
> They lowered him down as a king

Lowered down, as even a king will be in the end, and yet for Evers there is the ceremonial dignity of a royal burial, too. He is a king, not a pawn. Black and white. Black against white. In 1963 there was, as it happens, a king, Martin Luther King, whose name must have meant a great deal to the man named Medgar Evers. Five years later, when another killer had been taught "To keep up his hate", Martin Luther King was buried from the bullet he caught.

Pride

Like a Rolling Stone

The performers of the dance of death in *Tarantula* include tragedy. Or
rather Tragedy. Or even perhaps (the actor's throbstuff) Taragedy. But
be warned, there is a caveat. *Caveat*: let him beware, or at least be
wary. For although tragedy can be profound in its understanding of pride,
tragedy becomes shallow as soon as it does itself fall into pride. It should
not presume to look down on comedy, its otherwise inclined brother.
Tarantula contemplates "tragedy, the broken pride, shallow & no deeper
than comedy", tragedy in line for "the doom, the bending & the farce of
happy ending".[1]

Like a Rolling Stone, which looks into the depths of such comedy as is
savage farce (and yet is not without a happy ending of a weird kind),
is an achievement in which Dylan takes pride.[2] The song takes pride as
its target.

> Once upon a time you dressed so fine
> Threw the bums a dime in your prime, didn't you?
> People'd call, say, "Beware doll, you're bound to fall"
> You thought they were all kiddin' you
> You used to laugh about
> Everybody that was hangin' out
> Now you don't talk so loud
> Now you don't seem so proud
> About having to be scrounging your next meal

"Once upon a time": do remember how fairy-tales sally forth, but don't

---

[1] *Tarantula* (1966, 1971), p. 52.

[2] "*Like a Rolling Stone* changed it all; I didn't care any more after that about writing
books or poems or whatever. I mean it was something that I myself could dig. It's
very tiring having other people tell you how much they dig you if you yourself don't
dig you" (*Playboy*, March 1966).

forget how soon the darkness encroaches. For this nursery formula enters not as a sarcasm but as an irony.

The song bides its time before releasing "proud" (getting on for the sixtieth word), but we have got the picture. The posture, too, there in "Once upon a time you dressed so fine". (Of pride, the proverb says: "be her garments what they will, yet she will never be too hot, nor too cold".[1]) There, too, in "Threw the bums a dime in your prime, didn't you?", with its evocation of small-minded largesse (all change was small change to her in those days). Averse to advice, she saw no need to heed. "People'd call, say, 'Beware doll, you're bound to fall'". And why was she bound to fall? Because of what famously comes before a fall. This thought itself, within the song, comes before "proud".

Her misguided insouciance is guyed in the rhyme "didn't you?" / "You thought they were all kiddin' you". (A rhyme? That? You must be kidding.) "Now you don't talk so loud": but the song is, in its way, a talking song, a good talking-to. "Now you don't seem so proud": "seem" partly as a further rounding on her, but partly as an admission that he can't really be sure what is going on inside, as against how she seems.

> Now you don't seem so proud
> About having to be scrounging your next meal

Not at all the same thing as a meal, this phrase "your next meal". We know where "your next meal" is coming from. Scrounging your next meal means swallowing your pride.

So she *had it coming*? But Dylan knows that those who take pleasure in the words "had it coming" are themselves likely to be guilty of the complacency that they impugn. Or the callousness, dressed up so fine. Dylan's voice can be heard to disown the phrase at the heinous end of *Black Cross*, the story of Hezekiah Jones:[2]

> And they hung Hezekiah
> As high up as a pigeon
> White folks around said
> Well, he had it comin'
> Son-of-a-bitch never had no religion

[1] 1614; *The Concise Oxford Dictionary of English Proverbs*, ed. J. A. Simpson (1982).
[2] *Black Cross*, Lord Buckley's monologue from Joseph Newman's poem. Dylan recorded it (Michael Gray gives the date, 22 December 1961).

Not that a religion guarantees a good god. Samuel Butler transubstantiated the piety of "An honest man's the noblest work of God" into a provocative proverb: "An honest God's the noblest work of man". There are dishonest gods and goddesses. William James deplored "the moral flabbiness born of the exclusive worship of the bitch-goddess *success*. That − with the squalid cash interpretation put on the word success − is our national disease."[1] The woman in *Like a Rolling Stone* has been down upon her knees before the bitch-goddess, the goddess that failed and that made her fail. Fail, fall, feel.

Yet this relentless pressure (the drill of "How does it feel"), though it will not give up, is not without misgivings. They are what saves the song. Saves it from being − in all its vituperative exhilaration − even more damnably proud than the person whom it damns and blasts. For in the end the song doesn't only chastise, it finds itself chastened by its recognition of more feelings than it had at first bargained for. But perhaps not so much *more* feelings (I am thinking of the good old gibe, "I'm afraid this will hurt X's feelings, but then he has so many of them . . .") as different ones, feelings more at odds with themselves and with the revenge comedy that is the song.

You never turned around to see the frowns on the jugglers and the clowns
When they all did tricks for you

But the song eventually turns around, in the way in which Kipling's masterpiece of revenge, his story *Dayspring Mishandled*, turns around in some of its sympathies by the time it is through with the monstrous trick that the revenger plays upon someone who had it coming − someone who then turns out to have something more than a cruelly practical joke coming: the final fatal it.

The right characterization of the animus within the song, in my judgement, is not gloating but exulting. Dylan's judgement in the song, by the end, feels different from the one he was moved to make before it, outside it, about it. What do we really feel about its question "How does it feel?"? (A question within a question there.) How does it feel? Mixed: is that not how it feels? Not to be confused with Mixed-Up Confusion, but mixed feelings, nixed feelings.

[1] 11 September 1906; *Letters* (1920), vol. II, p. 260.

> How does it feel
> How does it feel
> To be without a home
> Like a complete unknown
> Like a rolling stone?

Those several questions amount to – they mount to – one question. Just how many questions the song puts is itself in question. "Threw the bums a dime in your prime, didn't you?": is that a question, exactly?

> As you stare into the vacuum of his eyes
> And say do you want to make a deal?

Doesn't this report a question rather than put one?

> Ain't it hard when you discover that
> He really wasn't where it's at
> After he took from you everything he could steal

It's not just the lack of a question-mark on the page that makes "Ain't it hard" feel obdurately uninquiring, beyond question. Still, the final verse is the only one of the four to have no question or question-type solicitation other than the single-minded tireless inquisition, "How does it feel?"

And does this question permit of a single-minded answer? If the song were nothing other than a triumph of gloating, then the hoped-for answer would be reduced to the broken admission, "Terrible, that's how it feels, if you must know." But there can be felt in the refrain an exhilaration and a further exultation, not just the one that is being bent upon this Princess (proverb: "Proud as a prince"), but a different one, some exultation that she herself may have come belatedly into possession of and be feeling even now. Allen Ginsberg caught Dylan's catching this, Dylan who is loved (Ginsberg said) "by every seeker in America who's heard that long-vowelled voice in heroic ecstasy triumphant. 'How does it feel?'"[1]

> How does it feel
> To be without a home

Does the answer have to be *terrible, terrifying*? Is there nothing about being

---

[1] Sleeve-notes to *Desire*.

without a home that could be, even if far short of *terrific*, at least freed from certain pressures or oppressions? (Ask any artist whose life, by and large, is on the road.) Or freed from certain sadnesses? Ask Philip Larkin.

HOME IS SO SAD

Home is so sad. It stays as it was left,
Shaped to the comfort of the last to go
As if to win them back. Instead, bereft
Of anyone to please, it withers so,
Having no heart to put aside the theft

And turn again to what it started as,
A joyous shot at how things ought to be,
Long fallen wide. You can see how it was:
Look at the pictures and the cutlery.
The music in the piano stool. That vase.

Not that the music in the piano stool was likely to include *Like a Rolling Stone*.

Again:

How does it feel
To be on your own

The point isn't that a positive answer can shove aside the negative one; rather, that if you acknowledge any possibility of a positive answer, you immediately grant mixed feelings as to how it feels, you concede that the song is alive to more than one kind of exultation, and your imagination reaches well beyond gloating. True, she lost a great deal of what had constituted her being, this princess. But did she gain nothing?

The refrain gains something. At first, it lacked this taunt or tint that subsequently comes to colour the song and make it its own:

How does it feel
To be on your own

It would be stubborn to acknowledge no thrill whatsoever when this arrives. You don't have to have led the life of the young Dylan to sense that something of power arrives with "To be on your own". And you have only to imagine the flash-lit life of a celebrity (goldfish-bowled) to feel a touch of yearning in "Like a complete unknown". Dylan's voicing of this includes something of relief, release, as though the exchange might, just might, have gone like this: *How does it feel? Good of you to ask, not at all bad, or at any rate not all bad.*

"Tragedy, the broken pride": her pride may have been broken ("Now you don't seem so proud"), but she may not have been. She is not altogether to be bullied into abjection by the school-bully named Life. Bully for her.

> You've gone to the finest school all right, Miss Lonely
> But you know you only used to get juiced in it
> Nobody's ever taught you how to live out on the street
> And now you're gonna have to get used to it

For in the end the finest school is the Little Red School of Hard Knox, the school that by the end may have taught you how to live out on the street. Like all of us, Miss Lonely bridles at the thought of being taught a lesson, but she may not be above learning her lesson, provided that it is hers, provided that it is something more than an exposure (though never less than that), an exposition in the song, not an imposition by the song.

> You said you'd never compromise
> With the mystery tramp, but now you realize
> He's not selling any alibis
> As you stare into the vacuum of his eyes
> And say do you want to make a deal?

But now you realize: there is much that she is coming to realize. For instance, that she can't claim to have somehow been someone else or somewhere else at the time ("He's not selling any alibis"), somewhere other than the pinnacled stage of life where she strutted and fretted.

> Princess on the steeple and all the pretty people
> They're all drinkin', thinkin' that they got it made
> Exchanging all precious gifts
> But you'd better take your diamond ring, you'd better pawn it babe

That word "pawn" may hold a grudge, yes, but then if you were a grudge, wouldn't you like to be held?

Realizing such things is a gain of a sort. Perhaps pure loss is as rare as any other purity. "Like a complete unknown": under one aspect this is a threat, but there are other aspects, and one of them would be the reminder that being like a complete unknown[1] might not feel as totally evacuated as being like a complete known. Think of the celeb, known not only to all but to sundry, and with no longer even a chance of going (a complete unknown) *incognito.*

Robert Shelton, then, was not being perverse (tactless, perhaps) when he retorted the song's question upon the singer. His interview in *Melody Maker* (29 July 1978) had the title *How does it feel to be on your own?*, and it began: "'How does it feel?' I teased Bob Dylan with his own famous question." And eight years later, Shelton's biography called itself simply *No Direction Home*. Simply, and simplifyingly, but still with a response to something positive, something liberating, in the thought of being without a home. (Which is not the same as being homeless.) *Like a Rolling Stone* put this complex plight in stages. The first time the refrain comes, the line is "To be without a home". Thereafter it recedes further: "With no direction home". From no home to no direction home. And yet neither of these is sheer.

Like a Rolling Stone is home to a great many home truths, valid home truths.

Home: That strikes home; that comes home to one; searching, poignant, pointed; effective, appropriate; to the point, close, direct. Now chiefly in *home question, home truth.*

(*The Oxford English Dictionary*)

Such is the song all right, earning all of those epithets. Its home question: How does it feel? Its home truth: Like a rolling stone. For those four words, the entitlement, are not just part of what you are being asked about ("How does it feel to be like a rolling stone?"), they constitute one answer, too: like a rolling stone, that is how it feels. And how does that feel? Exercise your imagination, as Keats did: "He has affirmed that he can conceive of a billiard ball that it may have a sense of delight from its own roundness, smoothness, volubility, and the rapidity of its motion."[2] A sense of delight within *Like a Rolling Stone*? Certainly, but what is not certain is that the

---

[1] The refrain, on its second appearance, does not say "Like a complete unknown", but – unmitigated – "A complete unknown".

[2] Richard Woodhouse to John Taylor, about 27 October 1818; *The Letters of John Keats*, ed. H. E. Rollins (1958), vol. I, p. 389.

delight is monopolized by the excoriator, with none of it seized by the excoriated. And the rapidity of its motion? "That was a great tune, yeah. It's the dynamics in the rhythm that make up *Like a Rolling Stone* and all of the lyrics."[1] Such is the source of the song's delight (energy is eternal delight, as Blake sensed), and since delight often overflows its bounds, then if the Princess is indeed like a rolling stone, some of this sense of delight just might roll her way. She can't simply be anathema to him, for the song rolls like an anthem.

Mustn't sentimentalize, true. I am not convinced that the song rises quite as high (or would be the better for rising quite as high) above its ugly truthful feelings as Paul Nelson's shining upward face suggests.[2] Ill-will is there, for sure, and critics have found the song distasteful in the charge that it brings, in the charge that it makes, and in the charge that it carries.[3] The song's recrimination might incriminate it. But just as creators are more magnanimous than critics, so creations – works of art – have a way of being more magnanimous than their creators. Dylan's conversational relish as to *Like a Rolling Stone* is no doubt true to the song's occasion and to its impetus, but the achievement is then the sublimation of all the dross that it knew it needed to start with or to start from. There is a process that transmutes what is acid and acrid and acrimonious. The original impulse and the original draft are something other than the song.

In its early form it was 10 pages long . . . It wasn't called anything. Just a rhythm thing on paper all about my steady hatred directed at some point that was honest. In the end it wasn't hatred, it was telling someone something they didn't know.

[1] *Playboy* (March 1978).

[2] "The finest song on the album, and Dylan's greatest so far, I think, is *Like a Rolling Stone*, the definitive statement that both personal and artistic fulfilment must come, in the main, by being truly on one's own. Dylan's social adversaries have twisted this to mean something very devious and selfish, but that is not the case at all. Dylan is simply kicking away the props to get to the real core of the matter: Know yourself. It may hurt at first, but you'll never get anywhere if you don't. The final 'You're invisible now, you got no secrets to conceal / How does it feel? / How does it feel? / To be on your own' is clearly optimistic and triumphant, a soaring of the spirit into a new and more productive present."

(*Sing Out!*, February/March 1966)

[3] "*Like a Rolling Stone* is of course a put-down – most likely the best Dylan ever wrote. What is annoying about it to me is its self-righteousness, its willingness to judge others without judging oneself, the proselytizing in disguise for Dylan's own way of life" (Jon Landau, *Crawdaddy!*, 1968).

Telling them they were lucky. Revenge! That's the better word. I had never thought of it as a song until one day I was at the piano and on the piano it was singing, How does it feel? in a slow motion pace, in the utmost of slow motion, following something. It was like swimming in lava. In your eyesight you see your victim swimming in lava. Hanging by their arms from a birch tree. Hitting a nail with your foot. Seeing someone in the pain they were bound to meet up with. I wrote it. I didn't fail. It was straight.[1]

"Revenge! That's the better word." But revenge within dark comedy, Dylan's or Shakespeare's, can be left to time, is time's business or pleasure. "And thus the whirligig of time brings in his revenges". His, Time's, quite as much as his, Dylan's. "Seeing someone in the pain they were bound to meet up with." But one thing that we know proverbially is that *pride feels no pain*. Or rather, that there is a paradox in pride's relation to pain: "Pride is never without her own pain, though she will not feel it" (1614). Will not: refuses to. As to the future, she will feel it.

The song moves, in its own pain, from the vindictive to a vindication of itself. It doesn't torture, it cauterizes. "You never understood": this arrives at an understanding that has its own sadness.

> You never turned around to see the frowns on the jugglers and the clowns
> When they all did tricks for you
> You never understood that it ain't no good
> You shouldn't let other people get your kicks for you

When Dylan elsewhere makes a joke in this vicinity, we shouldn't put the joke down to the vacuum that is flippancy.

How do you get your kicks these days, then?
"I hire people to look into my eyes, and then I have them kick me."
And that's the way you get your kicks?
"No. Then I *forgive* them. That's where my kicks come in."[2]

"As you stare into the vacuum of his eyes": "You shouldn't let other

---

[1] *Bob Dylan* by Miles (1978), p. 28 (not to be confused with the compilation by Miles, *Bob Dylan in His Own Words*, also 1978). Apparently from an interview with Jules Siegel (March 1966).
[2] *Playboy* (March 1966).

people get your kicks for you". I know, I know, Dylan is jesting when he
says "Then I *forgive* them", but it isn't an empty jest. Among the things
that *Like a Rolling Stone* does to her is forgive her. Many things protect this
against sentimentality; for one, the fact that forgiveness, which is styptic,
makes you wince.

> You used to laugh about
> Everybody that was hangin' out

The song doesn't laugh and it doesn't laugh at her. "You used to be so
amused": the song isn't amused or amusing. It is in earnest, and in its
turbulent way it gives an earnest of its mixed feelings. "You've gone to
the finest school all right, Miss Lonely": she is Miss Lonely, only, for she
is not Miss Lonelyhearts. But in the long run that is life, she isn't heartless,
and nor is the song.

This is what underlies the overlap between what the song sings of
her arrival at bleakness, and what on occasion Dylan is moved to say of
himself.

> When you ain't got nothing, you got nothing to lose

You must be vulnerable to be sensitive to reality. And to me being vulnerable
is just another way of saying that one has nothing more to lose. I don't have
anything but darkness to lose. I'm way beyond that.[1]

And for now? "The word 'NOW'"[2] has its penetrative immediacy:

---

[1] *Rolling Stone* (26 January 1978).

[2]
> Now you see this one-eyed midget
> Shouting the word "NOW"
> And you say, "For what reason?"
> And he says, "How?"
> And you say "What does this mean?"
> And he screams back, "You're a cow
> Give me some milk
> Or else go home"
> (*Ballad of a Thin Man*)

How now no brown cow.

Now you don't talk so loud
Now you don't seem so proud

And now you're gonna have to get used to it

      but now you realize
He's not selling any alibis

Go to him now, he calls you, you can't refuse
When you ain't got nothing, you got nothing to lose
You're invisible now, you got no secrets to conceal

Not since Marvell's *To His Coy Mistress* has there been such an upsurge of the urgency of *now*:

Now, therefore, while the youthful hue
Sits on thy skin like morning dew,
And while thy willing soul transpires
At every pore with instant fires,
Now let us sport us while we may;
And now, like amorous birds of prey,
Rather at once our time devour,
Than languish in his slow-chapped power.
Let us roll all our strength, and all
Our sweetness, up into one ball . . .

To His Coy Mistress is a love song. *Like a Rolling Stone* ("In the end it wasn't hatred") is an unlove song, *To His Coy Princess*: let us roll all our strength – this is no time for sweetness – up into one stone.

    There is now, and there was then. You can hear the different parts played by the simple words "used to", meaning sometimes "was what you did" and one time "get habituated to". The song sets the "used to" of "You used to laugh about" ("You only used to get juiced in it", "You used to ride on the chrome horse with your diplomat", "You used to be so amused") against this moment when what was habit has become the need to get habituated to the way life is: "And now you're gonna have to get used to it". And both of these are set against the different meaning of "used" as "made use of" (differently pronounced, too, this different usage) in

> You used to be so amused
> At Napoleon in rags and the language that he used[1]

It is the word "you" that is used to make her confront her self-abuse. Nearly thirty times in the song "you" is thrust at her, eight times in the last verse, where it is pressed home even further by its accomplices in rhyme:

> But *you*'d better take your diamond ring, *you*'d better pawn it babe
> *You* *used* to be so *amused*
> At Napoleon in rags and the language that he *used*
> Go to him now, he calls *you,* *you* can't *refuse*
> When *you* ain't got nothing, *you* got nothing to *lose*
> You're invisible now, *you* got no secrets to conceal[2]

The pronoun "you" is the song's pronouncement, this being a song in which, although "they" may for a while be hanging out with "you" ("They're all drinkin', thinkin' that they got it made"), and "he" may be doing so, too (even if "He's not selling any alibis"[3]), "you" will never, Miss Lonely, enjoy the company of "we" or "us", and never ever the company of an "I". Of all Dylan's creations this is the song that, while one of his most individual, exercises the severest self-control when it comes to never mentioning its first person. Never say I. Not I and I: you and you.

---

[1] "Napoleon in rags" is, among other things, the great man who has fallen. People'd call, say, "Beware, Boney, you're bound to fall"; he thought they were all kidding him. On Napoleon and his fall in relation to how language can be used, consider Byron on "the 'greatest living poet'": "Even I .../ Was reckoned, a considerable time,/ The grand Napoleon of the realms of rhyme. //... But I will fall at least as fell my hero" (*Don Juan*, XI, 55–6). My hero: compare Dylan's *Hero Blues*, "You need a different kind of man, babe / You need Napoleon Boneeparte".

[2] The "you" in "you're" is a different sound, and it does different work in the song (three times).

[3] There are two excruciating crescendos that writhe with "him" and "he":

> You used to ride on the chrome horse with your diplomat
> Who carried on his shoulder a Siamese cat
> Ain't it hard when you discover that
> He really wasn't where it's at
> After he took from you everything he could steal

> You used to be so amused
> At Napoleon in rags and the language that he used
> Go to him now, he calls you, you can't refuse

And yet, in the end, with mixed feelings about you.

The song's proverb has gathered its own mixed feelings over the years. "A rolling stone gathers no moss, and a running head will never thrive" (Gosson, 1579). Moss, it seems, is imagined there as a good thing (making you feel comfortable in some way). *The Oxford English Dictionary* says of the proverb that it is "used to imply that a man who restlessly roams from place to place, or constantly changes his employment will never grow rich. Hence, in *slang* or allusive use, *moss* occas. = money." By 1926, what with what, the proverb was ready to receive the Stephen Leacock treatment, which included Leacock's scepticism about home when success is at stake.

A ROLLING STONE GATHERS NO MOSS

Entirely wrong again. This was supposed to show that a young man who wandered from home never got on in the world. In very ancient days it was true. The young man who stayed at home and worked hard and tilled the ground and goaded oxen with a long stick like a lance found himself as he grew old a man of property, owning four goats and a sow. The son who wandered forth in the world was either killed by the cannibals or crawled home years afterwards doubled up with rheumatism. So the old men made the proverb.

But nowadays it is exactly wrong. It is the rolling stone that gathers the moss. It is the ambitious boy from Llanpwgg, Wales, who trudges off to the city leaving his elder brother in the barnyard and who later on makes a fortune and founds a university. While his elder brother still has only the old farm with three cows and a couple of pigs, he has a whole department of agriculture with great sheds full of Tamworth hogs and a professor to every six of them.

In short, in modern life it is the rolling stone that gathers the moss. And the geologists say that the moss on the actual stone was first started in exactly the same way. It was the rolling of the stone that smashed up the earth and made the moss grow.[1]

Modern life, 1926. By the mid sixties, the Rolling Stone had got on in the world even further, what with a heaven-sent magazine and a hell-bent group, with the song itself maintaining the momentum of a rolling stone, of rock 'n' roll. And no need to say a word about moss.

George Bernard Shaw protested in his preface to *Misalliance*: "We keep repeating the silly proverb that a rolling stone gathers no moss, as if moss

[1] Stephen Leacock, *Studies in the Newer Culture; Winnowed Wisdom* (1926), pp. 104–5.

were a desirable parasite." A desirable parasite does figure in Dylan's song. But what would be so great about gathering moss anyway? "Gather ye rose-buds while ye may": that, I can understand. Herrick, not To Miss Lonely, but *To the Virgins, to make much of Time.*

> Gather ye rose-buds while ye may,
> Old Time is still a-flying:
> And this same flower that smiles today,
> Tomorrow will be dying.

Gather ye rose-buds . . . But who could ever forget the great moment when Lou Costello suddenly says to Bud Abbott, "Gather ye moss, Bud, while ye may"?

Day of the Locusts

It is easy to make the mistake of supposing that a Dylan song is about Dylan, as against his being about it, its unmistakably manifesting him in his element. Don't break works of art back down into the biographical contingencies that contributed to bringing them into being but that are not their being. Don't track or trace him. Don't seek to interpret the life of his songs by resurrecting loathed people or loved people from his personal life. "My songs have a life of their own."[1] More, they lead their own lives. The impersonality that is one of art's strengths is a feat, and the artist has to exercise imagination to achieve it, to have the song be his but not he. More, even: to have it be true of his independent creations, as William Blake said of his, that "Though I call them mine, I know that they are not mine."

But there will sometimes be the special occasion, biographically and artistically, when we don't mishear a particular Dylan song if we bring it home to him and to the events of his life. *Day of the Locusts* preserves his life at what is not a stolen moment. The song alludes to what occasioned it. To allude is to call something into play, as Dylan does when he plays this song.

Alfred Tennyson in 1831 had not stayed to gain a degree from the University of Cambridge. His honorary degree twenty years later (from the University of Oxford . . .) both bestowed and earned honour. Robert Allen Zimmerman did not hang around – or in there – to gain a degree

[1] Interview, London (4 October 1997); *Isis* (October 1997).

from the University of Minnesota. In due course, ten years later, Princeton University gave Bob Dylan an honorary degree, a doctorate of music.

The artist can be and should be proud of such an honour. But this had better not tempt him or her into pride. One way to exorcize pride might be to write an unostentatious poem or song about the occasion, an occasional song. Careful now, for to ridicule the ceremony would be to demean not only it but oneself. But to rib it, fine. Comedy will save the day of the locusts.

"As I stepped to the stage to pick up my degree": of course no gentleman would ever mention that the degree in question was (don't you know) an honorary not an ordinary one. But there is bound to be at least the possibility of one's becoming a shade pompous in the circumstances. I remember when someone important and self-important put it to me once (over a glass of sherry) that he had a moral dilemma: could I help him with it? I shall do my best, I answered gravely. It is this: is it proper, do you think, to give exactly the same speech of thanks when I am given an honorary degree by the University of Middlemarch next week that I gave last week when I was given an honorary degree by the University of Barset? Well, I could see that there was a moral dimension to all this, but I wouldn't myself have located it quite where my affable inquirer did.

So how does Dylan's song protect itself against being affected by, infected by, pride? Humour is the penetrating disinfectant.[1] Which is why this song that sets the scene in the first verse – "As I stepped to the stage to pick up my degree" – will soon arrive in all innocence at a weather-report: "The weather was hot, a-nearly 90 degrees". My degree, 90 degrees. Did you realize, sir, before making such a song and dance about your honorary degree, that there are people out there who have been awarded nearly ninety degrees? Take the sage George Steiner, for one . . .

I am aware (as people say when too aware of themselves) that 90 degrees is a tot not of academic garlands but of heat. (90 honorary degrees would mean that you were a very hot property indeed, possibly even hot shit.[2])

---

[1] When Tennyson was about to be given his honorary degree at Oxford in June 1855, an undergraduate (recalling the first line of *The May Queen*: "You must wake and call me early, call me early, mother dear") called out as the long-haired honorand entered, "Did your mother call you early, dear?"

[2] Philip Larkin has a soundly patterned evocation of the bestselling novelist in lavish exile among glittering prizes: "the shit in the shuttered château / Who does his five hundred words / Then parts out the rest of the day / Between bathing and booze and birds" (*The Life with a Hole in it*). To bathe, not to bath, I take it.

But then Dylan is turning the word "degrees" through ninety degrees, so that this sense is at a tangent to the other one. Right angles, right? And that his song at this point has mental activity in mind (and how it can be too much of a good thing, the brainy season) is clear from how it echoes an earlier song. The rhyming in *Day of the Locusts* uses its old brain-pan:

> Outside of the gate the trucks were unloadin'
> The weather was hot, a-nearly 90 degrees
> The man standin' next to me, his head was exploding

"Sure was glad to get out of there alive". *From a Buick 6*:

> Well you know I need a steam shovel mama to keep away the dead
> I need a dump truck mama to unload my head

One way to unload your head is humour, and in *Day of the Locusts* humour has been the note from the word go (from the word Oh, actually).

> Oh, the benches were stained with tears and perspiration
> The birdies were flying from tree to tree
> There was little to say, there was no conversation
> As I stepped to the stage to pick up my degree

The grooves of Academe![1] "The benches were stained with tears and perspiration": people must have wept buckets of tears for the very benches to be stained. (Is this where the students sit their examinations? and exude their perspirations?) Mothers crying, fathers sweating at the high summer season of degrees? "Tears and perspiration" is itself a disconcerting combo:

[1] Matthew Arnold, on some verses by Wordsworth about education and its benches, verses grim in the extreme:

One can hear them being quoted at a Social Science Congress; one can call up the whole scene. A great room in one of our dismal provincial towns; dusty air and jaded afternoon daylight; benches full of men with bald heads and women in spectacles; an orator lifting up his face from a manuscript written within and without to declaim these lines of Wordsworth; and in the soul of any poor child of nature who may have wandered in thither, an unutterable sense of lamentation, and mourning, and woe!

(*Wordsworth*, 1879)

There was no conversation. "Benches full of men with bald heads": to baldism, I shall return.

wouldn't sweat be the word these days? (Not in the old days, when horses sweated, men perspired, and women glowed.) The first rhyme in the song is *perspiration / conversation*; but perspiration is not mentioned in polite conversation. Let alone sweat.

But perhaps "tears and perspiration" is to call up "tears and sweat" from Winston Churchill's wartime speech of 1940: "I have nothing to offer but blood, toil, tears and sweat." But why suppose an allusion here? Partly because the clarion call is very famous (no dictionary of quotations can afford to be without it). Partly because the song also has "I glanced into the chamber" (the chamber of the House of Commons is where the backbenchers and frontbenchers were listening to Churchill).[1] Partly because of the sense of a ceremonial occasion, of formalities that are not empty formalities. And partly because of what would be the comedy of reducing "blood, toil, tears and sweat" to "tears and perspiration". Sweat, within academic life as contrasted with war, has to become demure perspiration. As for blood, it is too high a price to pay for, or in, academic life. And toil had better not be invoked, since the degree is an honorary one, not earned by the sweat of one's high brow. Earned by past toil, no doubt, but not by toiling for the degree itself.

> Oh, the benches were stained with tears and perspiration
> The birdies were flying from tree to tree

Why is "birdies" so endearing there? I feel about it as a Kingsley Amis hero did about sex, that he knew why he liked it but why did he like it so much? Partly, the open poeticality of it, its calling up the songs of Robert Burns: "Ye birdies dumb, in with'ring bowers". Yes, the birdies are dumb in this song, they are not singing but flying, and they leave it to the locusts to be the songsters. And those "with'ring bowers"? "Benches stained with tears and perspiration"?

Or, watching the birdie, the songs of Tennyson: "She sang this baby song. / What does little birdie say / In her nest at peep of day?" Nothing about a doctorate of music, you may be sure of that – and yet the world of primary education is there, on its way to the tertiary.

But mostly it must be a matter of the sound-effect. "The birdies were flying from tree to tree": such a sweet melody as it flies from "bird*ies*" to

---

[1] A twist might then be given to "There was little to say", given that a *parliament* is a place to say things.

"*tree*" to "*tree*". And how enduringly this then becomes the song's sound throughout (*tree . . . degree . . . melody . . . me*), with this, the second line of the song, delivering it not just once or twice but thrice, thanks to "birdies".

Since Dylan is being honoured for his songs, and since an honorand always does well to be an honourer too (so that respect can form a humane chain), let seventeen lines of this thirty-three line song be a tribute to how others sing: not the usual poetical honorands (birds[1]) but locusts. Seventeen out of thirty-three: half a line more than half the song. This is exactly judged; there is no need to dance attendance on the locusts and their sweet melody, since your sweet melody is all but its equal . . .

> And the locusts sang off in the distance
> Yeah, the locusts sang such a sweet melody
> Oh, the locusts sang off in the distance
> Yeah, the locusts sang and they were sanging for me

As printed, "they were singing" but he sings "sanging": one form of the past ("they sang") finds itself tensely tucked up within another form of the past ("they were singing") to create not a continuous present but a continuing past, not an eternal present but an eternal past.[2] Thanks for the memory within a memory. "Off in the distance". And "sanging" has both aptness and comedy: there is something genially unpropitiatory about the way in which in this song about a university ceremony Dylan continues to be himself, grammatically, verbally, reprehensibly. Not just "they were sanging for me", repeatedly, but "it give me a chill", not "it gave", and – on the last occasion when the phrase comes – not "they were sanging for me", but "they was sanging for me". But then the locusts sang with one voice, very singularly. Heard one, heard them all.[3]

---

[1] Shakespeare, Sonnet 73: "Bare ruined quires, where late the sweet birds sang". The leafless branches as pews or benches.

[2] Tennyson, *Mariana*: "All day within the dreamy house, / The doors upon their hinges creaked; / The blue fly sung in the pane". A board of examiners would lower the mark (for sung read sang), but T. S. Eliot raised the mark: "*The blue fly sung in the pane* (the line would be ruined if you substituted *sang* for *sung*)" (*Selected Essays*, 1951 edition, p. 330). The words sing differently.

[3] Dylan's title has "day" in the singular, "locusts" in the plural. Nathanael West's had them both in the singular: *The Day of the Locust* (1939). He might have come to Dylan's mind, not only because he died the year before Dylan was born but because of the name-changing: Nathan Wallenstein Weinstein (1903–40) into Nathanael West; Robert Allen Zimmerman into Bob Dylan. West hadn't had Allen as his middle name, but he did have Allen within his middle name: Wallenstein.

The locusts sing freely, for free, and ask for no applause. "As I stepped to the stage to pick up my degree": this asks us to remember exactly what Dylan was being honoured for, as well as the fact that these academic ceremonies are themselves performances. But don't prance please. "You might be a rock 'n' roll addict prancing on the stage"[1] but no prancing at Princeton. That would strike a chill.

An unexpected moment, that, when Dylan sings: "And the locusts sang, yeah, it give me a chill". Unexpected, since you might have expected to be given not a chill but a thrill (a word that is then audible in the rhyme that follows, "trill"). But then there is a further unexpectedness in the turn by which "it give me a chill" turns out not to be simply ominous. True, there remains something chilling about the eerie wiry locusts at their tuning-up, but (no less truly) to be given a chill has something positive about it, given that "the weather was hot, a-nearly 90 degrees". Anyway, Dylan has some fellow-feeling for the locusts. They are not the only ones to have been accused of singing "with a high whinin' trill". Added to which, "they were sanging for me": first, in my honour (after their fashion), and second, relieving me of the need to sing, at least just this once. "They were sanging for me", instead of the usual story, my singing for others. And this sympathy with the locusts can be heard to overflow the closing of the song, when what had always been the last line of the refrain just can't keep from spilling over into reiterated happiness and gratitude, held in a small whoop on "well":

> Yeah, the locusts sang and they was sanging for me
> Sanging for me, well, sanging for me

Before the opening exclamation ("Oh, the benches . . ."), we had heard the crickety creaking of the locusts, and we hear it till the sweet end. There is a lot about locusts that goes to build up the atmosphere of the song, the active static in its air. Locusts are migratory (even to the point of getting a capital M: the Migratory Locust, *The Oxford English Dictionary*), like university populations. They, too, are innumerable. Locusts ravage localities, whole districts. (Bloomsbury in London, and Cambridge in Massachusetts, for a start.) How they soar (higher education). They constitute a plague – but

---

[1] *Gotta Serve Somebody*. As to the stage, compare *11 Outlined Epitaphs*: "who have no way of knowin'/that I 'expose' myself/every time I step out/on the stage" (*Lyrics 1962–1985*, 1985, p. 113). See p. 480, on *Eternal Circle*.

then a plague that may be God-given, providential even when punitive.[1] (They take up the housing, they bring in the money.) And they at once batten upon and are battened upon. "Locusts are in many countries used for food" (*The Oxford English Dictionary*). Leviticus 11:22: "Even these of them ye may eat: the locust, after his kind, and the bald locust after his kind."

The bald locust, now there's an image of the university teacher for you. Feeder and feeder-upon. Nourisher and nourishee. In a university, the young may be set against the old. (Dylan was very *young* for an honorary degree on 9 June 1970, not even thirty.) The Bible ponders the locusts within this context of old and young, of fathers and children, of hungry generations. Joel 1:

Hear this, ye old men, and give ear, all ye inhabitants of the land. Hath this been in your days, or even in the days of your fathers? Tell ye your children of it, and let your children tell their children, and their children another generation. That which the palmerworm hath left hath the locust eaten; and that which the locust hath left hath the cankerworm eaten.

"Benches full of men with bald heads", as Matthew Arnold glimpsed it.[2] W. B. Yeats saw another such contrast, that of the old scholar against the young poet from the old days. *The Scholars*:

> Bald heads forgetful of their sins,
> Old, learned, respectable bald heads
> Edit and annotate the lines
> That young men, tossing on their beds,
> Rhymed out in love's despair

[1] Exodus 10 has the word swarming through its verses:

tomorrow will I bring the locusts into thy coast . . . And the Lord said unto Moses, Stretch out thine hand over the land of Egypt for the locusts, that they may come upon the land of Egypt, and eat every herb of the land, even all that the hail hath left . . . and when it was morning, the east wind brought the locusts. And the locusts went up over all the land of Egypt, and rested in all the coasts of Egypt: very grievous were they; before them, there were no such locusts as they, neither after them shall be such. For they covered the face of the whole earth, so that the land was darkened.

Revelation 9:2–3: "and the sun and air were darkened by reason of the smoke of the pit. And there came out of the smoke locusts upon the earth: and unto them was given power." *Day of the Locusts*: "Darkness was everywhere, it smelled like a tomb".

[2] See footnote, p. 194.

> To flatter beauty's ignorant ear.
>
> . . .
>
> Lord, what would they say
> Did their Catullus walk that way?

An editor of Catullus may gain an honorary degree. Would Catullus have gained one?[1] Still, their Dylan walked that way, and the bald heads rallied and rose to the occasion. "Forgetful of their sins", they may have been. Dylan, though, was not forgetful of the need not to fall into the sin of pride.

The word that he sings most exultantly in the whole song is the last word before it enters the final lines of the refrain (four lines that now, for the first and last time, become five): "alive". "Sure was glad to get out of there alive". His voice rides the word in the wind, enlarging and enlivening it. Why does that word so deserve his educing so much from it? Because of what education is, because of the ancient doubt about the ancient universities (and about the new ones, too, come to think of it), that they not only lack life but stultify life. T. S. Eliot wrote to Conrad Aiken, 31 December 1914: "In Oxford I have the feeling that I am not quite alive – that my body is walking about with a bit of my brain inside it, and nothing else. As you know, I hate university towns and university people."[2] Eliot had written two months earlier: "I only mean that Oxford is not intellectually stimulating – but that would be a good deal to ask of a university atmosphere."[3] The life of the mind. The *life* of the mind? Eliot in 1914 may have hated university towns and university people, but in the fullness of time he reached nearly 90 degrees.

"Sure was glad to get out of there alive": Dylan doesn't treat with disrespect the university that had expressed its respect for him. He doesn't diss it but he does josh it. He had, after all, had his death-dealings with colleges. For he had once rhymed, in of all places *Tombstone Blues*, "the old folks home and the college" with "your useless and pointless knowledge". He had moved, in (again of all places) *11 Outlined Epitaphs*, from "get an A" to this:

---

[1] The painter Walter Sickert wrote about the patron Sir Hugh Lane: "Now that Sir Hugh Lane has been knighted for admiring Manet – (I wonder if Manet would ever have been knighted for *being* Manet?), it might perhaps be permissible without blasphemy to speak the sober, unhysterical truth about him" (*A Free House: Being the Writings of Walter Richard Sickert*, ed. Osbert Sitwell, 1947, p. 42).

[2] *Letters*, ed. Valerie Eliot, vol. I (1988), p. 74.

[3] To Eleanor Hinkley, 14 October 1914; *Letters*, vol. I, p. 61.

> an' I stopped cold
> an' bellowed
> "I don't wanna learn no more
> I had enough"
> an' I took a deep breath
> turned around
> an' ran for my life[1]

Thereby getting out of there alive.

The university can come to resemble legal chambers or a court of law, where the hanging judge may be sober but *veritas* is *in vino*. "I glanced into the chamber where the judges were talking". Judges, because of academic judgements. The robes that judges wear, as do dons. The black cap that the judge dons before passing sentence of death, suggestive of the academic cap or mortar-board. The judgments that are passed. But the song moves on from this adverse judgement of its own.

> I glanced into the chamber where the judges were talking
> Darkness was everywhere, it smelled like a tomb
> I was ready to leave, I was already walkin'
> But the next time I looked there was light in the room

Light, and even perhaps enlightenment.

So not all of the university's way of life smells of death. Nevertheless, the life of the song is there in its getting out of there alive. Getting away with it (*sanging!*) is as nothing compared with getting away from it. The rhyme of "my diploma" with "Dakota" (no, with "the black hills of Dakota", made famous in song by Doris Day[2] of the Locusts) good-naturedly invites banter all round.

> I put down my robe, picked up my diploma
> Took a-hold of my sweetheart and away we did drive
> Straight for the hills, the black hills of Dakota
> Sure was glad to get out of there alive

Only the final refrain remains. If this ending happily takes a-hold not only

[1] *Lyrics 1962–1985* (1985), p. 110.
[2] On Doris Day and the song, see Michael Gray, *Song and Dance Man III* (2000), p. 175.

of a sweetheart (the "sweet melody" issuing now in a "sweetheart") but of some sense of how these traditional departures go, it might be by courtesy of Tennyson. He liked nestlings, and within a sequence of poems called *The Day Dream* ("Day" once more) he has a sub-sequence, *The Sleeping Palace*, and this has within it *The Departure*, which has within it these lines:

> And on her lover's arm she leant,
> And round her waist she felt it fold,
> And far across the hills they went
> In that new world which is the old.

Up and away, and out into the university of life. No dropping in, no dropping out. Degrees of honour, but no honorary degrees. Wife to husband, waving a letter: "It's from the University of Life. You've been rejected."

What Can I Do for You?

Good question. Not least because it can range all the way from the least of questions, the inquiry by the shop-assistant (What can I do for you – other of course than imply p'litely that you do have the air of someone who is about to shop-lift . . .[1]), to the deepest of prayers.

> You have given everything to me
> What can I do for You?
> You have given me eyes to see
> What can I do for You?

This is addressed to God, for its profound pronoun is not "you" but "You". Giving this word a hearing is eternally different from giving it a seeing. "You have given me eyes to see", and it is the eyes that can take in with immediate confidence a distinction – that between "you" and "You" – that the ears cannot secure, although they may divine it. It is characteristic of Dylan's sense of how to effect such a distinction unobtrusively that the song should create room for just the one case of the casually lower case

---

[1] "May I help you" to stay out of trouble and the courts . . .

"you": "Soon as a man is born, you know the sparks begin to fly". God is You, but Everyman is you, you know.

Addressed to God, then, the question "What can I do for You?" does not just allow, it demands, the immediate recognition of two opposite answers.

From one point of view (man-the-poor-worm's eye view: *sub specie humanitatis*), the answer to "What can I do for You?", when addressed to the Absolute Being Who is God, is "absolutely nothing". Not "relatively nothing". But from another point of view (under the aspect of eternity: *sub specie aeternitatis*), the answer is "everything". T. S. Eliot wrote of such a condition with a hush that is audible in those sheltering parentheses of his that admit the point:

> A condition of complete simplicity
> (Costing not less than everything)
>   (*Little Gidding*)

What can I do for You? *Nothing.* This is the answer granted by humility. If this may be humiliating as an admission, it is none the worse for that, since without the possibility of humiliation there would never be the possibility of humility. *What Can I Do for You?* seeks humility, and so it comprehends pride. For Pride, alone of the seven deadly sins, has a good side. This isn't a matter of distinguishing a vice from an adjacent virtue (foolhardiness may look like courage but isn't truly courage) but of the distinction that attaches to pride in itself: that it is the word for a virtue, too. The sin that is Envy must often envy Pride this. We do well to have pride in, to take pride in, the right things. Which is where the other answer to the question "What can I do for You?" comes in. *Everything.* By the saving grace that's over me, this goes without saying – though not without praying.

The double assurance, nothing and everything, is an intensification of an interrogative urging of which Dylan has long heard the urgency. He has always felt the force of such questions as must be answered both *yes* and *no* – the force, not the convenience, of this, because having to give two answers, *yes* and *no*, is not at all the same as having recourse to the slurred syphonation of *yes-and-no*, evasively lazy in its lackadaisical lack of convictions. (Do you want to undertake this responsibility? We-ll, yes-and-no . . .) "I'm not askin' you to say words like 'yes' or 'no'" (*Mama, You Been on My Mind*) – but I may be asking you to say both the words *yes* and *no*.

William Empson once gave an example from, as it happens, a poet whom

Dylan – his true words spoken in jest – has respectfully bantered. (The interviewer asked why Dylan had deigned to come to the Isle of Wight. Answer: To see the home of Alfred Lord Tennyson.) Empson:

In place of stating a contradiction it is often possible to ask a question whose answer is both yes and no; this device is particularly frequent when an author is adopting a "poetical" style, so that he often wants to say things of greater logical complexity than his method will allow. It makes less parade of its complexity than any other.

> But who hath seen her wave her hand?
> Or at the casement seen her stand?
> Or is she known in all the land,
> The Lady of Shalott?

Yes and no. She is not *known* personally to anybody *in all the land*, but everybody *knows* of her as a legend. Both these facts heighten the dramatic effect, and they are both conveyed by the single question.[1]

Take the heightened dramatic effect of the soul-searching question "Are you ready?" You risk your soul if you answer this simply or solely *yes*, for that way the wrong kind of pride lies; but you had better not answer it simply *no*, for such simple soleness has a way of settling into the other complacency that is hopelessness. There are pincer-jaws you start to feel. As in the double admonition that Samuel Beckett attributed to St Augustine, although no one seems ever to have found the exact words there (I dreamed I saw in St Augustine . . .): "Do not despair, one of the thieves was saved; do not presume, one of the thieves was damned."

"Are you ready?": you might answer this, escaping both despair and presumption, as Dylan does in *Are You Ready?*, "I hope I'm ready." Another of these questionable interrogations is "How does it feel?", roundly revolved as though it were not just your common-or-garden rolling stone but the one that Sisyphus will eternally roll and re-roll. "How does it feel?" is a question that has to be answered *terrible* and *wonderful*. It is wonderful to be "on your own, with no direction home, like a rolling stone", but it is at the same instant terrible.

---

[1] *Seven Types of Ambiguity* (1930, second edition 1947), p. 182.

Dylan's imaginative decisions in the singing of *What Can I Do for You?* are an inseparable part (which is not to say that they are an indistinguishable part) of the song's penetrative power. You can feel it and you can hear it. For instance, in the way in which, from the beginning, the title question "What can I do for You?" is sung by him with an impetuosity, an eagerness, that runs slightly ahead of the music and of the other voices (a chorus that begs to differ).

The pattern is of a quatrain followed by a quintain, five lines following four lines; what saves this from being at sixes and sevens is the consummation of both shapings with the timed timeless question itself.

You have given everything to me
What can I do for You?
You have given me eyes to see
What can I do for You?

Pulled me out of bondage and You made me renewed inside
Filled up a hunger that had always been denied
Opened up a door no man can shut and You opened it up so wide
And You've chosen me to be among the few
What can I do for You?

You have laid down Your life for me
What can I do for You?
You have explained every mystery
What can I do for You?

Soon as a man is born, you know the sparks begin to fly
He gets wise in his own eyes and he's made to believe a lie
Who would deliver him from the death he's bound to die?
Well, You've done it all and there's no more anyone can pretend to do
What can I do for You?

By this point in the song it has become established that the words of the eternal question are not perfectly in time with the music that accompanies the question or with the accompanying questioners. This imperfection is a touching effect, a human haste, an anxious hopeful striving, and it is at the same time something less than a perfectly disciplined resignation to the will of God, something less than fitting. It is only in the last verse, in the very last line, that Dylan's voice reins itself in more to the music's timing and to a chastened patience – yet (and this is what saves the singing of the song from spiritual complacency) even there the congruity isn't quite perfect, isn't a claim to conclusive sanctity such as would be sanctimonious.

> I know all about poison, I know all about fiery darts
> I don't care how rough the road is, show me where it starts
> Whatever pleases You, tell it to my heart
> Well, I don't deserve it but I sure did make it through
> What can I do for You?

It is with tender unfieriness that he sings ruefully that he knows all about "fiery darts". The benevolent contrariety between the words and the voicing might take you back to its political counterpart, the freedom from aggression with which he softeningly sang "How many times must the cannonballs fly?", his pacific voice giving to the cannonballs the gentleness of cottonwool.[1] Except that Dylan doesn't sing simply "fiery darts" but something of a pun, combining "doubts" (sufficiently suggested for this to be the word that was printed in the *Saved* song-book, though *Writings and Drawings* and *Lyrics 1962–1985* have "darts") with "darts", the word that is asked for by both the rhyme (*darts / starts / heart*, positioned where the previous verses have given the sure-footed *inside / denied / wide*, and *fly / lie / die*) and by the biblical allusion: "The shield of faith, wherewith ye shall be able to quench all the fiery darts of the wicked" (Ephesians 6:16). Dylan's phrasing and voicing amount to a great act of quenching. The fiery darts of the wicked are quenched, first by the coolness of his voice's utterance and next by the tempering of the words, so that there is this tentative doubt as to whether we heard "darts" at all or "doubts". But then the fiery darts of the wicked may imperfectly well turn out to be those doubts with which the devil pricks us.

The effect of the doubt (doubts or darts?) is a very dramatic one, not only in its subdued intensity but in being characteristic of drama as a medium, for within a performing art – Shakespeare's tragedies, Dylan's songs – the ear possesses an extraordinary compensation for its sacrifice of the particular certainty that the eye can command. ("You have given me eyes to see", yet once more.) For the eye can see at a glance whether the word is "doubts" or "darts", with the page then being the gainer by this. And the loser by it.

[1] See p. 326.

For the ear that hears the echoes within recesses may be blessed as well as cursed by the doubt as to the very words. This, too, may be a two-edged weapon. Macbeth cries out that he should be the last person to murder Duncan:

> He's here in double trust;
> First, as I am his kinsman, and his subject,
> Strong both against the deed; then as his host,
> Who should against his murderer shut the door,
> Not bear the knife myself.
>
> (I, vii)

Not bear the knife, and not bare the knife. "Is this a dagger which I see before me? . . . I see thee yet, in form as palpable / As this which now I draw . . . / And on thy blade, and dudgeon, gouts of blood" (II, i).

When Dylan draws upon our doubts as to whether the word is doubts or darts, he is sounding a traditional doubt as to the word "doubt": that, being sturdily foursquare, it doesn't sound as though it doubts a bit, unlike (say) the breathy undulating word "hesitate". Samuel Beckett fastened on the discrepancy between what the word "doubt" sounds like and what it means, in arguing that the English language stands in need of James Joyce, the abstraction-buster:

It is worth remarking that no language is so sophisticated as English. It is abstracted to death. Take the word "doubt": it gives hardly any sensuous suggestion of hesitancy, of the necessity for choice, or static irresolution. Whereas the German "Zweifel" does, and, in lesser degree, the Italian "dubitare". Mr Joyce recognises how inadequate "doubt" is to express a state of extreme uncertainty, and replaces it by "in twosome twiminds".[1]

It is the song's progress that contains and releases these local movements of twimind as to darts and doubts. What the singer, like any devout lover, cannot but crave is entire reciprocity – and yet entire reciprocity with God is unimaginable, unthinkable, even blasphemous. It would be an act of pride, incompatible with the humility that occupies not the high moral ground but its opposite, the honourably low moral ground. From

---

[1] In *Our Exagmination . . .* (1929), p. 15. I discuss this in *Beckett's Dying Words* (1993), pp. 51–5.

the very beginning, we are taken down into a yearning for the perfect matching reciprocity of an answer, for a true fit: the divine justice of the true, the wholly true, and the nothing but the true, fit. And continually the song has the honest patience to deny us this. "Patience, hard thing", as Hopkins understood. Hard, as difficult to achieve, and as being a steeling of oneself.[1]

So the first line, "You have given everything to me", is not followed by – not matched with – the hollow insecurity of an echo (which would be "What can *I* give to *You*?"), but by the unremitting question that is central and yet at a tangent: "What can I do for You?"

It is this imperfect alignment that (throughout the opening verses) animates the relation of statements ("You have ... You have ..." – where Dylan divides the cadence and the words at exactly that point, repeatedly) to the succeeding question, "What can I do for You?" But then Dylan varies this pattern (as he so beautifully does, just when he would seem to have settled into cordial parallels and reversals, in *Do Right to Me, Baby*). For in these succeeding instances, he now comes very near to finding the reciprocity that he hungers for – and yet still not quite there. So near and yet not achieved so far. The second quintain ends with:

> Well, You've done it all and there's no more anyone can pretend to do
> What can I do for You?

– this offering a new parallelism in the return: "You've done it all" / "What can I do for You?" And then this is itself succeeded, in the third quintain, by a phrasing that varies the terms of this while repeating its shape:

> You have given all there is to give
> What can I give to You?[2]

But still neither of these is the exact, the exacting, fit, the perfect returning of a question to its acknowledgement, that is aspired to. For the move is neither (in the former instance) from "You've done it all *for me*" to "What can I do *for* You?", nor (in the latter) from "You have given *me* all there is to give" to "What can I give *to* You?"

[1] "Patience, hard thing! the hard thing but to pray, / But bid for, Patience is!"
[2] Sung so; as printed in *Lyrics 1962–1985*, "do for You".

It is at this point that Dylan reaches for – better, reaches – the realization that the question itself must be turned so that it will, in its very questioning, return a true answer:[1]

> You have given me life to live
> How can I live for You?

Not "*What* can I *do* for You?" – or "give to You?" – but "*How* can I live for You?"

The deepest question turns out not to be a *what* question but a *how* one – which is one true way of seeing the truth of gratitude and of a due humility, a due abstention from pride. "How can I live for You?" It is with this recognition that Dylan can then legitimately return to asking the good old (not the even better new) question, with his mild matching of "Whatever pleases" with "What":

> Whatever pleases You, tell it to my heart
> Well, I don't deserve it but I sure did make it through
> What can I do for You?

The key question, the one that unlocks the heart, has proved to be "How can I live for You?", but it is good that the other question, the question that gives the song not only its title but its refrain, is never shucked or shucksed: "What can I do for You?" In this, it resembles the words that come and go before the arrival at the best that (spiritually) the song can do. For instance, weight should be given to the fact that, alone of the three quatrains, the middle one is given no "given" (the others have it twice):

> You have laid down Your life for me
> What can I do for You?
> You have explained every mystery
> What can I do for You?

Or, as to recurrences, there is the fact – which asks some explaining – that the final verse, the one in which the singer comes closest to achieving the unegotistical state not just of mind but of soul that is sought, is the

---

[1] For Dylan on questions that truthfully answer themselves in some way, see p. 420.

one that most goes in for *I, me, my*: "me" and "my" once each, and "I"
six times.

> I know all about poison, I know all about fiery darts
> I don't care how rough the road is, show me where it starts
> Whatever pleases You, tell it to my heart
> Well, I don't deserve it but I sure did make it through
> What can I do for You?

How can this "I" be at one with humility, with the repudiation of egotism?
Because any such presence or absence of, say, the first-person pronoun is
always an axis, not a direction. "I don't care how rough the road is", and it
is characteristic of roads that they run in two opposite directions. Sometimes
the reluctance to say "I" may be the sign of humility, sometimes the very
opposite. ("I think" may be much less egotistical than "we think" – or than
"one thinks".) The reiteration of *I, me, my* is frank in its plea, its prayer, its
acknowledging that self-attention is inescapable and is not necessarily only
self-serving. "Show me" is not mealy-mouthed. "And You've chosen me
to be among the few". Matthew 20:16: "So the last shall be first, and the
first last: for many be called, but few chosen."

   Paul Williams, who was quick to see the power of Dylan's Christian
songs, was too quick to condemn what had become the song's ending,
preferring the earlier wording that Dylan had sung in the concerts of late
1979 ("I don't deserve it but I have made it through"):[1]

On *What Can I Do for You?*, which is either a song of total humility or else it's
nothing, an indication of the problem with the whole vocal (the attitude of the
vocal) can be found when Dylan sings, "I don't deserve it but I *sure did* make it
through". This bit of boasting shifts the focus of the song; the original lyrics and
performance here conveyed the subtly (but extremely) different message that "I
didn't deserve to survive, but You chose to bring me through and so my life is
Yours, please help me find a way to begin to show my devotion". Instead the
new vocal almost suggests that Dylan made it because he was smart enough to
buy a ticket on the right train. Ouch.[2]

To this, I would vouchsafe a counter-ouch. ("'How are you?' he said to

---

[1] *Saved* was recorded in February 1980.
[2] *Dylan One Year Later* (1980), p. 6.

me / I said it back to him".) For one thing, "almost suggests" is almost weasel-wording. For another, Williams mis-listens. "This bit of boasting"? Not so, for what is audible is not the squeak of pride (I knew it, I knew it) but the stilled voice of surprise (this, I could not have known, even though "I know all about poison, I know all about fiery darts"). "The new vocal almost suggests . . .": evasive. If it only *almost* suggests . . . then it doesn't suggest any such thing, does it? But anyway, where Paul Williams most goes wrong is exactly at the point where he announces – with pride – what is for him an indisputability: *What Can I Do for You?* is "either a song of total humility or else it's nothing". Rather the reverse, for the beginning of wisdom when it comes to humility will be the acknowledgement that *total* humility is totally out of the question. Anyone who believes that such a thing is possible to human beings, to say nothing of believing that he or she has achieved such a state, may proudly look forward to being in a very select circle of hell. Proudly, and conceitedly. "I do know that God hates a proud look" (Dylan, on *Biograph*).

Proverbs 26:12: "Seest thou a man wise in his own conceit? there is more hope of a fool than of him."

> Soon as a man is born, you know the sparks begin to fly
> He gets wise in his own eyes and he's made to believe a lie

Isaiah 5:20: "Woe unto them that are wise in their own eyes." Proverbs 3:7: "Be not wise in thine own eyes." To be wise in your own eyes is one thing; to get wise in your own eyes gets a further charge, a smouldering resentment ignited to aggression: Don't you get wise with me. The smouldering is anticipated by those sparks, where again Dylan both respects and recharges a biblical warning.[1] Job 5:7: "Yet man is born unto trouble, as the sparks fly upward." The sparks fly upward. Extinguished. The sparks begin to fly? *The Oxford English Dictionary*: "heated words are spoken, friction or excited action occurs". *American Speech* (1929) : "It was also said of an angry woman that 'she will make the sparks fly'." The sin of pride incites the sin of anger.

Dylan not only opens his Bible, he opens up its radiations and its

---

[1] Dylan, *Biograph*: "The Bible says 'Even a fool when he keeps his mouth shut is counted wise,' but it comes from the Bible, so it can be cast off as being too quote religious. Make something religious and people don't have to deal with it, they can say it's irrelevant."

revelations. Revelation 3:8: "I have set before thee an open door, and no man can shut it."

> Opened up a door no man can shut and You opened it up so wide

So wide a line, this, in the singing, opened so extensively. *What Can I Do for You?* is as deep as it is wide. And never wide-eyed.

When Robert Shelton reviewed *Saved*, he (even he who had, from the first, heard Dylan so well) announced that "three of the slower numbers" – one of them being *What Can I Do for You?* – "frankly don't touch me at all".[1] A blasphemous thought rises up, about Shelton and those three numbers: thou shalt deny me thrice. "You have given me eyes to see". Ears, too. He that hath ears to hear, let him hear. And having ears, hear ye not?

Disease of Conceit

> Comes right out of nowhere
> And you're down for the count

The pugilistic punch in *Disease of Conceit* does itself come right out of nowhere, suddenly, not even "*It* comes right out of nowhere", a right hook thirty-five lines into the song. (Where are we now, all of a sudden? In at the killing of Davey Moore?) But no amount of ducking or weaving will stop the blow from landing. "And you're down for the count". Eight . . . Nine . . . Ten. Not just down but out.

Who killed Davey Moore? "'Not I,' says the referee", and every other participant promptly joins in the chorus of refusals to think ill of oneself.

What kills? The disease of conceit, *I* and *I* again. Is it a coincidence that the lines of each verse in *Disease of Conceit* count to ten?

> There's a whole lot of people suffering tonight
> From the disease of conceit
> Whole lot of people struggling tonight
> From the disease of conceit
> Come right down the highway
> Straight down the line

[1] *Melody Maker* (21 June 1980).

> Rips into your senses
> Through your body and your mind
> Nothing about it that's sweet
> The disease of conceit

The verse's closing line, the line that reaches the "it's all over now" number that is ten, finds itself pounding away at the same spot, the four words that end both the second line and the fourth line of each verse: "The disease of conceit". But Dylan makes a final point of the final words of the song by having them take up into themselves not just those four words "The disease of conceit" but the deadly preposition "from" that so often introduces those words, right down the highway of the song: "From the disease of conceit". This five-word line tolls through the song, being the second and fourth line of all four verses. And yet in the tenth and closing line of the first three verses it doesn't take exactly this form, for there it doesn't insist, as the word "From" does, on the fatal infection, the cause. "The disease of conceit": that is how the first three verses end. But the termination of the song is the moment that records the infection's having spread terminally from the "From . . ." lines, and it presses this on us unrelentingly by pressing the "*from* = the cause" use of the preposition "from" against the other kind of "from", "*from* = the starting point". From starting point to finishing point.

> Then they bury you from your head to your feet
> From the disease of conceit

It is a graceless run of words, not a run but a ponderous plod, and you can imagine a misguided guide telling the author of it not to be so cumbrously stumbling, so lumpish on his feet. But just remember "the eagle eye with the flat feet" (Empson's phrase for George Orwell). And there is something indeflectibly honest about Dylan's flat-footedly pounding the lines here, policeman-like. Dylan as bobby. "From your head to your feet from"? But this uncouth refusal to have any mincing words or any mincing steps is the gawkily awkward right thing. Inelegant? True. Sorry about that, but such is the nature of the case.

> Nothing about it that's sweet
> The disease of conceit
>
> Ain't nothing too discreet
> 'Bout the disease of conceit

Nothing about it that's graceful, the disease of conceit. Ain't nothing too fleet of foot 'bout the disease of conceit.

> Then they bury you from your head to your feet
> From the disease of conceit

From . . . to . . . From: in death, there will be no further *to* to look forward to.

The song starts in the tone of, and with the idiom of, a ruminative report. "There's a whole lot of people . . .": this has a particular movement of the head as it reflects on life or reflects life, shaking its mind sadly over something, not pointing its finger sharply at something.

> There's a whole lot of people suffering tonight
> From the disease of conceit
> Whole lot of people struggling tonight
> From the disease of conceit

"There's a whole lot . . .", when it returns, has been contracted into a pensive puckering of the mouth: "Whole lot of people . . ." Not much may seem to change from the first two lines to the next two, but – all the same – things have changed: "There's a whole lot of people", pursed down to "Whole lot of people". And "suffering tonight / From the disease of conceit" is other than what off-rhymes with it: "struggling tonight / From the disease of conceit".[1] Struggling *from*? As a result of? Because of? But these are not the same. You know what he means, but he also means you to sense the counter-currents of the wording: you struggle with or you struggle against, you don't struggle from – though you do struggle to get away from. All sung more in sorrow than in anger.

Of the forty-four lines of the song, thirteen (not a lucky number) repeat "the disease of conceit": three in each verse, and the surprising one that begins the four-line bridge. Surprising, not because it comes out of nowhere but because it comes out of everywhere. After having already been warned nine times about "the disease of conceit", we nevertheless still need to be told that conceit is a disease.

---

[1] Off-rhyming here, just this once. The ensuing opening rhymes come straight down the line: *breaking tonight / shaking tonight, dying tonight / crying tonight*, and *in trouble tonight / seeing double tonight*.

> Conceit is a disease
> But the doctors got no cure
> They've done a lot of research on it
> But what it is, they're still not sure

The solemn assurance is grimly sardonic, you can be sure of that. Listen to how Dylan tilts the word "research": not "reséarch" but "rée-search", with réespect for the authorities even though they haven't yet made the medical breakthrough.

"Right down the highway". "Straight down the line". Down, down. "And you're down for the count". And don't forget that "You may be the heavyweight champion of the world" (*Gotta Serve Somebody*), "But you're gonna have to serve somebody". Which is the home truth that just might be the home remedy that you need against the disease of conceit.

But wait, the differences of weight must mean that this can't be a fair fight. I don't mean the fight between any one of us and our domesticated enemy, conceit. No, the fight between the words "disease" and "conceit". Disease is a heavyweight. Conceit is bantam weight. It is overweening (see the dictionary) but not overweight. What does the promoter think he's promoting? Where's the ref?

At which point the ref puts it to you that you're wrong about conceit. It may look slight on its feet, but it packs a punch. From the ring, you can't run away, so you will not live to fight another day.

> Comes right out of nowhere
> And you're down for the count
> From the outside world
> The pressure will mount
> Turn you into a piece of meat
> The disease of conceit

Conceit – which likes to come on as though it is no big deal – can be death-dealing, the disease of conceit. And as soon as conceit is at work inside you, a pressure inside you, then it will join forces with the outside world. The enemy is within the gates. The outside world – say, the world outside the ring, those who are yelling for blood, and who are putting mounting pressure on those slugging it out in the ring, and who are enjoying the thought that one or both of the boxers will be turned into a piece of meat: the outside world will be only too keen to collude with your intestinal disease. The pressure within Dylan's lines, the stress, isn't on the word "world", but on "outside": not "From the outside *world*", but "From the *outside* world / The pressure will mount". The inside world already has its swollen pressure from within. The pressure mounts; you mount above yourself. Doctor Faustus was uplifted –

> Till, swollen with cunning of a self conceit
> His waxen wings did mount above his reach.[1]

The disease has entered. The grim casualness of "Steps into your room" is followed at once by "Eats into your soul":

> Steps into your room
> Eats into your soul

– conceit behaving as "love that's pure" does not, for love that's pure "Won't sneak up into your room" (*Watered-Down Love*).

The song's pressures put all this to you, aware of the resistance that its severe judgement on conceit is likely to meet, aware that conceit is good at suggesting that its stakes are not high, let alone sharp. Like vanity,[2] conceit is shallow and petty, so can it really inflict any deep harm? Yes, for conceit, unlike pride and arrogance, wreaks its destruction by not seeming, on the superficial face of it, to be anything like as heftily dangerous as the other members of the Family.

There's a whole lot of contrarieties in *Disease of Conceit*. The jarring weight of the clangorous chords at the very beginning of the song, the sombre pace as though a judge in his grandeur were solemnly donning the black cap before passing the death sentence that is its final words:

> Give ya delusions of grandeur
> And an evil eye
> Give ya the idea that
> You're too good to die
> Then they bury you from your head to your feet
> From the disease of conceit

[1] Marlowe, *Doctor Faustus*, prologue.
[2] "God got the power, man has got his vanity" (*Ain't No Man Righteous*). Think how different "man has got his pride" would be, bringing home that pride, unlike vanity and unlike conceit, can be a good thing, self-respect for instance.

– *eye* into *idea* into *die*: these are weighty matters to ponder. Mark 7:22: "deceit, lasciviousness, an evil eye, blasphemy, pride, foolishness: all these evil things come from within, and defile the man". But at the same time there is this contradictory impulse, something sinisterly weightless. For the word "disease" has a kind of weight that the word "conceit" disarmingly and dangerously lacks, disarmed to the teeth. We know well enough, thank you, that conceit is not a good thing, but is it really such a destructively bad thing? Doesn't it suggest the hollow, the empty, the puffed up, as against the tonnage that terror carries? Pride, we admit, carries weight, and when Dylan summons the *Foot of Pride*, he brings it down with the biblical weight of the Psalmist's cry: "Let not the foot of pride come against me, and let not the hand of the wicked remove me."[1] But *conceit*?

Yet the swollen distention, with its pressure, can be that of disease. The Bible understands the gravity of conceit, and *Disease of Conceit* is, among other things, set upon restoring to what might seem to be a petty word a pressing sense of its ancient menace. "Wise in his own conceit": three times in one chapter of Proverbs alone.[2] Romans 12:16: "Be not wise in your own conceits." Which entails being wise about the word itself and how its modern-day triviality may disguise its deadliness.

Understatement is a way of ensuring that the song, though weighty, never becomes overweight. The unexpected epithets for conceit are those that say the most, to say the least.

> Nothing about it that's sweet
> The disease of conceit
>
> Ain't nothing too discreet
> 'Bout the disease of conceit

Itself very discreet, the word "discreet" there. Such words, "sweet" and "discreet", feel at once full and empty: full of an underlying understated threat, empty of any lying or huffing and puffing. And the same effect is created by the process and progress of the refrain. It is in the nature of a refrain that its reiteration makes it both more full and more empty every

[1] Psalms 36:11.

[2] Proverbs 26:5: "Answer a fool according to his folly, lest he be wise in his own conceit." 26:12: "Seest thou a man wise in his own conceit? there is more hope of a fool than of him." 26:16: "The sluggard is wiser in his own conceit than seven men that can render a reason."

time it returns. A refrain needs to be both concentrated and concentrated upon. So the deeply imaginative uses of refrain are always ones that don't just deny or deplore the fact that there is an emptying process that goes on when you say something again and again and again (your own name, for instance, getting more and more evacuated of you yourself as you go on repeating it). No, the intense resourcefulness of a refrain is shown when there is in the song or poem some appropriate engagement with this very condition: when getting at once fuller in some ways and emptier in other ways is the grim point, the poignant plight. Which is where conceit comes in, steps into your room, eats into your soul. The fuller you are of conceit, the emptier you are of everything else, including yourself, your self.

"Disease", when the word is figurative and not literal, means "a deranged, depraved, or morbid condition (of mind or disposition); an evil affection or tendency". 1607: "Ambitious pride that been [i.e. that was] my youth's disease"; or, the disease of pride. Conceit is "an overweening opinion of oneself; over-estimation of one's own qualities, personal vanity or pride". Granted, vanity and pride are often in the company of conceit, but they aren't the same and they don't have the same heft and weft. It may be worth calling up the old sense of conceit to mean "a (morbid) affection or seizure of the body or mind", that is, a disease. (To take a conceipt, or conceit, was to sicken.) Worth calling up, perhaps, not because Dylan is a great man for browsing in dictionaries (though he may very well be: *A-Bazouki*), but because anything that the English language has a way of comprehending (the relation of conceit to disease?) is likely to be something that a very resourceful adept of the English language may well be in touch with, in harmony with.

Two further pressures contribute to the saddened and saddening weight of the song. First, the disease of conceit is one that you can suffer from without really knowing it; you can suffer from it without exactly *suffering*.

> There's a whole lot of people suffering tonight
> From the disease of conceit

For the cunning of conceit (Marlowe's "cunning of a self conceit") is that it may find its pleasure in not giving you pain. At least, not yet a while. It is happy to bide its time, like the tumour that prefers to give no warning. "Comes out of nowhere". Some of the people glimpsed in Dylan's song clearly know that they are suffering even though they don't know what from: "There's a whole lot of hearts breaking tonight", "Whole lot of people crying tonight". But some do not. Seeing double, they don't see the half of it. T. S. Eliot saw this as an understanding bitterly arrived at in Djuna Barnes's novel *Nightwood*:

The miseries that people suffer through their particular abnormalities of temperament are visible on the surface: the deeper design is that of the human misery and bondage which is universal. In normal lives this misery is mostly concealed; often, what is most wretched of all, concealed from the sufferer more effectively than from the observer.[1]

Last, and lacerating, there is the fact that "conceit" is from the Latin for conceiving, conception. So there is something peculiarly horrible about all the death that conceit deals. It ought to be a word that is on the side of life. It isn't. Not least because it likes to "give ya the idea that / You're too good to die". Too bad, this thinking too well of oneself.

[1] Introduction to Djuna Barnes, *Nightwood* (New York, 1937).

The Virtues

Justice

The Lonesome Death of Hattie Carroll

Many of Dylan's songs hinge upon the cardinal virtue that is justice ("cardinal" means pertaining to a hinge). The songs turn upon justice, while – in the opposing or oppositional sense of "turn upon" – they turn upon *in*justice. There can be no grosser injustices than those perpetrated by the law itself, by justices, and the most heartfelt of Dylan's remonstrations is *The Lonesome Death of Hattie Carroll*. It is a song that brings home the falsity of the boast – on this occasion at the very least – that "the courts are on the level". This is why the song has not only to level with us but to be unremittingly level in its tone, verbally and vocally. Well judged in its dismay at what had been so ill judged.

The deadly sin of the aggressor who killed Hattie Carroll was anger, impatience bursting into unwarrantable anger. He is "the person who killed for no reason / Who just happened to be feelin' that way without warnin'". The truthful surprise is the double sense of "without warning" – without warning to other people but also without warning (since anger suddenly erupts) to Zanzinger himself. Zanzinger's name just happens to contain, in sequence, *a n g e r*. But he could not contain his anger. The song (a triumph that must never sound triumphant) movingly resists temptation and is patient, containing its anger. Oh, the anger is there all right, but to be contained, to be held in check in contrast.

The Lonesome Death of Hattie Carroll is the coinciding of a newspaper item with a cadence.

> William Zanzinger killed poor Hattie Carroll
> With a cane that he twirled around his diamond ring finger
> At a Baltimore hotel society gath'rin'

William Zanzinger, Hattie Carroll. The thing about those names – you might say that this starts as purely technical, but then, as T. S. Eliot said, "we cannot say at what point 'technique' begins or where it ends"[1] – is their

---

[1] *The Sacred Wood* (1920), preface to the 1928 edition, p. ix.

endings. What the killer and the killed have in common is that, in both their first names and their surnames, they've got feminine endings. She's Háttĭe Cárrŏll, where in both of her names the first syllable is stressed [Cárroll] and the last is unstressed [Carrŏll], and he's Wíllĭam Zanzíngĕr, where again his first name is stressed on the first syllable and where his surname, though it has the second syllable stressed, again has its last syllable unstressed. Dylan heard this, and the song is founded upon the particular cadence of their real-life names (except only that there should be a *t*: Zantzinger) and a real death.

It is a cadence that perhaps explains why Dylan wanted the word "lonesome" in the title, where it can evoke a contrast between the loneliness of dying, of her dying, and the crowded hotel ("At a Baltimore hotel society gath'rin'"). The word "lonesome" is not to be heard in the song itself, wisely, since there it might have invited a lover's complaint (within this particular song and its responsibilities, unlike in *Tomorrow Is a Long Time*, "lonesome would mean nothing to you at all"[1]), but the word does set a scene, or rather set a cadence: *Thĕ Lónesŏme Déath ŏf Háttĭe Cárrŏll.*

The first line of the first verse begins with his name and brings her name to its end: "William Zanzinger killed poor Hattie Carroll". The second verse begins with his name: "William Zanzinger, who had twenty-four years".[2] The third verse begins with hers: "Hattie Carroll was a maid in the kitchen" and it ends (leading into the refrain) with his name: "And she never done nothing to William Zanzinger". The fourth verse, the final verse, closes the case: "William Zanzinger with a six-month sentence". In this final verse he had been, at first, "the person who killed for no reason". At this appearance in the dock, he was not named.

The double challenge to the song lay in its duty not to yield to the anger that had seized Zanzinger, and in its duty to resist melodrama and sentimentality. Dylan knows what he does in adopting this cadence. For the feminine ending naturally evokes a dying fall or courage in the face either of death or of loss, something falling poignantly away. This can be heard in Wordsworth:

> The thought of death sits easy on the man
> Who has been born and dies among the mountains.
>   (*The Brothers*, 182–3)

---

[1] In the love songs *Tomorrow Is a Long Time* and *Boots of Spanish Leather*, the word means much.

[2] Dylan sings "had"; as printed in *Lyrics 1962–1985* (1985), "at".

The móuntăins. And it's imperative that the thought of death not sit easy on the man who has been born and dies among the *hills*, rocks, crags, or any of those words. The masculine ending ("the man", as it happens) is in tension with the feminine ending ("móuntăins"). Not this:

> The thought of death sits easy on the pérsŏn
> Who has been born and dies among the móuntăins.

And not this:

> The thought of death sits easy on the man
> Who has been born and dies among the hills.

What the voice has to do in apprehending Wordsworth's very wording, "Who has been born and dies among the mountains", is breathe life into the final syllable, as though it were a flag that will lapse into limpness unless it can be made to ripple out resiliently. The cadence will fall away unless the voice holds it up, holds it forth. The ending may choose to acquiesce, or it may resist: there is an axis, and the energies may run in either direction. These properties of language are like the paradoxical properties of everyday soap: the very thing that makes it so slippery when wet is what makes it stick so obdurately to the side of the bath as it dries.

In this cadence, Dylan fashioned his song, which is steeled and steely in support of "the gentle". From the start, he established this movement, inexorable in its sadness and in its curbed indignation. Duly monotonous, provided that we understand here what William Empson understood in the great double sestina of Philip Sidney: "The poem beats, however rich its orchestration, with a wailing and immovable monotony, for ever upon the same doors in vain."[1] Always, in the verses of Dylan's song, there is this last dying fall, a cadence that advances like nemesis. This is what Dylan hears from the beginning, having us not only hear it but listen to it.

> William Zanzinger killed poor Hattie Carroll
> With a cane that he twirled around his diamond ring finger

---

[1] *Seven Types of Ambiguity* (1930, second edition 1947), p. 36.

> At a Baltimore hotel society gath'rin'
> And the cops was called in and his weapon took from him

– where the fourth line is notably, differently, vivid, in bringing out that the feminine ending doesn't depend upon how many syllables there are in the closing word. It's not "his weapon took from *him*" (as against from someone else), it's "his weapon took *from* him", so that within "from him" the word "him", although it's a monosyllable, is a feminine ending, isn't where the stress is carried.[1] There is only one moment when this cadence of the verses is broken, and it's when he fells her. "Got killed by a blow, lay slain by a cane" – not "Got killed by a blow, lay slain by a trúnchĕon":

> Got killed by a blow, lay slain by a cane
> That sailed through the air and came down through the room

– not "came down through the lóbbў" or "came down through the chámbĕr". What happens in this terrible quiet moment is that there's an amputation, which is exactly understated and yet is registered. Something – a life – is cut short, curtailed by curt brutality, at that moment, and this without the song's having to melodramatize it. A cutting short of what had seemed an unchanging cadence: that will do it.

A cadence runs throughout the song. (Ah, but not quite so, for there is the refrain, for which we wait. And shall wait now for a moment.) There may be the effect of an internal rhyme (for there is no external rhyme, rhyme at the line-endings, in the body of the verses, as against the refrain), as when "Got killed by a blow, lay *slain* by a *cane*" comes back in the self-satisfaction of the judge: "he *spoke* through his *cloak*, most deep

---

[1] T. S. Eliot, in *Little Gidding*, II, has an alternation of feminine and masculine endings, arriving at the end of the seventh line at just such a monosyllable that is unstressed, a feminine ending ("sóund wăs"):

> In the uncertain hour before the morning
> Near the ending of interminable night
> At the recurrent end of the unending
> After the dark dove with the flickering tongue
> Had passed below the horizon of his homing
> While the dead leaves still rattled on like tin
> Over the asphalt where no other sound was

and distinguished". That's the only other moment when you've got a line that has this form of internal rhyme, and it's the moment when the judge had better remember that he is there because a woman "lay slain by a cane" (there's very strong assonance as well: *lay / slain / cane*).[1]

Hattie Carroll has her enslaved rhyming – or rather non-rhyming, since a rhyme would offer *some* change in wording, some relief from monotony – of "the table . . . the table . . . the table" as the grim ending of three consecutive lines:

> And never sat once at the head of the table
> And didn't even talk to the people at the table
> Who just cleaned up all the food from the table
> And emptied the ashtrays on a whole other level

She never appears by name in the final verse (but then he is not at first named there, though his turn will come), but she is still there, because when this verse begins –

> In the courtroom of honor, the judge pounded his gavel
> To show that all's equal and that the courts are on the level

– *gavel / equal / level* must call us back not only to the word "level" from before ("And emptied the ashtrays on a whole other level"), but to everything that has sounded within "Carroll", "table", "table", "table", "level". That's her sound, that *-l*. And it goes with the "gentle": Zanzinger with his cane had been "Doomed and determined to destroy all the gentle".

It's very brave not to mention her, or her name, at the end. It's not shrugging her off, it's shouldering what happened to her, and what then. For now it is too late. Now is the time for your tears. Or as he sings, "For now's the time for your tears". If I'd had the genius to come up with the song, I fear that – having sung "Now ain't the time for your tears" all

---

[1] Often noted in *Hattie Carroll* has been the spectral presence of Cain (identical with *cane* to the ear that hears, though not to the eye that reads): "slain by a cane". "To lay cane [*Cain*] upon Abel; to beat any one with a cane or stick" (Francis Grose, *Vulgar Tongue*). A rhyme is wielded in *Every Grain of Sand*: "Like Cain I now behold this chain of events that I must break", and Cain and Abel put in their appearance in *Desolation Row*. As for *Hattie Carroll*: "The table . . . the table . . . the table": does this *-able* prepare for the word that soon follows, "cane"? Cain and Abel, masculine and feminine endings.

the way through till now – I would have gratified myself emphatically by
singing "Now *is* the time for your tears". He doesn't sing "Now is", he sings
"Now's". The contraction at the very end quietly takes out anything hotly
hortatory.

The body of the song, the verse proper, refuses to rhyme (very unusually
for Dylan); instead it has the different relentlessness of the gentle, there
in the cadence with its feminine ending. But the refrain, the wheel, on
the contrary is distinctly, bracingly, different: it is all masculine endings
and it rhymes insistently: *disgrace / fears / face / tears*. There are two syllables
to "disgrace", but it's not a feminine ending, not dísgrace but disgráce.
So whereas the verses all the way through possess unrhymed feminine
line-endings, the clinching refrain doubly does the opposite – a refrain
that opens with the effect of a tank turret turning in threat, an iron
rhyme: "But you who . . ." This *you who* reminds me – and not as a
matter of sources or allusions, but as an analogue, a place of power –
of what Shakespeare does in the opening soliloquy of *Richard III*, when
Richard has chafed at the many maddening obstacles to his murderous
ambitions and then says, "Why, I, in this weak piping time of peace . . ."
Why, I. Again, the menace, the turret turning; Dylan's *you who*, this is the
levelled gaze.[1]

There are the effects of rhyme, then, including internal rhyming – and
including *not* rhyming when you might have expected it. (T. S. Eliot
once said that punctuation "includes the absence of punctuation marks,
when they are omitted where the reader would expect them".[2]) But two
things unexpectedly change in the final verse of *Hattie Carroll*. The first is
the sudden outbreak of a grim rhyme, an off-rhyme: *caught 'em / bottom*.
You haven't heard anything like this before in the song, whether in the
rhyming refrain or in the unrhyming verses.

> Once that the cops have chased after and caught 'em
> And that the ladder of law has no top and no bottom

– this is sardonic, Byronic, and it is en route to the end of this last verse,
repentance / sentence. This is the one and only full rhyme at a line-ending
in any of the four verses, and moreover it is a disyllabic rhyme (as against,

---

[1] Like the sharp identification in *The Waste Land*: "You who were with me in the
ships at Mylae!"

[2] A statement with Eliot's recorded reading (1947) of *Four Quartets*.

say, *pence / hence*). The rhyme *repentance / sentence* is poised to lead into the full, the fulfilling, rhymes of the final refrain after this clinching ruling:

> And handed out strongly, for penalty and repentance
> William Zanzinger with a six-month sentence

Unforgettably clear sense, this, while at the same time being tricky, hard to parse or to disentangle. "False-hearted judges dying in the webs that they spin" (*Jokerman*).

> *– The judge handed down a six-month sentence.*
> *– The judge handed out to William Zanzinger a six-month sentence.*
> *– The judge punished William Zanzinger with a six-month sentence.*
> *– The judge came out strongly against William Zanzinger.*

But he *handed out strongly (for penalty and repentance) William Zanzinger with a six-month sentence*? Any disingenuousness in this way of putting it is not to be laid at Dylan's door. "The courtroom of honor"? Not so, Your Honor.

Dylan's refusal to commit the sin that is Zanzinger's anger – however much such righteous anger might have claimed to be all in the good cause of giving a bad man some of his own medicine – is audible in the exquisite self-control of the pause in the singing (the least of pauses and therefore the most telling) after the word "a", in "with a [. . .] six-month sentence". The temptation at such a moment must always be to luxuriate in indignation: "With a [*pause*: For Christ's sake! Can you believe it?] SIX MONTH sentence!" All he does is just lengthen the toneless *a* [ə] to *a* [ei, as in *pain*], and then bide this micro-second of cold incredulity. Indignation may sometimes be a good servant but is always a bad master. Zanzinger should have curbed his temper; Dylan's is the timing that can temper steel.

Tempered, and temperate (temperance being another of the cardinal virtues). For it is a mark of Dylan's cooled control of this incendiary case that he watches his language. Aidan Day has said of Dylan's "vehement moral sense" that it "cauterised white judges who handed out six-month sentences to white murderers of black kitchen maids".[1] You can sympathize with

---

[1] *"Do You Mr. Jones?" Bob Dylan with the Poets and the Professors*, ed. Neil Corcoran (2002), p. 275.

Day's indignation (while glad that Dylan didn't yield to vehemence), but this is overheated, not only in its putting the case into the plural (judges? murderers? maids?) but in its unmisgiving use of a word that Dylan does not use: "murderer". Back at the time, *Sing Out!* used such terms ("She was murdered on February 8, 1963, by William Devereux Zantzinger"), though it did then acknowledge, even if reluctantly, that the court found him "guilty of manslaughter, dismissing charges of first and second degree homicide". The song rightly doesn't issue a ruling on this point. The police "booked William Zanzinger for first-degree murder", but the song, though it contests the sentence, does not contest the verdict. Far from weakening its cold contempt for the mildness of the sentence, this determination not to enjoy vehemence strengthens the contempt. It was a brutal indefensible killing, but you distort the horror of it all if you insist – without ever going into the evidence – that Zanzinger, in his drunken impatience, will have intended to kill her, that (and this is what we need to mean by murder) he murdered her. Dylan doesn't respect any such easy appeals to self-gratifying indignation. Think of what is going on in *Who Killed Davey Moore?* Of all the scoundrels with their excuses, the ugliest may be the gambler who bleats: "I didn't commit no ugly sin / Anyway, I put money on him to win". The boxer who killed Davey Moore is, horribly, both right and wrong in his defensive words: "Don't say 'murder'" – true, it wasn't murder in the ring – but "don't say 'kill'"? Don't say murder, *do* say kill. And don't, for Heaven's sake, go on, confident that this is the last word: "It was destiny, it was God's will".

The judge "handed out strongly, for penalty and repentance / William Zanzinger with a six-month sentence". Sentence and repentance were supposed to be how this case would close. The two words constitute an ancient rhyme, and they consummate Dylan's sentence. As with a prison sentence, there's a point of timing, of punctuation, here at the very end (which is then no end at all, given the perfunctory legal sentence). The Victorian book *Punctuation Personified* had characterized the full stop,

> Which always ends the perfect sentence
> As crime is followed by repentance.

Would that this were not just a true rhyme but true. Dylan in a recent interview quoted four lines from Rudyard Kipling's poem *Gentlemen-Rankers*, among them "We are dropping down the ladder rung by rung". The ladder and lawlessness. The thought that comes in Kipling three lines later, immediately after the lines that Dylan quoted, is "Our shame is clean repentance for the crime that brought the sentence".[1]

Words of clean truth, exactingly timed and voiced, are Dylan's throughout this song. He can crucially pivot a line-ending into an immediate rhyme at the head of the ensuing line: "That sailed through the air and came down through the room / Doomed . . ." It's a sickening rotation-repetition. You think at first that it's Hattie Carroll who was doomed, but it wasn't, it was Zanzinger with his cane: ". . . Doomed and determined to destroy all the gentle". In some terrible way, Zanzinger, too, is doomed, isn't in control not just of himself but of his life. Yet part of the feeling in the word "determined" is that he does will it, too. This is Freud's antithetical sense of primal words. "Determined" means either that you didn't have any choice in the matter (determinism), or, on the contrary, that you've chosen (determined) it, chosen in a fury to destroy all the gentle.

Richard III, the opening soliloquy again:

> And therefore, since I cannot prove a lover,
> To entertain these fair well-spoken days,
> I am determinèd to prove a villain,
> And hate the idle pleasures of these days.

The repetition at the line-ending, *these . . . days / these days*, has a grating resentment (Richard the hunchback, a victim of bodily deformity who is on the offensive) that is the counterpart to the defenceless victim's grind in *the table . . . the table . . . the table*.

Or take the double negative in the line that immediately follows: "And she never done nothing to William Zanzinger". In its positive power to elicit a simple pathos, this reverts to a child's sense of injustice, of injustice perpetrated against the powerless. James Baldwin moved this terrible turn of phrase beyond any possibility of condescension to Black English in his play *The Amen Corner*:

Such a nice baby, I don't see why he had to get all twisted and curled up with pain and scream his little head off. And couldn't nobody help him. He hadn't never done nothing to nobody.

"And she never done nothing to William Zanzinger": it takes you right

---

[1] *Rolling Stone* (22 November 2001).

back to a time when you believed, or hoped against hope, that there surely must be somebody who would see to it that such things didn't happen. The sadness and pathos are on her behalf, but they touch us all.

All this, though, without that human illusion of feeling that is sentimentality.[1] The song opens with a line that takes a risk: "William Zanzinger killed poor Hattie Carroll". But "poor" is saved from any soft pity because it is hard fact. The word is compassionate but it is dispassionate, too, for it does not lose sight of the plain reality that she is poor. Zanzinger, on the other diamond-ring hand, is not poor. He has "rich wealthy parents". They're not just rich, and they're not just wealthy; they're rich wealthy. Superfluous? You bet. Wasteful? But not a word is wasted.

"Rich wealthy parents who provide and protect him". Parents provide. True. But parents also provide for you. (When you are a child . . .) No, no: his parents didn't just provide for him, they provided him. And yet in the eerie way that may be true of these rich families, he both is owned by his parents and owns them in his turn:

> Owns a tobacco farm of six hundred acres
> With rich wealthy parents who provide and protect him

This doesn't say, as it might have said, that he is a man "With rich wealthy parents", but that he "Owns a tobacco farm . . . With rich wealthy parents".

Who provide him, not just provide for him? Some people say, well, that's just because Dylan couldn't get the word "for" in. But Dylan can always get into any line as many words as his art asks. Talk about Hopkins's sprung rhythm – this is more than sprung, it's highly sprung. When he sings "who provide and protect him", he means it. A poet, as G. K. Chesterton maintained, is someone who means what he says and says what he means.

"Provide" as against "provide for": a great deal may turn upon the unobtrusive difference between a transitive and an intransitive verb. The judge "Stared at the person who killed for no reason". There, one of the horrible things is that Dylan doesn't, as we might have predicted, call

[1] T. S. Eliot: "Stendhal's scenes, some of them, and some of his phrases, read like cutting one's own throat; they are a terrible humiliation to read, in the understanding of human feelings and human illusions of feeling that they force upon the reader" (*Athenaeum*, 30 May 1919).

Zanzinger "the person who killed Hattie Carroll". (The cadence would have been fulfilled, after all.) No, it's just "who killed". Period. For no reason. Killed as though with no object. The verb "to kill" doesn't mind being, as is its right on occasion, an intransitive verb, flat, hideous, indifferent.[1] The converse is true of the telling indictment of "you who philosophize disgrace and criticize all fears". Whereas "criticize" is its usual transitive self, "philosophize", which is usually intransitive, turns transitive. Usually you just philosophize, that is it. You don't philosophize something. So Dylan's sense becomes: you who hold forth and who spin philosophical excuses for what is simply disgrace, you for whom it's easy to be philosophical about these things since they don't really impinge on your daily life.[2]

He has a tobacco farm; she empties the ashtrays. He has parents; she gave birth to ten children. "Gave birth to" is piercing (how many lived?). It just reminds you that if you're poor, the infant mortality rate does not favour you. Or if you're black. The song never says she's black, and it's his best civil rights song because it never says she's black. Everybody knows she's black and it has nothing to do with knowing the newspaper story.[3] You just know that she must have been black. But then you know that Zanzinger is white, though it never says this either. It's a terrible thing that you know this from the story, and from the perfunctory prison sentence, even while the song never says so. It's white upon black, it's man upon woman, it's rich upon poor, it's young upon old.

William Zanzinger, who owns things, had "twenty-four years". Hattie

---

[1] Pope opens his *Epistle to Dr. Arbuthnot* with a chafed impatience that immediately repeats an imperative through clenched teeth: "Shut, shut the door, good John! fatigu'd I said, / Tie up the knocker, say I'm sick, I'm dead, / The Dog-star rages!" The Dog-star isn't the only thing that rages. Pope seizes the difference between repeating, say, an intransitive verb such as "Go" (where you could just say "Go, go" without necessarily being impatiently maddened), and repeating a transitive verb, "Shut, shut" as though unable to wait even a second for the object: "the door".

[2] Dylan: "I don worry no more bout the no-talent criticizers an know-nothin philosophizers" (*For Dave Glover*, programme for Newport Folk Festival (July 1963); *Bob Dylan in His Own Write*, compiled by John Tuttle, p. 7). Pope, again in his *Epistle to Dr. Arbuthnot*, sharpens the intransitive verb "hesitate" into a transitive: "Just hint a fault, and hesitate dislike". You can hesitate, and you can intimate dislike, but can you "hesitate dislike"? If you are cold sly Addison, you can.

[3] Dylan in concert (New York, 31 October 1964), when saying something to introduce the song, had a nervous laugh and uneasy wording, as though (touchingly) in awe of the greatness of what he must have known he had created: "This is a true story, right out of the newspapers again . . . The words have been changed around. It's like conversation really."

Carroll "was fifty-one years old". It is the simple or even casual word "old" that underscores the difference of age, without underlining anything. We don't have to be implying that someone is old when we use the phrase ". . . years old", but we ought to register what happens when you set "twenty-four years" against "fifty-one years old".[1] And, given her life and livelihood, Hattie Carroll is likely to be old at fifty-one.

Or there is the way in which nouns are seen as property.

> William Zanzinger killed poor Hattie Carroll
> With a cane that he twirled around his diamond ring finger

It's not that he had a finger that had a diamond ring on it; he had a diamond-ring-finger. He may well have had, too, an amethyst-ring-finger, an opal-ring-finger, and a ruby-ring-finger. His diamond ring finger has this extraordinary feeling of affluent agglomeration. "At a Baltimore hotel society gath'rin'". Add up the nouns like that and you're really propertied. Nouns are items, and you can possess them, you can own them. It's partly, yes, the feeling of a newspaper headline, BALTIMORE HOTEL SOCIETY GATHERING,[2] but it's also the way in which the nouns can be felt to bank up so very very powerfully.

Powerfully, and with rich insolence. For William Zanzinger

> Reacted to his deed with a shrug of his shoulders
> And swear words and sneering, and his tongue it was snarling
> In a matter of minutes on bail was out walking

Not walked out on bail but strolled out on bail: "In a matter of minutes on bail was out walking". One fine day. There you have it, leisure and freedom and amplitude. Meanwhile that "matter of minutes" anticipates another little lapse of time, that "six-month sentence". Such numbers are felt to figure all the way through, as with those twenty-four years and those fifty-one years old. Even the scale of the verses plays its scrupulous part. The verses build up. First, six lines plus the refrain. Then seven lines plus the refrain. Then

---

[1] There is this exchange with an interviewer: "Listen, how does it feel, Bob, when you're twenty-two years old and you go out on the stage at the Lincoln Center . . ." Dylan: "Old?" "Well you were twenty-two then." Dylan: "Oh yeah." (*Les Crane Show*, 17 February 1965; *Bob Dylan* by Miles, 1978, p. 24).

[2] The headline effect is there in the song from a newspaper report, *Talking Bear Mountain Picnic Massacre Blues*.

ten lines plus the refrain. And then the same again, for there it must stay, on the same scale, no longer lengthening. The final verse, pronouncing the sentence of (and upon) this court, must not be allowed to trump the life of Hattie Carroll. The scales of justice must hold perfectly level the scale of the two verses, however disgracefully the court failed to be on the level.

Hattie Carroll is a supreme understanding of the difference between writing a political song and writing a song politically. T. S. Eliot knew, and practised, the difference between writing religious poems and writing poems religiously. It is good to be able to write religious poems, but the great thing is being able to write poems religiously, to have religion be not the subject of a poem but the element. *Hattie Carroll* is one of Dylan's greatest political songs, not so much because it has a political subject as because everything in it is seen under the aspect of politics. Truly seen so.

One would need many more words of appreciation than Dylan needed of creation to bring out the living perfection, four square and subtle, of this great song. What Dylan said of the album *Time Out of Mind* should no less be said of the song *Hattie Carroll*: "There's no line that has to be there to get to another line."[1] Yet sometimes he is too modest.

Y'know, every one of my songs could be written better. This used to bother me, but it doesn't any more. There's nothing perfect anywhere, so I shouldn't expect myself to be perfect.[2]

But here is a song that could not be written better. Something perfect everywhere.

Seven Curses

Dylan raised the case of Hattie Carroll to mythic status without ever losing sight of the fact that the judicial hearing was fact: a real particular woman had been killed in 1963, a real particular man had just been brought to trial. So much was history. Dylan's art ensured that the death of Hattie Carroll was not degraded into either the transcendently mythical or the slang sense of *history*, something over and done with (forget it, it's history). But in a different

---

[1] *Newsweek* (6 October 1997).
[2] London, April 1965; *Bob Dylan in His Own Words*, compiled by Miles (1978), p. 77.

indictment of the law's corruptions, *Seven Curses*, the world is not that of historical fact, let alone recent fact, but that of myth. Truth is to be tested and manifested otherwise than in history. Folklore, ancient and modern, is felt to populate a worldly story that is at once that of Shakespeare and of Judy Collins.[1]

SEVEN CURSES

Old Reilly stole a stallion
But they caught him and they brought him back
And they laid him down in the jailhouse ground
With an iron chain around his neck

When Reilly's daughter got a message
That her father was goin' to hang
She rode by night and came by morning
With gold and silver in her hand

When the judge saw Reilly's daughter
His old eyes deepened in his head
Sayin', "Gold will never free your father
The price, my dear, is you instead"

"Oh I'm as good as dead," cried Reilly
"It's only you that he does crave
And my skin will surely crawl if he touches you at all
Get on your horse and ride away"

"Oh father you will surely die
If I don't take the chance to try
And pay the price and not take your advice
For that reason I will have to stay"

The gallows shadows shook the evening
In the night a hound dog bayed
In the night the grounds was groanin'
In the night the price was paid

---

[1] John Bauldie's sleeve-notes for *the bootleg series*, vols. 1–3: "The song's story is as old as the hills . . . but it seems likely that Dylan's direct source was a song called 'Anathea,' often performed by Judy Collins."

The next mornin' she had awoken
To find that the judge had never spoken
She saw that hangin' branch a-bendin'
She saw her father's body broken

These be seven curses on a judge so cruel:
That one doctor cannot save him
That two healers cannot heal him
That three eyes cannot see him

That four ears cannot hear him
That five walls cannot hide him
That six diggers cannot bury him
And that seven deaths shall never kill him

The sin is lust. It might have been covetousness, but the judge did not find himself tempted by the gold and silver. The first verse ends "With an iron chain around his neck". By the end of the second verse, the metal has become more precious, and the hope is to save his neck (the chain will otherwise become the rope around his neck) with the help of what is in her hand: "With gold and silver in her hand". Appealing to the sin of covetousness. But the judge isn't excited by money (although he is by her hand, which he wants, though not in marriage), as he makes clear with his nasty half-punning suggestivenesses with the words "free" and "dear":

> Sayin', "Gold will never free your father
> The price, my dear, is you instead"

The nauseating thing here is the travesty of the love between father and daughter: "The price, my dear, is you instead", enjoying its little libidinous suspension, pausing before and after "my dear" so that it may savour and purr the more. (Not "My dear, the price is you instead" or "The price is you instead, my dear", but "The price, my dear, is you instead".) Old Reilly is the older generation, like the judge:

> When the judge saw Reilly's daughter
> His old eyes deepened in his head

– sharply seen, this, in the way it catches the deep-set look of lust and of ageing (your eyes will deepen in your head, just as you will get long in the tooth because of those receding gums), so as to mean *His old eyes deepened still further in his head*. Bed–rheumy eyes. And then Dylan's sequence is perfectly clear and yet not quite what you expect:

> When the judge saw Reilly's daughter
> His old eyes deepened in his head
> Sayin', "Gold will never free your father . . ."

– *Sayin'*? It is as though his eyes were seen to say this in the split second before his lips did. Not *When the judge saw Reilly's daughter, he said*, but *His old eyes deepened in his head / Sayin'*.

When old Reilly hears of this (immediately, for the song cuts directly from the old judge's words to old Reilly's), he doesn't crawl:

> "And my skin will surely crawl if he touches you at all
> Get on your horse and ride away"

The vault into the saddle is from the creepily slow-paced "And my skin will surely crawl" into "Get on your horse and ride away".[1]

The horses, as so often in ballads and in Westerns (and in D. H. Lawrence's *St Mawr*), suggest energies that include sexual energies, as riding does. "Old Reilly stole a stallion". "She rode by night and came by morning".[2] "Get on your horse and ride away". But in the night ("In the night the price was paid") she submits to being not the rider but the ridden, mounted by her extortioner in his lust. Once again there might come to mind the opening soliloquy of *Richard III*, with its exacerbated sexuality:

> Grim-visaged War hath smoothed his wrinkled front,
> And now, instead of mounting barbèd steeds
> To fright the souls of fearful adversaries,
> He capers nimbly in a lady's chamber,
> To the lascivious pleasing of a lute.
> But I, that am not shaped for sportive tricks,
> Nor made to court an amorous looking-glass . . .

---

[1] Samuel Beckett plays "go" against "creeps": "We go wherever the flesh creeps least" (*Mercier and Camier*, 1974, p. 90).

[2] Intriguingly different uses of the preposition "by": "by night" is through the night, "by morning" is in time for morning.

One temptation that the song itself successfully resists is the sin of anger. (In *The Lonesome Death of Hattie Carroll*, the temptation might have been to respond in kind, whereas anger is not what besets the perpetrator in *Seven Curses*.) More pressing might have been – though there was never any real danger of this, given the character of Dylan's art – the sin of lust in its turn. For attacks on lust are often in collusion with it. Think of all those films that mount a crusade against pornography in a way that makes it deliciously necessary for them to show us a great deal of pornography.[1] Lust does not cease to be lust just because it is ostentatiously deplored. One of the sleaziest forms that lust can take is prurience. So it is greatly to the credit of *Seven Curses* that the song does not yield to self-righteous anger in the face of the judge's wrongdoing, and that it offers no combination of the high-minded and the low-bodied. D. H. Lawrence was repelled by such a combination in the eighteenth-century novelist who fascinatedly explored rape, "Richardson with his calico purity and his underclothing excitements".[2] *Seven Curses* does the decent thing, and this with controlled imagination, averting not only its eyes but its mind from what took place "In the night". This, as against the act itself, is an act of respect.

The story in Dylan's ballad is folklore, sometimes all too true: a judge says that he will refrain from carrying out the death-sentence provided that the woman who is pleading with him for someone's life will bribe him with her body. This story is at the heart of *Measure for Measure*.[3] Shakespeare's genius is in eliciting the hideous complexities that ensue when Angelo puts it to the virgin Isabella (pleading for the life of her brother, who has been condemned to death for fornication) that all she has to do is sacrifice her body. In Dylan's ballad the strength is in the simplicity, in what is *not* questioned, whereas the very different strength of *Measure for Measure* is in what is questioned. Yet it is crucial not to forget that both are grounded on the secure belief that what the judge does is heinous.

The contrasts are many.

In *Measure for Measure*, the justice of the sentence passed upon her brother is centrally vexed: death as the punishment for fornication? But that *is* the old law, there in Vienna, and the absent old Duke had said that he had

---

[1] "Adulterers in churches and pornography in the schools / You got gangsters in power and lawbreakers making rules" (*When You Gonna Wake Up?*).

[2] *Introduction to These Paintings* (1929); *Phoenix*, ed. Edward D. McDonald (1936), p. 552.

[3] When Pushkin re-created *Measure for Measure* as a poem, it was this crucial situation to which he gave salience.

been remiss in not enforcing the law, and venereal disease is death-dealingly rampant, and and and. And the man who now rules in the Duke's absence is not someone who is sympathetic to the lusts of the flesh. His lusts are of the spirit – or always had been until Isabella pleads with him on her condemned brother's behalf.

By contrast, there is nothing in *Seven Curses* to suggest that the horse-thief Reilly doesn't deserve to hang.[1]

> Old Reilly stole a stallion
> But they caught him and they brought him back
> And they laid him down in the jailhouse ground
> With an iron chain around his neck

The song simply sets aside the whole question of whether stealing a horse is justly punishable by death. The point is not that the song endorses the punishment; rather, that this never enters at all. All we know is that we are in a world where such a sentence is unmisgivingly passed. As often in such a case, the modern listener (or reader or viewer) is asked to be not a historian but an anthropologist – come on, you can imagine a society in which these severities make sense, however much they may strike you as cruel and unusual punishment. Reilly himself doesn't say a word about the sentence's being too severe, and nor does his daughter. And when the judge is judged "so cruel", this too doesn't invoke the harshness of the sentence itself, but the judge's lustful incitement of the sexual bribe and then his ratting on it after he has taken it, taken her.

But then there is a related impassivity in the face of bribery itself. Shakespeare's Isabella would never have dreamt of trying to bribe Angelo with gold and silver or with anything. So she could not have been met by any tacky snigger along the lines of "Wrong bribe, darling". ("The price, my dear, is you instead.") For Reilly's daughter, though, and for the chilly realism in such respects that is characteristic of a ballad, there is no question as to whether she should try bribery – the morality of bribery, like the justice (or not) of the sentence, just doesn't come up. Reilly's daughter brings gold and silver. Such is the way of the world, and the judge responds to it in his way of the world.

A further contrast between Shakespeare's play and Dylan's ballad would

---

[1] Contrast *Percy's Song* and the injustice, or not, of the sentence passed upon the driver of a car.

raise another question that the ballad, secure within its due limits, does not raise: is a judge the better for not acting on a bribe? Agreed, a judge should not accept a bribe, and certainly should not solicit one (a sexual solicitation here). But once he has taken the bribe, might it not be better if he went ahead with the sentence that had been passed? At least he would not then have perverted the course of justice. Now, a key difference between the play and the ballad is exactly here: would it be the course of *justice*, as against that of injustice, if Angelo were to proceed as though he had never incited and secured the bribe? Was the original sentence a just one? (But then might it not be a judge's duty to proceed with a sentence even if it were an unjust one?) Within the intricately philosophical and jurisprudential world of Shakespeare's play, a play of which the first sentence circuitously begins "Of government the properties to unfold . . .", it must be in question, however distastefully, whether a bribed judge does not do better by the world if at least he doesn't act on the bribe. He may be the worse person, intrinsically – but consequentially, as an officer of the law?

Such are the knotty complications, ethical and political, characteristic of *Measure for Measure*. But *Seven Curses* cuts all such knots. The judge incurs seven curses. His not acting on the bribe, far from being perhaps a mitigating circumstance, compounds his offence. Clean-cut simplicity, and clean lines – however dirty the world.

Another contrast such as brings out the ballad virtues of limits and of the off-limits: Reilly's daughter has no doubt at all that she must "take the chance to try". She knows that it is only a chance, for the judge – as is to be expected in such a case – will almost certainly renege. (As he does in the play, too. The person who acts on a bribe makes any subsequent accusation against him much more credible than if he just carries on in due process.) But she is sure in her own mind. To her father's protest that she must leave at once ("And my skin will surely crawl if he touches you at all"), she replies with her own *surely*:

> "Oh father you will surely die
> If I don't take the chance to try
> And pay the price and not take your advice
> For that reason I will have to stay"

It is up to her. Her father's cry is more than advice, but she judges it right not to heed his cry. Yet in *Measure for Measure* there is an unending contention both within Isabella and outside her. Is she right to repudiate

Angelo's hateful offer? She is sure of her spiritual duty – her body is not hers
to sacrifice, and the more so because she is a novitiate nun. And yet she is
agonized by her decision. Her brother at first rises to the high ground and
agrees with her – but then breaks down: What is a maidenhead compared
to a life? She repudiates him, furiously. But what price will she pay, for the
rest of her life, for her refusal to take the chance and try to save his life?

At which point a further contrast must surface, for Isabella is rescued from
having to live with such a decision not to save a life: the Duke returns, and
with providential powers he saves the day by now saving the night. Angelo
had been betrothed to Mariana, and Mariana is happy to take Isabella's
place by night, so that the bribe can be paid without Isabella's having to
pay it. So far, so good. But not so fast, not far enough, for Angelo does
the expected wrong thing, and – having (as he thinks) enjoyed Isabella –
means to proceed with the execution of her brother all the same. Once
again, the Duke must act fast if he is to prevent tragedy . . .

The point of retailing all this is to bring out the contrast with *Seven
Curses*. In the play, there is rescue, by the miracle that is providence and
that is tragicomedy. In the ballad, there is simply tragedy. Dylan's voice,
entirely without sentimentality, refuses to break or to break down, it simply
catches, at the moment when he sings the word "broken":

> She saw that hangin' branch a-bendin'
> She saw her father's body broken

The proverbial hope behind the antithesis of "bend" and "break" is lost in
tragedy. Wittgenstein: "You get tragedy where the tree, instead of bending,
breaks."[1] The hanging branch hangs there, and there it hangs people.

There is no hope that anything but what we know will happen will
happen. The daughter will sacrifice herself, to no avail. She and her father
are differently lost. And so, in a further different way, is the judge.

Not that there will be justice here on this earth. Whereas in the play's
world of strained hope, justice returns and the Duke effects a rescue, the
ballad has to despair of any trust in justice. Or even in revenge. *Measure for
Measure* has a great many complicated feelings and thoughts about justice,
as any Christian play ought to have, while containing Shakespeare's greatest
evocation of Christian mercy:

---

[1] Wittgenstein in 1929; *Culture and Value*, ed. G. H. von Wright, tr. Peter Winch
(1980), p. 1e [i.e., English].

ANGELO: Your brother is a forfeit of the law,
            And you but waste your words.
ISABELLA: Alas, alas:
            Why all the souls that were, were forfeit once,
            And he that might the vantage best have took
            Found out the remedy. How would you be,
            If he, which is the top of judgement, should
            But judge you as you are? Oh, think on that,
            And mercy then will breathe within your lips
            Like man new made.

Isabella's cry to Angelo is in vain, but her cry to the heavens is not, and justice comes. So revenge is not called for, is not called upon. But in *Seven Curses* there is simultaneously a justified craving for revenge and an unflinching recognition that it will not be forthcoming. There will be no Clint Eastwood armoured in white light. Unfortunately not, since revenge would be the real right thing. The ballad is as obdurate as was A. E. Housman: "Revenge is a valuable passion, and the only sure pillar on which justice rests."[1] Not the only pillar (that would be an exaggeration . . .), but the only sure one. So whereas the play can end with mercy of a kind, the ballad must end with its hopeless seven curses.

Simplicity is won, hard-won, but this doesn't mean that our response to it is uncomplicated. And it doesn't mean that the art of such simplicity is easy. Take the expunging of Reilly. "Old Reilly" opens the first verse, and "When Reilly's daughter"[2] the second. The third opens, "When the judge saw Reilly's daughter", and the fourth, "'Oh I'm as good as dead', cried Reilly". So his name has been heard, though differently, as each of the first four verses opens. But with the words "'Oh I'm as good as dead', cried Reilly", he goes, as good as dead, to be unnamed in the succeeding verses, all five of them. All that is left for him, and of him, is to hang there, in the last line of the last verse before the curses begin: "She saw her father's body broken". But then he had been as good as dead from the very first verse, where Dylan had made the tiny inspired change of the preposition "on" to "in". Originally he sang what is printed in *Lyrics 1962–1985*:

[1] To his publisher, Grant Richards, about another publisher, 21 August 1920; *The Letters of A. E. Housman*, ed. Henry Maas (1971), p. 177.
[2] As printed in *Lyrics 1962–1985*, and as sung on the Witmark demo tape, the second verse began: "Old Reilly's daughter". Released by Dylan in his *bootleg series*, the second verse begins "When Reilly's daughter", and has several other changes that matter.

> And they laid him down on the jailhouse ground
> With an iron chain around his neck

This became, in the performance that Dylan chose to release in his *bootleg series*, "And they laid him down in the jailhouse ground". As good as dead, "in the jailhouse ground". It will not be long before the diggers make actual what had been proleptic, and bury him.

The chilling effect when the name Reilly disappears is like that in T. S. Eliot's *Sweeney Among the Nightingales*, another poem about death expected and unexpected, where the first verse opens, "Apeneck Sweeney"; the second ends, "And Sweeney guards the hornèd gate"; and the third ends, "Tries to sit on Sweeney's knees" – whereupon Sweeney goes, as good as dead, unnamed in the succeeding verses, all seven of them. Yet it remains Sweeney's poem (he is in its title, as Reilly is not), since the poem consists of three sentences, and his name is in each of the three. For the first sentence is the first verse, and the second is the second verse, but the third is all the other verses, three to ten.[1]

We never learn the name of his daughter (the more strikingly in that Dylan has always loved what you can do with names), but then this is horribly true to her existing in this song, as far as this grim story goes, solely as old Reilly's daughter. The relation in *Measure for Measure* had been brother and sister, not father and daughter. But here: "And my skin will surely crawl if he touches you at all". Her skin is from his. In the play, Isabella had excoriated her brother when he weakened and wanted her to give herself up to Angelo:

> Oh you beast,
> Oh faithless coward, oh dishonest wretch,
> Wilt thou be made a man out of my vice?
> Is't not a kind of incest, to take life
> From thine own sister's shame? What should I think,
> Heaven shield my mother played my father fair,
> For such a warpèd slip of wilderness
> Ne'er issued from his blood.

---

[1] I am reminded of Eliot, who made much of the word "only", by Dylan's distinctive *only*: "It's only you that he does crave". This comes to more than just the father's insistence that "It's only that – it's just that – he craves you", for there is a faint suggestion that the line might be moving towards a lovingly grateful remark from the father whom she so loves: "*It's only you* who would even think of doing such a thing for me" or "*It's only you* I love".

It would have been no less a kind of incest, in *Seven Curses*, had Reilly chosen to profit from his own daughter's shame. Reilly urged her to ride away. She saw that she must defy him. And then, next day, "She saw her father's body broken" – as hers had, differently, been. The song never says that she is a virgin, but this is how it feels.

The song had vaulted into the saddle.

> Old Reilly stole a stallion
> But they caught him and they brought him back

"Catch" and "bring" do not rhyme, but "caught him" and "brought him" assuredly do, and rhyme is a means by which things are caught and brought. From the beginning, the song seizes and is seized by the life that is in rhyme. It might be a sudden leap of apprehension, as when the last line of the third verse, the judge's smirk, "The price, my dear, is you *instead*", prompts a sickening rhyme within the first line of the next verse: "'Oh I'm as good as *dead*', cried Reilly". I don't think that I'm imagining such effects but that Dylan imagined them, whether consciously or not – *caught him / brought him*, or *dead / instead* – and to put this weight on the word "instead" may be the more plausible in that this is the first full rhyme in the song. (The first verse, *back / neck*; the second, *hang / hand*; but the third, *dead / instead*.) In the spirit of ballads, there are alliteration and assonance to take and make their chances throughout, hauntingly at such moments as "stole a stallion" and "The gallows shadows shook the evening". But three verses place their strong internal sounding in the third line, in the ballad manner, and these lines constitute the plot. Verse 1, "And they laid him down in the jailhouse ground". Verse 4, "And my skin will surely crawl if he touches you at all". Verse 5, "And pay the price and not take your advice".

There are two verses that rhyme their first, second, and fourth lines: verse 5, which incarnates hope that tries to stay, *die / try / stay* (on edge as a rhyme), and verse 7, which is hope broken: *awoken / spoken / broken*.

> The next mornin' she had awoken
> To find that the judge had never spoken

There is a surprise to "she had awoken": could she have slept, you ask yourself, on such a night, a night of rape, her father's last night on earth? Yet it is not difficult to imagine her exhaustion, and it is proper to hope that she found mercy in oblivious sleep. When she wakes, though, it is to the terrible reality that she had known she would have to suffer. "Oh why did I awake? When shall I sleep again?"[1]

As in the very different feat that is *Hattie Carroll*, there is the sense of what it is to count. The phrase "the price" comes three times. First, the judge: "The price, my dear, is you instead". Second, the daughter: "And pay the price and not take your advice". Third, the narrator, in a stanza that then three times tolls the words "In the night":

> The gallows shadows shook the evening
> In the night a hound dog bayed
> In the night the grounds was groanin'
> In the night the price was paid

Seven verses precede the seven deadly curses. The final two verses, eight and nine, in their relentless telling and tolling of the curses, one by one, constitute the song's first – and therefore its one and only – momentum not within a verse but from one verse to the next. No longer is there a rhyme-scheme, which might offer something of a relief or release. Instead, an eternity of curses upon him:

cannot save him / cannot heal him / cannot see him

cannot hear him / cannot hide him / cannot bury him / shall never kill him[2]

The flat weight of this is the old torture visited upon you if you refused to plead guilty or not guilty, the flatly increasing weights that will make you speak or make you no longer alive to speak: *peine forte et dure*.

"And that seven deaths shall never kill him": this is the final curse, the ultimate and eternal one. The Book of Job saw "the bitter in soul; which long for death, but it cometh not; and dig for it more than for hid treasures" (3:23). The Book of Revelation foresaw that "in those days shall men seek death, and shall not find it; and shall desire to die, and death shall flee from them" (9:6). Exposed and humiliated, Angelo in *Measure for Measure* had begged His Grace the Duke for grace:

---

[1] Housman, *A Shropshire Lad*, XLVIII.

[2] For the first six curses, *Lyrics 1962–1985* prints "will not", which is what he sings on the Witmark demo tape; on *the bootleg series*, he sings "cannot". Both versions retain "shall never kill him" for the last curse. On *the bootleg series*, Dylan has a frighteningly beautiful suspension, instrumental, following the first of the curses, "That one doctor will not save him", as though biding his time, his eternity.

> But let my trial be my own confession:
> Immediate sentence then, and sequent death,
> Is all the grace I beg.

The Duke did not reply, or rather, replied with the words "Come hither Mariana". Again Angelo begs for mercy, but again the mercy of death:

> I am sorry that such sorrow I procure,
> And so deep sticks it in my penitent heart,
> That I crave death more willingly than mercy,
> 'Tis my deserving, and I do entreat it.

Again, no reply. Dylan:

> Can they imagine the darkness that will fall from on high
> When men will beg God to kill them and they won't be able to die?
> (*Precious Angel*)

Seven Curses, because it is myth, not history, is amenable to re-performance as *Hattie Carroll* perhaps is not. This is a question not of which version to prefer (Dylan preferred to release the Columbia studio recording), but of different facets catching different lights. The Witmark demo tape rendering is faster, with a brisker rhythm, with a dextrously plaited accompaniment, and with a voice that is less saddened or chastened. This Witmark rendering is closer to a traditional ballad, with something of the ballad's odd insouciance or impersonality, its risking the charge of heartlessness. "Get on your horse and ride away" – as though we, too, may need to do some such leaving. *the bootleg series* version is superb, and is (as it were) my choice, but something differently true is audible in the contrast with, and in the contrasts within, the Witmark one, something along the lines of William Empson's comments on the contrariety of the refrain in a traditional ballad (of illicit sexuality and betrayal) that is both discomfiting and comforting:

> She leaned her back against a thorn
> (*Fine flowers in the valley*)
> And there she has her young child born
> (*And the green leaves they grow rarely*)

Empson: "The effect of the contrast is not simple; perhaps it says 'Life went on, and in a way this seems a cruel indifference to her suffering, but it lets us put the tragedy in its place, as we do when we sing about it for pleasure.'"[1] The ballad bears the title *The Cruel Mother*, for it tells of her killing her illegitimate baby – a story, somewhere in the vicinity of *Seven Curses*, of tragic parental plight and of child sacrifice.

"It lets us put the tragedy in its place, as we do when we sing about it for pleasure." Dylan, too, undertakes the responsibility of putting tragedy in its place, Reilly's and his daughter's, so that he may sing about tragedy, strangely, for pleasure – and may bring us responsible pleasure.

Oxford Town

All because . . .: one frequent function of those two words is to introduce – courteously but firmly – a remonstration against injustice. It might be a political remonstration. A black man, down in Mississippi, has been not just mistreated or badly treated but badly mistreated, "All because his face was brown", or – soon pressing the same point slightly differently, as though wishing not to nag you but to urge you please to think again – "All because of the color of his skin".

> Oxford Town, Oxford Town
> Ev'rybody's got their heads bowed down
> Sun don't shine above the ground
> Ain't a-goin' down to Oxford Town
>
> He went down to Oxford Town
> Guns and clubs followed him down
> All because his face was brown
> Better get away from Oxford Town
>
> Oxford Town around the bend
> He come to the door, he couldn't get in
> All because of the color of his skin
> What do you think about that, my frien'?

The scene is set. The fate and the face of James Meredith were set. He was the first black to enrol – over what some whites said would be their

<hr>

[1] *The Structure of Complex Words* (1951), pp. 347–8.

dead bodies, although their hope was really that the dead body would be his – at the University of Mississippi. Oxford Town.

The haunted song is played by Dylan obliquely and yet unequivocally. But what was he playing at (equivocation?) when he said, on the *Studs Terkel Show*,[1] "Well, yeah, it deals with the Meredith case but then again it doesn't"? The right question to ask about this soft-shoe-shuffle of his is not "Is it true?" but "What truth is there in it?" And the answer radiates. Yes, *Oxford Town* deals with the Meredith case in the sense that as a matter of historical fact this was the place and this was the person there: the confrontation was altogether real, as the photos and footage of the siege in 1962 bear witness, and the challenge by Meredith – that the law be upheld, that his right to admission be admitted – was burlily and brutally met by a challenge to the law from the very officials whose duty it was to enforce the law. In Mississippi, "The leading institution of higher learning", recorded *The Oxford Companion to American History*,[2]

is the University of Mississippi (Oxford, est. 1848). Its campus was the scene (1962) of the most violent opposition to Federal court rulings since the Civil War, after the governor of the state in person sought to block the registration of a Negro student.

So the song deals with the Meredith case. But then again it doesn't. Not naming Meredith, it isn't handcuffed to a political particularity. It may be asked whether *The Lonesome Death of Hattie Carroll*, then, is limited to its occasion, but the cases are very different, not only as history but in the type of artistic realization that Dylan gives to them. The story of Hattie Carroll and of William Zanzinger is told in full and in detail; moreover, though it is dramatic, it is not told by a voice that is itself dramatized in the song. Nobody has been imagined by Dylan, the imaginer, as having this to say. He speaks, and sings, in his own voice, for all of us, and not as any dramatized imaginary one-of-us. But *Oxford Town* is not on the scale of such a tragic novel (an American tragedy, Hattie Carroll's life and death, and, yes, William Zanzinger's life, too); it is a sketch. Not sketchy at all, but offering in twenty short lines a picture of a different kind from that which is painted in the nearly fifty long lines of *Hattie Carroll*. Added to

---

[1] WFMT Radio, Chicago (3 May 1963). Dylan didn't perform the song on this show.

[2] (1966), ed. Thomas H. Johnson, under *Mississippi*.

which, the swift wretched tale of *Oxford Town* is told to us by someone who (it is imagined) was there. *Oxford Town* is sung with Dylan's voice but not sung in Dylan's voice exactly. For whereas the voice in *Hattie Carroll* is crucially not that of someone who had been present at the Baltimore hotel society gathering, down there in Oxford Town there we were,

> Me and my gal, my gal's son
> We got met with a tear gas bomb
> I don't even know why we come
> Goin' back where we come from

This is the only verse that doesn't include "Oxford Town", a name placed and pressed home three times in the first verse, twice in the second, once in the third and in the last, as if the song, like "Me and my gal, my gal's son", can't wait to get out of Oxford Town. "Goin' back where we come from". Where was that, exactly?

"I don't even know why we come". This is not the stuff of which heroes are made.[1] Oh, it took courage to be down there, in the midst of protest, the three of us. But there are limits. In the unmousy words of *Tarantula*: "it's every man for himself – are you a man or a self?"[2]

In *Some Other Kinds of Songs . . .*[3] Dylan imagines a scene:

> a loose-tempered fat
> man in borrowed stomach slams wife
> in the face an' rushes off t' civil
> rights meeting.

It would be nice to be sure that a man of this stripe was rushing off to the civil rights meeting in order illiberally to disrupt it, but we had better admit that he just might be going to it to support it. For many a good cause politically is supported by people who don't begin to practise at home what they preach abroad. "What do you think about that, my frien'?"

Oxford Town does not avert its eyes or ears from the fact that you can't

---

[1] On gals and heroes, see *Hero Blues*: "Yes, the gal I got / I swear she's the screaming end / She wants me to be a hero / So she can tell all her friends". "She wants me to walk out running / She wants me to crawl back dead". "You can stand and shout hero / All over my lonesome grave".

[2] *Tarantula* (1966, 1971), p. 81.

[3] *Lyrics 1962–1985*, p. 147.

count on liberals to be heroes. So? Why should you expect it of them? The song is not in the business of urging its listeners to feel superior to the voice they overhear, the voice of someone decent, who was up to going down there but who is not up to dealing with tear-gas bombs. Now is the time for your tears? – but it is not pleasant to think that now is the time and place for tear-gas tears. The idealism, though it is not ridiculed, is felt to falter, all too naturally:

> I don't even know why we come
> Goin' back where we come from

People do well not to go in for protestations about their protest-marches. Robert Lowell cast into verse a letter from Elizabeth Hardwick:[1]

> "I guess we'll make Washington this weekend;
> it's a demonstration, like all demonstrations,
> repetitious, gratuitous, unfresh . . . just needed."

Bigoted bullies like Bull Connor who wield cattle-prods against protesters, these *Oxford Town* has no time for, but this does not prevent it from setting reasonable limits to the amount of time that it has for liberal fellows or liberal fellow-travellers, the limits then being the amount of time that the liberals themselves will courageously commit themselves to. "Goin' back where we come from". I don't blame you. But I can't idolize you or idealize you either. And the song is saved from being in any danger of self-righteousness because it is mediated to us through the voice of someone who has no wish to be a martyr, makes no priggish claim to be a hero, and is not despised for not being a martyr or a hero. "I don't even know why we come".

> Oxford Town in the afternoon
> Ev'rybody singin' a sorrowful tune
> Two men died 'neath the Mississippi moon
> Somebody better investigate soon

"Ev'rybody singin' a sorrowful tune". Singing it insincerely? Hypocritically? Playing along with it? This line is parallel to the earlier one with which it is paired: "Ev'rybody's got their heads bowed down". In genuine sorrow?

---

[1] *Letter*, in *The Dolphin* (1973).

In pretended sorrow? Or prudentially, heads ducking below the parapet? The word "down" is bent on dragging the song down, four times in the first six lines, from "Ev'rybody's got their heads bowed down", through "Ain't a-goin' down to Oxford Town" and "He went down to Oxford Town", to "Guns and clubs followed him down".[1]

"Ev'rybody singin' a sorrowful tune". But as Robert Shelton wrote of this song, "Melody and tempo are jaunty, the lyrics are not."[2] The brisk buoyant strumming that opens the song does not ever let up or let you down in *Oxford Town*. It gives you something sorrowful, "but then again it doesn't", for the unsorrowful tune does not play along with what the words lay bare. Such counteraction is characteristic of a song that does so much interweaving. The "Ev'rybody" of "Ev'rybody's got their heads bowed down" and "Ev'rybody singin' a sorrowful tune" becomes, two lines later, the wistful wishful "Somebody" of

> Two men died 'neath the Mississippi moon
> Somebody better investigate soon

Somebody else, as always. Not *whatever*, but *whoever*. The patterned song is about patterns of behaviour. And "Sun don't shine above the ground", of the first verse, becomes in this last verse "Two men died 'neath the Mississippi moon". And just as "sorrowful tune" might have a romantic colouring, ugly in the circumstances, so another of the quiet horrors in the song is the contrast within the phrase "'neath the Mississippi moon", for it, too, might have a disconcertingly romantic colouring:

> Where I can watch her waltz for free
> 'Neath her Panamanian moon

That is *Stuck Inside of Mobile*. Fortunately you don't have to be stuck inside of Oxford Town. "Better get away from Oxford Town". The minimal hopeless "Better" of "Better get away" is not at all a good thing, and it returns in "Somebody better investigate soon", where nothing is any longer being shouldered and somebody is relapsing into shrugging the whole thing off.

Verse 1, "Ev'rybody's got their heads bowed down". Verse 2, "Better get

---

[1] What a contrast with the spirit in which Dylan sings *Baby, Let Me Follow You Down*.

[2] *No Direction Home* (1986), p. 156.

away from Oxford Town". Verse 3, "He come to the door, he couldn't
get in". Verse 4, "We got met with a tear gas bomb". "Got" and "get",
get it? At which point there is verse 5, which has got rid of "got" and
"get". Nobody is going to get caught or punished.

> Oxford Town in the afternoon
> Ev'rybody singin' a sorrowful tune
> Two men died 'neath the Mississippi moon
> Somebody better investigate soon

A silkily sinister ending. Even tinged, perhaps, with *hope they don't find out
anything*, a dark thought that is in touch with the bright thought that ends
a very different early song about politics, *Talkin' John Birch Paranoid Blues*:

> So now I'm sitting home investigatin' myself!
> Hope I don't find out anything . . . hmm, great God!

"Somebody better investigate soon". As printed in *Lyrics 1962–1985*,
though (and as can be heard on a bootleg tape), *Oxford Town* ended not
with this "soon" that will never be realized, but by circling back to repeat
the first verse of the song:

> Oxford Town, Oxford Town
> Ev'rybody's got their heads bowed down
> Sun don't shine above the ground
> Ain't a-goin' down to Oxford Town

Circling is good, both as being wary and as going nowhere, but there
is a more effective circling back without the repetition of the opening
verse (a touch easy, that), in the coming back round to the "Ev'rybody"
lines. "Ev'rybody's got their heads bowed down": "Ev'rybody singin' a
sorrowful tune".

The sorrowful tune is embodied in the sound that ends the word "tune"
or the closely related sound that ends the word "from". This sound has its
unremitting and encircling drone or hum. For all the lines of this song
rhyme, and every line can be heard to sound (like "line" and "rhyme") *n*
or (in the fourth verse) *m*. Not so, you might say, for what about "ground"
in the very first verse? But "ground" there is denied its *d* by rhyming with
"Town", even as "bend" in the third verse is denied its *d* by rhyming

with "frien'", and even as "bomb" – with its silent *b* – is rhymed with "from". And what might this steady drone or hum do within the song? Create a tone of semi-military menace without remission, not letting up, a background (or a backgroun') that bows heads down and brings everything down to Oxford Town. Think of the sounds of the bagpipe and of how the chanter's penetration is set against the drone, the brown air that the drone suffuses through it all.[1]

The short words go about their work. Meanwhile, "Mississippi" and "investigate" are the long words in the song, and there they are in two successive lines, the two closing lines.

> Two men died 'neath the Mississippi moon
> Somebody better investigate soon

Two men stayed in Mississippi a day too long. Somebody better see that justice is done to all this. As somebody truly did.

---

[1] About *Lay Down Your Weary Tune*, Dylan said: "I had heard a Scottish ballad on an old 78 record that I was trying to really capture the feeling of, and I couldn't get it out of my head. There were no lyrics or anything, it was just a melody – had bagpipes and a lot of stuff in it. I wanted lyrics that would feel the same way" (*Biograph*).

Prudence

And these few precepts in thy memory
Look thou charácter. Give thy thoughts no tongue,
Nor any unproportion'd thought his act . . .

Et cetera. Polonius, to his son, Laertes, in *Hamlet*. "These *few* precepts"? With a further twenty-two maxim-packed lines awaiting delivery? He must be kidding. You can feel the young man's relief when at last his father arrives at "This above all", with the end in sight or in hearing. Look out kid, one wants to say to Laertes, except that this is what his father (allowing for a change of idiom) is repeatedly saying to him. Polonius maximizes precepts. Some centuries later, such prudential considerations came to be the ammunition of the Maxim gun that is *Subterranean Homesick Blues*.

Look out kid
It's somethin' you did
God knows when
But you're doin' it again

Look out kid
You're gonna get hit[1]

        Beware
Of entrance to a quarrel, but, being in,
Bear't that th'opposèd may beware of thee.

Prudence says *Beware*, and *Be aware*, and *Be wary*. Whether or not the times are a-changin', time is of the quintessence. *No Time to Think*: such

---

[1] The fleet foot urgency and urging are audible within *Tarantula* (1966, 1971), "Note to the Errand Boy as a Young Army Deserter", a page that begins: "wonder why granpa just sits there & watches yogi bear? wonder why he just sits there & dont laugh? think about it kid, but dont ask your mother. wonder why elvis presley only smiles with his top lip? think about it kid, but dont ask your surgeon". It ends: "wonder why the other boys wanna beat you up so bad? think about it kid, but dont ask nobody".

is the title and the refrain of a timely song. American English, with its pleasure in and profit from built-in obsolescence, has its distinctive relation to time, to time's passing.[1] In terms of the transitory language, it is not that there is no time to think, but rather that one of the things that must be promptly thought about is that there's no time. The refrain that marks the particular whirligig of time that is *No Time to Think* makes a punctuation point of adding, every time, "And there's no time to think" – until the last time, the last verse. Then the refrain-line both expands and contracts. It expands, in that it takes over the whole of the last verse. It contracts, in that in the final end when the time comes for the last refrain, time so presses ("No time to lose") that, instead of "And there's no time to think", the refrain is curtailed to "And no time to think":

> No time to choose when the truth must die
> No time to lose or say goodbye
> No time to prepare for the victim that's there
> No time to suffer or blink
> And no time to think

"No time to lose or say goodbye": yet the song is about to effect its own way of saying goodbye (farewell is too good a word, so I'll just say goodbye), at once loyal to its refrain and departing not only with it but from it. Minutely. A prudent move, with perfect timing.

Prudence can sound something less than a virtue. Virtuous, merely? A soft touch, a touch too timid or tepid? Too puny to stand up there with Justice and Fortitude? Perhaps this virtue should be placed on a humbler plinth, alongside Temperance, the other less muscular one. But be careful (Prudence warns), for Prudence does have its glint, its steely sense of what a warning is and of how this differs from a threat – it then being understood that the difference may not be all that great. The pliability is wirier and wilier than you might think, and for Dylan it can grab best as "you better":

> You must leave now, take what you need, you think will last
> Whatever you wish to keep, you better grab it fast

[1] I draw on an essay of mine on *American English and the inherently transitory* (*The Force of Poetry*, 1984).

For "you better" grabs it even faster than "you'd better". Every letter, every microsecond, might count now that *It's All Over Now, Baby Blue*. Not that it is all over until the fat lady sings instead of the thin man.

"Look out the saints are comin' through". Prudence is always on the lookout. The advice that it gives may need to be repeated but will need to be varied, otherwise the hearer stops listening. "Take what you need" / "Take what you have gathered from coincidence". The taker, meanwhile, must be careful not to be taken.

> The lover who just walked out your door
> Has taken all his blankets from the floor

His blankets, your door. He'd probably take that too,[1] if he could, when taking his leave.

The first verse begins "You must leave now". The last verse gives notice of closing-time by opening with "Leave your stepping stones behind". How could you not? Stepping stones are more of a fixture than are Longfellow's footprints, Longfellow with his shipwrecked sailor (Dylan's sailors sound shipwrecked, too, seasick and rowing home):

> Lives of great men all remind us
>   We can make our lives sublime,
> And, departing, leave behind us
>   Footprints on the sands of time.
>
> Footprints, that perhaps another,
>   Sailing o'er life's solemn main,
> A forlorn and shipwrecked brother,
>   Seeing, shall take heart again.
>   (*A Psalm of Life*)

Take heart, take what you need (it may be heart).

---

[1]
> Well, I rush into your hallway
> Lean against your velvet door
> I watch upon your scorpion
> Who crawls across your circus floor
> Just what do you think you have to guard?
>   (*Temporary Like Achilles*)

Door again finds itself floored.

> Leave your stepping stones behind, something calls for you
> Forget the dead you've left, they will not follow you

In the making of those lines, something may have called to Dylan, don't forget, something that followed him and that at the same time he followed. For the meeting of stepping stones with the dead happens to resemble a meeting with a dead poet, a poet not forgotten – as is only right when his poem, remember, bears the title *In Memoriam*, and when we remark the same imaginative associations in the opening lines of section I:

> That men may rise on stepping-stones
> Of their dead selves to higher things.

And the more so if you hold in mind the whole opening verse:

> I held it truth, with him who sings
>   To one clear harp in divers tones,
>   That men may rise on stepping-stones
> Of their dead selves to higher things.

Dylan might get a rise out of the thought of himself singing to one clear harp in diverse tones, especially as his harp is heard immediately before this final verse of his. "Leave your stepping stones behind": earlier art may act as a stepping stone, as indeed it had for Tennyson himself, whose lines have as one of their own stepping stones a phrase ("their dead selves") from a poem that had been written twenty years earlier by a Cambridge friend of Tennyson's.[1] The affinity of Tennyson and Dylan is presumably a coincidence, but it is the kind of coincidence from which Dylan has been known to gather things.

> The highway is for gamblers, better use your sense
> Take what you have gathered from coincidence

While the phrase "you better" is brisker than "you'd better", even brusquer is "better": "better use your sense".

This cluster does its reminding and its foretelling in every kind of Dylan song. "You better go back to from where you came", counsels *Just Like*

---

[1] *The Poems of Tennyson*, ed. Christopher Ricks (1987), vol. II, p. 318.

Tom Thumb's Blues, which has much advice to air. ("Don't put on any airs", for instance.) In *The Times They Are A-Changin'*, "Then you better start swimming". In *Subterranean Homesick Blues*, "You better duck down the alley way", along with three more good *betters*.

> Better stay away from those
> That carry around a fire hose
>
> Better jump down a manhole
>
> You better chew gum

Subterranean Homesick Blues is sardonic but not exactly sarcastic, given that its advice is worth giving for all one's misgivings. Whether you'd have to be a complete cynic to act on such advice ("Keep a clean nose / Watch the plain clothes"), that is another matter, and almost as tricky as whether one should act on the principle that "Honesty is the best policy" – a principle that has been described as one on which no honest man ever acts. Worldly wisdom teases when it mouthes "Please her, please him", but this may still be a better use of the mouth than "Don't wanna be a bum / You better chew gum".

Satire, yes, these Skeltonic raids and forays, but the song is not ready for to fade into its own tirade. It has the wisdom to mock not only the complacencies of Polonius but the inverted (cynical) complacencies of Hamlet, who first mocks and then kills Polonius.

> Ophelia she's 'neath the window
> For her I feel so afraid
> (*Desolation Row*)[1]

The official precepts have a way of being, even if only confusedly, perceptive. To spit at them or spit them out is not really much wiser than swallowing them.

[1]
> – ok, so you used to get B's
> in the ivanhoe tests & A minuses
> in the silas marners . . . then you
> wonder why you flunked the hamlet
> exams – yeah well that's because one
> hoe & one lass do not make a spear –
> (*Tarantula*, p. 70)

Arthur Hugh Clough has a similar frictive rictus when he looks at the Ten Commandments. *The Latest Decalogue* refuses ever quite to settle into meaning merely the opposite of what it says:

> Thou shalt not kill; but needst not strive
> Officiously to keep alive.

> Thou shalt not steal; an empty feat,
> When it's so lucrative to cheat.

> Thou shalt not covet; but tradition
> Approves all forms of competition.

Subterranean Homesick Blues is likewise to be respected for preserving, however bitterly, some curious respect for the precepts that it owns, that it owns up to, that it won't altogether disown.

> Please her, please him, buy gifts
> Don't steal, don't lift
> Twenty years of schoolin'
> And they put you on the day shift

Look out kid, and keep a clean nose, but better not become the *Clean-Cut Kid*. We know what happened to him, how he was schooled.

> He was on the baseball team, he was in the marching band
> When he was ten years old he had a watermelon stand

> He was a clean-cut kid
> But they made a killer out of him
> That's what they did

The Times They Are A-Changin'

When I paint my masterpiece, I had better acknowledge that one day it may need to be restored. According to *Visions of Johanna*, "Mona Lisa musta had the highway blues", but the greens that are now highly visible in the painting are viewed with suspicion inside the museums-world. But then every restoration, whether political or painterly (the pristine Sistine?), goes up on trial. For history is like infinity [1] with its Louvre doors. "If the doors of perception were cleansed," William Blake said, "everything would appear to man as it is, infinite."

It is in an infinity of ways that *The Times They Are A-Changin'* has been restored by Dylan. Not that he has ever been stuck with a song, or stuck inside of one. (Maybe *Maggie's Farm*, there for dear life, until the worm farm.) The songs are on the move, although love-life, imagined within a song, may be rather the reverse:

> But it's like I'm stuck inside a painting
> That's hanging in the Louvre
> My throat starts to tickle and my nose itches
> But I know that I can't move
> > (*Don't Fall Apart on Me Tonight*)

Dylan, king of the cats, majestically lets the songs lead their own ninety-nine lives. His transfusion or transmission of the songs is his life's blood. Yet a problem may attend our reception. For well-known songs can become too well known, may no longer prove as open to our knowing them as they once were when we were all ears. Our having so often heard them may make it hard for us truly to listen to them. Now, if the *ears* of perception were cleansed . . .

Dylan can issue the songs anew, but can we admit them to ourselves anew? Like *Blowin' in the Wind*, *The Times They Are A-Changin'* may sometimes seem too much of a success for its own good. Those cards for *Subterranean Homesick Blues* that Dylan lackadaisically dandles as prologue to the film *Don't Look Back*, cards with some of the song's key-words on them, include one that simply reads S U C K C E S S. "Try to be a success", but there may be too much not only of nothing but of something, too much of a good thing.

One way perhaps of recovering for ourselves the very good thing that is *The Times They Are A-Changin'*, of having it become fresh to us again, or even fresh with us again, might be to go far back and guess at the process by which it grew to be itself. Not in order to track or trace its creator's own intuitions, let alone his deliberations as a conscious matter, but so as to

---

[1] In the Rome interview (2001), someone quotes to Dylan the words "Inside the museums history goes up on trial". Dylan, with infinite patience and corrugated brow: "Is it *history*?", and then "I don't think that's right . . . doesn't sound right − Is it right? It could be . . . Let me go look in the book." In this exchange, *infinity* is not the only thing that goes up on trial.

glimpse some of the possibilities as to where the effects may be coming from.

Like *Blowin' in the Wind*, *The Times They Are A-Changin'* is in essence its title-refrain, the title that is again almost, not quite, the refrain.

The waters have grown, and so has the song. Time involves evolution, such as the title-refrain knew. The acorn is presumably a thought from times long past, *tempora mutantur*. *Times change*. Then a series of new time began.

> Times change
> The times change
> The times are changin'
> The times are a-changin'
> The times they are a-changin'
> For the times they are a-changin'

The acorn has grown into a royal oak.

"Times change" is dubbed by grammarians the *simple present*. (The tone of "Times change" is something to come back to.) "The times are changing" offers something of a change, being a different *aspect* (the grammatical term) of the present tense. This aspect goes under several names. Not that Dylan, in order to be able to create intuitively from what grammar codifies, has any need to know what grammarians have to say. Knowing in a schoolish way about grammar is something other than having an instinct for the ways in which grammar itself is very knowing.

Two things about the "are changing" aspect are crucial to how Dylan wields it. First, that the terms for this aspect of the present tense are themselves intimate with what *time* is or what *the times* are, which may compound the thoughts and feelings that live within this title-refrain about time and the times. Second, that the terms are themselves suggestively at odds, which may have prompted some of the choppy energies of the song.

"The times change": *simple present*. "The times are changing": *present progressive* – a term, as it happens, that might epitomize this song about being progressive at present. The *present progressive*: "sometimes called the *durative* or *continuous* aspect". These two are epithets close to the heart of *The Times They Are A-Changin'* and its urgings. One of the things about such a present tense, whether you call it durative, continuous, or progressive, is its two-edgeness. For as the *Comprehensive Grammar*[1] shows, this form of

---

[1] *A Comprehensive Grammar of the English Language*, by Randolph Quirk, Sidney Greenbaum, Geoffrey Leech, and Jan Svartvik (1985), pp. 197–200.

the present tense catches "a happening IN PROGRESS at a given time".
A. E. Housman, exasperated by a dud scholar's having visited scepticism
upon a certain textual principle ("so we should be loth to assume it in a
given case"), tartly remarked that "Every case is a given case."[1] Likewise,
every time is a given time (the given times they are a-changin'?), with
the song powerfully intimating that *all* times are a-changin'. And *continuous*
as an alternative to *progressive* present? The "continuous" is admittedly not
the same as the "continual", but the interplay between those siblings might
foster some of the creative friction in the song, rather as the *durative* present
(if we were to prefer that term) at once insists upon and curtails duration.
The durative must last, endure, but only for a duration. For the duration
of the war, or of the battle outside that is raging.

We might see the key-phrase, "The times they are a-changin'", in the
light of what the *Comprehensive Grammar* comprehends: "The meaning of
the progressive can be separated into three components, not all of which
need be present":

   (a) the happening has DURATION
   (b) the happening has LIMITED duration
   (c) the happening is NOT NECESSARILY COMPLETE

The first two components add up to the concept of TEMPORARINESS.

It is timely that the words "The times they are a-changin'" add up to the
concept of TEMPORARINESS,

As the present now

Will later be past

But then, just as nothing proves more permanent than a temporary solution,
so temporariness is itself a permanent condition.

The Times They Are A-Changin' expresses its termination by means of
-ing, or rather of the pliant *-in'*. The title-refrain commands the other such
endings in the song, almost all of which are in the present progressive.

That it's namin'

Ragin'

---

[1] *The Application of Thought to Textual Criticism* (1921); *Collected Poems and Selected Prose*,
ed. Christopher Ricks (1988), p. 334.

> Your old road is
> Rapidly agin'
>
> The order is
> Rapidly fadin'

But of the many progressive presents that the song gives us, only one has its nature reinforced by the prefix that in itself emphasizes process: "*a*-changin'". The title-refrain enjoys the monopoly of this tiny touch within the song, a touch of which Dylan well understands the effect,[1] and one that, because it has weathered into archaism, is well adapted to times and their changing.

> Bye, baby bunting,
> Daddy's gone a-hunting

– nursery rhymes and songs apart, it is mostly time to say bye to the prefix *a-* in this sense, the prefix that denotes "in process of, in course of". 1 Peter 3:20, "in the days of Noah, while the ark was a-preparing".

> If your time to you
> Is worth savin'
> You better start swimmin'
> Or you'll sink like a stone
> For the times they are a-changin'

Or, "while the ark was a-preparing wherein few, that is, eight souls were saved".

Times change. And one exercise in which an imaginative writer takes delight is to change some time-worn thought about the times. Take the wit that Dickens brings to holy writ. Ecclesiastes, opening chapter 3: "To every thing there is a season, and a time to every purpose under the heaven: a time to be born, and a time to die . . ."[2] Dickens, opening chapter 1 of *A Tale of Two Cities*: "It was the best of times, it was the worst of times, it was the age of wisdom, it was the age of foolishness . . ." Times have

---

[1] "As the night comes in fallin' . . .": how very different this would be from Dylan's "As the night comes in a-fallin'" (*One Too Many Mornings*), and not only for rhythmical reasons.

[2] A few verses later: "a time to cast away stones, and a time to gather stones together". Dylan's song happens to have "time", "cast", "stone", and "gather".

changed, and so have the things that need to be said about the times. The same goes for the relation between the ways in which things stay the same and the ways in which they do not, within the world evoked by *The Times They Are A-Changin'*.

Back to the ancient adage. *Tempora mutantur nos et mutamur in illis.* "Times change, and we change with them." Or, in words from long ago that invoke a longer ago: "The times are changed as Ovid sayeth, and we are changed in the times" (1578). It has been crucial to the saying, whether in Latin or in English, that "we" be in it. But "we" is a word and a thought strikingly absent from *The Times They Are A-Changin'*. Strikingly, as having been struck out of it.

But then most of the pronouns, having been told "Don't stand in the doorway", have been shown the door. It is *you* who will apparently get to stay. For this is another of the great Dylan *you* songs.

> Come gather 'round people
> Wherever you roam
> And admit that the waters
> Around you have grown
> And accept it that soon
> You'll be drenched to the bone
> If your time to you
> Is worth savin'
> Then you better start swimmin'
> Or you'll sink like a stone
> For the times they are a-changin'

Six times in this first verse, *you* – plus a *your* thrown in, en route to the next verse, which may be free of *you* but does need what are *yours*. The song chides but it hopes not to nag, which is one reason why *you* is used more sparingly after the first verse, even while the word *your* keeps the thought of you unremittingly in play, twice in the second verse ("your pen", "your eyes"), twice in the third ("your windows", "your walls"), and five times in the fourth verse ("Your sons and your daughters", "your command", "Your old road", "your hand"). As for the shorter sharper word, although *you* is off convalescing during the second and third verses, *yous* return with certain values in the fourth verse: "What you can't understand", rhyming with (and parallel to) "If you can't lend your hand".

The pronunciamento is willing to acknowledge, for a brief moment, the word "he", provided that this pronoun identifies no one in particular ("For he that gets hurt / Will be he who has stalled"). There are plenty of occasions for "they" – but only on condition that the word refer not to people, solely to the times: "For the times they are a-changin'". The alignment of the song is the human "you" and the larger-than-human "they" of the times. And of these two, only the latter is left in the last verse, a verse that has no other pronoun except, be it noted, "it", the forgettable pronoun that at last comes into its own, the little "it" that has figured four times earlier but only now finds its opening, an opening that – with an emphatic syntactical redundancy of "it" – draws its two lines tightly parallel:

> The line it is drawn
> The curse it is cast
> The slow one now
> Will later be fast
> As the present now
> Will later be past
> The order is
> Rapidly fadin'
> And the first one now
> Will later be last
> For the times they are a-changin'

Not just "now", and not just the admonitory "now, now", but three times the urgency of "now" at the line-ending. All the verses until this last one have launched an imperative address: "Come gather 'round people", "Come writers and critics", "Come senators, congressmen", "Come mothers and fathers". But when the last verse comes, it is too late for any such injunctions. The line is drawn under all that.

This final verse, rising exhilaratedly above any accusatory "you", might invite us once more to set the refrain, "For the times they are a-changin'", against its forebear: "Times change". And then to feel the transformation of tone that Dylan effects. "Well, times change, I guess": this remark from 1949 is quoted in Bartlett Jere Whiting's *Modern Proverbs and Proverbial Sayings* (1989), and although "Times change" wouldn't *have* to carry this tone of concessive reluctant acquiescence, this is a tone that comes naturally to it. "Times change": granted, it does lend itself to shrugging (I guess) more than to shouldering. But "The times they are a-changin'": this squares its shoulders while it rounds on people.

> Come gather 'round people
> Wherever you roam

Dylan once said "I've never written any song that begins with the words 'I've gathered you here tonight . . .'"[1] True, literally, but it is an unexpected thing for him to say, given that he has written "Come gather 'round people", to say nothing of "Come gather 'round friends / And I'll tell you a tale"; "Come around you rovin' gamblers and a story I will tell"; "Come you ladies and you gentlemen, a-listen to my song"; or "Come you masters of war".[2] What can Dylan have been thinking of, then, with this claim, "I've never written any song that begins . . ."?

Yet there are differences in the air. *The Times They Are A-Changin'* is unlike *North Country Blues*, or *Rambling, Gambling Willie*, or *Hard Times in New York Town*, each of which tells a story. Nor is it like *Masters of War*, which foretells a story. *The Times They Are A-Changin'* admonishes, that is for sure, but it doesn't take the tone of "I've gathered you here tonight . . .". Its imperatives, immediately after the first one (which is simply "Come gather 'round"), put it to you at once that you already know the truth that is being pressed upon you: "And *admit* that . . ." And the recurrent urging finds its humanity and its decency in its own admission that it is putting to you something that you have already (come on, admit it) put to yourself. Admit it, and accept it.

> Come gather 'round people
> Wherever you roam
> And admit that the waters
> Around you have grown
> And accept it that soon
> You'll be drenched to the bone
> If your time to you
> Is worth savin'
> Then you better start swimmin'
> Or you'll sink like a stone
> For the times they are a–changin'

---

[1] "I'm not about to tell anybody to be a good boy or a good girl," he went on. *Playboy* (March 1966).
[2] *North Country Blues, Rambling, Gambling Willie, Hard Times in New York Town,* and *Masters of War.*

As so often in Dylan, it is words of scripture that may be the bridge by which one word of his has crossed over to another.

> Come gather 'round people
> Wherever you roam
> And admit that the waters

Where might we gather that the waters are from? From a biblical gathering together? Perhaps Genesis 1:9, "Let the waters under the heaven be gathered together." More probably, Exodus 15: "the waters were gathered together", given that this same chapter gives us a song ("Then sang Moses and the children of Israel this song unto the Lord, and spake, saying, I will sing unto the Lord"), a song that exults in terms that may sound the depths of Dylan's song:

Pharaoh's chariot and his host hath he cast into the sea: his chosen captains also are drowned in the Red sea. The depths have covered them: they sank into the bottom as a stone.

"Or you'll sink like a stone". "The curse it is cast". Or, in the very different accents of exuberant word-work from the moment *When the Ship Comes In*:

> And like Pharaoh's tribe
> They'll be drownded in the tide

Dylan's words are never quite what you might have expected. "If your time to you / Is worth savin'": we know perfectly well what it perfectly means, but if this were a crossword clue, given the context of drowning the four-letter word -*i*-*e* would probably be filled in, not as *time*, but as *life*. (The time of your life, but not with the usual pleasure in the thought.) If your *life* is worth savin', you better start swimmin' or you'll sink like a stone: isn't that a line of thought?

Saving your life is one idiom; saving time is another; and the two mingle fluidly. Is time worth saving, however short? (Is it worth saving a few minutes?) And then there is a third way of putting it that may mingle with the others: "If your time is worth" – not *saving* but – "anything". All this, with "your time" set against what immediately ensues, "the times".

And with the words "Or you'll sink like a stone" sung by Dylan a moment ahead of the music, as though plummeting, "sink" sung out of synch.

The second verse comes in with a word that is both new (not in *The Oxford English Dictionary* . . .) and true:

> Come writers and critics
> Who prophesize with your pen

What's the matter, Dylan, the verb "to prophesy" not good enough for you?

That's right, not good enough here because what's needed is something that will not sound good: to *prophesize*, which gets and whets its sardonic edge from what the suffix *-ize* often implies, that the whole thing has become a predictable formula or an empty abstraction, complacently explaining away. You can hear this in the Dylan sleeve-notes for Peter, Paul and Mary,[1] from the same year: "At these hours there was no tellin what was bound t happen – Never never could the greatest prophesizor ever guess it –". No tellin what,

> And there's no tellin' who
> That it's namin'

But you'll know what I mean by "Who prophesize", you who "criticize / What you can't understand", or (elsewhere) "you who philosophize disgrace" (*The Lonesome Death of Hattie Carroll*).

The coinage rings true because "prophesize" chimes naturally with "to prophesy" and with "prophesied": "Who prophesy with your pen", say, or "Who prophesied with your pen". "My tongue", says the singer of Psalm 45, "is the pen of a ready writer." Dylan's tongue curls at the thought of the too-ready writers.

> Come writers and critics
> Who prophesize with your pen
> And keep your eyes wide
> The chance won't come again

[1] To *In the Wind*, December 1963; *Bob Dylan in His Own Write*, compiled by John Tuttle, p. 23.

We may need to keep our wits about us when we hear "And keep your eyes wide". *The Oxford English Dictionary* points out that "wide" is in some respects "now superseded in general use by *wide open*". But "wide-eyed" has changed with the times. It used to be "having the eyes wide open, gazing intently", with D. H. Lawrence urging upon the human soul the duty of "wide-eyed responsibility" (*Man and Bat*). But then it comes to mean naivety, true or simulated: "You ask him all those wide-eyed innocent questions about making profits from cheap labour" (Len Deighton, 1983).

It was back in 1894 that the New York *Forum* praised Madison's "wide-eyed prudence in counsel". The virtue that is urged and celebrated in *The Times They Are A-Changin'* is prudence. This virtue asks courage and great good sense, and is to be distinguished from petty caution, in the knowledge that few things are more dangerous than playing safe. Tough maxims can be plaited into a rope that is thrown to you.

> Then you better start swimmin'
> Or you'll sink like a stone
>
> And keep your eyes wide
>
> And don't speak too soon
>
> Don't stand in the doorway
> Don't block up the hall
> For he that gets hurt
> Will be he who has stalled

"Stalled", as *come to a halt* and (an altogether different verb) as *prevaricated*. Very apt to *The Times They Are A-Changin'*, since to stall is to play for time or temporize. Anyway, be warned. Prudence, though mannerly, *demands*. Be advised.

Dylan's writings are happy to give advice, often of a derisory kind. *Advice for Geraldine on Her Miscellaneous Birthday*, which appears in *Lyrics 1962–1985* as the conclusion to the songs from the *Times They Are A-Changin'* album, is a formidable sequence of prudential assurances. It begins:

> stay in line. stay in step. people
> are afraid of someone who is not
> in step with them. it makes them
> look foolish t' themselves for

being in step. it might even
cross their mind that they themselves
are in the wrong step. do not run
nor cross the red line.

Stay in line, do not cross the red line. The line it is drawn.

> say what he
can understand clearly. say it simple
t' keep your tongue out of your
cheek.

The Times They Are A-Changin' says what we can understand clearly, and is determined to *say it simple*. Not "simp*ly*". Yet in *Advice for Geraldine*, too, this wasn't so simple. "Say it . . ." looked likely to be completed with "simp*ly*", right after "understand clear*ly*". What "say it simple" does is join forces with "keep it simple", the word "keep" then immediately surfacing: "say it simple / t' keep your tongue out of your / cheek".

"This was definitely a song with a purpose," Dylan said of *The Times They Are A-Changin'*. "I knew exactly what I wanted to say and for whom I wanted to say it to" (*Biograph*). A characteristic touch, this, in its throwing in more prepositions than it might seem to need.[1] Which do you want to say, sir, "for whom I wanted to say it", or "whom I wanted to say it to"? Both, because "to whom" is *as addressed to*, but "for whom" is *on behalf of*. It may seem surprising that so combative a song could be on behalf of those whom it berates, but salutary words are words on behalf of those who stand in need of them. As will later be realized.

> For the loser now
> Will be later to win

Again, there is the small but telling divergence from the likely ways of putting it. Will be later *the winner*? Will be later *the one to win*? (Will be *certain to win*?) The word "later" comes early in the song (this second

---

[1] Of old: "They said who they fought an what they fought for an with what they fought with" – enemy and weapon (*For Dave Glover*, programme for Newport Folk Festival, July 1963; *Bob Dylan in His Own Write*, p. 8). Of late: "For whom does the bell toll for, love?" (*Moonlight*).

verse) but it is only late in the song, the last verse, that its time comes, its triple time:

> The line it is drawn
> The curse it is cast
> The slow one now
> Will later be fast
> As the present now
> Will later be past
> The order is
> Rapidly fadin'
> And the first one now
> Will later be last
> For the times they are a-changin'

Matthew 19:30: "But many that are first shall be last; and the last shall be first." This is the last verse of the chapter, even as it is the last admonition of the song.[1]

The song has its pattern, and – as T. S. Eliot knew – the crucial thing for the artist is the "recognition of the truth that not our feelings, but the pattern which we may make of our feelings, is the centre of value".[2] Dylan: "Anyway it's not even the experience that counts, it's the attitude toward the experience" (*Biograph*). Things not only may but must change, but the refrain at the end of each verse is itself unchanging: "For the times they are a-changin'". In performance, the song is free to be always changing. Dylan knew better than to heed his own sombre warning in *Advice for Geraldine on Her Miscellaneous Birthday*:

> do Not create anything, it will be
> misinterpreted. it will not change.
> it will follow you the
> rest of your life.

The capital *N* on "Not" is Notoriously the only capital letter in the

---

[1] In the preceding verse of Matthew: "father, or mother, or wife, or children, or lands". "Come mothers and fathers / Throughout the land / . . . / Your sons and your daughters".

[2] *A Brief Introduction to the Method of Paul Valéry*, *Le Serpent* (1924).

hundred-and-more lines of *Advice*, and Dylan did well Not to obey it but, instead, to be beyond his own command. Children of the sixties still thrill to *The Times They Are A-Changin'*, kidding themselves that what the song proclaimed was that at last the times were about to cease to change, for the first and last time in history. Was not enlightenment dawning, once and for all?

But the times they are still a-changin', and for decades now when Dylan sings "Your sons and your daughters / Are beyond your command", he sings this inescapably with the accents not of a son, no longer perhaps mostly of a parent, but with grandparental amplitude. Once upon a time it may have been a matter of urging square people to steel themselves to accept the fact that their children were, you know, hippies. But the capacious urging could then come to mean that ex-hippie parents had better accept that their children looked like becoming yuppies. And then Repupplicans . . .

The Fourth Times Around Are A-Changin'.

We Better Talk This Over

"We better" is more magnanimous than "You better", in that anyone who says "We better" doesn't, on the face of it, exempt himself (or herself) from the advice that is recommended or commended. But magnanimity is well advised to stay sober. The first rhyme of *We Better Talk This Over* is furrily slurred: *over / sober*.

> I think we better talk this over
> Maybe when we both get sober

It matters that the song is not called, cumbrously and with a touch of the pretend-tentative, *I Think We Better Talk This Over*. This would have been the wrong first line to take. The words "I think" are decent of him (don't want to press the point) but are not about to weaken into any doubt on the matter. The same goes for "Maybe", which amounts to "really" really. "It really would be prudent of us to leave it till we both get sober". (Both? The hint may be that one of us is already sober. Me, I take it.) And the run of the words and of the voice is prudently precise about where to place that "Maybe". Not "We better talk this over, maybe" – no, that we'd better talk this over is a sure thing, for all the courtesy of "I think" – but "Maybe when we both get sober". It is only the "when" that is in question.

Delicately done, again. It would be quite a different story if the song were
called, as in those vibrant moments in films, *We Need to Talk*.

> I think we better talk this over
> Maybe when we both get sober
> You'll understand I'm only a man
> Doin' the best that I can

"The *best* that I can" seizes the chance to justify itself, to feel that it really
does follow climactically, by following the words "we *better*". Meanwhile
the pronouns are doing "a downhill dance" of a sort: *I we we / You I I*.
There could easily have been a "he": "I'm only a man / Doin' the best
that he can". But this would have been too easy. This man won't duck.
"Only a man", which is engendered by the sexual situation, both is and
is not gendered (someone, this particular someone, then, speaking from a
man's eye view all right). "Only a man" is not asking for a fight, it is on
this occasion gender-pacific. And the phrase both concedes and intercedes:
come on, there's a limit to the best you should hope from a man, given the
run of men, to say nothing of original sin. Anyway, maybe you're only a
woman, doing the best that you can.

Twos and threes: these are set before us in this first shaping of pronouns
and in the verse-form itself. It looks as though it is constituted of twos, pairs,
couplets or couples whether happy or not. The song is about coupling, "the
bed where we slept", and about uncoupling:

> The vows that we kept are now broken and swept
> 'Neath the bed where we slept

Couplets, then, from the start: *over / sober*, *man / can*. And this isn't only
a matter of the look on the page but of the weight in time and in speed in
the singing. But the verse-form could be lineated on the page as a supple
couplet followed by a tripping triplet:

> I think we better talk this over
> Maybe when we both get sober
> You'll understand
> I'm only a man
> Doin' the best that I can

Or, in verse 2, there can be felt both this shaping spirit of imagination:

> This situation can only get rougher
> Why should we needlessly suffer?
> Let's call it a day, go our own different ways
> Before we decay

and this different unauthorized lineation:

> This situation can only get rougher
> Why should we needlessly suffer?
> Let's call it a day
> Go our own different ways
> Before we decay

The one verse-form goes its own different ways.

The bridge then takes the form of a duly undulating couplet:

> You don't have to be afraid of looking into my face
> We've done nothing to each other time will not erase

Yet even here, two and three are heard to interplay, for laced with the rhyme *face / erase* there is the strong assonance *afraid / face / erase*. And this sound, too, is followed up in the downhill momentum of the song, in the very next phrase, "I feel displaced".

> We've done nothing to each other time will not erase
>
> I feel displaced, I got a low-down feeling
> You been two-faced, you been double-dealing
> I took a chance, got caught in the trance
> Of a downhill dance

The "low-down feeling" (he is feeling low, his spirits are down, because she has behaved in a low-down way) will be felt to be warranted when he gets down to "a downhill dance", but on the way he will let her know that he knows, letting us in on a fact: "You been two-faced, you been double-dealing". Two-faced, so maybe it isn't altogether true that "You don't have to be afraid of looking into my face". My one face. My integrity, your duplicity, your double-dealing. You and I have ceased to be a twosome. Two and four, now, perhaps, since the verse's opening couplet might now take the lineated shape of a foursome:

> I feel displaced
> I got a low-down feeling
> You been two-faced
> You been double-dealing

And from such a two-cum-four to three again: *chance / trance / dance.*

It is immediately following this accusatory verse that there comes the only other one that sets itself to the two-cum-four rhyming of the opening couplet. A sudden pang is felt, a wish that there had been no need to accuse, a longing for what had been fantasized but could not be realized:

> Oh, child, why you wanna hurt me?
> I'm exiled, you can't convert me
> I'm lost in the haze of your delicate ways
> With both eyes glazed

Or:

> Oh, child
> Why you wanna hurt me?
> I'm exiled
> You can't convert me

This is cryptic, as though unable to bring itself to declare all that it is feeling. There is no difficulty in understanding "I'm exiled" – she has done this to him, has banished him, even though she may not have known that this would be the upshot of the downhill dance. And there is no difficulty with "You can't convert me". A lost soul, "I'm lost in the haze". Lost time is not found again, nor is lost faith. But what is the relation between "I'm exiled" and "You can't convert me"? Exiled afar to another country, another continent? Beyond the reach of conversion, beyond the reach of even the best-positioned missionary? The elusiveness fascinates.

> I'm lost in the haze of your delicate ways
> With both eyes glazed

He admits it, he sees the haze clearly, he even sees that his eyes are glazed. This, too, is delicately done. "Both eyes": no one-eyed jack or jill. If he needs a third eye, he just can't grow it. "Why should we go on watching each other through a telescope?" The days when each was under the other's loving microscope have gone.

The acknowledgement that their number is up comes when he breaks into this dusty answer:

> The vows that we kept are now broken and swept
> 'Neath the bed where we slept

Or in this lineation:

> The vows that we kept
> Are now broken and swept
> 'Neath the bed where we slept

Three in the bed of rhyme. There were three in the bed, and the little man said, Roll over, roll over. So they all rolled over, and one fell out. The little man, for once, before the end. Displaced. There were two in the bed, and the little man said, "I guess I'll be leaving tomorrow", leaving the other two to it. The eternal triangle? No, not eternal, for time is the mercy of eternity. "Oh, babe, time for a new transition".

The song, which gambols and gambles, is one form of a numbers game. "Two-faced" will face off, not only against "my face", but against "this universe", both of these being variants on the old one-two, or on two to one.

> You don't have to yearn for love, you don't have to be alone
> Somewheres in this universe there's a place that you can call home

This universe may be vast but it is one, a single whole, or it would be a multiverse.[1] One is one and all alone, and evermore shall be so. But you don't have to be alone. "Somewheres" is a word that is happy to play its part or parts, feeling plural while being singular. This form of the word

---

[1] Dr Clark Kerr, of the University of California, earned the credit or the discredit for coining "multiversity" in the 1960s. The protests at his Berkeley, though, were about the war in Vietnam.

has come to feel singularly American, and it is true that *The Oxford English Dictionary*, which introduces it with a quotation from *Bartlett's American Dictionary* (1859), does label it *dial.* or *vulg.* But "somewheres" doesn't mean exactly the same as "somewhere", any more than the American "quite a ways" means quite the same as "quite a way", and Robert Louis Stevenson was safe in employing it in *Treasure Island*: "I know you've got that ship safe somewheres." Not just some place but a great many possible places. "Somewheres in this universe there's a place that you can call home".

Throughout the song, Number One ("one's self, one's own person and interests", *The Oxford English Dictionary*) is being looked after, reasonably enough, while looking towards two, even as two can look towards three. So that when the rhyme of "half" with "laugh" arrives, it is not only comic relief but fun and games with numerations.

> I guess I'll be leaving tomorrow
> If I have to beg, steal or borrow
> It'd be great to cross paths in a day and a half
> Look at each other and laugh

The couplet *tomorrow / borrow* tucks up within itself a borrowing of the notoriously unscrupulous triplet, "beg, borrow, or steal". A borrowing, but a twisting, too: Dylan's "beg, steal or borrow" has a happy ending, or at any rate what may be an honest one. ("Neither a borrower nor a lender be", in Polonius's words, but if you do borrow, please return.) "If I have to beg, steal or borrow" does not, unlike "beg, borrow or steal", descend to a life of crime, it just flirts with stealing and then steals on. Dylan doesn't borrow things without making them his own. But the telling stroke is "in a day and a half". It'd be great to cross paths in a day or two, surely . . . A day and a half? The divisive calculation is perfectly calculated to lead into the inexorable "But" which introduces a further subtraction:

> But I don't think it's liable to happen
> Like the sound of one hand clappin'

Zen and the art of rhyme. What would it be, in the total absence of any other word, for one word to rhyme? What is the rhyme-sound of one rhyme-word when it does "have to be alone"? The amiably impudent rhyme *happen / clappin'* conveys the truth that a worthwhile rhyme is a happenstance worthy of our applause, while wittily confirming the impossibility that it sets itself to imagine – and of which it speaks with a becoming tentativeness (we better not be too sure about those Masters of Zen): "But I don't think . . ." On the other hand, we can not only imagine but we can see and hear "one hand waving free" in *Mr. Tambourine Man*.[1] Yes: "Yes, to dance beneath the diamond sky with one hand waving free". No downhill dance, this glimpse.

The song is about making an end, or rather, about not flinching from the fact that a love has ended. That the end draws near is intimated to us by Dylan's changing what had been the manifest pattern within the song. Three times there has been unfolded for us a particular pattern: two quatrains, followed by the bridge-couplet. But on the third occasion, this trio is succeeded, not by a quatrain but by the bridge-couplet again, a bridge having led not to a destination but to a further bridge. And only after that is there a final quatrain, standing alone as no previous quatrain had done. Not four, four, two, but two, two, four. The word "Eventually" earns its placing, as does the invocation of "a new transition". The sequence is by no means tangled, but this end is twisted and turned and justified.

> Don't think of me and fantasize on what we never had
> Be grateful for what we've shared together and be glad, oh
>
> Why should we go on watching each other through a telescope?
> Eventually we'll hang ourselves on all this tangled rope
>
> Oh, babe, time for a new transition
> I wish I was a magician
> I would wave a wand and tie back the bond
> That we've both gone beyond

There is something very wasteful about what has happened to the word "share" in modern English, whether American or British. Hardly a day goes by without your reading somewhere that they share something in common, or that they both share it. So I hope that I am right in feeling grateful for Dylan's line "Be grateful for what we've shared together and be glad". Not the usual unthinking redundancy, but a sense of the overflowing gladness of what was once the case. "Shared together": we have shared a bed, "the bed where we slept" (as he sang a moment ago), and we have slept together, and we have been in bed together. "Be glad".

[1] See p. 138.

Rhyme can be a magic wand. I wish. The rhyme *transition / magician* is saucy sorcery, audible, too, in the swish of *wish / magician*, unsentimentally aware of all the things that no amount of rhyming can effect or affect. The finality of this consummation is there in the triplet's fourfold rhyming, the first and last such patterning, going beyond its previous bonds of rhyming:

> I would wave a *wand* and tie back the *bond*
> That we've both *gone beyond*

"Oh, babe". It's all talked over now.

Do Right to Me Baby (Do Unto Others)

Couched both as plea and as pledge, all the admonitions in *Do Right to Me Baby (Do Unto Others)* are addressed to a woman, but they start by invoking an admonition from the Lord, his having counselled prudence. He had said "Judge not, that ye be not judged. For with what judgment ye judge, ye shall be judged: and with what measure ye mete, it shall be measured to you again" (Matthew 7:1–2). The first words of the song, courting blasphemy with their tone of casual indifference, as good as tell the Lord not to worry: "Don't wanna judge nobody". No need to counsel me not to do it, don't wanna do it. So the question doesn't arise, except that of course it does. For the terms of the divine advice do beckon him on, and "Don't wanna judge nobody" is succeeded by "don't wanna be judged". Except, again, that this isn't quite how the impulse of the song impels the two halves of the thought. For whereas Christ gave it as the *reason* why it would be, to say the least, imprudent for us to go around judging (you don't want to *be* judged, do you?), in the song's case any such argumentation is presented as another of the things he doesn't wanna bother with. There is no counterpart in the song to the train of reasoning that is "Judge not, *that* ye be not judged. *For* with what judgment ye judge, ye shall be judged." Think ahead. "A prudent man foreseeth the evil" (Proverbs 22:3). "I wisdom dwell with prudence" (Proverbs 8:12).

　　"Don't wanna judge nobody, don't wanna be judged". Here the second thought, instead of following from the first, merely follows it, and this flatly, fatiguedly. *Do Right to Me Baby (Do Unto Others)* is apparently in no mood for mounting arguments or surmounting them. All it really wants to do is run through – or trudge through – the long list of all the things that it don't wanna do. If it weren't for the pluck and luck of the blithe light-fingered music, twinkling like light on water as it flows (it is the first thing we hear, instrumentally and mentally alert, not lethargic in the least), you might fear that what stretches in front of you is an unremitting teen-age reiteration of *Don't wanna*, a phrase that, by the end, we shall have heard thirty-three times, a phrase that might seem doomed to be leaden or sullen. The wannabe may be bad news but is not as bad company as the don't-wannabe.

> Don't wanna judge nobody, don't wanna be judged
> Don't wanna touch nobody, don't wanna be touched
> Don't wanna hurt nobody, don't wanna be hurt
> Don't wanna treat nobody like they was dirt

But hang in there, there will be a "But".

> But if you do right to me, baby
> I'll do right to you, too
> Got to do unto others
> Like you'd have them, like you'd have them, do unto you

It's a deal. *Don't*, seven times, but then *Do . . . do . . . do . . . do*: a done deal.

"Do unto others . . .": is this the worse for sounding like a deal? Is it, like any other quid pro quo, a double-dealing, a temptation, a lapse into accountancy?

> It's the last temptation, the last account
> The last time you might hear the sermon on the mount
> > *(Shooting Star)*

There hangs about any such thought that we should "do unto others . . .", even though it has behind it the authority of Christ,[1] the suspicion that it

---

[1] Michael Gray is humanely attentive to the Sermon on the Mount (Matthew 7). "Christ's injunction 'all things whatsoever ye would that men should do to you, do ye even so to them' is rendered in modern Bibles as 'do unto others as you would have them do unto you'" (*Song and Dance Man III*, 2000, p. 244 n.)

may come down to no more than *You scratch my back, I'll scratch yours.*[1]
The challenge, then, when it comes to embodying "Do unto others . . ."
in art, is how to cleanse it of any such whiff of the reduction of love and
morals to calculating-machine machinations. An unsanitary whiff, if not
worse. Milton, in *Lycidas*, had to practise an imaginative hygiene when it
came to acknowledging the motive, or rather, one of the motives, moving
him to honour a dead friend.

> So may some gentle Muse
> With lucky words favour my destined urn,
> And as he passes turn
> And bid fair peace be to my sable shroud.

What protects this against any merely grubby reciprocity is, first, the tender
tone of the turn, and then the exquisite modesty of the wish, the wish
that a later poet, in passing, might in turn wish – for Milton, who will
have passed away – not (as you might have anticipated) fame, but peace,
fair peace.

   Do Right to Me Baby (Do Unto Others) is not concerned to be exquisite.
Instead, it finds its hygienic turn in humour, turning to those small unsettling
thwartings of expectation in which humour teasingly delights. The humour
is not frivolous, for serious matters are at stake, salvation and damnation,
that sort of thing. The good words of the good book are touched upon
from the start.

> Don't wanna judge nobody, don't wanna be judged
> Don't wanna touch nobody, don't wanna be touched
> Don't wanna hurt nobody, don't wanna be hurt
> Don't wanna treat nobody like they was dirt

From the Sermon on the Mount ("Judge not . . ."), to the garden of the
sepulchre (John 20:17), where Mary Magdalene hails the resurrected Jesus
as master: "Jesus saith unto her, Touch me not." Don't wanna be touched. It
sounds better perhaps in Latin: *Noli me tangere.* Dylan's moving at once from

---

[1] Greil Marcus, itchy and scratchy, put it like that, to back up his version of this song:
"Dylan's received truths never threaten the unbeliever, they only chill the soul, and
that is because he is offering a peculiarly eviscerated and degraded version of American
fundamentalism" (*New West*, 24 September 1979). It is not the unbeliever that this is
quick to threaten.

judging to touching (his off-rhyme, the putting-off-rhyme *judged / touched*, is well judged) owes something to this biblical moment, and something perhaps (given that this is so bodily a song) not only to Thomas's wish, later in this same chapter of St John, to verify Jesus's resurrection by touching His body, but also to Mary Magdalene's having formerly lived by prostitution. Her eternal life, she earned quite otherwise, by (for instance) hailing Jesus as master.

The subsequent words are likewise simple enough, and so is the pivotal equilibrium that they maintain – "Don't wanna hurt nobody, don't wanna be hurt" – but all this, too, may carry biblical weight. Isaiah 11:9: "They shall not hurt nor destroy in all my holy mountain." Even what might seem the most down-to-earth of such moments, "Don't wanna treat nobody like they was dirt", may be compounded not only of the everyday idiomatic contempt but of the everlasting biblical punishment (God and His ministers having retained the right to hurt) that awaits the enemies of the Lord. Psalms 18:42: "Then did I beat them small as the dust before the wind: I did cast them out as the dirt in the streets".

Yet it would be uncharacteristic of Dylan, even in so religious an album as *Slow Train Coming* (watch out, *Slow Train* urges: be prudent), to make his words gain their authority solely from the word of God. "Don't wanna touch nobody, don't wanna be touched": this is rightly, in human terms and for two reasons, the first of the senses of which the song speaks, though the song itself does, naturally, engage us by virtue of hearing.

The sense of touch has been traditionally (and unjustly?) rated below the sense of sight and the sense of hearing, touch having been rated and berated as basely bodily. Any chance of redeeming this? The line may sound negative to the point of monkishness, "Don't wanna touch nobody, don't wanna be touched", but we know from the title and from the refrain that *nobody* does carry the courtesy "present company excepted". Don't wanna touch nobody else, baby. "But if you do right to me, baby . . ."

Moreover, touch is the only one of the senses that is reciprocal or mutual. I can see you without your seeing me, or hear you without your hearing me, or taste you without your tasting me, or smell you without your smelling me – despite the fact that the verb "to smell", like the verb "to taste", can be in this particular way either transitive or intransitive: I can smell you, or I can smell (pure and simple), and I can taste good things, or I can taste good. But alone of the five senses (the sixth sense is a touch more mysterious), to touch *is* to be touched. I cannot touch you without my being touched. So that although "Don't wanna touch nobody, don't wanna be touched" may sound as though it is exactly parallel to "Don't wanna judge nobody, don't wanna be judged", the thought about judging simply juxtaposes its constituents, whereas the thought about touching can establish its elements as inseparable, as symbiotic, as each inconceivable without the other. As, in short, a doing unto others as you would they should do unto you.

The song may disavow, or make a show of disavowing, a good many of the sins. Pride: "Don't wanna judge nobody". Covetousness: "Don't wanna cheat nobody", as well as "Don't wanna marry nobody if they're already married". ("Thou shalt not covet thy neighbour's wife" – here lust gets a look in.) Anger: "Don't wanna shoot nobody". These sins, and perhaps envy: "Don't wanna defeat nobody who's already been defeated". There is nothing about greed, who is presumably dining out, and sloth is still in bed. But the song's impetus is not exactly to do right, in itself, as God does (Genesis 18:25): "Shall not the Judge of all the earth do right?" (Wanna judge everybody.) "God is still the judge and the devil still rules the world so what's different?" (*Biograph*).

Do Right to Me Baby ought to set us half wondering what it is to do right *to* somebody –

> But if you do right to me, baby
> I'll do right to you, too

– as against doing right by somebody, or (in the good old phrase) doing somebody right (granting them "just or equitable treatment; fairness in decision; justice"), or doing (say) justice to somebody. Do right to me: this looks like a very small deviation from the wording that might have been expected. But then the whole song is founded on such deviations, where a pattern is created and respected but then finds itself modified – modified, should this turn out to be the way to do right by it and to it. So in the opening verse, after three lines that balance equably the enterprise that is activity against that which is passivity:

> Don't wanna judge nobody, don't wanna be judged
> Don't wanna touch nobody, don't wanna be touched
> Don't wanna hurt nobody, don't wanna be hurt

– the fourth line wants, not to be a swaying pair of scales, but to exercise its sway, and to do so by waiving any such antithetical predictability: "Don't wanna treat nobody like they was dirt". This singularity in the last line of the quatrain then becomes expected, naturally, as part of the pattern. So in the second verse (following the refrain quatrain), there is what might seem to be the same trick again: the move from this –

> Don't wanna shoot nobody, don't wanna be shot
> Don't wanna buy nobody, don't wanna be bought
> Don't wanna bury nobody, don't wanna be buried

– to this: "Don't wanna marry nobody if they're already married". But then this is not really the same structure as "Don't wanna treat nobody like they was dirt", even while it might remind you that one way of treating people like dirt is running off with a spouse. For this time the fourth line might look as if it has the antithesis that we are used to ("shoot" / "be shot", and so on), for it does play "marry" against "married". The banter is in the fact that you couldn't have had a hinged line this time, *Don't wanna marry nobody, don't wanna be married*, not unless you didn't mind the mindlessness of putting it like that. To marry somebody, like it or not, *is* thereupon to be married. You can't marry somebody and not be married, though admittedly people are in a sense trying it all the time. "Don't wanna marry nobody if they're already married": this respectfully takes a turn for the better.[1]

Then in the third verse, a further liberty is taken, pattern-wise. This time, there turn out not to be three hinged lines –

> Don't wanna judge nobody, don't wanna be judged
> Don't wanna touch nobody, don't wanna be touched
> Don't wanna hurt nobody, don't wanna be hurt

that are followed by a single sweep of a line:

> Don't wanna treat nobody like they was dirt

---

[1] *Some Other Kinds of Songs*:

> as i vanish down the road
> with a starving actress
> on each arm
> (for better or best
> in sickness an' madness)
> i do take thee
> i'm already married
>
>   (*Lyrics 1962–1985*, 1985, p. 155)

This had been the pattern of the next verse, too:

> Don't wanna shoot nobody, don't wanna be shot
> Don't wanna buy nobody, don't wanna be bought
> Don't wanna bury nobody, don't wanna be buried

– into:

> Don't wanna marry nobody if they're already married

But what now ensues is a different pattern, an alternation of a hinged line with a single direct one, one by one, a couple of times, not three to one.

> Don't wanna burn nobody, don't wanna be burned
> Don't wanna learn from nobody what I gotta unlearn
> Don't wanna cheat nobody, I don't wanna be cheated
> Don't wanna defeat nobody if they already been defeated

What keeps the song on its toes, and us on ours, too, is the feeling, gradually forming, that all these frustrations of expectation can be trusted to become the source of new satisfactions. The course of true love songs never did run smooth. So "Don't wanna burn nobody, don't wanna be burned" is followed by "Don't wanna learn . . ." – at which point, thinking for yourself, you'd better hear in a flash that it can't possibly move on to anything resembling "don't wanna be learned". Time to realize that you may need to unlearn some habits. (But then, "Study means unlearning".[1]) "Don't wanna learn from nobody what I gotta unlearn". Whereupon the quatrain does the same again, this not being the same as what the previous verses had done:

> Don't wanna burn nobody, don't wanna be burned
> Don't wanna learn from nobody what I gotta unlearn
> Don't wanna cheat nobody, I don't wanna be cheated
> Don't wanna defeat nobody if they already been defeated

It isn't (I admit) that I don't want to defeat anybody, it's just that there is no challenge in defeating someone who is down, who has been downed.

---

[1] Lord Bryce, quoted in *Geoffrey Madan's Notebooks*, eds. J. A. Gere and John Sparrow (1981), p. 28.

Patterns are habits forming. The fourth verse finds a different way of being different. It starts as though it might be going to repeat the previous verse's shape, antithesis of active and passive followed by a straight-forward jet:

> Don't wanna wink at nobody, I don't wanna be winked at
> Don't wanna be used by nobody for a doormat

But then, with a wink, the lines are used, not as a doormat, but as a launching pad. For the shaping that then ensues is one that we have not had before, with the *closing* two lines having the antithetical form of every quatrain's *opening* lines – and with the added amusement (no confusement) of the particular tone with which they rhyme, both within themselves and with one another, happy to mount from the simple truth to an outrageous untruth that nevertheless has a serious truth ensconced within it:

> Don't wanna wink at nobody, I don't wanna be winked at
> Don't wanna be used by nobody for a doormat
> Don't wanna confuse nobody, don't wanna be confused
> Don't wanna amuse nobody, I don't wanna be amused

I Don't Believe You (He Acts Like We Never Have Met His Expectations).
Which leaves only the finishing end, the verse that comes up with yet more ways of being itself while not snubbing the other verses and their selves.

> Don't wanna betray nobody, don't wanna be betrayed
> Don't wanna play with nobody, don't wanna be waylaid
> Don't wanna miss nobody, don't wanna be missed
> Don't put my faith in nobody, not even a scientist

First line, as expected or even agreed: "betray" into "be betrayed". But the second line, with its "play" into "be waylaid"? This last rhyme-word (double, really, *way-laid*) is a comical breach of faith, way out. Not till now had we ever been given to understand that when the active verb changes to the passive, it would be permissible, would be fair play, to change the verb, too. A dozen times we had accepted that we were being trained to shape up. But now, "Don't wanna play with nobody" – fine, only to be succeeded,

not by "don't wanna be played with", but (waylaying us) by "don't wanna
be waylaid". Clearly, he *does* wanna play with somebody. With her. But
fortunately with us, too. Love is teasing, love is pleasing.

But we know where we are with "Don't wanna miss nobody, don't
wanna be missed". (A thought of which we will miss the range unless we
call to mind the very different things that the word "miss" may mean.)
And then the last line of the song (followed by the final refrain): "Don't
put my faith in nobody, not even a scientist". Again we know where we
are with this: that is, in a place where we haven't been before. For this
Don't wanna song has suddenly changed what it most needs to say. No
longer what he doesn't want to do, but what he doesn't do. "Don't put
my faith in nobody, not even a scientist". The song, which had begun
with the Christian faith, rounds in the end upon the presumptuous gullible
faith that believes itself to have taken the place of religion or to have put
religion in its place. "Not even a scientist" – the phrase arrives from outer
space. "Don't put my faith in nobody", but again, with the tacit "present
company excepted". Have faith in me, as I have in you. Be faithful, he
says to her but also to himself. For such is one of the ways in which you
do right to somebody.

> But if you do right to me, baby
> I'll do right to you, too
> Ya got to do unto others
> Like you'd have them, like you'd have them, do unto you

And in doing right to one another, they will have a good chance of
doing right by others, even as the song in its well-weighed comedy does
right by us.

Temperance

Love Minus Zero / No Limit

"Arise, arise," he cried so loud
In a voice without restraint
"Come out, ye gifted kings and queens
And hear my sad complaint"

I Dreamed I Saw St. Augustine. I dreamed I heard him, too. When (wide-awake) you chance to read his Confessions, which amount to more than a sad complaint, it is a voice with restraint that you hear. With passion, yes, and with convictions, but not without restraint. In Dylan's evocation, the very rhyme acts – as rhyme often does – as a restraint, as a way of containing emotions.

A voice without restraint would be a voice without Temperance. This virtue, like its sister Prudence, may not seem robust enough to be more than an associate member of The Cardinals, but one should never underestimate the power that derives from not overestimating things. The family of words to which temperance belongs may not appear to claim very much – moderation, measure, sobriety, self-control, self-restraint – but then not claiming very much is part of their point. And as to the forms that may be taken by knowledge, one of the best is knowing when one has had enough. Also known as temperance.

The practice or habit of restraining oneself in provocation, passion, desire, etc.; rational self-restraint. (One of the four cardinal virtues.)

Self-restraint and moderation in action of any kind, in the expression of opinion, etc.; suppression of any tendency to passionate action; in early use, esp. self-control, restraint, or forbearance, when provoked to anger or impatience.

(The Oxford English Dictionary)

Temperance is a virtue that, though not worldly, knows the world.

> She knows there's no success like failure
> And that failure's no success at all
>
> She knows too much to argue or to judge

Benjamin Franklin: "Three may keep a secret, if two of them are dead." Benjamin Jowett: "Cheat as little as you can" (to a grocer who said it was impossible for an honest tradesman to live). Benjamin Disraeli: "Next to knowing when to seize an opportunity, the most important thing in life is to know when to forgo an advantage."[1] And that's just the Benjamins.

There is, it need hardly be said (a temperate idiom, this), a countering culture that sees Temperance as no more than a *nom de guerre* for temporizing, weakness, flight. Temperance fugit.

> Those who restrain desire, do so because theirs is weak enough to be restrained; and the restrainer or reason usurps its place & governs the unwilling.
>
> And being restrain'd, it by degrees becomes passive, till it is only the shadow of desire.
>
> (*The Marriage of Heaven and Hell*)

William Blake, who constitutes the greatest Intemperance Society, may exclaim "Enough! or Too much", and may aver that "If the fool would persist in his folly he would become wise", and that "The road of excess leads to the palace of wisdom." But he did have the grace to call these provocations Proverbs of Hell.[2] And he might have acknowledged that W. H. Auden was within his rights to retort that "The road of excess leads to the slough of despond".

Even when a Dylan song pleads for more, it will often plead, not for more and more and more, but for "one more": *One More Weekend, One More Cup of Coffee, One More Night,* or (one more instance) *Honey, Just Allow Me One More Chance.* Get along with you.[3] It is all a matter of

---

[1] Franklin, *Poor Richard's Almanack*, July 1735. The other two of the three: *Geoffrey Madan's Notebooks*, eds. J. A. Gere and John Sparrow (1981), pp. 112, 52.

[2] Blake was hard on Prudence, too: "Prudence is a rich, ugly old maid courted by Incapacity." See p. 359.

[3] Beckett, *Mercier and Camier* (1974), p. 31:

Good evening, my children, said Mercier, get along with you now.

But they did not get along with them, no, but stood their ground, their little clasped hands lightly swinging back and forth.

setting a limit to what is asked. And the song that has the word "limit" within its title, though crucially never within the limits of the song itself, is a temperance song: *Love Minus Zero/No Limit*.

No limit: this must sound intemperate, and is so, consciously, when Dylan sings (in *Sugar Baby*) "There ain't no limit to the amount of trouble women bring". The line is sung most sadly, with the sadness deriving not really from the truth or falsity of the charge itself but from any such sad complaint's needing to be resorted to when there never turns out to be any comfort in such blame-shifting. Is there no limit to the amount of blame we all try to cast? *Sugar Baby* broods on this, limitlessly.

> Sugar Baby, get on down the line
> You ain't got no brains, no how
> You went years without me
> Might as well keep going now

No limit: as when the sky's the limit. ("And but for the sky there are no fences facin'".[1]) But the title *Love Minus Zero/No Limit*, while remaining mysterious, was clarified a fraction by Dylan when, just for once, he uttered the title of a song, and uttered this one as "*Love Minus Zero* over *No Limit*", calling it "sort of a fraction".[2] The song engages with temperance, which becomes fractured, divided. *Love Minus Zero* being divided by *No Limit*? It defies explaining or even imagining, but does itself thereby set limits to what one can explain or imagine. And is a joke of a curious sort.

Auden proposed that one tantalizing distinction is between poems whose titles you could guess from the poem, and poems whose titles you couldn't. Not that the one kind is superior to the other, simply that they may be of crucially different kinds. There would be something wrong with you if you were unable to guess from the words of the particular song the title *Blowin' in the Wind*, say, or *Sad-Eyed Lady of the Lowlands* or *If Not For You*. Then along the way there are some songs where you might need luck to guess the title with precision (*Slow Train*, given that its title is not *Slow Train Coming*, and *Abandoned Love*). And then, at the other end, there are those songs where, let's face it, there would be something wrong with you if you supposed even for a moment that you could ever have guessed the title. No way, when it comes to *Love Minus Zero/No Limit*. Not only that,

[1] *Mr. Tambourine Man.*
[2] Newcastle (9 May 1965); released as one of the bonus tracks on the DVD of *Dont Look Back* (1999).

but it is rare for you to hear a title. For the title of a song almost always goes unuttered, and this means that it is not at all the same as the title of a poem, which is there for the eye to take in exactly as the eye will then proceed to take in the poem. Even when the poem is offered to the ear (at a poetry reading), the poet will vouchsafe the title.

Positively 4th Street. Just Like Tom Thumb's Blues. And *Love Minus Zero/ No Limit.* These titles, in their variously bizarre ways, are off-limits. Off the limits of the song proper. Heard melodies are sweet, but those unheard are sweeter. Unheard titles to heard melodies, titles unheard on the album and rarely heard in concert, titles (moreover) undivinable, have a way of being sweet and sour.

William Blake once more:

Without Contraries is no progression. Attraction and Repulsion, Reason and Energy, Love and Hate, are necessary to Human existence.

The contraries are at once necessary to the existence of *Love Minus Zero/ No Limit.*

> My love she speaks like silence
> Without ideals or violence

A deep rhyme, for all kinds of reasons. Rhyming on such a word as "silence" is likely to intrigue, because a rhyme is a sound; there's something askew about the criss-cross of the meaning of the word and the fact that you're using it for a sound effect. *Silence / violence*: it's not exactly a violent rhyme (exactly not a violent rhyme?), but you can hear that it isn't a perfect rhyme, either. (*Is* there a perfect rhyme for "silence"? This song has a way of making you want to ask questions parenthetically.) So the nature of violence is brought up at the very beginning, and yet the rhyme fits or kinda fits. As, with its own violence, does Ben Jonson's tour de force, *A Fit of Rhyme against Rhyme.*[1]

---

[1] Including:

> He that first invented thee,
> May his joints tormented be,
> Cramped forever;
> Still may syllabes jar with time,
> Still may reason war with rhyme,
> Resting never.

[*syllabes*: syllables]

Silence and violence: and do ideals and violence fit together, too, and unexpectedly, too? Robert Lowell said that "Violence and idealism have some occult connection."[1] Asked about the violence of the USA, Lowell spoke of an idealistic crusading history, a nation "founded on a declaration", but he admitted that there is no knowing: "I think that it has something to do with both the idealism and the power of the country. Other things are boring for these young people, and violence isn't boring." Lowell, like Dylan, knows that the difficulty comes when something more than silence is called for, when you must speak.

At the beginning of *King Lear*, Cordelia does not know how she will be able to reply to her father's insistence that his three daughters announce their love for him. She has an aside (an aside being a combination of speech and silence, as speaking to oneself is): "What shall Cordelia speak? Love, and be silent." Her love, it speaks like silence. Or she hopes it will. But this, in the unjust upshot, does not satisfy Lear. Her silence, which becomes her refusal to placate him (let us not talk falsely now), moves him to violence.

> "What can you say to draw
> A third more opulent than your sisters? Speak."
>
> "Nothing, my Lord."
>
> * * *
>
> "So young and so untender?"
>
> "So young, my Lord, and true."

True like ice, like fire, and true moreover as love. When Dylan puts a question and answer, the exchange may find itself harboured within parentheses, themselves carrying a suggestion of the unspoken, the silent.

> (you ask of love?
> there is no love
> except in silence
> an' silence doesn't say a word)[2]

Or, in the words said by Blake:

---

[1] I draw on an essay of mine on Lowell, *The Force of Poetry* (1984), pp. 263–5. Lowell's words are from 1965.

[2] 11 *Outlined Epitaphs*, in *Lyrics 1962–1985* (1985), p. 114.

> Never seek to tell thy love,
> Love that never told can be.
> For the gentle wind does move
> Silently, invisibly

The rhyme of "silence" and "violence" is at once forced and easy enough, and it is a rhyme that Lowell needed in his translation of Racine's *Phèdre*. Lowell gives a greater strain to the rhyme than Dylan does, by insisting metrically (Dylan did the opposite) on the extra syllable in "violence":

> Lady, if you must weep, weep for your silence
> that filled your days and mine with violence.

The edge or edginess is different from Dylan's opening couplet:

> My love she speaks like silence
> Without ideals or violence

But both Dylan and Lowell invite you to think about, even if not to speak about, the occult connection between idealism and violence. A much later Dylan song, *Union Sundown*, an overtly political song that scowls at violence, is closer to Lowell's sense of the world:

> Democracy don't rule the world
> You'd better get that in your head
> This world is ruled by violence
> But I guess that's better left unsaid
> From Broadway to the Milky Way
> That's a lot of territory indeed
> And a man's gonna do what he has to do
> When he's got a hungry mouth to feed

The dark comedy here is not that of rhyming "silence" with "violence", waywardly yet gently, but of positioning (with a grimace) "violence" so that it leads, not to silence, but to "But I guess that's better left unsaid", as though by a rhyming of sense, not of sound. The word that is better left unsaid, and unsounded, is "silence", for all its willingness to make up to "violence" elsewhere. And when "territory" is reached, there is a feeling, given the insistence that "This world is ruled by violence", that territory there may be tinged with terror. As the head becomes the mouth, and as the Milky Way breastfeeds the hungry mouth,[1] the world of *Union Sundown* ("From Broadway to the Milky Way") widens voraciously. Fortunately, prudence has put in a word, has put in the words that come naturally to it: "You'd better" and "I guess that's better left unsaid".

The loved one in *Love Minus Zero/No Limit* leaves things unsaid:

> My love she speaks like silence
> Without ideals or violence
> She doesn't have to say she's faithful
> Yet she's true, like ice, like fire
> People carry roses
> Make promises by the hours
> My love she laughs like the flowers
> Valentines can't buy her

The rhyme-scheme is simplicity herself. The first and second lines rhyme (*silence/violence*); so do the fourth and eighth lines (*fire/buy her*); and so do the sixth and seventh lines (*hours/flowers*). Which leaves only the third and fifth lines not rhyming. A tacit intricacy is set up so that nothing rhymes with "faithful", and nothing rhymes with "roses". (And yet the roses and the flowers, paired at their line-endings, clearly chime in sense.) This ought to lure us into wondering about the relationship not only between the lines that rhyme (we are used to doing this), but between the lines that don't. Her being faithful doesn't have anything to do with roses. Anyway, it doesn't say – it doesn't have to say – she's faithful, any more than she has to. It's written all over her. And all through this praise of her.

"People carry roses": "carry" there suggests a certain gait, and something of an errand, and even perhaps weapons in the war between the sexes, a war that may entail winning women over. But it isn't because people carry roses (to her or in the wider world of their amorous solicitations) that she's faithful. It doesn't turn on that. Anyway, people in life often carry roses because they have been – or have been tempted to be – *un*faithful. The bouquet bought on the way home. Nothing in her has any wish that *roses*

---

[1] The Milky Way is far away, but the thought is not far-fetched given the origin of the phrase, the milk from a mythical breast. Also *OED*, 2b: The region of a woman's breast.

should rhyme, or that *faithful* should, either. An end in itself, in herself, being faithful. People carry roses. She carries it off.

> My love she laughs like the flowers
> Valentines can't buy her

Flowers laugh in the classical application of such words as "laugh" or "smile", in that they not only make you happy but look happy themselves.

All three pairs of rhymes in the first verse have something in common, an undulation, a hesitation as to exactly how many syllables they ask. There is a play of the two syllables of "silence" against the two or three of "violence", and of the two syllables of "buy her" against the one or two of "fire" – with then a variation on this with "hours" and "flowers", hoverers both.[1] There is another kind of hovering here, too, in the unobtrusive word "by": "Make promises by the hours". What begins as the "by" of "in terms of swearing or adjuration" – "make promises by . . ." – becomes in time the "by" of time: "by the hours".

But it is time for the second verse. Whereas in the first verse, lines one and two had rhymed:

> My love she speaks like silence
> Without ideals or violence

the next verse varies this, so that the third line maintains the initiating rhyme, with "repeat" to make sure that although this may surprise us, it will not startle us:

> In the dime stores and bus stations
> People talk of situations
> Read books, repeat quotations
> Draw conclusions on the wall

But it is not only that the double rhyme becomes a triple one (*stations / situations / quotations*), and not only that "situations" so completely engrosses or swallows up "stations", but that the abstract suffix, *-ions*, keeps pressing on,

[1] Lowell feels the poignancy in such a hovering: "often the old grow still more beautiful, / watering out the hours, biting back their tears". Both "hours" and "tears" are uncertain as to how long they have. (*Mother and Father 1*, in *History*, 1973.)

until it reaches "conclusions". People (again this faintly dismissive locution: people carry roses, people talk of situations) read the writing on the wall, and among the quotations that they repeat there is one that is itself a conclusion that speaks of the future.

> Draw conclusions on the wall
> Some speak of the future

Conclusions *on*, not conclusions *from*, though the latter will be drawn soon enough. The Book of Daniel, chapter 5:

In the same hour came forth fingers of a man's hand, and wrote over against the candlestick upon the plaster of the wall of the king's palace.

And this is the writing that was written, MENE, MENE, TEKEL, UPHARSIN. This is the interpretation of the thing: MENE; God hath numbered thy kingdom, and finished it. TEKEL; Thou art weighed in the balances, and art found wanting.

Later in the song, "the candlestick" furnishes Dylan not only with "the candles" but with "matchsticks" to light the candles, and the word "numbered" may have its relation to *Minus Zero*. This same chapter of Daniel has "people", "tremble", "wise men", and "gifts"; also "spake" ("speaks"), "said" ("say"), and "that night" ("the night" and "at midnight"). "The king" is reduced to "the pawn".[1]

"Thou art weighed in the balances, and art found wanting". Who, in the end, in the song, will be weighed in the balances and found wanting?

In this verse, the rhyme-scheme – since "wall" and "all" rhyme, and so in their hollow way, disconcertingly, do "future" and "failure" – leaves only the fifth line not rhyming: "My love she speaks softly". It is a lovely touch, this not rhyming (so hushedly) on "softly", and yet the line in other respects rhymes with, pairs with, something elsewhere, since it picks up "My love she speaks like silence", and "softly" is after all both more and less *hushed* than is silence. The sequence of thought remains elusive, or even illusory:

---

[1] This chapter of Daniel may contribute to *Dark Eyes*, where "the falling gods of speed and steel" are the accelerated modernized compacting of "the gods of gold, and of silver, of brass, of iron, of wood, and of stone" who are twice invoked.

Some speak of the future
My love she speaks softly

"Some speak of the future": this does not proceed to usher in any anticipated contrast by way of what my love speaks of. *Of the future* as against what, exactly? "My love she speaks" – wait for it – "softly". Is it that people who speak of the future speak with hardness and with loudness? Yes, actually, they often do, in the self-gratifying heat not just of prophesying but of prophesizing. So my love, she speaks not of the future but – softly.

Her voice was ever soft,
Gentle, and low, an excellent thing in woman.
(*King Lear*, V, iii)

No limit to the amount of trouble generalizations about women bring. Lear, in his recovered love as he stands over the body of Cordelia, speaks of the past. She, who at the beginning of the play, could say "Nothing", can now say nothing.

"My love she speaks softly": softly, because the past and the present may have some power to hush us into speaking more quietly, more temperately. The future, on the other hand, is up for grabs, and grabs can be noisy. A friend of mine, Mark Halliday, once proposed, a quarter jokingly, a sequence of thought that might have met one's expectations:

Some speak of the future
My love she's into Now

– a burlesque that does bring out how powerfully inconsequential these alignments may be.

The third verse of *Love Minus Zero / No Limit* has always baffled and delighted me. One of Dylan's most suggestive surrealist sequences, it eludes paraphrase and translation, and it teases us into and out of thought – and back into thought again.

The cloak and dagger dangles
Madams light the candles
In ceremonies of the horsemen
Even the pawn must hold a grudge
Statues made of matchsticks

> Crumble into one another
> My love winks, she does not bother
> She knows too much to argue or to judge

My love winks, and an equivocal wink it is, too, and an equivocal thing a wink is, too. Like the lines themselves, with all their secretive nudges, she seems to be sharing a joke with us while not actually letting us in on the joke. Could it be that she is conniving? Powerfully attractive women sometimes are. "Connive": from the Latin, "to wink". *The Oxford English Dictionary* brings out the disconcerting shifts and shiftiness of the word "connive", from

To shut one's eyes to a thing that one dislikes but cannot help, to pretend ignorance, to take no notice

("My love winks, she does not bother") – through to a really rather different sense of what is going on:

To shut one's eyes to an action that one ought to oppose, but which one covertly sympathizes with; to wink *at*.

This verse of the song winks, tipping us the wink and advising us likewise to know too much to argue or to judge, or perhaps reminding us that we know too little to be able to do either. The rhyme *dangles/candles* has the melting touch of Salvador Dali; the rhyme *grudge/judge* returns us promptly to the real world of solid sullenness; and the other rhyme, *another/bother*, very appropriately does not bother and should not bother us. Imperfect, but what's so good about being perfect? Such is the rhyme's air. Which leaves, as the only line-endings that are left unrhymed, "horsemen" and "matchsticks". I have no idea what to make of the teeming and the provocation here, or what Dylan made of them except mischief and glee and shadows. The "ceremonies of the horsemen" suggest the chessboard knights (lording it over the pawn) as well as the Changing of the Guards, but what game or ceremony is going on here? "The cloak and dagger" is transformed by "dangles", as though by a conjuror, into a medal or decoration, like the Star and Garter (he was awarded the Cloak and Dagger; there it is, dangling or daggling from his breast). At a leap, the world of the song has become "espionage, secrecy, intrigue, etc." (a good dark *etc.*), a world – *The Oxford English Dictionary* reminds us – of "drama or stories of intrigue and romantic or melodramatic adventure, in which the principal characters are taken from that class of society which formerly wore cloak and dagger or sword".[1] And which formerly frequented brothels: "Madams light the candles". A sinister business.

> Madame de Tornquist, in the dark room
> Shifting the candles.[2]

It is all a dreamscape in which there is much to be felt and little to be learnt.

> At dawn my lover comes to me
> And tells me of her dreams
> With no attempts to shovel the glimpse
> Into the ditch of what each one means
> (*Gates of Eden*)

The interpretation of dreams? Again the Book of Daniel, chapter 5:

And the king spake, and said to the wise men of Babylon, Whosoever shall read this writing, and shew me the interpretation thereof, shall be clothed with scarlet, and have a chain of gold about his neck, and shall be the third ruler in the kingdom.

These wise men, unlike the Christmas ones, do not bring gifts, yet the successful interpreter is promised a gift of gold, though not of frankincense or myrrh.

Visions and dreams are among the limitlessnesses, and the final dream-vistas of the song are at once continuous with the previous glimpses and newly disturbingly disjointed:

> The bridge at midnight trembles
> The country doctor rambles
> Bankers' nieces seek perfection

---

[1] "You came in like the wind, like Errol Flynn" (*You Changed My Life*). "Sing me one more song, about ya love me to the moon and the stranger / And your fall-by-the-sword love affair with Errol Flynn" (*Foot of Pride*). One more song, that's all he asks, temperately. But the next two lines, despite their further "one more", have had enough of temperance: "In these times of compassion when conformity's in fashion / Say one more stupid thing to me before the final nail is driven in".

[2] T. S. Eliot, *Gerontion*.

Expecting all the gifts that wise men bring
The wind howls like a hammer
The night blows cold and rainy
My love she's like some raven
At my window with a broken wing

This is exquisitely evoked, both line by line and in its mounting. The rhyme *trembles / rambles* engages auditorily in those two activities, and "bring" duly brings in "wing", or rather, "bring" spreads its wing to become *broken wing*. The off-rhyme *rainy / raven* thinks better than to seek perfection, and yet the laminations of the lines are perfect in their way. "The bridge at midnight trembles": who (it may be wondered with a slight tremble) can be out there at this time of night? "The country doctor rambles": rambling in his mind, is it? or a house call, at this hour? "Bankers' nieces seek perfection": where have they impertinently arrived from? Not who do they think they are, but who do we think they are? And what kind of perfection, exactly? "Expecting all the gifts that wise men bring": but the wise men were bringing gifts to the infant Christ, a very different perfection from any that is likely to figure in the calculations of bankers' nieces.

But then again (for the suggestions twist and turn) perhaps the Three Wise Men are not in fact the wise men in question, not because they are shadows of their former selves but because they are later selves. For is it not the earlier wise men, the wise men of the Book of Daniel, who take precedence? "The wise men of Babylon", "Then came in all the king's wise men", "the wise men, the astrologers". Far wiser than the wise men, the prophet Daniel went without gifts: "Then Daniel answered and said before the king, Let thy gifts be to thyself, and give thy rewards to another."

The riches of the song, of its instigations and recesses, constitute in themselves a range of gifts. Yet there remains something deeply dark about the song's ending. The crucial decision by Dylan can be felt in his leaving unrhymed in this last verse the words "perfection" and "hammer". What is perfection up against? A hammer.[1] And this involves the question of how it is, and of why it is, and of whether it believably is, that

My love she's like some raven
At my window with a broken wing

---

[1] *Sugar Baby*: "I got my back to the sun 'cause the light is too intense / I can see what everybody in the world is up against".

This is another of the occasions in my experience of Dylan, my experience moreover of his greatest songs (for the other instances of my perturbation are *One Too Many Mornings* and *Positively 4th Street*), when I don't know what to think, or what to feel, or quite how to argue and to judge. For there is at the end of the song what feels like a curious rounding on the woman. She has been evoked throughout the song in a way that is on the face of it incompatible with her being like some raven with a broken wing. Why is she like some raven with a broken wing? Because she has now been hit with a hammer?

The end of the song should be felt as something of a surprise, to put it mildly. The beautiful equanimity of Dylan's voicing and of the tune itself should not disguise this from us, although clearly to speak of disguise may do the enterprise less than justice: not, perhaps, an attempt to evade the contrariety, but to bring home an evasiveness or a self-deception that threatens all such laudatory lovings. The song seems to me to turn out to be saying something along these lines: "What I like about her is that she is so wonderfully independent of me, she doesn't really need me, other people do this, that, and the other, and she deliciously doesn't, she, she, she – actually, come to think of it, far from being what I like about her, it's why . . ." – exit, muttering darkly something about going to get a hammer, and maybe breaking more than her wing, her spirit . . . She had been valued for not needing to need him, yet now there is felt a need to be needed by her, a need that she *not* be so strong.

A fascinating situation, if I read it aright (and no doubt if I don't), but one that raises – as so often do the love poems of Donne – the question of whether the situation is being dramatized or not. Dramatized or inadvertently advertised? Are the feelings in the song realized as to their true nature, as inevitably tinged with falsity, their wresting of feelings from what is true like ice, like fire? Does the doctor ramble, or can he be trusted to diagnose truly?

The song had begun with a simple haunting asseveration:

> My love she speaks like silence
> Without ideals or violence

It ends no less simply but now differently haunted:

> My love she's like some raven
> At my window with a broken wing

The violence that had been disavowed in the beginning has come to constitute the end. For violence is just below the surface of the lines:

> The wind howls like a hammer
> The night blows rainy

All but silently (that is, tacitly), this invokes the raining of blows on somebody with a hammer.[1] When "rain" and "blows" and "hammer" go together, "perfection" is set to meet "hammer", without rhyme but with reason. (So different from the unrhyming relationship of "faithful" to "roses", or from the unique and delicate unrhymedness of "softly".) Is her perfection to be broken by some phantom hammer? Or was she never as perfect as we – going along with her, going out with her – had supposed?

Dylan has had lots of shots at that line "The night blows rainy." You can hear him sing in a 1965 out-take "The rain blows cold". But then "cold" has no rhyme at all, with a very chilling effect. On another occasion, you can hear him sing what is printed in *Lyrics 1962–1985*, "The night blows cold and rainy" – which separates the word "blows" from *rain / rainy*, and so does something to mitigate the incipient violence. "Even the pawn must hold a grudge". Even the king? Even Dylan, whom I ungrudgingly admire?

The choice is, in my judgement, stark. If it is granted that the end must be allowed to retain its surprise, its shock even, then the question (when it comes not to valuing the song, but to valuing it at its true worth) is whether the end is apprehended in the course of the song. And apprehended has to mean understood, or – to invoke Henry James's term – "placed".[2] So from the wing of a raven to *The Wings of the Dove*. The elaborations are those of love and resentment:

He was walking in short on a high ridge, steep down on either side, where the proprieties – once he could face at all remaining there – reduced themselves to his keeping his head. It was Kate who had so perched him, and there came up for him at moments, as he found himself planting one foot exactly before another, a sensible sharpness of irony as to her management of him. It wasn't that she had put him in danger – to be in real danger with her would have had another quality. There glowed for him in fact a kind of rage at what he wasn't having;

---

[1] I believe that it was Tom Davis, in Birmingham long ago, who pointed out to me some of these dark energies.

[2] See p. 437.

an exasperation, a resentment, begotten truly by the very impatience of desire, in respect to his postponed and relegated, his so extremely manipulated state. It was beautifully done of her, but what was the real meaning of it unless that he was perpetually bent to her will?

All he had originally felt in her came back to him, was indeed actually as present as ever – how he had admired and envied what he called to himself her direct talent for life, as distinguished from his own, a poor weak thing of the occasion, amateurishly patched up; only it irritated him the more that this was now, ever so characteristically, standing out in her.[1]

There she is, there they are, in Henry James's imagining. And, if we allow for this and that, in Dylan's imagining.

Every time I write a song, it's like writing a novel. Just takes me a lot less time, and I can get it down . . . down to where I can re-read it in my head a lot.[2]

Read books, repeat quotations, draw conclusions.

Sugar Baby

When it comes to the way they walk, there are songs that stroll and songs that stride, those that prance and those that saunter. Amble or gambol, meander and maunder. Foxtrot, lope, and pace. How a song moves those who hear it, this will be intimate with how it does itself move, particularly when it is of movement that it sings. Just imagine all the ways there are to talk the walk. Indefatigable: *Pressing On*. Pricked: *If You Gotta Go, Go Now*. Hobbling: "My toes too numb to step". (I don't believe you, thought Mr. Tambourine Man.) Hobbled: *Cold Irons Bound*. Or following a direction: "Sugar Baby get on down the road".

Matthew Arnold heard the truth, long ago, far away:

The superior character of truth and seriousness, in the matter and substance of the best poetry, is inseparable from the superiority of diction and movement marking its style and manner.

[1] Book Eighth, chapter 1.
[2] *Whaaat?* (the 1965 interview with Nat Hentoff, in full, differing from *Playboy*, March 1966), p. 6. See p. 25.

The Study of Poetry. The same would go for the study of song, the study of how song goes. Especially when a song's concern is a going one.

Two idioms were the parents of this Sugar Baby, parents who – despite not exactly getting on with one another – were determined to make a go of it. They are the idioms *to go without* ("You went years without me") and *to keep going* ("Might as well keep going now"). Their child would be *keep going without*. Meanwhile, lurking in the brains behind pa and ma is the thought of getting going, which is why the words "get" and "got" get to usher in "went without" and "keep going":

> Sugar Baby get on down the road
> You ain't got no brains, no how
> You went years without me
> Might as well keep going now

Might as well keep going? Or might as well keep going without me? Might as well keep going, without any mention of "me".

When something is sung, a vocal fluctuation can make it impossible even to imagine what the counterpart would be in a poem, let alone what an equivalent would be. *Sugar Baby* depends upon the way in which (outside the refrain that furnishes the contrast) the music and the voice, from the beginning, are reluctant to accommodate themselves to the shaping that the words' sense-units would demand, were the words not in a song but in a poem. A poem may play one system of punctuation (the usual marks) against another (the line-ending that has no terminal punctuation), and to this, a song may add the unexpected tilt or pause, the hesitation or edge, that the voice and the music can express and impress.

Metre, prosody, lineation, rhythm: time for a crèche course. Accent, or stress, is what we are to hear – and listen for – in poetry, particularly poetry in the English tradition. This might take the line that no poet ever quite perpetrates: *ti tum, ti tum, ti tum, ti tum, ti tum.* That is, an unstressed syllable and then a stressed one, all the way to "Detroit Detroit Detroit Detroit Detroit". Or, with the stress the other way round, the vast vista in *King Lear*, never to be forgotten:

> Thou'lt come no more,
> Never, never, never, never, never.

But then the complication, as we all know, is that there are degrees of stress, so that in conversation as well as in poetry, the life in any utterance is not disposed to have its sounds be simply either stressed or unstressed, either the one or the other. For life and verse like to touch upon matters diversely, with gradations, taking the measure of things.

In music, the principle of measurement (for that is what metre means) will subordinate accent or stress to quantity or length: how long it takes to utter something. Bars come in lengths. Quantity or length, it is true, was also in some classical poetry the ground rule (Greek more than Latin),[1] and there have been intermittent attempts in English poetry to imitate this classical precedent. More memorably, there have been poems (for instance, by William Cowper and by Thomas Hardy) that sound as though they are setting the one principle and practice against the other, quantity or length against stress or accent.

How long it takes to utter something is not the same as how much stress you put on it, for there may be a word that takes little emphasis but has a clutch of consonants and vowels reluctant to slip along. An effect of stress versus quantity, then, can act as an embodiment of a human contrariety: fate versus resolution, say, or stoicism versus pain, or grief versus relief. Of a particular motion of mind that you are brought to hear, you may feel that it is somehow not natural to move in this way or in these contrarious ways. But art, naturally, cannot afford to limit itself to movements that are natural. For it may be under strain that a truth will be found to reveal itself, brought to light's intensity from the hiding places of its power. "Plenty of places to hide things here if you wanna hide 'em bad enough".

We feel a strain in the strains of *Sugar Baby*. "You got a way of tearing the world apart. Love, see what you've done". What, on the face of it, could be simpler than the words "a way of"? But the simplicity is torn. For in terms of accent or stress (poetry's terms), the words would run equably from the stressed into the unstressed: "wáy of". But in terms of length or quantity, the two words are granted, by the music and the voice, and by the bleak break after the word "of", a plain equality: "wáy óf".

> You got a way of
> tearing the world apart
> Love
> see what you've done

The effect has something of the off-rhyme about it. For the unmistakable

---

[1] Kenneth Haynes helped me to see and hear this.

rhyme *love/of*, see or rather hear *City of Gold*, a song that he performed in 1980, now covered by the Dixie Hummingbirds on the CD of *Masked and Anonymous*:

> There is a city of love
> Far from this world
> And the stuff dreams are made of
> Beyond the sunset
> Stars high above
> There is a city of love

"And the stuff dreams are made of": good Shakespearean stuff, benign enough, unlike the growl of Philip Larkin:

> Ah, were I courageous enough
>   To shout *Stuff your pension!*
> But I know, all too well, that's the stuff
>   That dreams are made of.
>
> (Toads)

"*Love* rhymes with *of*". Such is the title of a generously revelatory essay by Anne Ferry.[1]

There is "a wáy of", and there is "a wáy óf". The one way of apprehending those words is pitched against another. There is a dual possibility in the very word "stress". *Sugar Baby* deals in stress, deals with it.

Prudence and temperance set themselves to engage stress, responsibly

---

[1] In MODERNISM/*modernity*, vol. 7, 2000. "Rhymes like *love : of* have signifying possibilities that were first taken seriously in the early twentieth century because they satisfied the intentions of the modernist aesthetic." Such a rhyme is felt to be "mismatched", marked by "incongruent effects", because of the tradition that deemed certain classes of word to be below the dignity of rhyming, even of comic rhyming. Prepositions, for instance (though phrasal verbs or prepositional verbs were granted some licence: "Shakespeare's 'drinkes it vp': 'cup'; Herbert's 'creepes in': 'sinne'"). Edward Bysshe, in *The Art of English Poetry* (1702), had issued a list of the parts of speech that should not be rhymed on, for instance "the Particles *An, And, As, Of, The,* &c." Anne Ferry writes with imaginative acumen about what it is to rhyme on such a word as "but" or "of", even – Marianne Moore's inaugurative move in 1916 – to have an end-rhyme of "the" with "be". The essay is on poetry, not song, but much in it would illuminate Dylan's decisions in timing and in a kind of rhyming that his lineation, as voiced, can bring home.

anticipating all such movements as may prove incautious or immoderate. *Sugar Baby* opens with open eyes, thanks to a prudent decision as to where to place oneself:

> I got my back to the sun 'cause the light is too intense
> I can see what everybody in the world is up against
> You can't turn back – you can't come back, sometimes we push too far
> One day you'll open up your eyes and you'll see where we are

Prudence and temperance do not shrink from giving advice or from issuing admonitions such as these. For instance, don't be too intense. Prudence and temperance concur in such a turn of phrase as "Might as well . . .", which is at once prudential and temperate, careful not to be precipitate or to overdo things, careful not to insist *Easily the best thing would be to . . .* or *Much better to . . .* Settle for "Might as well keep going now": this, as the conclusion of the refrain, both precedes and succeeds another recommending of prudence, "Try to make things better for someone, sometimes, you just end up making it a thousand times worse" – a serpentine line that warns against the danger of spilling and flooding.

Look before you leap, but first of all, station yourself, not where you look best but where you can best look.

> I got my back to the sun 'cause the light is too intense
> I can see what everybody in the world is up against

Position yourself where you can best see (and can least be seen back?), where you can see not only what everybody in the world is up against but what everybody in the world is up to. Bear in mind, and not only there, that – in the harsher terms from *Foot of Pride* –

> There ain't no goin' back
> When your foot of pride comes down
> Ain't no goin' back[1]

"You can't turn back – you can't come back": two halves of truths, these,

---

[1] Three lines later in *Foot of Pride*: "He looked straight into the sun and said revenge is mine". Blind revenge. As for me: "I got my back to the sun 'cause the light is too intense".

and saved from being virtue-ridden only by the touches of comedy. First, that even if you can't come back, the word "back" can, since here it is, coming back – after just a couple of lines – from "I got my back to the sun": back as "You can't turn back", and then, not only coming back but coming back again, as "you can't come back". Second, by a memory that comes back, the memory of *Mississippi* earlier on *"Love And Theft"*, which had been happy to qualify what, for its part, it felt obliged to say on the matter: "You can always come back, but you can't come back all the way".

In *Sugar Baby* the succeeding thought that opens ominously with "One day you'll . . ." is out to lace a warning with a threat. Prudence and temperance, who need to watch their propensity to italicize their wisdom (*mark my words*), do well to remember that they have the duty not only of offering good advice but of offering advice well. That is, in such a way as to maximize the chances of people's being willing to take it. "Sometimes we push too far", not just go too far. And this goes even for the high-minded virtues themselves, for here, too, we must not go too far. T. S. Eliot cautioned against too much prudence and temperance:

Of course one can "go too far" and except in directions in which we can go too far there is no interest in going at all; and only those who will risk going too far can possibly find out just how far one can go.[1]

"One day you'll open up your eyes and you'll see where we are". But on this particular day, listening to this song, we have to open up not our eyes but our ears, since *Sugar Baby* is not verse-lines on a page but a sound-sequence on the waves. Which means that the things that might be said about the song's movements will be more than usually useless to anyone who does not have the song in the head.

As printed in the lyrics, the song's opening is cast as four lines, two couplets that rhyme *intense / against* and *far / are*. But as voiced there are twelve units. You might think of these as constituting a twelve-line verse, or as taking care to register within the location of those four long lines several edged divisions, but, either way, such is Dylan's way with these sub-units of his devising. This is not only where the song goes but how it goes. Get on down the lines when the lineation is set as sung:

[1] Preface to Harry Crosby, *Transit of Venus* (1931), p. ix. On temperance in relation to "no limit" (which in *Sugar Baby* is "There ain't no limit to the amount of trouble women bring"), see p. 289.

I got my back
to the sun 'cause
          the light is too intense
I can see what
everybody
          in the world is up against
You can't turn back –
you can't come back,
          sometimes we push too far
One day
you'll open up your eyes and
          you'll see where we are

The instrumental bass-line that has opened the song, and that precedes any of the words, may be heard as one sequence that is divided:

dark dark Darktown   dark dark Darktown   dark dark Darktown
dark . . .

Immediately following the instrumental opening there are the opening words. Looking down the line:

I got my back to the sun 'cause the light is too intense

But, heard and not seen, it goes like this:

I got my back
to the sun 'cause
          the light is too intense

Not "to the sun / 'cause the light . . .", but "to the sun 'cause / the light is too intense". As a friend of mine once turned it, comedy is the secret of timing. But then so is tragedy.

The song's beat is fourfold, and the rhythm of the instrumental opening is immediately confirmed by there being four syllables in each of the first two units. But the words that provide the title and that later open the refrain,

"Sugar Baby",[1] have their four syllables two by two, 2 x 2. The rhythm of the words "Sugar Baby" is a dual rhythm, fourfold and twofold. And in pacing the song, Dylan pauses at certain points so as to make two syllables occupy the time and space that in the basic scheme of things will be expected to be occupied by four syllables. It is this movement in the voicing, with its pauses (contemplative, disconcerted, riven, chary, sardonic, shifting its grounds), that gives to the song its unique gait. The song does proceed down the road, down the line, but it never puts only its best foot forward and it never marches. More, the song always plays the slow troubled subdivisions of the verse-lines against the single-minded momentum of the speedy refrain (wishing her God speed?), the lines of which always get on with it, without a break, getting on down the road and down the line.

A shape in space for the song's shaping in time might look like this.

SUGAR BABY

I got my back
to the sun 'cause
     the light is too intense
I can see what
everybody
     in the world is up against
You can't turn back –
you can't come back,
     sometimes we push too far
One day
you'll open up your eyes and
     you'll see where we are

---

[1] There is many a song called *Sugar Baby*, and Dock Boggs has one. (It is in the recorded *Anthology of American Folk Music*, edited by Harry Smith.) The first citation for "sugarbaby" in the OED ("sugar" as a term of endearment) is from *Gone with the Wind* (1936), chapter XXVI: "Scarlett said gratefully: 'Thank you, Sugarbaby'." (In *Sugar Baby* the regrets are tinged with weary thanks, less said than glimpsed – thanks, I suppose.) The instance in *Gone with the Wind* is presumably no more than a coincidence, but the ferret enjoys unearthing the fact that the preceding sentence in the novel ends "in the sun". (Dylan, "to the sun".) Dylan famously sings "gone with the wind" in *Song to Woody*, which shares with *Sugar Baby* the phrase "down the road" (and mentions "Walkin' a road") and which has "a thousand miles" (*Sugar Baby*, "a thousand times"), as well as "It looks like it's a-dying an' it's hardly been born" (*Sugar Baby*, "Just as sure as we're living, just as sure as you're born").

Sugar Baby get on down the road, you ain't got no brains, no how
You went years without me, might as well keep going now

> Some of
> these bootleggers,
>   they make pretty good stuff
> Plenty of places
> to hide things here if
>   you wanna hide 'em bad enough
> I'm staying
> with Aunt Sally,
>   but you know, she's not really my aunt
> Some of these memories
> you can learn to live with
>   and some of 'em you can't

Sugar Baby get on down the line, you ain't got no brains, no how
You went years without me, you might as well keep going now

> The ladies down in
> Darktown
>   they're doing the Darktown Strut
> Y' always got to
> be prepared but
>   you never know for what
> There ain't no limit
> to the amount of trouble
>   women bring
> Love is pleasing,
> love is teasing,
>   love not an evil thing

Sugar Baby get on down the road, you ain't got no brains, no how
You went years without me, might as well keep going now

> Every moment of
> existence seems
>   like some dirty trick

Happiness can
come suddenly and
   leave just as quick
Any minute
of the day
   the bubble could burst
Try to make things better[1]
for someone, sometimes, you just end up
   making it a thousand times worse

Sugar Baby get on down the road, you ain't got no brains, no how
You went years without me, might as well keep going now

Your charms have
broken many a heart
   and mine is surely one
You got a way of
tearing the world apart
   Love, see what you've done
Just as
sure as we're living,
   just as sure as you're born
Look up, look up –
seek your Maker –
   'fore Gabriel blows his horn

Sugar Baby get on down the line, you ain't got no sense, no how
You went years without me, might as well keep going now

All the pauses are designed to give us pause. Attentive to the mobility of the heart and head, which are often at odds with one another (and neither of them simply of one mind), the pauses repay attention.

   One day
   You'll open up your eyes and
      you'll see where we are

[1] But with a saddened impetuosity, only the slightest of breaks in the run of the words.

With the doubled weight not of four syllables but of two, "One day" is
dilated so as to occupy – while speaking of time – the time that on all the six
previous occasions in this opening verse has been occupied by the expected
count of four syllables that confirms the fourfold beat of the song:

> I got my back
> to the sun 'cause

and

> I can see what
> everybody

and

> You can't turn back –
> you can't come back

Instead of those foursomes, a twosome: "One day". This vocal dwelling
upon "One day"[1] is then succeeded at once by the local housing within
the next line, this time not of two syllables instead of four, but of seven
syllables instead of four:

> One day
> you'll open up your eyes and

Opening up, yes indeed. Especially when this expanded syllabification is
then compounded by the reach of the open "and", out on the end of
the arm of the line. This is a line that does not run, as it does on
the page,

> One day you'll open up your eyes and you'll see where we are

– or, as the sense-units would have it,

---

[1] The time-word "day" again gets the time of two syllables later in the song:

Any minute	[the expected four]
of the day	[three, two of them allotted to *day*]
the bubble could burst	

> One day you'll open up your eyes
> And you'll see where we are

— but is audible as the footfalls of this:

> One day
> you'll open up your eyes and
> you'll see where we are

At the brink, "and". In *The Waste Land* T. S. Eliot transformed Oliver Goldsmith's song by a tiny unsettling re-settling, re-setting on the page Goldsmith's conjunction "and" in an inspired disjunction. Goldsmith:

> When lovely woman stoops to folly,
> And finds too late that men betray,
> What charm can soothe her melancholy,
> What art can wash her guilt away?

Eliot:

> When lovely woman stoops to folly and
> Paces about her room again, alone,
> She smoothes her hair with automatic hand,
> And puts a record on the gramophone.

The record could not, except in *Back to the Future*, have been *"Love And Theft"*, but love and theft are in evidence there in Goldsmith — and in Eliot, whose lines pace about the room with a different view of these matters.

A road may have cracks where you had better step with caution. The movement from one verse of *Sugar Baby* to another is not a train of thought that moves on metalled ways but is firmly footing. What is it, for instance, that grounds the move from "you'll see where we are", via the refrain ("get on down the road"), to "Some of these bootleggers"?

> Some of
> these bootleggers,
> they make pretty good stuff

> Plenty of places
> to hide things here if
>   you wanna hide 'em bad enough

"Some of": these well-judged words stay with their thought (taking the time of four syllables, not of only two). Only some of these bootleggers, don't forget. The bootleggers are the fire-water ones of Prohibition, not the cassetteers to whom Dylan in concert mostly turns a blind eye. It is blind, not just blind drunk, that the bootleggers' concoctions may make you if the bootleggers have made not good but bad stuff. ("I can see", "open up your eyes": no harm done, as yet.) But this prospect is tinged with a characteristic comedy when the rhyme is of "good stuff" with "bad enough".

As the lines make their painstaking quick-witted way, they often pause and look up, alert. He who hesitates may be saved. For instance, there is that cocked "if".

> Plenty of places
> to hide things here if
>   you wanna hide 'em bad enough

A thousand times less vigilant, these words would be here if – instead of the pitch and swivelling poise in "here if" – you were to take them at the run of the page, toeing the line of the printed lyrics:

> Plenty of places to hide things here if you wanna hide 'em bad enough

Anyway the bootleggers doubly earn their living in the song, given what is hidden (street-legal and road-wise) in the word: boots, legs. Get on down the road. For my part, I'm not on the road for now.

> I'm staying
> with Aunt Sally,
>   but you know, she's not really my aunt
> Some of these memories
> you can learn to live with
>   and some of 'em you can't

Again, the staid humour, with "to stay with" being both very like and very unlike "to live with". Swap them, handy dandy? He could, after all, have been living with Aunt Sally (especially as she's not really his aunt), and then in life there are some memories that you learn to stay with.

Aunt Sally may or may not be a lady, and where she lives is not dwelt upon. But where the ensuing ladies live, this location is stayed with, "Darktown" occupying in its time twice the usual space, not four syllables but two. The dark is so intense.

> The ladies down in
> Darktown
>> they're doing the Darktown Strut
> Y' always got to
> be prepared but
>> you never know for what

One of the things that you've got to be prepared for is having the break in the voicing be somehow against nature.

> Y' always got to
> be prepared but
>> you never know for what

True to human nature, though. As for the limit of which this verse goes on to speak ("There ain't no limit to the amount of trouble women bring"), the breaks have set their own limits with a feeling for both caution and brinkmanship: "down in / Darktown", "got to / be prepared but / you never know for what". Just so.

Since in the midst of life we are in death, be on the *qui vive*. Tread carefully. Which means moving your foot carefully forward, here in Darktown where we all live, respectful of "of", and "can", and "and", feeling for the ledge or step:

> Every moment of
> existence seems
>> like some dirty trick
> Happiness can
> come suddenly and
>> leave just as quick

Insecure, we all are, you do have to feel. It is only in the last half of the final verse that there arrives a certain security of mind.

> Your charms have
> broken many a heart
> and mine is surely one
> You got a way of
> tearing the world apart
> Love, see what you've done
> Just as
> sure as we're living,
> just as sure as you're born
> Look up, look up –
> seek your Maker –
> 'fore Gabriel blows his horn

True, there is still a touch of the cautious or the tentative at some of the unit-breaks: "have / broken many a heart" is itself a broken effect; "a way of / tearing the world apart" does find itself torn apart in the utterance; and "Just as / sure as we're living" cannot but sound less sure than it claims. But at least each of the four central breaks, or caesurae, is at last at one with the sense of the phrasing, so that "and mine is surely one" can stand surely on its own feet, as can "Love, see what you've done", and "just as sure as you're born", and "'fore Gabriel blows his horn". At long last, it has become time to modulate in the final refrain from "You ain't got no brains, no how" to "You ain't got no sense, no how". From "the light is too intense" to "you ain't got no sense".

What makes me think that this is the line to take with and to this song? A couple of contrasts. First, the contrast with the rhythm and movement of other Dylan songs that imagine being on the road.

> I'm walkin' down that long lonesome road, babe
> Where I'm bound, I can't tell
> Goodbye is too good a word, babe
> So I'll just say fare thee well
> (*Don't Think Twice, It's All Right*)

Jaunty, the manner and movement of that. Not that *Sugar Baby* just says fare thee ill, but it does feel Darktown bound, and it does think twice and even suggest Do Think Twice, It's All Right.

"Get on down the line"? Take *Walkin' Down the Line*. What it does with the road is hit it.

> Lord, I'm walkin' down the line
> Walkin' down the line
> An' I'm walkin' down the line
> My feet'll be a-flyin'
> To tell about my troubled mind[1]

There he may go on to sing "I got a heavy-headed gal", but the song is never heavy-headed and is always light-hearted even when you might have expected otherwise. Its gait never trips, it trips along, for all its troubled mind.

> I got a heavy-headed gal
> I got a heavy-headed gal
> She ain't a-feelin' well
> When she's better only time will tell

She ain't a-feelin' well, but he might as well keep going now.

Even a particular break in the timing that might have been expected to call up the tone of *Sugar Baby* turns out to feel nothing like the later song. Never mind the quality, feel the width between this and that. Between this positioning:

> I see the morning light
> I see the morning light
> Well, it's not because
> I'm an early riser
> I didn't go to sleep last night

And this, which is from *Sugar Baby*, thirty-eight years later and light-years away:

> I got my back
> to the sun 'cause
>   the light is too intense

But a more intense light is thrown by a song of 1928 without which *Sugar*

---

[1] As printed in *Lyrics 1962–1985*, not "Lord" but "Well, I'm walkin' down the line". But seek your Maker.

Baby would never have been born in 2001: Gene Austin's *Lonesome Road*.[1] Right from the opening instrumental bass-line, in which Dylan's melody totally immersed itself –

dark dark Darktown   *dark dark Darktown*   *dark dark Darktown*
dark . . .

– the resemblances would be uncanny if they were not canny.

> Look down, look down that lonesome road before you travel on,
> Look up, look up and seek your Maker, 'fore Gabriel blows his horn.
> Weary totin' such a load, trudgin' down that lonesome road,
> Look down, look down that lonesome road before you travel on.

> True love, true love, what have I done that you should treat me so
> You caused me to walk and talk like I never done before.
> Weary totin' such a load, trudgin' down that lonesome road,
> Mmmm . . .

> [Whistle]

> Weary totin' such a load, trudgin' down that lonesome road,
> Mmmm . . .

Sugar Baby is full of things that are not to be found in the fine song *Lonesome Road*. But is it fine for Dylan to have treated Austin so? Yes, partly because of the comedy that enters with the crucial verbal borrowing (the music is its own other matter), "Look up, look up and seek your Maker, 'fore Gabriel blows his horn". In both of the songs, the Maker is the Lord. But in Dylan's song there is this further maker, Austin. For us there is another further maker, Dylan. Anyway Dylan is not blowing his own horn. And he achieves his own re-working and re-playing of the original by being, himself, in certain respects original with the minimum of alteration (the phrase is T. S. Eliot's): that is, by having *Sugar Baby* exercise its imagination

[1] Dylan-lovers posted word of this soon after "*Love And Theft*" appeared, but I should never have known of the Austin/Shilkret song were it not for my colleague Jeremy Yudkin, who generously made a tape of it for me in November 2001; I am much in his debt.

in a particular way that Austin never does. Austin positions his words securely even when poignantly. At every point in Austin, the words and the music and the voice are fittingly in place. In Dylan, they are at odds. They move as the spirit takes them, and their spirit engages not only with the precious but with the precarious.

"Look up, look up, seek your Maker": behind Dylan is Austin, and behind Austin is a long tradition from which such an urging derives. It is there for all to hear (at least, all who can spare a moment not only to look up but to look up a medieval moment) in Chaucer's *Balade de Bon Conseyl*, his ballad of good counsel to the pilgrim who is to get on down the road:

> Flee from the press, and dwell with soothfastness.   [*truth*]
> Forth, pilgrim, forth! Forth, beast out of thy stall!
> Know thy countrý, look up, thank God of all!
> Hold the highway, and let thy ghost thee lead;   [*spirit, soul*]
> And truthë shall deliver, it is no dread.

Truth will deliver you. The highway is that of the Way, the Truth, and the Life.

Ye shall know the truth, and the truth shall make you free. They answered him, We be Abraham's seed, and were never in bondage to any man: how sayest thou, Ye shall be made free? Jesus answered them, Verily, verily, I say unto you, Whosoever committeth sin is the servant of sin.

(John 8:32–4)

Fortitude

Blowin' in the Wind

> How many roads must a man walk down
> Before you call him a man?

Dylan's greatest hit is a song that sustains fortitude in an appeal for justice. Two of the four cardinal virtues for the pricelessness of one.

"Equality, liberty, humility, simplicity": in due course, *No Time to Think* came to be sardonic about such abstract nouns and their lending themselves so obligingly to sloganry. But Dylan is aware that these concepts are indispensable aspirations. In *Blowin' in the Wind*, simplicity is everything, the everything that sets itself to promote equality, liberty, and humility. (Fraternity, too, my friend.) Which means that to expatiate on *Blowin' in the Wind* is to risk detracting from its simplicity. Yet it would be a detraction to suppose that simplicity has no truck with the subtle or suggestive or wayward. For it is characteristic of true simplicity that there may radiate from its utmost directness a good many glinting things.

The refrain of *Blowin' in the Wind* is simplicity itself, simply repeated:

> The answer, my friend, is blowin' in the wind
> The answer is blowin' in the wind

Could it be that by now we all know these words too well, and that we no longer listen to them but only hear them? It would be good if they could again become a surprising thing to hear. The refrain, even while it sounds like an assurance or reassurance, ought on reflection to continue to give us pause, ought even to be understood as insisting that there will always be some pause that we human beings will have to be given.

"This land is your land". "We shall overcome". "Which side are you on?" Those are words entirely without misgiving, and there are good things that such a way of putting it can give us.[1] But "The answer is blowin' in the wind"? This is a very different proposition.

---

[1] Dylan pinpoints and punctures such a political rallying-cry as "Which side are you on?": "Praise be to Nero's Neptune / The Titanic sails at dawn / And everybody's shouting / 'Which Side Are You On?'" (*Desolation Row*).

There ain't too much I can say about this song except that the answer is blowing in the wind. It ain't in no book or movie or TV show or discussion group. Man, it's in the wind – and it's blowing in the wind. Too many of these hip people are telling me where the answer is, but oh I won't believe that. I still say it's in the wind and just like a restless piece of paper it's got to come down some time . . . But the only trouble is that no one picks up the answer when it comes down so not too many get to see and know it . . . and then it flies away again.[1]

What Dylan has to say there about the refrain is corroborated or authenticated by his comments' taking up so many of the words that constitute the song. Over and above the simple quotation ("the answer is blowing in the wind"), there are these overlappings of the song's words with those of Dylan thinking about it:

The Song	*The Comments*
many roads	*many* of these
a *man*	*Man*
walk *down*	come *down*
many *times*	some *time*
cannon balls *fly*	*flies* away
some people	*some* time / hip *people*
just doesn't	*just* like
doesn't *see*	to *see*
look *up*	picks *up*
one man	no *one*
he *knows*	*know* it
too many	*too many*

[1] *Sing Out!* (October / November 1962), reporting Dylan in June 1962. Dylan at Carnegie Hall in 1963, introducing the song: "Met a teacher who said he didn't understand what *Blowin' in the Wind* means. Told him there was nothin' to understand, it was just blowin' in the wind. If he didn't feel it in the wind, he'd never know. And he ain't never gonna know, I guess. *Teachers*." (Anthony Scaduto, *Bob Dylan*, 1971, revised edition 1973, p. 157.)

One of the things that makes *Blowin' in the Wind* so good is that it never says, or even hints, that "The answer, my friend, is this song that I have written, called *Blowin' in the Wind*". The answer? "It ain't in no book or movie or TV show or discussion group" – nor is it in this song itself. The "restless piece of paper" comes briefly to rest, and "then it flies away again". For what would it be, for an answer to be blowing in the wind? Assuredly, the opposite of anything assured, final, achieved once and for all. The song staves off hopelessness and hopefulness, disillusionment and illusion.

Fortitude is in demand, for there is no assurance that all that is in question is *when* justice will come, there being (we should prefer to think) no question as to *if*. Fortitude finds itself in need, not of a fellow-virtue, but of a grace: Hope. "We shall overcome"? Realism does not shake its head, or take its head in its hands, but does have to be hard-headed. Cynicism always has an easier time. The *Onion* offered one of its memorable news items and a headline (30 January 1968):

Martin Luther King: 'Perhaps We Shall Not Overcome After All'

KNOXVILLE, Tenn.—In a speech at First Baptist Church in Knoxville, civil-rights leader

Dr. Martin Luther King Jr.

Dr. Martin Luther King Jr. acknowledged that he and his fellow negroes may not overcome, after all.

"For many long years, the rallying cry of our movement has been, 'We shall overcome,'" King told the capacity crowd. "But, having taken a few steps back to examine all sides of the situation, I have come to a new conclusion: that we most likely shall not."

As the assembled churchgoers listened intently, King continued: "For all our bravery in the face of hatred and intolerance, it appears that the white power structure is simply too powerful and entrenched to be overcome. I hope not, obviously, but it is very much starting to look that way."

"Nonetheless," King continued, "with deep faith in ourselves, and even deeper faith in God, we hope that our children and our children's children will, in time, come to witness an end to racial hatred, and that they will know freedom and equality."

"But I would not count on it happening any time soon."

Dylan was straightforward in commenting on the song's not saying straightforwardly what you might have expected or preferred it to say. His comments are fully borne out by the song's words as soon as you think about them. But thinking about them did soon become difficult, given that the song was so easily and promptly memorable as to become at once a memory of itself. A song that so immediately adheres to us, especially a song that is an adjuration, must always be in some danger of settling down as its own enemy – not its own worst enemy, its own best enemy, but an enemy in some ways still.

> Fearing not that I'd become my enemy
> In the instant that I preach
> (*My Back Pages*)

Very tempting, even in the moment of hearing the song for only the second time, to substitute a memory of it for the experience anew of the song. But to have the song itself be the answer would be to forgo the truth there in its lucid cryptic refrain.

There is nothing dubious about the questions (the warnings, the pleas, the admonitions and premonitions) that shape the song. But the assurance as to the answer does have its small skilful doubt as to just how it is about to be taken. For the formulation *The answer is . . .* might have been expected to culminate differently. Whereas the refrain's culmination is a location or an *en route* ("The answer is blowin' in the wind"), you might have hoped for a different kind of answer, not a where but a what. The answer is tolerance. The answer is desegregation. Or faith in the Lord. Similarly, the answer to "How many . . ." could have been an actual figure, preposterous though it might sound ("How many roads . . . ?" – 61 Highways, actually). Such a numerical answer is unthinkable, which is not the same as supposing that the thought shouldn't even cross your mind. Matthew 18:21: "Lord, how oft shall my brother sin against me, and I forgive him? till seven times? Jesus saith unto him, I say not unto thee, Until seven times: but, Until seventy times seven."

"Blowin' in the wind": in the end the answer is not in words but in music, there in the final harmonica, a wind instrument to be blown.[1] Still,

---

[1] At Gerde's, April 1962, the song opens with harmonica introduction and has the harmonica between verses and at the end. The Witmark demo tape, July 1962, has no harmonica. *The Freewheelin' Bob Dylan*, July 1962, does best by the song, establishing itself as the performance against which all others are heard and (though not necessarily measured) weighed: it opens with guitar, but has harmonica between the verses and at the end. Blown with breath's wind. Dylan does not sing the verses in the order in which they have been printed in *Lyrics 1962–1985* (1985). The printed sequence is: the first verse, but then the last one sung, and then the second that is sung. But *Broadside* (late May 1962) printed the verses in the order in which he sings them.

Dylan's words abide our question. For instance, the words "in the wind".
The Oxford English Dictionary:

a. in reference to something which can be scented or perceived by means of
   the wind blowing from where it is.
b. *fig.* So as to be "scented" or perceived.
c. predicatively: Happening or ready to happen; astir, afoot, "up". 1535 A thing
   there is in the wind . . which I trust in God will one day come to light.

If you want somebody you can trust, trust in God. "How long, O Lord,
how long?" But the phrase "in the wind" can catch a cross-current, and
within the sequence *to hang in the wind* the sense is "to remain in suspense
or indecision". "I still say it's in the wind and just like a restless piece of
paper, it's got to come down some time . . . and then it flies away again."
Not indecision, perhaps, but re-decision, decision that will always have to
be taken, taken up, again.[1]

The song made a great bid for popularity (a bid that was not beyond
its means), in its tune and in the simplicity of its words. A man should
stand up. As yet, there are not many men to stand up in this cause
and be counted, but there is a confidence that the cause will be joined
by many others. The song's claims to courage, and its asking courage
of others, its incipient solidarity, all required that it convey a certain
political loneliness, and it effected this by continually playing plurals against
singulars:

> How many roads must a man walk down
> Before you call him a man?

Each of the three verses includes five words that are plurals; every word
of the refrain is resolutely in the singular.

How many times is the phrase "how many" tolled in this song? Nine
times, with three of them being "How many times" – and then the

---

[1] The song was recorded on 9 July 1962. Harold Macmillan's words, which became
famous at once, had been delivered on 3 February 1960 in Cape Town: "The wind of
change is blowing through this continent and, whether we like it or not, this growth
of national consciousness is a political fact." *Forever Young*: "When the winds of changes
shift". What a singular difference the plurals make.

once-and-for-all chiming (immediately before the final refrain) of "too many": "That too many people have died". Dylan sings this line with timing that both seizes and touches: accelerating slightly, just ahead of the music, as though time and patience are running out.

The last verse begins "How many times"; each verse has this phrase, but the others have it not as their first but as their last question.

The first verse begins "How many roads must a man walk down", and the last begins "How many times must a man look up".

A man, not because of thoughtlessness or a hidden gender. Or because of misogyny. A man has no monopoly of common humanity or of mankind. But "a man" here because of the forms that a man's courage may have to take, forms different from those of a brave wise woman up against aggressive swaggering, a woman of the kind honoured in *License to Kill*:

> Man thinks 'cause he rules the earth he can do with it as he please
> And if things don't change soon, he will
> Oh, man has invented his doom
> First step was touching the moon
>
> Now, there's a woman on my block
> She just sit there as the night grows still
> She say who gonna take away his license to kill?

A man, because of particular men on particular roads, men who got themselves killed for the rights that were theirs and others'. And a man, because this can then be held in tacit tension with the "she" of the song, she who had originally been a "he":[1]

> How many seas must the white dove sail
> Before she sleeps in the sand?
> Yes, 'n' how many times must the cannon balls fly
> Before they're forever banned?

[1] "Before he sleeps in the sand" in the early sheet-music (*Broadside*, late May 1962). *Lyrics 1962–1985* prints "a white dove", but Dylan sings "the white dove": of peace in the world, of mercy from the Flood, and of pentecostal message. True, he wasn't a Christian in 1962, but he copyrighted *Long Ago, Far Away* long ago, in the same year as *Blowin' in the Wind*. "And to talk of peace and brotherhood / Oh, what might be the cost! / A man he did it long ago / And they hung him on a cross". Several of the early songs have more than a turn-of-phrase that is Christian.

"Let the bird sing, let the bird fly" (*Under the Red Sky*). Let the cannon balls no longer fly. Let all such weapons become as archaic as cannon balls.

But then Dylan has already done something to see the cannon balls off by voicing the words with such soft roundedness as to mollify their military mettle into cotton-wool, or into the feathered texture of a dove.

In March 1962, just a few months before the song was released like a dove, the *Broadside* lines had been abroad:

> How many roads must a man walk down
> Before he is called a man?

Revised, the song calls you on this. "Before you call him a man". This is the only "you" in the song, right there at the start, and it points to you and perhaps at you, even while it isn't as simply accusatory as it would be if the words "you call him" couldn't carry, too, the sense "before he is called". The song addresses someone, or many a one, throughout. "The answer, my friend, is blowin' in the wind". And we need to be mindful of the equivocal tone of "my friend". Perhaps you are indeed a friend to me and to this cause, so that before too long the implication of "my friend" will be able to be "my friends" or even "friends". But what protects the song against credulity (for there are murderous enemies out there, or the song wouldn't have had to be written) is the other possibility in the words "my friend", the edge of possible reprimand in it: What you don't seem to understand, my friend, is that . . . Such an edge is sharpened in another chilling civil-rights song, *Oxford Town*:

> He come to the door, he couldn't get in
> All because of the color of his skin
> What do you think about that, my frien'?

In *Blowin' in the Wind*, the words "my friend" are not the threat that they constitute in *Desolation Row* ("And someone says, 'You're in the wrong place, my friend / You better leave'"). But they are salty, too, not just sweet.

Roads and seas and times are plurals set against a man or a mountain, a man or one man. One particular resourcefulness not only turns to the sound of words ("can a mountain" / "can a man turn") but does so with the help of the very word "turn": "How many years can a mountain exist" turns into "How many times can a man turn his head". This is in touch with the ancient good sense that even the prophets must acknowledge: "If the mountain will not come to Mahomet, Mahomet must go to the mountain." This is good sense that Dylan in an interview brought down from the mountain to the plains or the plain:

"Just getting on a Greyhound bus for three days; and going some place".
Can you do that now?
"I can't do that any more. It's up to . . . y'know, get the Greyhound bus to come to *me*."[1]

The man and the mountain meet in *Blowin' in the Wind*, in tune with Blake's political scale:

> Great things are done when men and mountains meet;
> This is not done by jostling in the street.

The song is itself one of these great things, one that then – like Blake's poems – conduced to the great things of social conscience:

> How many years can some people exist
> Before they're allowed to be free?

The tone of the phrase "some people" is not casual or perfunctory (for the history of a people may be a justifiably proud one, and in this sense a people is not merely some people), but "How many years can some people exist" is designed to bring home, very simply, in common humanity, that a people is people – you know, *people*. A people *is*, or *are*? For the word "people" is a singular that constitutes a plural, too.[2]

What does it ask? It asks fortitude. The song is determined to keep asking its searching questions, indeflectibly. But it is sensitive to the difference between pressing a point and nagging, so the voicing has its concessive gentleness. A phrase like "How many times must" could very easily have found itself hardened into aggression (How many times must I tell you . . .)

[1] *Whaaat?* (the 1965 interview with Nat Hentoff, in full, differing from that in *Playboy*, March 1966), p. 10.
[2] The rhyme, as it were, of "exist" with "exist" (no shifting or paltering) lends to the people something of a heartening geological stubbornness: "Yes, 'n', how many years can a mountain exist / Before it is washed to the sea? / Yes, 'n' how many years can some people exist / Before they're allowed to be free?"

– Dylan wants the hint of steel but only the hint. And the same goes for another reiterated turn: "Yes, 'n'". Dylan has it once in the first verse, and three times in each of the other two verses,[1] culminating in the question that is asked of "a man", of everyman:

> Yes, 'n' how many deaths will it take till he knows
> That too many people have died?

Like "How many times", "Yes, 'n'" could easily manifest too much negativity. *And another thing . . . .*: such is the proclivity of "Yes, 'n'" to lean in for a quick jab. But Dylan doesn't let this happen; his tone of voice is *Let me put this to you*, not *Let me tell you*.

The song has entire singleness of purpose and of tone, but it would not be as supple (and as fertile of new performances) were it not for the modulations of the patterns that it establishes. Take the word "must" again. "How many roads must a man walk down". In the first verse, this is the insistence, twice more ("how many seas must a white dove sail", "how many times must the cannon balls fly"). The second verse weaves around, as though seeking a different point of entry into consciences, and the crux becomes a different form of necessity and contingency, not "must" but "can": "how many years can a mountain exist", "how many years can some people exist", "how many times can a man turn his head". And then the final verse reverts to "must" (". . . must a man look up", "must one man have"), only to change the whole timbre of the questioning by having the last instance of all be neither "must" nor "can" but the poignant ordinary cry, "will it take": "how many deaths will it take till he knows / That too many people have died?". And this thought, which is simple enough (God knows), has its recesses, being not only about how many deaths it will take but about how many lives will they take. Yet fortitude has what it takes.

But the word for which "must" and "can" and "will it take", each in its turn, stands by is the obdurately waiting word "Before".

> How many roads must a man walk down
> Before you call him a man?

And "Before" is soon compounded by the sounding sequence: "Before

---

[1] He sings it otherwise than as printed in *Lyrics 1962–1985*, dropping it (in singing) from the third line of the first verse, but adding it at the start of the second and third verses.

they're forever banned". *Before . . . forever*: yet let us not have to wait forever. Hope deferred maketh the heart sick. Even fortitude has its limits.

But how many times does a man have to maintain that *Blowin' in the Wind* is at once simplicity and multiplicity? "Man, it's in the wind – and it's blowing in the wind." You don't need to make heavy weather, man, to know which way the wind blows.

A Hard Rain's A-Gonna Fall

> But when I came to man's estate,
>   With hey, ho, the wind and the rain,
> 'Gainst knaves and thieves men shut their gate,
>   For the rain it raineth every day.

Shakespeare's Song, its refrain to be adapted as that of *Percy's Song*: "Turn, turn to the rain / And the wind". *Blowin' in the Wind* – Freewheelin' along – turns to rain, to *A Hard Rain's A-Gonna Fall*.

It's a hard song to befall the critic. (Tempted to take a hard rain check.) For one thing, it declines to be an allegory. If someone were to ask, "What does it mean, *I saw a white ladder all covered with water*?", might you reply "It means what it says"? T. S. Eliot was once asked what a line of *Ash-Wednesday* meant, "Lady, three white leopards sat under a juniper-tree". The answer: "Lady, three white leopards sat under a juniper-tree".[1] And there is another thing: that (as with *Blowin' in the Wind*) we may well know the song too well, which can easily mean too easily. "I'll know my song well before I start singin'": that's for him to say, or rather to sing, as he does at the end of *A Hard Rain's A-Gonna Fall*, in the instant before drawing to a close the curtains of his cosmic stage. Alexander Pope drew *The Dunciad* to an end with an apocalyptic vision:

> Lo! thy dread Empire, CHAOS! is restor'd;
> Light dies before thy uncreating word:
> Thy hand, great Anarch! lets the curtain fall;
> And Universal Darkness buries All.

In the universe of Dylan, there is the final rain to come.

[1] Eliot in 1929, recalled in B. C. Southam, *A Guide to the Selected Poems of T. S. Eliot* (sixth edition 1996), pp. 225–6.

And I'll stand on the ocean until I start sinkin'
But I'll know my song well before I start singin'
And it's a hard, it's a hard, it's a hard, and it's a hard,
It's a hard rain's a-gonna fall

He knows his song well. But as for us: instead of being kept on our toes, we may find ourselves resting on his laurels when we know his song well before he starts singing. Similarly with what it means for a prodigious performer to sing "I heard ten thousand whisperin' and nobody listenin'". We've all been at Dylan concerts when this was infuriatingly the case, except that the ten thousand weren't whispering, they were talking or shouting. Or *singing along* . . . They know his song well before he starts singing. Know it backwards. Would that they would just let the song surge forwards.

He will not have forgotten what it was like to be out in front of a dozen dead audiences. Bad trips. To be on the road is to be on a quest. *A Hard Rain's A-Gonna Fall* tells of a quest, which spells the opening of a question. So each verse will open with some variation of the initiating inquiry:

Oh, where have you been, my blue-eyed son?
And where have you been, my darling young one?

The immediate question about this question is "And you, where have you been, my blue-eyed son?" Dylan knows, and trusts us to know, just where this question has been, has come from. Sure enough, this particular source and resource we are all soberly aware of.[1]

O where ha you been, Lord Randal, my son?
And where ha you been, my handsom young man?

Not a source only, but an allusion, calling something into play – as will happen with the opening of *Highlands*,[2] where if you fail to recognize that you are in Robert Burns country you must be a pad-eared laddy of the lowlands.

The sinewy ballad *Lord Randal* prompted a structure within *A Hard Rain's*

[1] "Lord Randall playing with a quart of beer" (*Tarantula*, 1966, 1971, p. 82). Early nineteenth century, *Lord Randal* is in most anthologies of ballads or of Scottish verse.
[2] Dylan: "Well my heart's in the Highlands gentle and fair". Burns: "My heart's in the Highlands, my heart is not here".

A-Gonna Fall: its having for each verse both an inaugurative question and the concluding refrain. The song, like the predecessor ballad, takes poison, and it knows what impends: hell.

But the ways in which Dylan then chooses to depart so wide-rangingly from the original song of sin are one source of the achievement that is *A Hard Rain's A-Gonna Fall*. The ballad's questions and answers ask the justice of being here in full.

LORD RANDAL

"O where ha you been, Lord Randal, my son?
And where ha you been, my handsom young man?"
"I ha been at the greenwood; mother, mak my bed soon,
For I'm wearied wi hunting, and fain wad lie down."

"An wha met you there, Lord Randal, my son?
An wha met you there, my handsom young man?"
"O I met wi my true-love; mother, mak my bed soon,
For I'm wearied wi hunting, and fain wad lie down."

"And what did she give you, Lord Randal, my son?
And what did she give you, my handsom young man?"
"Eels fried in a pan; mother, mak my bed soon,
For I'm wearied wi hunting, and fain wad lie down."

"An wha gat your leavins, Lord Randal, my son?
And wha gat your leavins, my handsom young man?"
"My hawks and my houns; mother, mak my bed soon,
For I'm wearied wi hunting, and fain wad lie down."

"An what becam of them, Lord Randal, my son?
And what becam of them, my handsom young man?"
"They stretched their legs out and died; mother, mak my bed soon,
For I'm wearied wi hunting, and fain wad lie down."

"O I fear you are poisoned, Lord Randal, my son!
I fear you are poisoned, my handsom young man?"
"O yes, I am poisoned; mother, mak my bed soon,
For I'm sick at the heart, and I fain wad lie down."

> "What d'ye leave to your mother, Lord Randal, my son?
> What d'ye leave to your mother, my handsom young man?"
> "Four and twenty milk kye; mother, mak my bed soon,
> For I'm sick at the heart, and I fain wad lie down."
>
> "What d'ye leave to your sister, Lord Randal, my son?
> What d'ye leave to your sister, my handsom young man?"
> "My gold and my silver; mother, mak my bed soon,
> For I'm sick at the heart, and I fain wad lie down."
>
> "What d'ye leave to your brother, Lord Randal, my son?
> What d'ye leave to your brother, my handsom young man?"
> "My houses and my lands; mother, mak my bed soon,
> For I'm sick at the heart, and I fain wad lie down."
>
> "What d'ye leave to your true-love, Lord Randal, my son?
> What d'ye leave to your true-love, my handsom young man?"
> "I leave her hell and fire; mother, mak my bed soon,
> For I'm sick at the heart, and I fain wad lie down."

Throughout, a question is at once asked twice; there is vouchsafed the briefest of answers; and then there is heard an exhausted plea on the verge of death.

Dylan's creative departure from the shaping spirit of *Lord Randal* establishes his territory immediately.

> Oh, where have you been, my blue-eyed son?
> And where have you been, my darling young one?
> I've stumbled on the side of twelve misty mountains
> I've walked and I've crawled on six crooked highways
> I've stepped in the middle of seven sad forests
> I've been out in front of a dozen dead oceans
> I've been ten thousand miles in the mouth of a graveyard
> And it's a hard, it's a hard, it's a hard, it's a hard,
> It's a hard rain's a-gonna fall

Where have I been? Where fortitude and powers of endurance were called for. There, where I stumbled and walked and crawled. There, where I was the only human being – more, the only sentient being. There, where there was no bed for me to lie down upon, and no succumbing to weariness. The travelling: travail. The landscapes: lethal. This first verse establishes the impulse of the song, a willingness if need be (not a masochistic wish) to take the path of most resistance. Hard going. Thorough going. "I fain wad lie down". But I'm pressing on.

What *Lord Randal* may help us to grasp, by taking the force of the contrasts, is the form that Dylan has given to fortitude.

The lineaments of *Lord Randal* are these. First, that every verse is divided equally between mother and son, between question and answer: two lines apiece. Second, that every verse is therefore of identical size, a quatrain that asks and gives no quarter. Third, that every verse is possessed by not just the same rhyme-scheme but the same rhyming words: *son / man* [Scottish *mon*]; *soon / down* [Scottish *doun*]. Fourth, that because so much of each verse is constituted of a question that will be sealed in due course by the refrain, it follows that pitilessly few of the words ever change from verse to verse, and this means an unremitting indeflectibility and then a ratcheted force exerted by those few words that do change, the words that are tortured into telling all.

Dylan, for all his respectful gratitude to *Lord Randal*, abides by none of these precedents that it sets. Such is his right. His making his own way may clarify the lines followed by his song – and to what end.

First, Q. and A. to weigh the same? But in Dylan's song the question is always outweighed by the scale of the answer, and furthermore this scale itself then varies. The first verse consists of the opening couplet that is the question, followed by five lines of narrated endurance, and then by the two-line refrain – or is the refrain all one line really? (The refrain comes as five asseverations: "it's a hard . . .", heard five times before being completed.)

> And it's a hard, it's a hard, it's a hard, and it's a hard,
> It's a hard rain's a-gonna fall

There were, at first, five lines of narrative at the centre; this is varied by expanding to seven such lines and then to six, but with the last verse, doubled up but not flinching in pain, encompassing twelve lines of narrative. Conclusively.

For his part, Lord Randal can do no more than urge again his fatal fatigue: "For I'm wearied wi hunting, and fain wad lie down". Will we weary of hearing this? Such is the question that every refrain has to put to itself. But no, we don't weary, and this partly because here is no ordinary tiredness, "wearied wi hunting", rather the pangs of what will soon prove a cruelly altered refrain, with a death different from hunting: "For I'm sick at the heart, and I fain wad lie down". All the more *sick at the heart*, love-sick, because it was she who administered the poison, "my true-love".

Far from working with the steeled unchanging penetrations of *Lord Randal*, Dylan needs a different – a widespread – monotony, something like what Dryden evoked as the infernal ruin that fell to Lucifer after the war in heaven:

> These regions and this realm my wars have got;
> This mournful empire is the loser's lot:
> In liquid burnings, or on dry to dwell,
> Is all the sad variety of Hell.[1]

As to rhyme-scheme, *A Hard Rain's A-Gonna Fall* doesn't have one. Or much rhyming, come to that. This, despite its starting with a rhyming couplet that will be varied crucially but never relinquished at any verse's head:

> Oh, where have you been, my blue-eyed son?
> And where have you been, my darling young one?

The moment that it moves from this rhyming couplet (immediately, that is), the song sets itself at a great distance from how the ballad had enforced its sombre cross-examination. The song proceeds to work upon us – after every opening question – not by rhyme but through an insistent cadence, the unstressed final syllable that is the feminine ending: "I've stumbled on the side of twelve misty móuntains".[2]

The most common feminine ending in the language, my darling young one, is *-ing*. Or *-in'* in Dylan's voicin' – though not invariably. ("I heard

---

[1] T. S. Eliot in his essay *John Dryden* (1921): *The State of Innocence and Fall of Man* "is an early work; it is on the whole a feeble work; it is not deserving of sustained comparison with *Paradise Lost*. But 'all the sad variety of Hell'! Dryden is already stirring" (*Selected Essays*, 1932, 1951 edition, p. 312).

[2] For the feminine ending *móuntains* (as against *hílls*), see the commentary on *The Lonesome Death of Hattie Carroll* (pp. 223–4), where again the body of the song is a cadence; both songs play the dying fall of the feminine ending against a refrain of masculine ending or endings. *A Hard Rain's A-Gonna Fall* hoops together the opening and the closing of each verse by beginning and ending with the masculine: *son* (as it happens) / *one* and *hard* / *fall*.

many people laughin'", but "I met a young woman whose body was burning" – "laughin'" is one thing, "burning" is no laughing matter.) Against the future that is *a-gonna fall*, the present participles from the past in the song are an ominous presence. If we pluck out the endings of the lines, we see or hear that the first verse (surprising, in retrospect) has no truck with *-ing*. What it confronts at the line-endings is a mounting of nouns: "son", "one", "mountains", "highways", "forests", "oceans", and (finally) "graveyard" – the mouth of the graveyard at once closing hard on the rhyme as it swings around:

> I've been ten thousand miles in the mouth of a graveyard
> And it's a hard, it's a hard, it's a hard, it's a hard,
> It's a hard rain's a-gonna fall

There will later be a variant of this vocal grimace at the end of the fourth verse: "I met another man who was wounded in hatred, / And it's a hard, it's a hard . . ." – where "hatred" swallows "hard".

Only one of the first verse's noun-endings will return to such a position: "forests", which (as "forest") comes to darken the last verse within a sequence of words that – given "deepest" – makes "forest" feel less like a noun than an adjective in the superlative, an extremity: "I'll walk to the depths of the deepest dark forest".[1]

The lines come to an end with fateful nouns, and Dylan's forests and mountains are in tune with those of Philip Sidney. The double sestina in *Arcadia* opens:

> You goat-herd gods, that love the grassy mountains,
> You nymphs that haunt the springs in pleasant vallies,
> You satyrs joyed with free and quiet forests,
> Vouchsafe your silent ears to plaining music,
> Which to my woes gives still an early morning,
> And draws the dolour on till weary evening.

William Empson's eliciting of Sidney's greatness could be vouchsafed to Dylan's plaining music:[2]

The poem beats, however rich its orchestration, with a wailing and immovable

---

[1] Dylan sings "dark"; as printed in *Lyrics 1962–1985*, "black".
[2] *Seven Types of Ambiguity* (1930, second edition 1947), pp. 36–7.

monotony, for ever upon the same doors in vain. *Mountaines, vallies, forests; musique, evening, morning*; it is at these words only that Klaius and Strephon pause in their cries; these words circumscribe their world; these are the bones of their situation; and in tracing their lovelorn pastoral tedium through thirteen repetitions, with something of the aimless multitudinousness of the sea on a rock, we seem to extract all the meaning possible from these notions.

mountains: they suggest being shut in, or banishment; impossibility and impotence, or difficulty and achievement; greatness that may be envied or may be felt as your own (so as to make you feel helpless, or feel powerful); they give you the peace, or the despair, of the grave.

forests: though valuable and accustomed, are desolate and hold danger; there are both nightingales and owls in them; their beasts, though savage, give the strong pleasures of hunting; their burning is either useful or destructive.

music: may express joy or sorrow; is at once more and less direct than talking, and so is connected with one's permanent feeling about the characters of pastoral that they are at once very rustic and rather over-civilised; it may please or distress the by-standers.

The *meaning* of Dylan's music of joy and sorrow? "I would suggest", T. S. Eliot said, "that none of the plays of Shakespeare has a 'meaning', though it would be equally false to say that a play of Shakespeare is meaningless."[1] The first verse of *A Hard Rain's A-Gonna Fall*, while far from meaningless, is *-ing*less. The pressure is on in the second and third verses, in both of which there is this present tension in successive lines, first two lines, then three lines (from within which you might add the ten thousand whisperin'):

> I saw a black branch with blood that kept drippin'
> I saw a room full of men with their hammers a–bleedin'
>
> I heard one hundred drummers whose hands were a-blazin'
> I heard ten thousand whisperin' and nobody listenin'
> I heard one person starve, I heard many people laughin'[2]

The fourth verse has, on her own (and on its own as not *-in'*), "I met a young woman whose body was burning". And then the last verse insists that there is no escape, that there ain't no going back. First, there arrive

---

[1] *Shakespeare and the Stoicism of Seneca* (1927); *Selected Essays*, p. 135.
[2] This picks up a warning from earlier in the verse: "I heard the sound of a thunder that roared out a warnin'".

the two participles — *a-goin'* and *fallin'* — that you have been waiting for ever since you heard that "a hard rain's a-gonna fall": "I'm a-goin' back out 'fore the rain starts a-fallin'". A-going back out: going to back out? Never. (This will be the last verse all right: no previous one has mentioned rain except as forming part of the refrain.) Next and last, there is the beginning of the final end in the reiteration *I start sinkin'* / *I start singin'*:

> And I'll stand on the ocean until I start sinkin'
> But I'll know my song well before I start singin'
> And it's a hard, it's a hard, it's a hard, and it's a hard,
> It's a hard rain's a-gonna fall

And the nub of it all? The pearly grit that is "it". All the way from the specific identifications of "it" in "Oh, what did you see?":

> I saw a newborn baby with wild wolves all around it,
> I saw a highway of diamonds with nobody on it

— through to the unspecified final "it" that is it all:

> And I'll tell it and speak it and think it and breathe it,[1]
> And reflect from the mountain so all souls can see it

The refrain is sequential and torrential:

> And it's a hard, it's a hard, it's a hard, and it's a hard,
> It's a hard rain's a-gonna fall

Its oppressive force is built by the repeated withholding of the other four-letter word, so that "It's a hard, it's a hard, it's a hard, it's a hard" must leave us waiting for "rain". "Or else expecting rain".[2] The scale of this protraction will be the clearer if we think of another refrain that works by deferral, not massively amassed but quietly insistent or persistent: "There's a slow, slow train comin' up around the bend"

---

[1] In singing, Dylan transposes the printed words, "think it and speak it".
[2] *Desolation Row*. "Everybody is making love / Or else expecting rain". The train of thought? That the recumbent lovers share an intuition with the cows, who lie down (keeping that patch dry?) when expecting rain.

(*Slow Train*).¹ Not "There's a slow, there's a slow, there's a slow, there's a slow, and there's a slow train comin' up around the bend". Things have changed when it becomes a matter of waiting for a train.²

Waiting, because fortitude, like patience, is a relation of the present to both the past and the future. In this, it differs from, say, courage, which may be shown suddenly here and now. Courage need make no claim as to what it was and what it will be. True, the habit of being courageous ("May you always be courageous", *Forever Young*) is one to be cultivated, yet courage does not have the habitual built into its very constitution. But patience and fortitude give, in the present, an assurance about what their past has been and what their future has every chance of being; they are constituted of the three tenses, the three dimensions of past, present, and future. The past is summoned by the first four questions: "Oh, where have you been, my blue-eyed son?", "Oh, what did you see . . . ?", "Oh, what did you hear . . . ?", and "Oh, what did you meet . . . ?" But the final verse is spurred into the future:

> "And what'll you do now, my blue-eyed son?"
> "I'll tell it and speak it and think it and breathe it"

The final panorama could be seen as a journey into the depths of the word "resolution". In the words of *The Oxford English Dictionary*:

Determination; firmness or steadiness of purpose; unyielding temper.
I'll walk to the depths of the deepest dark forest

A statement upon some matter; a decision or verdict on some point; a formal decision, determination or expression of opinion.
Where black is the color, where none is the number

The process by which a material thing is reduced or separated into its component parts or elements.
Where the pellets of poison are flooding their waters

---

¹ That Dylan hadn't forgotten *A Hard Rain's A-Gonna Fall* when he came by *Slow Train* is suggested by the endings upon "it": "Oh, you know it costs more to store the food than it do to give it" / "They talk about a life of brotherly love, show me someone who knows how to live it" / "A real suicide case, but there was nothin' I could do to stop it".

² "I'm well dressed, waiting on the last train" (*Things Have Changed*). "There's a long-distance train rolling through the rain" (*Where Are You Tonight?*)

The act, process, or capability of rendering distinguishable the component parts of an object or closely adjacent optical or photographic images, or of separating measurements of similar magnitude of any quantity in space or time.

And I'll tell it and speak it and think it and breathe it
And reflect from the mountain so all souls can see it

Fortitude is the supreme virtue of the quest. *A Hard Rain's A-Gonna Fall* calls up the quests both of the medieval world and of the medievalizing world of later art. "I had so long suffered in this quest": the poem that in some ways most breathes the pestilential air of Dylan's song (as against being the ballad that launched his song) is not medieval but Victorian, Browning's *"Childe Roland to the Dark Tower Came".*[1] Like the song, it is a vision of judgement. "'Tis the Last Judgement's fire must cure this place". It ends, after a daunting parade of all those who had failed in the quest, with – dauntless all the same – fortitude, *fortissime*:

> in a sheet of flame
> I saw them and I knew them all. And yet
> Dauntless the slug-horn to my lips I set,
>   And blew. *"Childe Roland to the Dark Tower came."*

But when you have a trumpet at your lips (or a harmonica, for that matter), you cannot ask or answer questions, and *A Hard Rain's A-Gonna Fall* is built, above all and below all, on its being – as Browning's poem is not – antiphonal. Like *Lord Randal*, Q. and A. Unlike *Lord Randal*, not equally Q. and A. Alternation with alteration. Q.E.D.

[1] Browning knew Shakespeare's song well before he started writing. From *King Lear*: "Childe Roland to the dark Tower came, / His word was still, fie, foh, and fum, / I smell the blood of a British man". Michael Gray is good on Dylan and Browning (*Song and Dance Man III*, 2000, pp. 64–70), but doesn't mention this instance. In the order of the song, the two have these in common (but I'm assimilating, for instance, singulars and plurals: Dylan, "highways" / Browning, "highway"): "mountains", "highways", "dead", "mouth", "what did you see" / "Not see?" (at the start of the verse), "a baby", "black", "blood", "water", "what did you hear" / "Not hear?" (at the start of the next verse), "starve", "laugh", "a man", "burning", "dark", "poison", "executioner" / "hangman", "ugly", and "the souls". Stronger may be the relation of Dylan's "the roar of a wave that could drown the whole world" not only to Browning's "my whole world-wandering" but to Browning's immediately succeeding his other phrase, "the whole world", with a ship's going down in a storm.

But this does itself raise a Q. For while there is no doubt at all as to who asks

> O where ha you been, Lord Randal, my son?
> And where ha you been, my handsom young man?

– there is doubt as to who opens by asking

> Oh, where have you been, my blue-eyed son?
> And where have you been, my darling young one?

Moreover, antiphonal structure is markedly unusual in Dylan. *Blowin' in the Wind* has the asker be the answerer. *Who Killed Davey Moore?* has its question answered one by one by all those around the boxing ring. True, there is one song, alive with questions, that does set out as antiphonal: *Boots of Spanish Leather*, which alternates the verses until the seventh verse, when the dark truth dawns, with one of the interlocutors now becoming the narrator for the last three verses, verses that no longer have any place for questions. Though Dylan songs often turn upon questions, none of them has any such sequence of exchanges as makes *A Hard Rain's A-Gonna Fall* distinctive.

Added to which, "Oh, where have you been, my blue-eyed son?" doesn't sound like the sort of thing that one asks oneself – unlike, say, *Are You Ready?* ("I hope I'm ready"). And Dylan will not have failed to register that *Lord Randal* is not only antiphonal, it is an interrogation, an inquiry that becomes an inquisition. "My son" . . . "Mother", in every verse. What is so horrible about this murder story is how close the whole scene is to the banality of every mother to every son.

> "O where ha you been, Lord Randal, my son?"
>
> "An wha met you there, Lord Randal, my son?"
>
> "And what did she give you, Lord Randal, my son?"
>
> "An wha gat your leavins, Lord Randal, my son?"
>
> "An what becam of them, Lord Randal, my son?"
>
> "What d'ye leave to your mother, Lord Randal, my son?"
>
> "What d'ye leave to your sister, Lord Randal, my son?"

"What d'ye leave to your brother, Lord Randal, my son?"

"What d'ye leave to your true-love, Lord Randal, my son?"

"What was school-lunch like, Lord Randal, my son?"

"What do her parents do, Lord Randal, my son?"

Which is where another unforgettable ballad comes into the grim picture.[1] A man with his sword-blade a-bleedin'. Mother and son, antiphonally, her "Edward, Edward" being met always by his "Mither, mither".

> "Why dois your brand sae drap wi bluid,
> > Edward, Edward,
> Why dois your brand sae drap wi bluid,
> > And why sae sad gang yee O?"
> "O I hae killed my hauke sae guid,
> > Mither, mither,
> O I hae killed my hauke sae guid,
> > And I had nae mair bot hee O."

Whereupon the mother insists "Your haukis bluid was nevir sae reid" ("My deir son") – alternating her four lines with his four again, as in all seven of the verses. "O I hae killed my reid-roan steed". She again refuses to believe him. And he: "O I hae killed my fadir deir, / Mither, mither".

> "And whatten penance wol ye drie for that,
> > Edward, Edward?
> And whatten penance wol ye drie for that,
> > My deir son, now tell me O."

He will set sail, journeying into exile.

> "And what wul ye doe wi your towirs and your ha'?"
> "Ile let thame stand tul they doun fa"

> "And what wul ye leive to your bairns and your wife?"
> "The warldis room, late them beg thrae life"

[1] The eighteenth-century ballad *Edward, Edward* was and is in *The Oxford Book of English Verse*, as well as in most anthologies of ballads and of Scottish verse.

And then the devastating desolate end:

> "And what wul ye leive to your ain mither deir,
>   Edward, Edward?
> And what wul ye leive to your ain mither deir,
>   My deir son, now tell me O."
> "The curse of hell frae me sall ye beir,
>   Mither, mither,
> The curse of hell frae me sall ye beir,
>   Sic counseils ye gave to me O."

Like *Lord Randal*, this ends with the curse of hell, levied again upon a woman, this time not a true-love but (even more hideously) no truly loving mother or wife.

A Hard Rain's A-Gonna Fall is a vision of judgement, a scouring vision of hell. Hell on earth. And who is the mother who asks "Oh, where have you been, my blue-eyed son?"? Mother Earth.

Milton has his *Paradise Lost*, where the fallen angels in hell, "with impious hands, / Rifled the bowels of their mother Earth". A. E. Housman has his Paradisal Shropshire Lost: "The earth, because my heart was sore, / Sorrowed for the son she bore". Dylan has his Paradise Lost: "There's a million dreams gone, there's a landscape being raped" (*Where Are You Tonight?*).

Mother Nature. And Mother Earth. If you don't care for the old girl, you call her "beldam earth", and leave her to her unlovely landscape of cosmic indigestion:

> Diseasèd Nature oftentimes breaks forth
> In strange eruptions; and the teeming Earth
> Is with a kind of colic pinched and vext
> By the imprisoning of unruly wind
> Within her womb: which for enlargement striving,
> Shakes the old beldam Earth, and tumbles down
> Steeples and moss-grown towers.
>   (*I Henry IV*, III, i)[1]

Browning had shown her in a bad light and a bad mood, bitching about what had become of her landscape:

---

[1] Beckett: "It is made of dead leaves. A reminder of beldam nature" (*Closed Place*).

> "See
> Or shut your eyes," said Nature peevishly,
> "It nothing skills: I cannot help my case:
> 'Tis the Last Judgement's fire must cure this place,
> Calcine its clods and set my prisoners free."
>
> (XI)

The damp dirty prisoners. But in *A Hard Rain's A-Gonna Fall* Dylan sorrows for the mother who is being lost to all her sons. Mother Earth and Mother Nature are imperilled by the hard rain. And by the pellets of poison. And by so much else that haunts the song. Not just the one Dead Sea, but a dozen dead oceans.

Childe Roland had asked "Who were the strugglers, what war did they wage?", with the adversaries "Crouched like two bulls locked horn in horn in fight". It might be wondered why my commentary says nothing about the Cuban crisis of October 1962, about the fact that – as Dylan himself said – the song was written when it seemed that Khrushchev and Kennedy were head-to-heading towards the war to end life. What Dylan says about the song – *said*, one should say, since it was all back then – earns respect and asks thought:

It's not atomic rain, though. Some people think that. It's just a hard rain, not the fall out rain, it isn't that at all. The hard rain that's gonna fall is in the last verse, where I say the "pellets of poison are flooding us all" ["flooding their waters"], I mean all the lies that people are told on their radios and in the newspapers, trying to take people's brains away, all the lies I consider poison.[1]

"Every line of it is actually the start of a whole song." "Line after line after line, trying to capture the feeling of nothingness. I kept repeating things I feared." Feared, but imagined facing with fortitude.

> And I'll stand on the ocean until I start sinkin'
> But I'll know my song well before I start singin'
> And it's a hard, it's a hard, it's a hard, and it's a hard,
> It's a hard rain's a-gonna fall

What precipitated the song was the Cuban crisis. Agreed. But the song,

---

[1] *Studs Terkel Show*, WFMT Radio, Chicago (3 May 1963).

being a work of art, is always going to be larger than and other than what precipitated it. *The Oxford English Dictionary*: "Hence the frequent precipitation of heavy rain, and the banks and sheets of morning cloud which veil the tree-clad peaks" (1859). The misty mountains. And there remains the solitary man, whose individual suffering asks no less fortitude. "I met one man who was wounded in love". Next, "I met another man who was wounded in hatred". In English, you can be in love, and you can say something in hatred, and you can be wounded by or with hatred[1] – but "who was wounded in hatred"? Terribly damaged and damaging: in hatred with her or him or them, as if hatred were an ethos and an atmosphere.

The man who is left alone may stand in need of fortitude. You can feel it and you can hear it in *Most of the Time* or (with an alien sense of desertion) in *I Believe in You*. "They'd like to drive me from this town".

I Believe in You

There was once a "righteous king who wrote psalms". *I and I* is at one with *I* and *You*, there in *I Believe in You* – which sings "And I, I", and which is a psalm. As always in the Psalms, the unrighteous are the enemy. *You*, though, are my enemy's enemy, thank the Lord.

The stronger the unrighteous are, the more will fortitude be called for and called upon. "I will be sorry for my sin. But mine enemies are lively, and they are strong: and they that hate me wrongfully are multiplied" (Psalms 38:18–19). "Deliver me from my persecutors; for they are stronger than I" (Psalms 142:24).

The unrighteous are *they*. Unidentified, nameless. Psalm 3 begins: "LORD, how are they increased that trouble me! Many are they that rise up against me". Five verses later, it confronts those "that have set themselves against me round about". *I Believe in You* begins:

> They ask me how I feel
> And if my love is real
> And how I know I'll make it through
> And they, they look at me and frown
> They'd like to drive me from this town
> They don't want me around
> 'Cause I believe in you

[1] As printed in *Lyrics 1962–1985*: "wounded with hatred".

Me around / me round about.

They prowl in and around the song. They are in the first and second verses, and they return to lurk at the last. But the hope that is fortitude ("I know I'll make it through") is at the heart of the song, for the word "they" is not to be heard in the central sequence of it: not in the bridge the first time (beginning "I believe in you even through the tears and the laughter"), and then not in the central verse ("Don't let me drift too far"), and then not in the bridge the second time ("I believe in you when winter turn to summer"). That there exists this they-free zone puts hope in me: you and I can be there on our own together. Yet we need to be still aware of the threat, since the bridge – the second time – has to acknowledge "though my friends forsake me". (Psalms 38:11, "my friends stand aloof from my sore; and my kinsmen stand afar off".)

"And they, they" rings out its duplicity only once. "And I, I . . ." counters this twice with its refusal to flinch: "And I, I walk out on my own", "And I, I don't mind the pain".[1]

> They show me to the door
> They say don't come back no more
> 'Cause I don't be like they'd like me to

The bad grammar is up to no little good, since it is not a matter of slumming or of dumbing down but of intimating something different. Instead of the expected "Because I'm not like they'd like me to be", the turn of phrase makes "I don't be" take into itself both "I won't be" and "I can't be" (*like they'd like me to be*). My choice and at the same time my destiny.[2] People, uglily, will like you for being like what they want, which usually means like them.[3] The pressure that whets the word – "be like they'd like me to" – is the malign counterpart to what had been for John Keats a happiness about what this little word "like" (likewise near "because") could do in the right hands: "You will by this time think I am in love with her; so before I go any further I will tell you I am not . . . I like her and

---

[1] Printed in *Lyrics 1962–1985*, "And I walk out on my own". Dylan sings "And I, I walk out on my own".

[2] "Well, if I don't be there by morning / I guess that I never will" (*If I Don't Be There by Morning*, Dylan with Helena Springs).

[3] "Well, I try my best / To be just like I am / But everybody wants you / To be just like them" (*Maggie's Farm*).

her like because one has no *sensations* – what we both are is taken for
granted."[1]

> 'Cause I don't be like they'd like me to
> And I, I walk out on my own
> A thousand miles from home
> But I don't feel alone
> 'Cause I believe in you

These lines contain in themselves all that they simply need, so they don't
stand in any *need* of our remembering an earlier song of Dylan's in which he
didn't feel alone because he believed in someone. Still, the relation between
the two songs may have something to proffer.

> I'm out here a thousand miles from my home
> Walkin' a road other men have gone down
> I'm seein' your world of people and things
> Your paupers and peasants and princes and kings
> *(Song to Woody)*

Including the righteous king who wrote psalms?

It isn't that *I Believe in You* in any way reneges on the having believed in
Woody Guthrie; rather that what had been social conscience has become
religious conscience. "I'm seein' your world" has become seeing a world
that is not any man's, even an especially good man who was a true artist.
"For me He was rejected by a world that He created" (*Solid Rock*). Woody
Guthrie is not rejected by *I Believe in You*, but the song witnesses to
belief in One who was despisèd and rejected, rejected of men (Handel's
compassionate setting in *The Messiah*), and witnesses to how this has led
to being despised and rejected.[2] Being so, not just feeling so. For the
song moves past *feeling*. The first verse begins "They ask me how I
feel", the second has "But I don't feel alone", and the bridge has "this
feeling's still here in my heart". So we might have expected that every
verse would want to speak of feeling. But the remaining twenty lines of
the song choose not to do so – they evince a great deal of feeling, but

---

[1] 14 October 1818; *Letters*, ed. H. E. Rollins (1958), vol. I, p. 394.
[2] "They don't want me around" and "A thousand miles" / Psalms 3:6: "I will not be
afraid of ten thousands of people, that have set themselves against me round about".

all the more for making no further announcement. There is no longer any going along with the terms initially set by the unrighteous: "They ask me how I feel".

"And how I know I'll make it through": and as we make it through the song (process, not product, constituting any Dylan song), the word "through" modulates into the word "though", which then becomes the excrucial turn within the song. Dylan brings this about ("I believe in you when winter turn to summer") through having "even through" turn to "even though" (and on to "even on"):

> I believe in you even through the tears and the laughter
> I believe in you even though we be apart
> I believe in you even on the morning after
>
> I believe in you even though I be outnumbered

Whereupon "even though" is at once clipped back to the root of the matter:

> Oh, though the earth may shake me
> Oh, though my friends forsake me
> Oh, even that couldn't make me go back

Dylan's vocal punctuation is dramatically other than that of his page: he takes back the snarled and yelping "Oh" so that it clutches all but desperately at the previous line of bridge no. 1 and of bridge no. 2:

> Oh, when the dawn is nearing   Oh,
> when the night is disappearing   Oh,
> this feeling's still here in my heart
>
> Oh, though the earth may shake me   Oh,
> though my friends forsake me   Oh,
> even that couldn't make me go back

– with the strangled voicing of "heart" and of "back" bearing witness to his nerving himself not to be forsaken by fortitude.

"They" may start as though solicitous, but their string of questions (like those bent upon Christ) is meant to entangle him:

> They ask me how I feel
> And if my love is real
> And how I know I'll make it through

No answer is ever given to their asking – except the answer that is the song itself. Nothing is said to them ("no matter what they say"). Everything that is said is said to the One and to oneself, as with a psalm or a prayer. They may issue an imperative: "don't come back no more". But the song counters this with a plea, or rather two parallel pairs of pleas, set together not only by their syntax and their strong assonance but (I believe) by their invocation of the Psalms:

> Don't let me drift too far
> Keep me where you are
>
> Don't let me change my heart
> Keep me set apart

"O Lord, be not far from me" (Psalms 35:22). "Know that the Lord hath set apart him that is godly for himself" (Psalms 4:3).

Fortitude means keeping going. Which means, in its turn, that a song of fortitude must face something of the same challenge as a song of gratitude. The ending must maintain something. That the word "maintain" may itself be doubly a rhyme (it rhymes within itself and with other words)[1] might prompt us to notice how Dylan at the very end, for the first and last time, brings it about that the refrain, "'Cause I believe in you", is the culmination not of a single rhyme but of something that is doubly a rhyme, when two consecutive words rhyme, and are later rhymed with: *do pursue / you*.

> Don't let me change my heart
> Keep me set apart
> From all the plans they do pursue
> And I, I don't mind the pain
> Don't mind the driving rain
> I know I will sustain
> 'Cause I believe in you

---

[1] See how *Señor* ends with what is doubly a rhyme: *for, Señor.*

They have their form of persistence ("all the plans they *do pursue*"). The answer must be my better form of it.

> And I, I don't mind the pain
> Don't mind the driving rain
> I know I will sustain
> 'Cause I believe in you

The confidence, which is quite other than a boast, is realized in the syntax of "sustain", by which the breastplate of righteousness is variously buckled into place. First, "I don't mind the driving rain that I know that I will sustain, and the reason that I don't mind is that I believe in you." Second, "I don't mind the driving rain that I know that I will sustain because of (as a result of) my believing in you." Third, "sustain" not as a transitive but as an intransitive verb, absolutely: "I don't mind the driving rain, for I know that I will sustain, because I believe in you."

The English language ordinarily has "sustain" be transitive, but would, I am sure, be willing to entertain an imaginative exception. As it did in the old days, when "sustain" could be intransitive (*The Oxford English Dictionary*: "to bear up, hold out") and when Wyclif could translate – as it happens – Psalm 130: "If wickedness thou shalt all about keep, LORD: LORD, who shall sustain?"[1] And it is the Psalms that sustain the close of *I Believe in You*. Psalms 3:5–6: "for the LORD sustained me". Psalms 55:22, "Cast thy burden upon the LORD, and he shall sustain thee".

"I know I will sustain". That this possibility, even if it is misguided, is not the extravagance of one man alone is borne out by Robert Shelton's having ended his review of *Slow Train Coming* with the words "He will sustain". Two men alone, maybe.

But, as everyone has noticed, *I Believe in You* begins with a tantalizing echo of an earthly love song of unearthly loveliness: *Smoke Gets in Your Eyes*.[2] The echo is in the music (just listen to Dylan's opening) no less than

---

[1] Psalms 130:3: "If thou, LORD, shouldest mark iniquities, O LORD, who shall stand?"
[2] Music by Jerome Kern, words by Otto Harbach. Kern: "They asked me how I knew / My true love was true?". Dylan: "They ask me how I feel / And if my love is real / And how I know I'll make it through". There are other small overlaps. In the order within the Kern song: "here inside" / [Dylan] "here in"; "laughed" (and "laughing") / "laughter"; "my love"; "today"; "friends"; "Tears"; "say"; "heart"; "realize" / "real". And there is "doubt" against "I believe". It is extraordinary how different in its effect, as a cadence and a sentiment, is "Smoke gets in your eyes", from the wording elsewhere in Dylan: "Smoke is in your eye" (*When the Night Comes Falling from the Sky*).

in the words. The words went to the making of Dylan's song, however different his world on this occasion, sacred, not secular – or rather, sacred, and therefore willing to accommodate the secularly human (whereas the secular is usually loth to accommodate the sacredly divine).

SMOKE GETS IN YOUR EYES

They asked me how I knew
My true love was true?
I of course replied
Something here inside
Cannot be denied

So I chaffed them and I gaily laughed
To think they could doubt my love
Yet today
My love has flown away
I am without my love

Now laughing friends deride
Tears I cannot hide
So I smile and say
When a lovely flame dies
Smoke gets in your eyes

They said someday you'll find
All who love are blind
When your heart's on fire
You must realize
Smoke gets in your eyes.

In addition to what is unmistakable in the openings, the Kern / Harbach *I knew / true* furnished Dylan with "I know" and with his rhyming refrain. "My true love was true?" became his "if my love is real". The object of my love is real, or my love? For while "true" might ask "Faithful?", "real" might ask "Actually exists?" To believe in a human being may be to trust her or him. To believe in God is to believe in his existence – or rather, in His. (Or Hers, granted, though not in the world of the Psalms.)

"I of course replied": I of course did *not* reply (in *I Believe in You*) to those who deride and who are false friends. "So I chaffed them and I gaily laughed"? No, they chafed me and I didn't laugh. Yet the world of Jerome Kern may meet the world of the Psalms even here: "laughing friends deride" may combine with "my friends stand aloof" (Psalms 38:11) to precipitate "though my friends forsake me".

I Believe in You cannot but bring to mind the words that it never says: "Smoke gets in your eyes". And even there it may remember, too, the righteous, summoned by the Book of Proverbs 10:25–7.

The righteous is an everlasting foundation. As vinegar to the teeth, and as smoke to the eyes, so is the sluggard to them that send him. The fear of the LORD prolongeth days: but the years of the wicked shall be shortened.

Most of the Time

Are you sure? Few questions are more sure to make you unsure of yourself. The required answer, not always vouchsafed (let alone amicably), is "Well, I had thought so. But I suppose . . ." On an inspired occasion, the question may manage to contain its own answer.

"There's only one 'aspirated s' in English: the word sugar."
"Are you sure?"[1]

Usually, the question is not one that you put to yourself directly. *Am I sure?*: you might muse this, but would probably be averse to interrogating it. Compare the exchange in a Beckett novel:

> Do you feel like singing? said Camier.
> Not to my knowledge, said Mercier.

Dylan feels like singing most of the time.

> Most of the time
> I'm clear focused all around
> Most of the time

[1] R. A. Knox's question-and-answer. *Geoffrey Madan's Notebooks*, eds. J. A. Gere and John Sparrow (1981), p. 17.

> I can keep both feet on the ground
> I can follow the path, I can read the signs
> Stay right with it when the road unwinds
> I can handle whatever I stumble upon
> I don't even notice she's gone
> Most of the time

Most of the time, *Most of the Time* consists of repeating the words "Most of the time". But there you go again, immediately exaggerating in a way that the song itself is vigilant about – and is keen to quiz.[1] For there are forty-four lines to the song, and the four words "Most of the time" amount to only fourteen of the forty-four.

Those reiterated words are an inescapable admission. Admit it to yourself (the person whom you most wish to deceive): it is not *all of the time* that you can live up to the fortitude that you try to live by. The song embodies and scrutinizes the difficulty of being entirely honest with yourself when still in pain, especially when there is another self involved, a loved one who has gone and with whom you are doing your best to be no longer involved.

"I know exactly where it all went," Dylan sings, but then exactitude is the exacting thing. Being able to get over – or away from or past or beyond (what *is* the right preposition?) – a lost love, to recover even while acknowledging that the loved one (like the past) is irrecoverable: any of us might manage something of this, but not *all of the time*. Yet honesty will entail not exaggerating the other way either, not being luxuriously lugubrious. So not *none of the time*. And not, since a fair degree of resilience is proving possible, merely *some of the time*. *Much of the time*? No, "Most of the time": this is on the up, even though not yet completely on the up and up. And at the same time, bizarrely, it has the air of being on the level, being sung throughout very levelly. Perhaps it judges truly.

If we detect in the protestations of the song (not sung by Dylan protestingly but always resignedly on the face of it, with an unsettling mildness) somewhat too much of an insistence, are we sure that *detecting* is the right mode for us to practise when we are in the immediate company of suffering?

---

[1] As to exaggeration and artistic accomplishment, there is T. S. Eliot on how Pope's *Epistle to Dr. Arbuthnot* "depends upon the justice and reserve, the apparent determination not to exaggerate" (*John Dryden*; *Selected Essays*, p. 310).

Is the man protesting too much? (As to his lady.) "The lady doth protest too much, methinks": we all like to quote knowingly those words about assurances of fidelity, but most of the time we forget that the lady who says them – Hamlet's mother caught in the mousetrap, watching the play within the play – has fallen short of fidelity and is missing the point, is missing all the points.

Dylan has said that "songs need structure, stratagems, codes and stability".[1] This particular song is about the understandable human need to have stratagems and codes with which to outwit or outmanoeuvre – or, if need be, outfrown – the losses and the losings. And if we find (as this song understands) that such a human need may on occasion have to make do either with an honesty that perseveres for sure but does fall short of perfection, or with a courage that cannot always be as entire as we would wish, we might try compassion. And acknowledgement that the sufferer is proving pretty good at not taking it too badly. We all whistle to keep our courage up. This is an achieving of courage, not a lapsing from it. And what we whistle we may sing. Or enjoy the singing of, even while it is a curious business, art's enjoying the evocation of suffering. The plaintiff manages not to succumb to the plaintive.

The song sets itself to steer between the opposing threats to the peace of mind that is craved, a peace of mind that is apparently making its way but is taking its time. So timing is of the essence of the song. Take, as one of the self-protecting moves that it knows that this state of mind needs, its only slowly being able to bring itself to mention the woman at all. We hear at once that, "most of the time", he can see well, can press on well, can handle obstacles well – but it is not until the eighth line of the nine-line opening verse that he can bring himself to open up and say what all this is about and up against:

> I don't even notice she's gone
> Most of the time

(A telling pause in the singing, after "notice", a wince on the brink of a gulf.) Not that the previous lines have been marking time, leave alone wasting it, but they have been only gradually gaining the confidence to come right out with it. They have had to nerve themselves. For until

[1] *Irish Times Magazine* (29 September 2001), the Rome interview.

"I don't even notice she's gone / Most of the time", there has been this
touchingly natural bobbing and weaving. For instance, in the all-but-clichés
that then interknit: "clear focused all around" (quite a claim, when you focus
on it) into "I can read the signs"; or "I can keep both feet on the ground" into
"I can follow the path", with the feet then walking into the bodily oddity
of "I can handle whatever I stumble upon". The *handle / stumble* movement
is itself something of a stumble (hands and feet), and "stumble upon" isn't
quite what you expect – *stumble over* would feel glumly more like it, since
what he is coming up against these days doesn't sound promisingly fortuitous
(by a bit of luck, I stumbled on the answer) but more than accidental,
accident-causing.

She comes into the song with the words "she's gone", with only the
refrain of the first verse still to go or still to come. "I don't even notice
she's gone / Most of the time". She next gets admittedly thought about,
openly, at just the same place in the next verse, and with just the same
pressure in the words that introduce her.

> Most of the time
> It's well understood
> Most of the time
> I wouldn't change it if I could
> I can make it all match up, I can hold my own
> I can deal with the situation right down to the bone
> I can survive, and I can endure
> I don't even think about her
> Most of the time

The fact of her is being acknowledged but staved off as long as possible.
The third verse, again, doesn't speak of her until exactly this same point
when it is about to close, though this time, when it comes, the memory
is all the more urgently whole because it is of a part of her, part of her
physical being and of their love:

> Most of the time
> My head is on straight
> Most of the time
> I'm strong enough not to hate
> I don't build up illusion till it makes me sick
> I ain't afraid of confusion no matter how thick

> I can smile in the face of mankind
> Don't even remember what her lips felt like on mine
> Most of the time

The *illusion/confusion* rhyme, at once overt and covert (it rings out, but within the lines, not concluding them), has no counterpart elsewhere in the song, perhaps because it is the nub.

Cutting back on "I don't even remember", "Don't even remember" is clipped as tight-lipped hardihood chooses to be. *She*, as time passes, may gradually be becoming abstract (which would be a mercy), but her lips and what they felt like on mine: this is the body of the words. And Dylan has given it this reality, this corporeality, by means of what would ordinarily be only a commonplace, the phrase "in the face of":

> I can smile in the face of mankind
> Don't even remember what her lips felt like on mine
> Most of the time

There is no smile on the face of the line that leads to those lips of hers and of mine. Yet Dylan sings the word "face" there with a curled courage, a thrust of the jaw, that gives them a differently saddened contour from the lines that grace the next song on the album, *What Good Am I?*, "What good am I if I say foolish things / And I laugh in the face of what sorrow brings".

The final verse stays with the secure staving when it comes to letting her explicitly, for the last time, into the reckoning: once again it is the penultimate line that admits her.

> Most of the time
> I'm halfways content
> Most of the time
> I know exactly where it all went
> I don't cheat on myself, I don't run and hide
> Hide from the feelings that are buried inside
> I don't compromise and I don't pretend
> I don't even care if I ever see her again
> Most of the time

This stoical assurance shouldn't simply be credited, but it is to the credit of the speaker – and of the song – that there is recognition of the price that is being paid. The opposite of a claim is not a disclaim. Is it a disclaimer, of which the song is full? Is he a disclaimer?

But the song doesn't consist only of its four verses. Even as it is the penultimate line of each verse that thrusts home what is at stake, so it is the penultimate sequence within the song that bares the ways in which there can be something obsessive about needing to rid oneself of being obsessed with someone. For it is the bridge, carrying us into the last verse, that is the mordancy of the song. Whereas each of the nine-line verses speaks only once of what she once was, the eight-line bridge, whatever it needs to hear itself saying, has her not just in mind but in mouth all the way through: six times, "she" and "her".

> Most of the time
> She ain't even in my mind
> I wouldn't know her if I saw her
> She's that far behind
> Most of the time
> I can't even be sure
> If she was ever with me[1]
> Or if I was ever with her

Those last two lines writhe as though in hell. For what the hell is the difference between her being with him, and his being with her? Ah, but . . . And anyway it is one of the strengths of this song about fortitude that it keeps its lips sealed ("Don't even remember what her lips felt like on mine") about all the rights and wrongs of the love that came and went. T. S. Eliot's praise of a poet's "justice and reserve, the apparent determination not to exaggerate",[2] can be granted here. *Most of the Time* has no time for giving its side of the story, or even for giving the story. There is a sudden flash, as though he might be going to let slip or let rip, in the phrase "I don't cheat on myself" – which is not at all the same as cheating myself and which might be about to say that she cheated on him (or, darkly, that he cheated on her). But then it thinks better of this – no need for others to think the worse of her, or of either of them. No vindication is sought, and there is no vindictiveness. And no trying to recover her, only to recover

---

[1] In the bridge here, the only word at the end of any line that doesn't have a link to another end word is "me". This uniqueness has its poignancy and oppugnancy.

[2] See footnote, p. 352.

himself. In this, it is in another world from a song that might have breathed the same air, *Don't Think Twice, It's All Right*. Try not to think about it or about her, but it's not all right yet. And may not be for quite a time. If ever. "I don't even care if I ever see her again / Most of the time".

What is painful in the song, in its comprehension of pain, is how hideously much must be being conceded, all the way through, with those words "most of the time". For the admission within "most of the time" is that some of the time – perhaps even much of the time – he is *not* clear focused (not that anybody can be clear focused *all around*), and *can't* keep both feet on the ground, or follow the path, or stay right with it, or handle whatever he stumbles upon. Or – as the assurances to himself mount (self-assurings, not self-assurance) – make it all match up, or hold his own, or deal with the situation, or (with fortitude fully explicit) *survive* or *endure*. And so it goes, unadvancingly, a chilling marshalling of all that cannot be denied: that he does (at least some of the time) cheat on himself, and run and hide, and compromise, and pretend – and *care*. This is the horror upon which all these asseverations insist. The horror is not the whole story, for there is nothing hollow about the counter-insistence, that most of the time he has the fortitude to survive and to endure. He knows his own strength, which means acknowledging its limitations: "Most of the time / I'm strong enough not to hate". (The immediate *time / I'm* rhyme at the turn of the line is prosecuted three times in the song.) "I'm strong enough not to hate": this is not nothing. But it has to be understood as conceding that some of the time he is not strong enough not to hate. Only enough is enough.

> But, for the unquiet heart and brain,
>   A use in measured language lies;
>   The sad mechanic exercise,
> Like dull narcotics, numbing pain.
>   (*In Memoriam*, V)

The measured language of the song – measured as metre, and measured as grimly temperate – is a tissue of tensions. Eleven times, "I can", but not a single time in the bridge or in the final verse; "I can't", once only. Ten times, "I don't"; never, "I do". Three times, "I am"; once, "I ain't". The state of mind, and of heart, is one that is necessarily self-absorbed as it tries in vain to absorb the pain. Again and again we hear "I", "my", "mine", "me" (nearly forty times in the forty-four lines); very seldom, for all her unignorability, "she" or "her". And "I", "my", "mine" all throb through the song because of their assonance with the refrain that opens and closes each verse, *Most of the time*. Exactly half of the lines, twenty-two of them, toll this.

> Most of the time
> I can't even be sure
> If she was ever with me
> Or if I was ever with her

Just so, to be sure. To assure. To reassure, or – as this song reiterates – to re-re-re-reassure. It is others that we assure (let me assure you, or I assure you), but then the state of mind in *Most of the Time* is one in which *I am*, or as Rimbaud put it – albeit in French – *I is another* (or an other). And "sure" has long been a curiously unsure word, since it has to be both *Oxford English Dictionary*, III, "Subjectively certain" ("Certain in mind; having no doubt; assured, confident"), and IV, "Objectively certain". One would have thought that these two meanings would not lie down happily together in the one word. Added to which, there is that tricky little colloquialism by which "Sure" both intensifies and slackens. (Another drink? Sure.) "Used to emphasize *yes* or *no*", quoting Lady Bird Johnson in 1970: "If it had been a request to chop off one's right hand one would have said, 'Sure.'" "I can handle whatever I stumble upon." Sure.

> Most of the time
> I'm halfways content

What is so well judged is that the word "content" is itself already a halfways thing, so that what is being drawn may amount to being quartered. *The Oxford English Dictionary* is more than usually acute and illuminating here, quoting the dictionary of Samuel (not to be confused with Lady Bird) Johnson:

content Having one's desires bounded by what one has (though that may be less than one could have wished); not disturbed by the desire of anything more, or of anything different; "satisfied so as not to repine; easy though not highly pleased".

It is only most of the time that the man in this long black song succeeds in being *not disturbed*. But he is halfways there. On the other hand, "She's that far behind". One too many mornings and a thousand miles behind, to be exact.

Not Dark Yet

Apocalypse Now may be less disturbing than Apocalypse Soon. The former does at least promise a prompt *No more*: over and done with (*former*, really). The latter mutters "Later", and just gets on (in its own good time) with doing away with. In this waiting game, the stakes may be higher – and sharper. That cardinal virtue Fortitude may be even more called for.

Dylan has always been alert to the dark spectre and spectrum of imminence, the different time-scales where we are weighed in the balance and found wanting. There is the apocalyptic-cryptic *A Hard Rain's A-Gonna Fall*. There is the scorpion song that stings itself to death, rounding fierily on itself, as *All Along the Watchtower*. "Two riders were approaching, the wind began to howl": at which conclusion, it is as if the song bizarrely begins at last, and as if the myth began again.

Or, altogether other, there is the bone-deep acquiescent fatigue in *Going, Going, Gone*. Never has the auctioneer's cutting-off point sounded more gravelled, less gavelled. No more auction block. Only writer's block. "There's not much more to be said": you can say that again. Or sing it again. But was it prudent to grant this so early in a song, in the very first verse? Prudence is another of the cardinal virtues, but that doesn't stop Prudence from sometimes being, as Blake had it, "a rich, ugly, old maid courted by Incapacity".

> I've just reached a place
> Where the willow don't bend
> There's not much more to be said
> It's the top of the end
> I'm going
> I'm going
> I'm gone
>
> I'm closin' the book
> On the pages and the text
> And I don't really care
> What happens next

> I'm just going
> I'm going
> I'm gone

This knows all about the sin that is Sloth (the Sloth that may be in or beneath the tree), but it knows too that Sloth long ago came to an understanding with Fortitude. Sloth doesn't really care what happens next, but then nor does stoical Fortitude. This exquisitely threaded song has no place for anger, being all languor. Once again, it's got to be done sometime so why not do it then? "Now, I've just got to cut loose / Before it gets late": on purpose this doesn't try to effect any purposeful impact of *cutting* (on the contrary, there is a furrily blurred edge), and what do you mean, before it gets late? It isn't only the world of *All Along the Watchtower* that ought to remember "the hour is getting late". The self-attender in *Going, Going, Gone* takes his time, not least by expanding those three words into "I'm just going, I'm going, I'm gone". But is the time his to take, exactly? Philip Larkin hovers at the brink of dismay: his poem's title is *Going, Going*, with *Gone* either already gone or not yet quite gone. "Well the future for me is already a thing of the past" (*Bye and Bye*).

Many of Dylan's songs issue a penultimatum. Looking through the telescoped: *Whatcha Gonna Do When the Night Comes Falling from the Sky*. Or, "Only a matter of time 'til night comes steppin' in" (*Jokerman*).

One of the most enduring of Dylan's only-a-matter-of-time songs will be *Not Dark Yet*. But anyone who gets his or her kicks from biographizing Dylan's songs is likely to end up with a medical condition: *Dylan's heart-trouble at the time* . . . It wasn't "at the time" (*Time Out of Mind* was recorded before the illness), but then it is true that poets are often very good at premonitions. Anyway, what a fun thing heart-fungus can be for the song-explainer! But you don't have to be near death to fear death. Philip Larkin saw that these things go beyond the biographical and the medical, saying of death in his poem *Aubade*: "Most things may never happen: this one will". Still, the newspaper *USA Today* had a right word, without knowing all the reasons (but who could ever do that? not even the man himself), when it announced: "Heart-ache. The word literally and figuratively defines Bob Dylan in 1997." Presumptuous, plainly – defining Bob Dylan, or anybody else for that matter, is nobody's business, and as for the idea that one word, even a compound word such as "heart-ache", could *define* him . . . But heart-ache does catch. It is a memento mori. "My heart aches": so it is that Keats opens the *Ode to a Nightingale*.

My heart aches, and a drowsy numbness pains
   My sense, as though of hemlock I had drunk,
Or emptied some dull opiate to the drains
   One minute past, and Lethe-wards had sunk:

Well my sense of humanity has gone down the drain
Behind every beautiful thing there's been some kind of pain

I don't believe that Keats's poem is *alluded to* in Dylan's song. That is, called into play, so that you'd be failing to respond to something crucial to the song unless you were familiar with, and could call up, Keats's poem. Dylan enjoys allusion all right (those lovely mermaids in *Desolation Row*, where the captain's tower housed T. S. Eliot, are both more and less desolate because they have flowed over from *The Love Song of J. Alfred Prufrock*), but *Not Dark Yet* doesn't seek any such crystallizing by name. I'd not mind the likeness between *Not Dark Yet* and the *Ode* being called a coincidence, provided that it wasn't called a mere coincidence. For coincidences can be deep things, and if two artists were to arrive independently at so many similar turns of phrase, figures of speech, felicities of rhyming, then my sense of humanity might go up a plane. We might learn something about what is behind every beautiful thing (a thing of beauty is a joy for ever), about the ways in which the minds of Keats and of Dylan have large movements of mind behind them. But I don't myself believe that the likenesses are coincidental; I believe that Dylan knows the famous more-than-anthology-piece, and that he had it in mind, even if not consciously or deliberatedly in mind, when he created his own re-creation of so much of it. After all, he did once rhyme "owed" with the line "He examines the nightingale's code".[1] *Not Dark Yet* is owed to a nightingale. And Dylan has given advice: "To the aspiring songwriter and singer I say disregard all the current stuff, forget it, you're better off, read John Keats, Melville, listen to Robert Johnson and Woody Guthrie" (*Biograph*).

The memories of *Ode to a Nightingale* in *Not Dark Yet* come from throughout the *Ode*, diffusedly there. The parallel passages are dark passages, to take up the term (itself repeated, in parallel) of Keats's profound letter on Shakespeare, Milton, and Wordsworth – and on fortitude:

However among the effects this breathing is father of is that tremendous one

---

[1] *Visions of Johanna*, when sung in Los Angeles (30 November 1965) and in New York (21 January 1966).

of sharpening one's vision into the heart and nature of Man – of convincing ones nerves that the World is full of Misery and Heartbreak, Pain, Sickness and oppression – whereby This Chamber of Maiden Thought becomes gradually darken'd and at the same time on all sides of it many doors are set open – but all dark – all leading to dark passages – We see not the ballance of good and evil. We are in a mist – *We* are now in that state – We feel the "burden of the Mystery," To this point was Wordsworth come, as far as I can conceive when he wrote "Tintern Abbey" and it seems to me that his Genius is explorative of those dark Passages.[1]

Heartbreak, heart-ache. The "burden of the Mystery" was to weigh in and weigh upon Dylan, too: "Sometimes my burden is more than I can bear".

Forbearance, and even perhaps fortitude, may now be asked of the reader who is about to be confronted with a tabulation. For the parallels may be more audible if spelt out.

ODE TO A NIGHTINGALE

I

My heart aches, and a drowsy numbness pains
   My sense, as though of hemlock I had drunk,
Or emptied some dull opiate to the drains
   One minute past, and Lethe-wards had sunk:
'Tis not through envy of thy happy lot,
   But being too happy in thine happiness –
      That thou, light-wingèd Dryad of the trees,
      In some melodious plot
Of beechen green, and shadows numberless,
   Singest of summer in full-throated ease.

II

O, for a draught of vintage! that hath been
   Cooled a long age in the deep-delvèd earth,
Tasting of Flora and the country green,
   Dance, and Provençal song, and sunburnt mirth!
O for a beaker full of the warm South,

---

[1] To J. H. Reynolds, 3 May 1818; *Letters*, vol. I, p. 281. Keats's spelling is retained.

Full of the true, the blushful Hippocrene,
   With beaded bubbles winking at the brim,
      And purple-stainèd mouth,
That I might drink, and leave the world unseen,
   And with thee fade away into the forest dim –

III

Fade far away, dissolve, and quite forget
   What thou among the leaves hast never known,
The weariness, the fever, and the fret
   Here, where men sit and hear each other groan;
Where palsy shakes a few, sad, last grey hairs,
      Where youth grows pale, and spectre-thin, and dies;
        Where but to think is to be full of sorrow
         And leaden-eyed despairs;
Where Beauty cannot keep her lustrous eyes,
   Or new Love pine at them beyond to-morrow.

IV

Away! away! for I will fly to thee,
   Not charioted by Bacchus and his pards,
But on the viewless wings of Poesy,
   Though the dull brain perplexes and retards.
Already with thee! tender is the night,
      And haply the Queen-Moon is on her throne,
        Clustered around by all her starry Fays;
         But here there is no light,
Save what from heaven is with the breezes blown
   Through verdurous glooms and winding mossy ways.

V

I cannot see what flowers are at my feet,
   Nor what soft incense hangs upon the boughs,
But, in embalmèd darkness, guess each sweet
   Wherewith the seasonable month endows
The grass, the thicket, and the fruit-tree wild –
      White hawthorn, and the pastoral eglantine;
        Fast fading violets covered up in leaves;
         And mid-May's eldest child,

The coming musk-rose, full of dewy wine,
  The murmurous haunt of flies on summer eves.

VI

Darkling I listen; and, for many a time
  I have been half in love with easeful Death,
Called him soft names in many a musèd rhyme,
  To take into the air my quiet breath;
Now more than ever seems it rich to die,
  To cease upon the midnight with no pain,
    While thou art pouring forth thy soul abroad
      In such an ecstasy!
Still wouldst thou sing, and I have ears in vain —
  To thy high requiem become a sod.

VII

Thou wast not born for death, immortal Bird!
  No hungry generations tread thee down;
The voice I hear this passing night was heard
  In ancient days by emperor and clown:
Perhaps the self-same song that found a path
  Through the sad heart of Ruth, when, sick for home,
    She stood in tears amid the alien corn;
      The same that oft-times hath
Charmed magic casements, opening on the foam
  Of perilous seas, in faery lands forlorn.

VIII

Forlorn! the very word is like a bell
  To toll me back from thee to my sole self!
Adieu! the fancy cannot cheat so well
  As she is famed to do, deceiving elf.
Adieu! adieu! thy plaintive anthem fades
  Past the near meadows, over the still stream,
    Up the hill-side; and now 'tis buried deep
      In the next valley-glades:
Was it a vision, or a waking dream?
  Fled is that music — Do I wake or sleep?

NOT DARK YET

I

Shadows are falling and I've been here all day
It's too hot to sleep, time is running away
Feel like my soul has turned into steel
I've still got the scars that the sun didn't heal
There's not even room enough to be anywhere
It's not dark yet, but it's getting there

Dylan's Verse 1

first line: Dylan and Keats, *shadows*

                  Dylan, *day* / Keats, *days*

second line: Dylan, *too hot* / Keats, *too happy*

                  Dylan and Keats, *sleep*

                  Dylan and Keats, *time*

                  Dylan, *running away* / Keats, *fade away; fade far away; Away! away!*

third line: Dylan, *my soul* / Keats, *thy soul; my sole self*

fourth line: Dylan, *sun* / Keats, *sunburnt*

sixth line: Dylan, *dark* / Keats, *Darkling; darkness* [this, in the closing line of
                  each Dylan verse]

So there is only one line from Dylan's first verse that has no Keatsian parallels: "There's not even room enough to be anywhere", and even this might be thought to be touched by Keats's words "But here there". Here, there, and everywhere. Or anywhere. Beckett, *The End*: "I didn't pay attention. Strictly speaking I wasn't there. Strictly speaking I believe I've never been anywhere." Beckett, *For to End Yet Again*: "And dream of a way in a space with neither here nor there where all the footsteps ever fell can never fare nearer to anywhere nor from anywhere further away."[1]

2

Well my sense of humanity has gone down the drain
Behind every beautiful thing there's been some kind of pain

[1] Dylan does not have to owe to anyone his title for the album on which *Not Dark Yet* appeared: *Time Out of Mind*. But Beckett's *Lessness* opens: "Ruins true refuge long last towards which so many false time out of mind". And it includes: "Blacked out fallen open true refuge issueless towards which so many false time out of mind". *Lessness* consists of twenty-four paragraphs or blocks (one for each hour of all day), and of sixty sentences, each of which comes twice (minutes and seconds).

> She wrote me a letter and she wrote it so kind
> She put down in writing what was in her mind
> I just don't see why I should even care
> It's not dark yet, but it's getting there

Verse 2

first line: Dylan, *Well my sense* / Keats, *so well*; *My sense*
                Dylan, *the drain* / Keats, *the drains*

second line: Dylan, *pain* / Keats, *pains* [with the same rhyme]

third line: Dylan, *so kind* / Keats, *so well*

3

> Well, I've been to London and I've been to gay Paree
> I've followed the river and I got to the sea
> I've been down on the bottom of a world full of lies
> I ain't looking for nothing in anyone's eyes
> Sometimes my burden is more than I can bear
> It's not dark yet, but it's getting there

Verse 3

first line: Dylan and Keats, *well*

second line: Dylan, *the river* / Keats, *the still stream* [and *Lethe*, the river
                that in *Too Much of Nothing* flows into Dylan's "waters of
                oblivion"]
                Dylan, *the sea* / Keats, *seas*

third line: Dylan, *been down* / Keats, *tread thee down*
                Dylan, *world full of lies* / Keats, *world*; *full* [five times, of which four
                are *full of*, one being *full of the true*]

fourth line: Dylan and Keats, *eyes*

fifth line: Dylan, *Sometimes* / Keats, *oft-times*; *many a time*

4

> I was born here and I'll die here against my will
> I know it looks like I'm moving, but I'm standing still
> Every nerve in my body is so vacant and numb
> I can't even remember what it was I came here to get away from
> Don't even hear a murmur of a prayer
> It's not dark yet, but it's getting there

Verse 4

first line: Dylan, *was born* / Keats, *wast not born*

             Dylan and Keats, *die* [and Keats, *dies, death*]

second line: Dylan, *standing still* / Keats, *stood; still stream; Still*

third line: Dylan, *numb* / Keats, *numbness*

fourth line: Dylan, *can't even remember* / Keats, *I cannot; quite forget*

             Dylan, *get away from* / Keats, *fade away; fade far away; Away!*

               away

fourth into fifth line:

             Dylan, *I came here* > *Don't even hear* [this verse of Dylan has

             here . . . here . . . here . . . hear > *there*] / Keats, *Here where men*

             sit and hear each other groan

fifth line: Dylan, *a murmur* / Keats, *murmurous* [and this on *summer*

             eves, too]

Enough.

No such parallels ever amount to proof (literary judgements don't admit of proof, only of evidence), but there are too many likenesses for it to be likely that they are coincidences. T. S. Eliot said, about the "borrowings" of the Elizabethan dramatist George Chapman, that the scholar's "accumulation of probabilities, powerful and concurrent, leads to conviction"; and Eliot wrote similarly on another occasion, of "many other parallels, each slight in itself but having a cumulative plausibility".[1]

It adds a further dimension to these affinities that *Not Dark Yet* stands to Keats's *Ode* very much as Keats's *Ode*, in its turn, stood to Shakespeare's Sonnet 73, "That time of year thou mayst in me behold". The continuity and community of the poets constitute a success that is a succession. And even as Dylan doesn't exactly allude to Keats, but has a different, a diffused, gratitude to his art (more than a source, a resource), so Keats doesn't allude to the Shakespeare sonnet – and yet just about every word of the sonnet takes its place and its turn within the *Ode to a Nightingale*. What in Shakespeare at first is a "time of year", and then becomes a time of day, is all along a time of day for Keats – as it was to prove, in due course, for Dylan. Sonnet 73 has its own way of saying and of singing "It's not dark yet, but it's getting there".

---

[1] *TLS* (24 December 1925, 25 July 1929); for the contexts, see Eliot's *Inventions of the March Hare: Poems 1909–1917* (ed. Christopher Ricks, 1996), p. xxviii.

That time of year thou mayst in me behold,
When yellow leaves, or none, or few do hang
Upon those boughs which shake against the cold,
Bare ruined choirs, where late the sweet birds sang.
In me thou seest the twilight of such day
As after sunset fadeth in the west,
Which by and by black night doth take away,
Death's second self that seals up all in rest.
In me thou seest the glowing of such fire
That on the ashes of his youth doth lie,
As the death bed, whereon it must expire,
Consum'd with that which it was nourisht by.
    This thou perceiv'st, which makes thy love more strong,
    To love that well, which thou must leave ere long.

Shakespeare speaks explicitly of night, "black night". Keats is explicit, too; his *Ode to a Nightingale* has "tender is the night", "this passing night", "the midnight". But it is one of Dylan's dark forbearances that "night" is never once brought into the light of day in *Not Dark Yet*. Oh, night casts its shadow throughout but is best left unsaid. And you can feel this whether or not the song brings the sonnet or the *Ode* to your mind. I'm not offering the absence of the word "night" as evidence of the presence of Shakespeare and Keats, for in terms of an argument this would be having it both ways. But there is a strong affinity with Keats in the way that in the song *night* colours, darkens, the whole atmosphere while never being spoken of. For *winter* colours and darkens Keats's *To Autumn*, being the only one of the four seasons *not* mentioned in this profound poem to a season.

When you say that *It's not such-and-such yet, but it's getting there*, the such-and-such could be many a different word. But think how much thinner Dylan's refrain would have been as "It's not night yet, but it's getting there". And this is a matter not only of understanding why night should be an intimation of mortality, not an announcement, but also of sensing how much the refrain gets from the fact that we don't speak of *getting night* but we do speak of *getting dark*. So that when we hear, and hear again and again, "but it's getting there", the word "getting" is getting its full due, a simple inexorable compacting of the two things that it is up to: getting there and getting dark.

Keats said, with touching modesty and confidence in the face of the personal extinction that he knew would soon be his, "I think I shall be among the English poets after my death". To set Dylan among the poets, there with Keats, is to give both poets their due. Not as a matter of the culture wars.[1] But because gratitude to Dylan is at one with his gratitude to Keats. Gratitude disowns envy. "'Tis not through envy of thy happy lot".

Perhaps the *Ode to a Nightingale* came particularly to mind for Dylan's song because the *Ode* is a poem couched always in song: "singest of summer in full-throated ease", "Provençal song", "Still wouldst thou sing", "self-same song". When Dylan sings "Sometimes my burden is more than I can bear", he may want us to recall that a burden may be a refrain, one that singers were said to bear. Keats, elsewhere: "Bearing the burden of a shepherd song" (*Endymion*, I, 136).

Dylan's refrain or burden is "It's not dark yet, but it's getting there". He bears it and bares it beautifully, with exquisite precision of voice, dry humour, and resilience, all these in the cause of fortitude at life's going to be brought to an end by death. And the word "burden" itself carries for Dylan, though not only for him, a sense of sin: in *Dear Landlord*, "Please don't put a price on my soul / My burden is heavy"; in *Yonder Comes Sin*, "The old evil burden that's been dragging you down"; and in *Foot of Pride*, "how to carry a burden too heavy to be yours".[2] There was a

---

[1] On the stage fight, or staged fight, "Keats vs Dylan", see Michael Gray, who points out that it was in 1992 that the playwright David Hare set up this show.

Never mind that Bob Dylan had spent the previous three decades with his face set firmly against the vulgar and the cheap, or indeed that John Keats had been a cockney oik and upstart himself. Such was the climate of opinion still that Hare's comically inaccurate personifying of the divide caught on like a pop craze itself. Within minutes, that doyenne of the literary clerisy, A. S. Byatt, could go on B.B.C.'s all-purpose arts programme, *The Late Show*, and pronounce that the qualitative difference between Keats and Dylan is that with Keats, she could take you through one of his poems and reveal many layers . . . She couldn't take you through a Dylan lyric because she wouldn't know where to begin. What's disgraceful is not the preference for Keats, nor the ignorance about Dylan: it is the malappropriate self-confidence.

(*Song and Dance Man III*, p. xviii)

Gray, with appropriate self-confidence, remarks that it was (in the year 2000) nearly thirty years since he began to argue "the case for Dylan's being, if you must, on the same side as Keats".

[2] *Than I can bear* may carry something of the sin that is often in Dylan's mind, the sin of Cain: "And Cain said unto the LORD, My punishment is greater than I can bear" (Genesis 4:13).

characteristically memorable mixture of the direct and the circuitous in Dylan's remark in an interview: "I sure would like to be spared of the burden to muse about what my fans think about me or my songs."[1] Not just spared the burden but spared of it, compacting "spared" and "relieved of", and with "muse" perhaps in touch with those presiding forces without which we wouldn't be inspired into the arts at all. (Keats mused in the *Ode* about "many a musèd rhyme".) Some burdens Dylan is spared (how right he is about the artist's at least having the right not to have to muse about his art), but not the burden that he has taken it on himself to sing. From refrains he cannot refrain.

Not Dark Yet seeks – in the great phrase from Freud – to make friends with the necessity of dying. This is fortitude not only as the subject of the song but as its element, its air. Like Keats in the *Ode*, Dylan understands what it is to go even beyond making friends with this necessity, and he is willing to be – as human beings sometimes should be – half in love with easeful death. Keats:

> Darkling I listen; and, for many a time
>   I have been half in love with easeful Death,
> Called him soft names in many a musèd rhyme,
>   To take into the air my quiet breath;
> Now more than ever seems it rich to die,
>   To cease upon the midnight with no pain,

– and yet a painful thought. "Half in love with easeful Death": but only half.

There's much more to *Not Dark Yet* than time – its subject and its element – permits of. Oh, its being a song that starts with "Shadows are falling and I've been here all day" – and then its having twenty-four lines, one for each hour of all day.[2] And the rapt beauty of the long instrumental patience – a full minute – both before the final verse, and, of the same length, after it: not . . . yet, not . . . yet.

Or there are the felicities of rhyming, including the rhyming that is included within lines. Say, those that open and close upon the same sound.

---

[1] London (4 October 1997); *Isis* (October 1997). *USA Today* (28 September 1997): "Making *Time Out of Mind* was a liberating experience for Dylan who can feel burdened by the weight of his legend."

[2] See footnote, p. 365, on Beckett's *Lessness*.

This may feel like pincers or forceps: "Feel like my soul has turned into steel". Yet even this is about making friends with something (again, it feels to me, friends with the necessity of dying), since "The friends thou hast", we are urged in *Hamlet*, "Grapple them to thy soul with hoops of steel" ("soul" again steeled into "steel"). And I can't imagine a tauter evocation of hoops of steel than this having the line itself be hooped: "*Feel* like my soul has turned into *steel*". (Dylan voices a pause after "has", the caesura there, so that "turned" is the turning point.) And with "steel" turned into "still" two words later ("into steel / I've still got") – and then with "still" still there in the last verse: "I'm standing still".

To start and end the line upon the same sound may be to fold the room of the line ("*There*'s not even room enough to be any*where*"). Or – in assonance, this time – to fold the world of the line or (fourfold) of two successive lines:

> *I*'ve been down on the bottom of a world full of *lies*
> *I* ain't looking for nothing in anyone's *eyes*

And it is especially by assonance, at once massive and as though passive, that the song brings home the impossibility of escaping the self that is *I*:

> *I* just don't see *why I* should even care

> *I* was born here and *I'll die* here against my will
> *I* know it looks *like I'm* moving, but *I'm* standing still

> *I* can't even remember what it was *I* came here to get away from

At which point (the point of a line that is elongated into the drolly dramatic, given its meaning) we would do well to register the way in which "away" turns out to be what you can't get away from, with the first verse's "It's too hot to sleep, time is running away" returning in this final verse (via that excursion to "gay Paree") as "I can't even remember what it was I came here to get away from" – an extensively protracted line, with scarcely a caesura at all in the length of it, as if, despite everything, the singer can still remember having world enough and time. "Away" as what there's no getting away from (Keats's "Away! away!"), and with "from" rhyming with "numb" ("so vacant and numb") as the first and last imperfect rhyme in the entire song, a rhyme that numbs and that turns slightly away from our hope of rhyme's satisfactions.

"There is a singer everyone has heard". So says, or sings, Robert Frost. The song is that of *The Oven Bird*, and Frost's sonnet comes in the end to paradox and pathos:

> The bird would cease and be as other birds
> But that he knows in singing not to sing.
> The question that he frames in all but words
> Is what to make of a diminished thing.

Among the other birds may be numbered the nightingale. As to all the diminished things of life, Tennyson's Ulysses – ageing and agèd – urged fortitude:

> Though much is taken, much abides; and though
> We are not now that strength which in old days
> Moved earth and heaven, that which we are, we are.

Not Dark Yet is committed to fortitude in the face of mankind's darker acknowledgement. Since much is taken, little abides. But not nothing. It is through the small recurrent thought, *not even*, that so much is acknowledged:

> There's not even room enough to be anywhere
>
> I just don't see why I should even care
>
> I can't even remember what it was I came here to get away from
> Don't even hear a murmur of a prayer

And perhaps the encroaching *even* even has some relation to what *evening* is. Hopkins saw it as *Spelt from Sibyl's Leaves*. "Evening strains to be tíme's vást, ' womb-of-all, home-of-all, hearse-of-all night". "Óur évening is óver us; óur night ' whélms, whélms, ánd will énd us".

Musically, vocally, and verbally *Not Dark Yet* makes real the force that is at once active and passive in it: "I know it looks like I'm moving, but I'm standing still". Looks like – and what does it sound like? Both moving and standing still. So I'm reminded of two lovely evocations of such a paradox. First, Coleridge, whose words about "the reader" will have equal though different force if we substitute the listener (not just the hearer):

The reader should be carried forward, not merely or chiefly by the mechanical impulse of curiosity, or by a restless desire to arrive at the final solution; but by the pleasureable activity of mind excited by the attractions of the journey itself. Like the motion of a serpent, which the Egyptians made the emblem of intellectual power; or like the path of sound through the air; at every step he pauses and half recedes, and from the retrogressive movement collects the force which again carries him onward.

(*Biographia Literaria*, chapter 14)

And next T. S. Eliot, on what it was, in religious apprehension from the seventeenth century, to seem to stand still: "In this extraordinary prose, which appears to repeat, to stand still, but is nevertheless proceeding in the most deliberate and orderly manner, there are often flashing phrases which never desert the memory."[1]

"It's not dark yet, but it's getting there": no coming on strong, and no letting off weakly. Dylan chafed at some of the responses to *Time Out of Mind*:

People say the record deals with mortality – *my* mortality for some reason! [*Laughs*] Well, it *doesn't* deal with my mortality. It maybe just deals with mortality in general. It's one thing that we all have in common, isn't it? But I didn't see any one critic say: "It deals with *my* mortality" – you know, his *own*. As if he's immune in some kind of way – like whoever's writing about the record has got eternal life and the singer doesn't. I found this condescending attitude toward that record revealed in the press quite frequently, but, you know, nothing you can do about that.[2]

A smaller matter than mortality, such condescension, and yet it, too, in daily life, asks of us a certain fortitude. You know, nothing you can do about that.

Alone of the four cardinal virtues, fortitude does not go in for an adjective or an adverb. Temperance is happy to grant us temperate and temperately; prudence, prudent and prudently; justice, just and justly. But fortitude declines to allow fortitudinous and fortitudinously.[3] "A multitude of sins" (as Dylan sings in *Something's Burning, Baby*) is happy to countenance

[1] *Lancelot Andrewes* (1926); *Selected Essays*, p. 349.
[2] *Rolling Stone* (22 November 2001).
[3] The *OED* records that Fielding and Gibbon in the eighteenth century tried "fortitudinous". But the language wasn't having it.

the multitudinous, and as for a platitude, few things give it greater pleasure than the thought of the platitudinous. But with fortitude, there is the staunch four-square noun, and that is it. This has great simplicity, as has Dylan's song itself and its refrain. And, as Eliot knew, such simplicity is one way of worsting and besting sin.

Great simplicity is only won by an intense moment or by years of intelligent effort, or by both. It represents one of the most arduous conquests of the human spirit: the triumph of feeling and thought over the natural sin of language.[1]

"Feel like my soul has turned into steel".

[1] *Athenaeum* (11 April 1919).

The Heavenly Graces

Faith

A true thing was said about art by the arty old fraud Jean Cocteau, that if artists have a dream, it is not of being famous but of being believed. Dylan's Christian songs ask to be believed. This isn't to say that the personal faith of the artist, which is a matter of biography and of change, and which might not become artistic creation, is the point. No, an artist is someone who is especially good at, generous about, imagining beliefs that he or she doesn't hold.

A lot of Dylan-listeners, though, persist in treating the Christian songs as if they were a personal affront, rather than as achievements to meet with flexibility; as if such songs only have either the passive low-level interest of a biographical report (one, moreover, that has become superseded) or the actively repellent fascination of an allegiance we don't share, thank you. Yet to trust that these songs, like others of Dylan's, ask to be believed is quite different from concluding that if you don't share or don't come to share their beliefs, then there's nothing really in them for you. To take this party line is to curtail what we have art and imagination for at all. Art becomes then only a matter of preaching to the converted, a rally for the faithful, instead of being a magnanimous invitation, myriad-minded.

One of the ways in which art is invaluable is by giving us sympathetic access to systems of belief that are not our own. How else could it enlarge our sympathies? It is our responsibility not only to believe but to learn how to entertain beliefs. In the words of William Empson:

It seems to me that the chief function of imaginative literature is to make you realise that other people are very various, many of them quite different from you, with different "systems of value" as well.

The main purpose of reading imaginative literature is to grasp a wide variety of experience, imagining people with codes and customs very unlike our own.

It strikes me that modern critics, whether as a result of the neo-Christian movement or not, have become oddly resistant to admitting that there is more than one code of morals in the world, whereas the central purpose of reading imaginative literature is to accustom yourself to this basic fact. I do not at all mean that a literary critic ought to avoid making moral judgements; that is useless as well as tiresome, because the reader has enough sense to start guessing round it at once.[1]

There is no great religious poetry that does not raise – as crucial to its enterprise – the question of whether it is open to the charge of blasphemy, even as there is no great erotic art that does not raise the question of whether it is open to the charge of pornography. And it is true, too, as T. S. Eliot said, that blasphemy is possible only to a believer – or at least only to someone who half fears he may be a believer, and who kicks against the pricks. For Eliot, the decay of blasphemy is a symptom of the decay of belief. "Genuine blasphemy, genuine in spirit and not purely verbal, is the product of partial belief, and is as impossible to the complete atheist as to the perfect Christian."[2] This last, it may be added, explains why the *possibility* of being accused of blasphemy is essential to Christian poetry, since without such a possibility the poetry would announce itself as that of a perfect Christian, something no good Christian would claim. Eliot in 1927 saw "the twelfth century anomaly – and yet the essential congruity – of the finest religious verse and the most brilliant blasphemous verse. To the present generation of versifiers, so deficient in devotion and so feeble in blasphemy, the twelfth century might offer an edifying subject of study."[3]

> God said to Abraham, "Kill me a son"
> Abe says, "Man, you must be puttin' me on"
> God say, "No." Abe say, "What?"
> God say, "You can do what you want Abe, but
> The next time you see me comin' you better run"
> Well Abe says, "Where do you want this killin' done?"
> God says, "Out on Highway 61"
>
> (*Highway 61 Revisited*)

I am not myself a Christian believer, being an atheist. One delight of

---

[1] *Argufying*, ed. John Haffenden (1987), p. 13, a letter from Empson; *Argufying*, p. 218; *Using Biography* (1984), p. 142, from an essay on Fielding published in 1958.

[2] *Baudelaire* (1930); *Selected Essays* (1932, 1951 edition), p. 421.

[3] *TLS* (11 August 1927).

Dylan's Christian songs can arise from finding (to your surprise and not chagrin) that your own system of beliefs doesn't have a monopoly of intuition, sensitivity, scruple, and concern. Most Dylan-lovers are presumed to be liberals, and the big trap for liberals is always that our liberalism may make us very *il*liberal about other people's sometimes letting us all down by declining to be liberals. The illiberal liberal has a way of pretending that the page that he would rather not read is illegible: "he's not talking about one of his most illegible back pages: that conservative, born-again-Christian phase that blindsided his liberal, secular fan base some 15 years ago".[1] Blindsided? But Dylan shows perspicacity when he imagines someone who concedes "I'm a little too blind to see" (*Precious Angel*). I'm a little on the blind side. Blindsided? "Everybody's shouting/'Which Side Are You On?'"

Bob Dylan has left the side of free-thinking, socially aware, sometimes cynical humans trying to make ethical choices in a modern world ripped apart by war and hate and prejudice. For him, all is solved in one simple act: accepting God.

Where are the de-programmers when we really need them?[2]

Sorry, I didn't quite catch that – who is it who's doing the over-simplification? And who is it who's colluding with *hate and prejudice* exactly?

"Rip down all hate, I screamed" (*My Back Pages*).

You can believe whatever you like so long as it's liberal: this isn't any less dogmatic than Christianity, and has its own way of being menacingly coercive.

The gratitude that I feel for the best of Dylan's Christian songs arises from my finding them among his supreme acts of gratitude. His songs of faith are continuous with all his other gratitudes, to singers and to songs, to loved ones and respected ones. "I've been saved/By the blood of the lamb":

> And I'm so glad
> Yes, I'm so glad
> I'm so glad
> So glad
> I want to thank You, Lord

[1] *Newsweek* (6 October 1997), on Dylan.
[2] Michael Goldberg, *New Musical Express* (November 1979).

> I just want to thank You, Lord
> Thank You, Lord

Those last three words don't just say something yet again, for the third time, because what had been something *I want to* do has become my doing it: "Thank You, Lord". Not a curtailment of what had first been said and then slightly expanded ("I want to thank You, Lord / I just want to thank You, Lord"), but an expansion of it, though (strangely) in fewer words, an expansion into doing it, a consummation of the two lines that lead into it. "Thank You, Lord": this, which is lovingly performed by Dylan, is a performative utterance, in the sense of the philosopher J. L. Austin. Like "I promise", the words are not a statement that could be true or false (though the promise might be kept or broken): the words simply do what they say. "I thank you", or "Thank You, Lord".

My own thanks come to this: that it is inspiriting to meet a heartfelt expression of faith that would constitute – if, say, you were ever to find yourself converted – so true an example as to become a reason. If I were ever to become a Christian, it would be because of the humane substantiation that is to be heard in many a poem by George Herbert. And in many a song by Dylan.

Words ask trust, and they can keep faith. They are built upon faith, the faith that people will tell the truth – or at any rate that people may betray themselves when they are failing to do so. The distress of lying is sharply evoked in *Fourth Time Around* and *Ballad in Plain D*. "The truth is true whether you wanna believe it or not, it doesn't need you to make it true . . . That lie about everybody having their own truth inside of them has done a lot of damage and made people crazy."[1]

Social life could not exist if it weren't believed that people are to be believed. Sometimes this faith is misplaced, but this is not as corrosive as it would be for us not to place faith at all. And language itself is built not only *upon* but *of* faith. A language is a body of agreements and acts of trust. A word is not a matter of fact or a matter of opinion, it is a social contract. Like all contracts, its life is a pledge and a faith. (And, like all contracts, it can be dishonest, suspect.) Songs and poems likewise keep faith alive. They "strengthen the things that remain" – words of the Book of Revelation, the force of which is revealed anew in *When You Gonna Wake Up?*

Faith in Dylan: this needs to encompass his having faith and our having

---

[1] *Biograph*'s ellipsis.

faith in him. There are sure to be occasions when we are not sure. For he has written very many songs, has sung them very variously, and has lived thoroughly in the world of an art the nature of which is that it reaches its particular heights by not being "high art". By being, rather, an intensely popular art – where anything might (sometimes) go? Was that weird wording of his a slip of the lip or was it his speaking in tongues? Did he make a dextrous move, or am I – when I exclaim at how intriguing some turn of phrase is – just going through the critical motions?

The choice can be stark.

> Now there's spiritual warfare, flesh and blood breaking down
> Ya either got faith or ya got unbelief and there ain't no neutral ground
>
> *(Precious Angel)*

Faith or unbelief: Dylan characteristically places the words in a pair of scales that we must ponder. For there isn't any longer[1] a noun "unfaith" to match "faith" (despite *unfaithful / faithful*), and though Dylan's word "unbelief" does have an antithesis, "belief", and although the opposite of a believer is an unbeliever, the word "belief" wouldn't make the true fit that he needs, for to have belief is something very different from having faith.

Again and again, confronted with one of Dylan's quirks of wording or phrasing or cadencing or sentencing, you find yourself having to choose between having faith and having unbelief, and there's no neutral ground. For the words insist that either Dylan is a sloven or he is up to something, something unexpected, diverting.

On *Planet Waves*, the song *Going, Going, Gone* goes like this:

> Grandma said, "Boy, go and follow your heart
> And you'll be fine at the end of the line
> All that's gold isn't meant to shine
> Don't you and your one true love ever part"

At the Budokan concert in 1978, he can be heard to slide a slyness into this:

---

[1] *OED*, "unfaith": lack of faith or belief, esp. in religion. From 1415, and including Tennyson: "Faith and Unfaith can ne'er be equal powers". But there is no instance since 1870, and the word would now feel strained.

You'll be fine at the end of the line
All that's gold wasn't meant to shine
Just don't put your horse in front of your cart

What was that? We shouldn't take this from Dylan unless we take it as
seizing a double-take. For in front of your cart is exactly where you'd better
put your horse. Straightfacedly in blinkers, with equine equanimity Dylan
does not nag you about putting the cart before the horse. This is comically
preposterous of him. Preposterous: before / after, "Having or placing last
that which should be first" (*The Oxford English Dictionary*).

Or there is the mid-stride footing in *Trouble in Mind* as it moves:

You think you can hide but you're never alone
Ask Lot what he thought when his wife turned to stone

Take this with a pinch of salt, or a column of it.

For Dylan has a great ear for these swerves and shifts that keep a mind
– and a language – not only alive but up to the mark. T. S. Eliot praised as
the accomplishment of Jacobean drama "that perpetual slight alteration of
language, words perpetually juxtaposed in new and sudden combinations,
meanings perpetually *eingeschachtelt* [compactly ordered] into meanings,
which evidences a very high development of the senses, a development
of the English language which we have perhaps never equalled".[1]

One development of the English language has been American English:
its licence and liberties and liberty. Don't follow leaders? But you cannot
lead yourself, except perhaps by the nose. And as to trust: *Trust Yourself*
urges you to be vigilant about the very thing that you are listening to,
but he does sing it trustworthily, whatever it may say:

Trust yourself
Trust yourself to do the things that only you know best
Trust yourself
Trust yourself to do what's right and not be second-guessed
Don't trust me to show you beauty
When beauty may only turn to rust
If you need somebody you can trust, trust yourself

[1] *Philip Massinger* (1920); *Selected Essays*, p. 209.

"Don't trust me to show you beauty" – except insofar as Keats (or his Urn) is right to hope that beauty is truth, truth beauty. Philip Larkin: "I have always believed that beauty is beauty, truth, truth, that is not all ye know on earth nor all ye need to know."[1]

"If you need somebody you can trust, trust yourself". But don't be too trusting even there, or particularly there. For if you really never trusted anyone or anything other than yourself, you'd not in fact be in any position to trust yourself.

Precious Angel

Should you ever be visited by an angel, first make sure that a fallen one has not befallen you, and then trust yourself as to its trustworthiness. *Precious Angel* yearns to express immediately its gratitude to a loved woman who is loved moreover for having brought the singer to the love of God. Perhaps he can enfold these double thanks, human and divine, by calling her an angel. So at once, "Precious angel": words upon entering that are sung by Dylan with a tauntingly expressive flat-tongued unexcitement, as if doing no more than giving her her due.

> Precious angel, under the sun
> How was I to know you'd be the one
> To show me I was blinded, to show me I was gone
> How weak was the foundation I was standing upon?

But does this grateful paean have a strong foundation? Are not "precious" and "angel" too weak as words, too usual, to be the ones?

A century ago, Gerard M. Hopkins, disapproving of his friend Dixon's lines of verse ("Each drop more precious than the gems that stud / An angel's crown"), said that this "strikes me as poor, indeed vulgar; I think angels are the very cheapest things in literature."[2]

How, then, does Dylan redeem this from cheapness, and justify our faith in him and in bandied words like "precious" and "angel"? By a

---

[1] *Further Requirements*, ed. Anthony Thwaite (2001), p. 39.
[2] To Dixon, 23 October 1881; *The Correspondence of Gerard Manley Hopkins and Richard Watson Dixon*, ed. Claude Colleer Abbott (1935, 1955 edition), p. 77.

simple profound stroke of imagination, this sequence: "Precious angel, under the sun". *The Oxford English Dictionary*, "under the sun": on earth, in the world. Her angelhood is in no respect diminished by being "under the sun", for she can descend to earth without condescension, and this is very endearing of her. It is not so much that the phrase humanizes her as that she humanizes herself. (As, within Christian history, did a spirit greater even than the angels.) Moreover, "under the sun" gives to her something superlative, unique, and complete, without ever having to trumpet it. For you don't ordinarily say "under the sun" without a large explicit claim. As the instances in *The Oxford English Dictionary* show, "under the sun" invites the superlative (no braver soldier under the sun), or the unique (the only honest man under the sun), or the complete (every single nation under the sun). "Using all the devices under the sun" (*Solid Rock*). "Don't you know there's nothing new that's under the sun?" (*Ain't No Man Righteous, No Not One*).[1] But make it new, as when a form of words succeeds in invoking a superlative that it need never mention, a supreme praise yet understated to the point of being unstated. Tact tucked into the tacit. Word perfect. No one under the sun can create these felicities better than Dylan.

Yet, as the word "felicities" implies, and as is true of any artist who seizes an opportunity, the effect is not one that is of his making alone, or such that it could simply be willed into being. For the line "Precious angel, under the sun" has something else stirring under it: the interplay of this unspoken superlative that informs *under the sun* (with its particular preposition, "under") against a different preposition and so a different stationing of the angel in relation to the sun: "And I saw an angel standing in the sun" (Revelation 19:17).

The song asks with insistence "Sister, lemme tell you about a vision that I saw", and this chapter 19 of Revelation is a vision of the evil forces "gathered together to make war against him". Gather from this what may underlie the song's conviction that "Now there's spiritual warfare".

Precious angel, shine your light on me. Revelation 21:11: "and her light was like unto a stone most precious". "I believe in the Book of Revelation," Dylan said.[2] The terms that most matter are those of his art, not those of

---

[1] *Don't you know?* This should not be news to you, given Ecclesiastes 1:9: "The thing that hath been, it is that which shall be; and that which is done, is that which shall be done; and there is no new thing under the sun."

[2] Interview with Kurt Loder, *Rolling Stone* (21 June 1984).

proselytizing, for his mission has never been that of a missionary. Even songs of conversion (his, he believed, and others', he hoped) are converted by him from faith healing to art healing. So that his believing in the Book of Revelation comes to include comprehending that his revelations will need to make manifest some quite other vista. Hear how differently he delivers his opening line, "Precious angel, under the sun" (in utter quietude), from how the line from Revelation evoked its ensuing voice: "And I saw an angel standing in the sun; and he cried with a loud voice."

Precious Angel, being voiced, enters us through our ears, not our eyes, and all the more insinuatingly because it is of the eyes that it persistently elects to sing. This vision will be heard and not seen – except that the human imagination (a visual word, "imagination": "Can they imagine the darkness that will fall from on high") is amazingly able to gather one sense under the aegis of others. Faith, which resists sin, welcomes synaesthesia. *The Oxford English Dictionary*:

1c. Production, from a sense-impression of one kind, of an associated mental image of a sense-impression of another kind: [including] "when the hearing of an external sound carries with it, by some arbitrary association of ideas, the seeing of some form or colour" (1903).

2. The use of metaphors in which terms relating to one kind of sense-impression are used to describe sense-impressions of other kinds: [e.g.] "loud colours" (1901).[1]

"Whatever colors you have in your mind / I'll show them to you and you'll see them shine": not "arbitrary" when within art. The artist is not arbitrary but is an arbiter.

Not since *King Lear* has there been so tensile a tissue of eyes and seeing (of being blinded or blind, of the bodily and the spiritual) as is woven through *Precious Angel*. "To show me I was blinded": this should not be seen as the same as being blind ("I was blinded by the devil", *Saved*), any more than "to show me" should be seen as the same as, say, "to tell me". "Shine your light, shine your light on me": this should not be seen as the same as shining it *for* me. (For I understand the risk of shame in the prospect that who I am and what I am will be seen in the naked light.) "I'm a little too blind to see":

---

[1] The *OED* citations include E. H. Gombrich, *Art and Illusion* (1960): "What is called 'synesthesia', the splashing over of impressions from one sense modality to another, is a fact to which all languages testify."

this should be seen as enlisting the understatement with which stoicism understandably keeps its courage up. Understatement has two cousins in the dictionary, *meiosis* ("A figure of speech by which the impression is intentionally conveyed that a thing is less in size, importance, etc., than it really is") and *litotes* ("A figure of speech, in which an affirmative is expressed by the negative of the contrary"). Both of these relate to the sort of laconic admission that puts something aside, or puts it mildly: "Ya know I just couldn't make it by myself / I'm a little too blind to see". Not precisely *Shine your litotes on me*, but *Shine your light on meiosis*.

There are, out there, some terrible casualties of spiritual casualness. The song eyes them.

> My so-called friends have fallen under a spell
> They look me squarely in the eyes and they say, "Well, all is well"

Complacency could not be better caught than in that "Well . . . well" self-satisfaction,[1] where the final assurance – "Well, all is well" – is reduced to little more than the lubricating "Well" of facile conversation. *The Oxford English Dictionary*:

well: Employed without construction to introduce a remark or statement, sometimes implying that the speaker or writer accepts a situation, etc., already represented or indicated, or desires to qualify this in some way, but frequently used merely as a preliminary or resumptive word.

"They look me squarely in the eyes": square eyes are what you get from watching too much television,[2] and it is intriguing that in *T.V. Talkin' Song* the scene in Hyde Park – "where people talk / 'Bout all kinds of different gods" – should have the soap-box orator seeing things in quite the way that he did:

> There was someone on a platform talking to the folks
> About the T.V. god and all the pain that it invokes
> "It's too bright a light", he said, "for anybody's eyes
> If you've never seen one it's a blessing in disguise"

[1] As printed in *Lyrics 1962–1985* (1985), simply, singly, "they say, 'All is well'".
[2] *OED*, "square-eyed": "*jocular*, affected by or given to excessive viewing of television" (1976). One of the television reviewers in *Private Eye* bears the name Square Eyes.

Don't shine your light, don't shine your light on me. Or in my eyes. Or in "anybody's eyes". Fortunately, blessedly, there is in *Precious Angel* the benign counterpart to too bright a light: "You're the lamp of my soul, girl, you torch up the night"[1] – and then, immediately following this faith in her, there comes the recognition of what such faith is up against, with "the eyes" frighteningly unspecified (whose, exactly? we don't know where to look):

> But there's violence in the eyes, girl, so let us not be enticed
> On the way out of Egypt, through Ethiopia, to the judgment hall of Christ[2]

"Princes shall come out of Egypt; Ethiopia shall stretch out her hands unto God. Sing unto God" (Psalms 68:31–2). And so he does. "Lo, he doth send out his voice, and that a mighty voice" (says the next verse).

It is in its way a violent and yet enticing rhyme, *enticed / Christ*, by way of being a judgement hall itself, and a judgement call. Choose between these two words that rhyme, the one the temptation to sin, the other the overcoming of sin in the face of judgement. There is a poem by George Herbert called *The Water-Course*.[3]

> Thou who dost dwell and linger here below,
> Since the condition of this world is frail,
> Where of all plants afflictions soonest grow;
> If troubles overtake thee, do not wail:
>   For who can look for less, that loveth $\left\{ \begin{array}{l} \text{Life?} \\ \text{Strife?} \end{array} \right.$

> But rather turn the pipe and water's course
> To serve thy sins, and furnish thee with store

---

[1] Dylan sings "torch"; as printed in *Lyrics 1962–1985* "touch".

[2] *Precious Angel*, "so let us not be enticed"; *T.V. Talkin' Song*, "It will lead you into some strange pursuits, / Lead you to the land of forbidden fruits". *T.V. Talkin' Song*, "His voice was ringing loud"; Revelation, "And I saw an angel standing in the sun; and he cried with a loud voice." The phrase "There's violence in the eyes" swerves from the expected body-parts: "The violence of your hands" (Psalms 58:2); "the act of violence is in their hands" (Isaiah 59:6).

[3] "An artificial channel for the conveyance of water. The alternate rhymes in lines 5 and 10 suggest the turning of the pipes 'up' or 'down'." John Tobin, *George Herbert: The Complete English Poems* (1991).

Of sov'reign tears, springing from true remorse:

That so in pureness thou mayst him adore,

Who gives to man, as he sees fit $\left\{\begin{array}{l}\text{Salvation.}\\\text{Damnation.}\end{array}\right.$

We are to wonder for a moment whether there are before us ten lines or twelve lines: does the insistence that there are two very different destinations mean that we should hear the last line of each verse ring twice in our ears until it arrives at the choice that it sets before us?

Threading through *Precious Angel*, we may wonder about its arrival at "the judgment hall of Christ" as its destination and destiny, and in particular about the inescapability of *judgement*. Might there be a memory of a twofold saying of Christ, of promise and of threat? "And Jesus said, For judgement I am come into this world, that they which see not, might see; and that they which see might be made blind" (John 9:39). This chapter of John, on the miracle that heals the blind man, is one that gained Dylan's attentive respect, even if his memory couldn't then place it:

I get very meditative sometimes, and this one phrase was going through my head: "Work while the day lasts, because the night of death cometh when no man can work." I don't recall where I heard it. I like preaching, I hear a lot of preaching, and I probably just heard it somewhere. Maybe it's in Psalms, it beats me. But it wouldn't let me go.[1]

And as Jesus passed by, he saw a man which was blind from his birth. And his disciples asked him, saying, Master, who did sin, this man, or his parents, that he was born blind? Jesus answered, neither hath this man sinned, nor his parents: but that the works of God should be made manifest in him. I must work the works of him that sent me, while it is day: the night cometh, when no man can work. As long as I am in the world, I am the light of the world.

(John 9:1–5)

Shine your light, shine your light on me, who am a little too blind to see; even as Christ – the light of the world – once did on him, the man who was from birth too blind to see. "To show me I was blinded": these are words heard elsewhere with a difference:

---

[1] *New York Times* (29 September 1997).

> I was blinded by the devil
> Born already ruined
> > (*Saved*)

I was blinded; the eye was blind. To the ear, although not to the eye, *I* and *eye* are as indistinguishable as *I and I*. "How was I to know", "I was blinded", "I was gone", "I was standing upon": the first four lines of the song will lead to the thought that there's violence in the *I*'s.

The sinner in Herbert's *Love* tries in his shame to disown the generosity gently offered by Love:

> Love bade me welcome: yet my soul drew back,
> > Guilty of dust and sin.
> But quick-eyed Love, observing me grow slack
> > From my first entrance in,
> Drew nearer to me, sweetly questioning,
> > If I lacked anything.

> A guest, I answered, worthy to be here:
> > Love said, You shall be he.
> I the unkind, ungrateful? Ah my dear,
> > I cannot look on thee.
> Love took my hand, and smiling did reply,
> > Who made the eyes but I?

(Hear, within this sweet questioning, how "eyes" in this verse is three times preceded by and then succeeded by "I".) The shamefaced sinner tries to avert his eyes, but Love looks him squarely in the eyes, and says – not "Well, all is well" – but rather, in the words of Julian of Norwich that T. S. Eliot made his own and everyone's, words recalling that although sin is inevitable we must not despair:

> Sin is Behovely, but
> All shall be well, and
> All manner of thing shall be well.
> > (*Little Gidding*)

Saving Grace

"My faith keeps me alive". And will keep me alive past death. Thanks to the Redeemer. *Saving Grace* must itself then exercise a power to redeem, to bring to life or back to life ("then come the resurrection") what are otherwise only religious lip-services, too easily passing for faith.

> If You find it in Your heart, can I be forgiven?
> Guess I owe You some kind of apology
> I've escaped death so many times, I know I'm only living
> By the saving grace that's over me

Start with how each verse ends. Once upon an eternity, "saving grace" was a term of deep redemption, alive to damnation and to salvation, "that saving grace of imputation which taketh away all former guiltiness" (Richard Hooker, 1597). Back then, "saving" had not spent its force. "*Theological*. That delivers from sin and eternal death by the power of God's grace" (*The Oxford English Dictionary*).

But the concept of salvation can suffer attenuation, and "saving grace" was gradually weakened into meaning merely "a quality, 'redeeming', exempting from unqualified condemnation or censure". And so, in due slack course, "saving grace" turns into just a turn of phrase, amounting to no more than "Well, I suppose there is this at least to be said for it . . ." Such a redeeming quality amounts to all but nothing, and certainly not to redemption. The instances of "saving grace" from the dictionary verge on the blasphemous in being so devoid of spiritual seriousness.

    1910 "But I had the saving grace, I trust, to remember . . ."
    1932 "Here, in its plain lack of ideas, is the saving grace of this dull company."
    1978 "In all the shouting, the bitter recriminations, there was the saving grace of native good humour."

Native good humour is a good thing, but it is not a saving grace. Except in a world of very low ideals.

Dylan's song seeks to redeem the quality of the term, though not to spurn the everyday use of it, the negligent demeaning of its meaning.

Such wide-open songs as his cannot afford not to save what can be saved. They must not sound superior to how we have got into the way of putting things. So he sets the timbre of the ancient phrase "saving grace" against our modern casualness. The phrase is not reached in the song until we have passed through the downmarket place, where can be heard the betrayingly uneasy shuffle of "Guess I owe You some kind of apology". That is no way to speak to Almighty God – except that it may be, provided that it is understood to be only a stage in learning how to speak to Him, to You (not you). The capital *Y* in "You" from the start of the song ("If You find it in Your heart, can I be forgiven?") is a supreme ineffability of the kind that religious faith acknowledges with humility; the eye can see, all but effortlessly, the difference between "You" and "you", but the voice cannot indubitably voice this difference, though the voice may be able to intimate it in awe. A world will separate (faith knows) the pronoun in "If You find it in Your heart . . ." from the one in "The wicked know no peace and you just can't fake it".[1] The voicing of a true song about God and man will carry within itself the admission that the voice of God puts the voice of even a genius to shame, that *vox Dei* is not to be identified even with *vox Dylani*. But then art often delights in creating something from a sense of the limits of its own possibilities as a medium. A song may be proud of all that voicing can accomplish while being humble as to all that it cannot. Confidence in the voice (a word in your ear) will bring it about that the words "sole" and "soul" will be one, as they cannot be to the eye that sees a poem on the page:

> I put all my confidence in Him, my sole protection
> Is the saving grace that's over me

By the same token, the ear must yield to the eye when it comes to "eye" as against "I", or to "You" as against "you". Meanwhile, "confidence" has faith at the heart of it, the Latin *fides*.

And then "some kind of apology" is another case for redemption. The word "apology" might itself seem to call for some kind of apology when addressed to God, since it falls so far short of contrition's depths. It sounds offhand, even, as though not mindful that "The Lord shall judge his people.

---

[1] For "know no", in relation to both the negative and the positive, see the discussion of *Blind Willie McTell* (p. 68), with *Paradise Lost*: "No happier state, and know to know no more".

It is a fearful thing to fall into the hands of the living God."[1] Guess I owe you some kind of apology: this really does sound as though it might not be much more than a social shrug. We would, for instance, be surprised to find the Psalmist telling God that he owed Him some kind of apology. And yet (once upon that time, again) there was a sense of the word that had dignity and gravity. The citations in *The Oxford English Dictionary* establish this. The saints used it so. ("Defence of a person, or vindication of an institution, from accusation or aspersion".) St Thomas More, for one: *Apology of Sir Thomas More, Knight; made by him, after he had given over the Office of Lord Chancellor of England* (1533). Baxter's *Saints' Rest*, for others: "Now they shall both by Apology be maintained just" (1650). St Paul, for yet another: "And before the same great court of Areopagites Paul made his Apology" (Sherlock, in 1754). Even *An Apology for the Bible*, by Bishop Watson (1796).

The point, not for the first time, isn't that Dylan gives his days to the dictionary, but that he does know what the dictionary is worth.

"But if we know anything about God, God is *arbitrary*. So people better be able to deal with that."
Is there something about the word "arbitrary" that you would like to clarify or perhaps that I'm not understanding?
"No. I mean, you can look it up in the dictionary."[2]

I mean what the word means.

Dylan's instincts when it comes to words are at one with how the language has realized things over the years. "Apology" is a word that has come down in the world, which is why the line "Guess I owe You some kind of apology" does feel as though it is taking rather a rueful line. But at the same time, or in those unsame times that we can yet bring back to mind, "apology" was a word that did not apologize.

Faith is inspired guesswork. Faith assures you that you know and that you do not *know* exactly – since knowledge would vitiate the act of faith, the particular virtue that is faith. *Saving Grace* rings its changes on these terms that both rise to the occasion and fall short of it, inadequate and indispensable. So "Guess I owe You some kind of apology" gives way to "I know I'm only living/By the saving grace that's over me", with the transition from "Guess" to "know" brought home with the support of "I

[1] Epistle to the Hebrews 10:31.
[2] *Rolling Stone* (22 November 2001).

owe"/"I know". But there can be no securely ascending graph in these matters of faith. That way, foolish pride would lie, and the song warns against the sin of pride, or rather against its shallow brother, vanity: "But to search for love, that ain't no more than vanity". Vanity, vanity, all is vanity. Even the search for love, and even perhaps love itself. For Dylan's "*that* ain't no more than vanity" does not issue a ruling on whether it refers to the search for love or to love in itself.

There is no complacent assent, then, after the movement from guessing to knowing, for in no time "I know" is followed by the idiomatically quizzical "I would have thought" – or rather, by "I'd have thought" – or rather, by "I'd a-thought":

> By this time I'd a-thought that I would be sleeping
> In a pine box for all eternity
> My faith keeps me alive, but I still be weeping
> For the saving grace that's over me

"I'd a-thought" refuses to stand on ceremony. "I still be weeping", going beyond this, refuses to stand by the rules of grammar. The Gospel songs are where Dylan most feels free to do such a thing, as though celebrating a freedom gained. Yet there must still be a sense of responsibility. For "but I still weep" or "but I still am weeping" would not come to quite the same thing as "but I still be weeping". What the shift in the grammar does (over and above giving a hint of Gospel English)[1] is create "I still be weeping" by sliding together "I still am weeping" and "I'll still be weeping". And why slide together the present and the future? Because of "for all eternity". In eternity, and in the eyes of God, there can be no distinction of past, present, and future. True, we will still need to speak in such terms ("My faith keeps me alive"), but we should do so with intimations that the terms – in the more than long run that is eternity – will not ever do.

> Well, the death of life, then come the resurrection
> Wherever I am welcome is where I will be

What a pregnant phrase "the death of life" is, at once simple-minded and ghostly. And "then come the resurrection": its central sense is the one that

---

[1] For "'Cause I don't be like they'd like me to" (*I Believe in You*), see p. 345.

we hear in "come Christmas, I shall have retired",[1] but the idiom has feelers out to some variations: then comes the resurrection? then will come the resurrection? then may there come the resurrection? (Till kingdom come, His kingdom.) Again there is the merging of present and future, further blended with the trust and the prayer that constitute faith in the future, not only in the words "then come" but "where I will be". How unerringly the coming to the final point is conducted: "Wherever I am" is both contracted and expanded as "where I will be" ("Wherever" contracted to "where", "I am" expanded to "where I will be"). And this is interleaved with the more ample contraction and expansion (contraction of seven words down to one, expansion into eternal hope) that brings "*Well*, the death of life, then *come* the resurrection" down to the sheer succinctness of the one word "welcome". "Wherever I am welcome is where I will be". Humility (I am happy to leave it to Him), and assurance (for in His will is not only my peace but my happiness).

The fourth word of the song is "it": "If You find it in your heart, can I be forgiven?" Tiny and indispensable, it – or rather, "it" – does not recur until the final verse, four times there:[2]

> The wicked know no peace and you just can't fake it
> There's only one road and it leads to Calvary
> It gets discouraging at times, but I know I'll make it
> By the saving grace that's over me

Very capacious, the atom of the word "it". Its irreducibility is at one with its richness of suggestion. "There's only one road and it leads to Calvary / It gets discouraging at times": oh, not just the road gets discouraging, but the whole thing. And "I know I'll make it / By the saving grace that's over me": how are we to take "By" there? Is "By" the means by which I come to know this truth? (*By the saving grace that's over me, I know I'll make it.*) Or is "By" the means by which I'll make it? (*I'll make it by the saving grace that's over me.*) "By" is bifold here, but faith rightly refuses to make the distinction. "I'll make it": nothing could be more unspecified and yet nothing could be more assured – by the grace of grace. Yet even at this height of the song

---

[1] *OED* 36a, "used with a future date following as subject . . . 'come Easter'; *i.e.* let Easter come, when Easter shall come". The first citation is 1420: "twenty year come Easter". Come Easter; that is, "come the resurrection".

[2] In the penultimate verse, what is printed in *Lyrics 1962–1985* is "Well, the devil's shining light, it can be most blinding", but he sings ". . . that can be most blinding".

there needs to be something low-key. Which is how and where the rhyme *fake it / make it* comes in. It is different not only in tone (its slangy "fake it") from all the previous such rhymes but also in its constitution, being the song's only rhyme that is comprised of two words.[1]

The song itself, by its nature, is words and music and a voice. The voice enters immediately (less common than you might think in a Dylan song), with the words of admission, "If You . . .", immediately, a beat or so ahead of the music, as though not wishing to miss a beat when it comes to expressing contrition, gratitude, and faith. Self-attention, self-absorption, must be acknowledged as inescapable: the last word of each verse is "me". But the voicing of "me", and of its rhyming precedent in each verse,[2] changes as the song moves and moves us. There is an ever increasing elongation in "over *me*", the word being brief and to the point in the first verse and then gradually straining and strained as the stations of the Cross ("it leads to Calvary") proceed. It is with the fourth verse that the strain tells, in the racked or throttled throating: "vanity" becoming a drowning gurgling. And so to the final verse, where "times" pleads for mercy as though tortured ("Time is the mercy of eternity", said Blake), and where the last "it" – "make *it*" – wrests the two-letter word into becoming a several-syllable word. Of Dylan's first album, Robert Shelton wrote unforgettably: "Elasticized phrases are drawn out until you think they may snap."[3] But the phrasing of *Saving Grace* is not elastic, it is taut wire.

All roads lead to Rome. The Romans were good at roads, and good at making sure where they led in the end. But the Roman Empire, in the person of Pontius Pilate, was not able to destroy Christian revelation and the Cross. "There's only one road and it leads to Calvary". The song puts unbelievers on the spot (a good place to be, actually), though Kurt Loder in *Rolling Stone*[4] preferred to feel otherwise:

Saving Grace is so persuasive on its own terms that one can disregard the lyrical lapses ("There's only one road and it leads to Calvary") and accept the track as a genuinely moving paean to some non-specific Providence.

I beg your pardon? Or his pardon? Or His pardon? I guess you owe both

---

[1] The sequence is *forgiven / living; sleeping / weeping; resurrection / protection; blinding / finding*; but then *fake it / make it*.
[2] The sequence: *apology / me; eternity / me; be / me; vanity / me*; and then *Calvary / me*.
[3] *New York Times* (29 September 1961).
[4] 18 September 1980.

him and Him some kind of apology. Loder is a listener who is not among those who have ears to hear. *The Road Not Taken*, in Robert Frost's phrase. Even the road (Loder maintains) that nobody chooses to take. Or, with the belated creative negation in which "Wayne's World" specialized, *The Road Taken – Not*.

"Some non-specific Providence"? Of course if the listener "can disregard" the line about Calvary, and fall into pretending that it is a "lyrical lapse" (no, it isn't, it is a lyrical redemption of the Fall of Man), then he may deign to accept the track, etc. But this amounts to not accepting the track or the road down which it beckons you. "There's only one road and it leads to Calvary", which is where the song leads. But let us at least acknowledge that the song puts the road to Calvary before us and takes it for all that it is worth.

You Angel You

In the emporium of the empyrean, there are many orders for angels, for archangels, cherubim, seraphim, thrones, dominations, virtues, princedoms, powers . . . In the Dylan spheres, too, there are varieties of angel. The one who is hailed as "precious angel" is human but heavenly, mediating between the singer and the Mediator. The one in *You Angel You*, on the other wing, is human and earthly. Not that it would be right of us to set sacred love against profane love, for she is not what you'd call profane, she is simply down to earth. About faith in her there can be no doubt.

> You angel you
> You got me under your wing
> The way you walk and the way you talk
> I feel I could almost sing

The song is lithe and blithe. It flies lightly, takes wing, but is happy to settle down to her human touches, her walking and talking. So let us not be heavy-footed.[1]

[1] As performed on *Planet Waves* (reissued on *Biograph*), the song swerves within the second line. Dylan sings "You angel you" but follows this by starting upon "You're as . . ." ("You're as fine as anything's fine"); he splits the second, and proceeds, "got me under your wing". The recovery is so prompt as to make the slip of the lip all but imperceptible. There is something simply unfussed (and delightfully appropriate to the spirit of the song) in his letting it stand, in his letting it go. Not at all "Go to hell", this unruffled imperfectionism, rather "Go to Heaven, there's an angel".

Yet sheer simplicity always has its reserves of power. "The way you walk and the way you talk": we can wonder about, as well as at, the way the song talks and the way it walks. (Very different from the cynical political cut, *He can talk the talk, but can he walk the walk?*) The song is on the balls of its feet, trippingly (again not tripping), the music dancing with the words, the music doing the leading. The whole thing is as modest, as fine, as can be, endearingly slight (as against slightly endearing), light-hearted, and enterprising.

Dylan is modest about the song but doesn't slight it: "I might have written this at one of the sessions probably, you know, on the spot, standing in front of the mike . . . it sounds to me like dummy lyrics" (*Biograph*). But what may begin as dummy lyrics, filling in a melody with the first words that come to mind (and to heart and to tongue), can then grow wings.[1]

"You got me under your wing": not your thumb, agreed? And what is then so buoyant in the song is its freedom from the thought that anybody (the singer, the sung-to, *anybody* in its carefree zone) stands in need of shelter. *The Oxford English Dictionary*, "under the wing of": under the protection, care, or patronage of. But here there is no need for protection, and there is no patronage and no patronizing – or matronizing, since men don't have the monopoly of condescension. Two lines that Dylan printed in *Lyrics 1962–1985* but didn't sing had risked condescension, very sweetly it is true: "The way you smile like a sweet baby child / It just falls all over me". Seeing her as a child might run athwart the childlike sweetness of the song itself. He sings instead "The way you walk and the way you talk / Is the way it ought to be". Way way way better.

"They say ev'ry man needs protection / They say ev'ry man must fall"[2] – but not the man in *You Angel You*. For he has a guardian angel. He may say that he can't sleep, but this then takes the form of having him sound brimmingly wide awake. He may say that at night he gets up and walks the floor, but he makes even this feel as exuberantly tireless as her way of walking.

> You know I can't sleep at night for trying
> Yes I never did feel this way before
> Never did get up and walk the floor

[1] For *Lay, Lady, Lay* and Dylan's sense of how it sprang from the fillers "la la la", see p. 155.
[2] *I Shall Be Released.*

> If this is love then gimme more
> And more and more and more and more[1]

The glee with which this is sung must mischievously counteract any uneasy sense of the words. Whatever the feeling may be ("Yes I never did feel this way before": what way, exactly?), then – as to love – gimme more and more and more and more. He says that he used to have no such churning ("Never did get up and walk the floor") but it comes out sounding just the opposite: as though "Never did" (in the old days) "get up and walk the floor" really wants to convey "Never do" (in these good new days) "get up and walk the floor" – at least never do those things in any way that would have me bowed down and bent.

The effect is exactly the reverse of that in the song whose gravity of expiration is the opposite of the inspired levity of *You Angel You*: *Mama, You Been on My Mind*, where he assures the woman in whom he misplaced his faith, "I do not walk the floor bowed down an' bent, but yet / Mama, you been on my mind". So you say – but, in the singing, every single syllable of all those one-syllable words ("Mama" making the only twofold impression) does feel bowed down and bent, burdened by those damnable *b*s and *d*s. "Mama, you been on my mind": nothing could be more distant from the turning of this phrase in *You Angel You*:

> I just want to watch you talk
> With your memory on my mind[2]

We expect "I just want to watch you *walk*". Not only because we've already heard "The way you walk", and not only because of what would be the claims of alliteration: *want . . . watch . . . walk / With* (into *memory . . . my mind*). For the happiness of watching a beautiful woman walk is clear enough. Dylan, as the creator of a song called *On the Road Again* (not the first song to bear such a title), might like the company of the man who wrote the poem *On the Road*,

---

[1] He sings "Yes I never did feel . . ."; as printed in *Lyrics 1962–1985*, "Never did feel . . ." (which is what he sings in the return of the bridge). And he sings "Never did get up and walk the floor"; as printed, "I get up at night and walk the floor".

[2] Dylan sings it so; as printed in *Lyrics 1962–1985*, "The way you talk and the way you walk / It sure plays on my mind". The word "plays" plays along nicely with the talk of singing, but perhaps the punning suggestion then of "preys on my mind" has a darkness out of place in light of the song. "*Mama*, you been on my mind" is transformed, in Dylan's memory, into "your *memory* on my mind".

William Barnes, who ends it with a sequence of ways of walking, all observed with affection and the last of them with immensely more than affection:

> There the horse would prance by, with his neck a high bow,
> And would toss up his nose over outspringing knees;
> And the ox, with sleek hide, and with low-swimming head;
> And the sheep, little kneed, with a quickdipping nod;
> And a girl, with her head carried on in a proud
> Gait of walking, as smooth as an air-swimming cloud.

But "watch you *talk*"? Yet it is an evocatively lovely and humorous moment; he doesn't need to hear what she is saying, he just loves the sight of her talking, maybe to him (his mind and heart on her, not, I'm afraid, on what she is saying, but she will forgive that), or the sight of her in conversation. And even while watching her (with good pride in her) in the present, he can fuse this with his sense of what she has been in the past and continues to be: "With your memory on my mind". One tribute to Dylan in concert would be to murmur "I just want to watch you sing with your memory on my mind".[1]

"The way you walk": *do* angels walk? They can, as birds can, and Heaven has been known to witness a ceremony:

> Now walk the angels on the walls of Heaven
> To entertain divine Zenocrate.
> (Marlowe, *Tamburlaine*, Part 2, Act II)

Sometimes angels deign down to our level, to our element. Very good of them. But again a comic glimpse nestles before gliding from the wing to walking. Edward FitzGerald birdwatched:

> The Bird of Time has but a little way
> To fly – and Lo! the Bird is on the Wing.

Time duly brought the notorious retort: The bird is on the wing? No, the wing is on the bird.

---

[1] On seeing and hearing, there is a good junction in Alex Ross (*New Yorker*, 10 May 1999): "I had just seen Dylan sing *Hattie Carroll*, in Portland, and it was the best performance that I heard him give."

The discreet slide from "wing" to "walk" is given salience by the
alliteration, helped on its way by "way" and then walking on its way
with that word again:

> You got me under your wing
> The way you walk and the way you talk

– whereupon the next rhyme comes winging in: "I feel I could almost
sing". This, which is all the more winning because it is itself being sung
to us (not being read by us), has many facets to catch a twinkling light,
but at this moment in the song it is offered so as to be suspended,
patiently awaiting its comical confirmation in the very last line of the
song. Later.

Meanwhile:

> The way you walk and the way you talk
> I feel I could almost sing

The first line of that sequence does not walk straightforwardly into the sec-
ond line. For "The way you walk and the way you talk" proceeds to proceed
nowhere in a way – which is where the subdued exclamatory excitement
comes from. The effect is of an awed musing happiness blossoming then
and there: "The way you walk and the way you talk / I feel I could
almost sing". It is quietly jumping for joy from the one line to the next,
a dawning joy.

One of the things that makes the song feel so simple, so trusting, is its
being happy just to repeat those few things it has to say, giving them
again without any misgivings. Not just "You angel you", rejoicing, and
not only the bridge crossed over again, but "The way you walk and the
way you talk" three times relished. What I tell you three times is true.

But then again it is of the nature of love to continue to be the same
without being exactly the same or being merely the same again. We thrill
to "You're as fine as anything's fine", which is fine but which, when it
returns, is heard to make even more of a claim: "You're as fine as can be".
Not just as fine as what *is* but as what *can be*. Or there is "feel" feeling
its way on within the song, from "I feel I could almost sing" into "Yes I
never did feel this way before". This is a song in which a man's feeling for
a paramour is paramount. And how effortlessly "feel this way before" has

some feeling for our having so heard the word "way" before, way before: "The way you walk and the way you talk".

"Seems like I been down this way before" (*Señor*). Dolefully, there. Delightfully, here.

Some such things escalate in the song, but one imaginative thing does the opposite. The first time, the exultation goes like this:

> Yes I never did feel this way before
> Never did get up and walk the floor
> If this is love then gimme more
> And more and more and more and more

"If this is love . . .". So how about "If music be the food of love, play on, / Give me excess of it" (the opening words of *Twelfth Night*). *Give me*, the swell of the Duke, gets informally urgent as *gimme*: "then gimme more / And more . . .". In Dylan's song, as in the Duke's speech, there is homage to love, and the Duke's words would catch the spirit of the love in *You Angel You*: "O spirit of love, how quick and fresh art thou". But the Duke himself, unlike the spirited singer, does not stay quick and fresh. No, everything quickly turns blah-blah-blasé:

> Enough, no more,
> 'Tis not so sweet now as it was before.

In Dylan's song, "more" likewise rhymes with "before", but "Enough, no more" is the very last thing that it would want to say. Moreover, we are not over with "more"; the reiteration of "more and more" does itself come back for more. But the second time, it goes like this:

> Never did feel this way before
> Never did get up and walk the floor
> If this is love then gimme more
> And more and more and more

Not five but four, one fewer "more", or less more.

There is more to come, though: the final verse.

> You angel you
> You got me under your wing

> The way you walk and the way you talk
> I swear it would make me sing[1]

The earlier bemused gratitude, "I feel I could almost sing", has become an amused gratification, "I swear it would make me sing". This goes singing on its way, but does not (dear auditor) issue any vaunt along the lines of "I swear it has made me sing". This, because whether Dylan *sings* is the comic backupdrop to the song. I feel he could almost sing. I swear it has made him sing!

Your music is great, but you'd be greater if you could kinda sing a little bit better.
"I appreciate that . . . a good solid rock-bottom foundational criticism and that just sinks it right in."
Not everybody has the courage to tell Bob the truth.
"Not everybody has the courage to sing like I do."[2]

John Berryman, who had been fond of Dylan Thomas, once exploded: "I can never forgive that young upstart for stealing my friend Dylan's name." "Yes, but don't you agree he's a poet?" "Yes, if only he'd learn to sing."[3]

Those of us who love to hear him sing may recall Shakespeare's "I love to hear her speak". Sonnet 130 brings together a loved woman, music, talking, and walking, always refusing to sentimentalize:

> I love to hear her speak, yet well I know
> That music hath a far more pleasing sound.
> I grant I never saw a goddess go,
> My mistress when she walks treads on the ground.

Goddesses can fly, as can angels.[4] But the way she walks . . . In the unabashedly human words of Keats about mythological loves:

---

[1] He sings this; as printed in *Lyrics 1962–1985* it says "It says everything".
[2] *Bob Fass Show* (WBAI-FM, New York, January 1966).
[3] John Haffenden, *The Life of John Berryman* (1982), p. 353.
[4] As to "on the ground", Dylan sings with special tenderness Willie Nelson's *Angel Flying Too Close to the Ground* (B-side of a single, 1983). She, an angel (not a raven) with a broken wing, is grounded for a while.

Let the mad poets say whate'er they please
Of the sweets of Faeries, Peris, Goddesses,
There is not such a treat among them all,
Haunters of cavern, lake, and waterfall,
As a real woman.[1]

"The way you walk and the way you talk": so what exactly is an angel anyway? An angel is a messenger. Translating the Greek word, and the Hebrew, which was in full "messenger of Jehovah". And what does a messenger have to be able to do? Deliver. Walk and talk. The song is free to take wing.

And the difference between words in a song and in a poem? That in song there can be this thing called *melisma*, where "one word flowers out into a passage of several notes". Or rather, not one word but one syllable can do so. *God Save the Queen*: "long to- oo rei- eign over us", where "to" and "reign" are not just extended through time, not just held longer, but are granted two notes, not left as one note per syllable. Dylan's imaginative decisions as to when and when not to take this responsible liberty would furnish matter for a whole book.

Song has a different system of punctuation from those of both poetry and prose, and there is no equivalent outside song to what song does when it separates one syllable to live within more than one note. The human voice can sing this flowering out into several notes, but the human voice cannot say it. (For a voice to change inflection when saying something is not the same thing as having one syllable be extended through more than one note.) So it is a profoundly simple accomplishment that has only one word in the whole of *You Angel You* be committed to melisma, this aspect of the art of song: the very last word of the song, the word "sing" itself: "I swear it would make me sing". And this had not been the case with this line's partner at the end of the first verse, when "I feel I could almost sing" had been happy to have the word "sing" be musically one simple syllable. It is only now, in the final moment of the song, that "sing" differently has the last word, and has it as a word to sing because the one syllable takes to itself more than one note. Unique to singing, this, and a unique moment within this particularizing song. How very many different aspects of art it reconciles.

Hopkins, who complained about "precious" in the vicinity of "angel",

[1] *Lamia*, I, 328–32.

was adamant. "I can never be reconciled to calling men or women angels; there seems something out of tune in it."[1] But then Hopkins never had the chance to hear Dylan's tune in it.

Boots of Spanish Leather

"Have you ever been", she asked him, "faithful?" It was meant to give him a turn, this turn at the last moment. The lover in *Boots of Spanish Leather*, a leather lover it turns out in the end, has misplaced his faith – not in the sense that he can't for the moment put his hand on it ("Has anybody seen my love?"),[2] but in that he placed his faith in someone who no longer has any place for it. Faith, it becomes clear, has been betrayed by infidelity, or by the thought of it, the possibility of losing her now, there in their immediate future.

In *Boots of Spanish Leather*, an indestructible song about the destruction of love, the artistic self-discipline is inseparable from the self-control of the one who comes to learn what it is to be let down. Bitterness, which will not yet let up, is tinglingly contained. Here is a song in which alternately a man and a woman exchange words of love.[3] The song avails itself of the fact that you are not sure who speaks first. Because it is a song by Dylan sung by Dylan, the natural assumption is that the man does so:

> Oh, I'm sailin' away my own true love
> I'm sailin' away in the morning

Usually, after all, or before all, it was the man (in the old days) who had to leave for work, to set sail. Oh, it's the opening of *Farewell*:

> Oh it's fare thee well my darlin' true,
> I'm leavin' in the first hour of the morn

[1] To Dixon, 26 September 1881; *The Correspondence of Hopkins and Dixon*, p. 65.
[2] *Tight Connection (Has Anybody Seen My Love)*.
[3] On the antiphonal in Dylan's songs, and particularly in *A Hard Rain's A-Gonna Fall*, see p. 340. As to Dylan's taking the dramatic role of a woman in a song, singing so throughout, there is (of his songs) only *North Country Blues*: "As I quit in the spring / To marry John Thomas, a miner". *House of the Rising Sun* (which he sings feelingly but which is not his song) is likewise in a woman's voice throughout: "It's been the ruin of many a poor girl, / And me, O God, I'm one".

– where, immediately following those lines in *Farewell*, and bound for the Spanish place-names of *Boots of Spanish Leather*, there comes this:

> I'm bound off for the bay of Mexico
> Or maybe the coast of Californ

So the initial alternation of verses in *Boots of Spanish Leather* might be heard as a man's question issuing in a woman's response. Still, it is clear that whose-voice-is-whose isn't (or isn't yet) cleared up. The song holds its cards close to its chest. A treasure chest of silver or of golden.

The first verse opens with "Oh"; the second, with "No", though proffering itself positively.

> Oh, I'm sailin' away my own true love
> I'm sailin' away in the morning
> Is there something I can send you from across the sea
> From the place that I'll be landing?
>
> No, there's nothin' you can send me, my own true love
> There's nothin' I'm wishin' to be ownin'
> Just to carry yourself back to me unspoiled
> From across that lonesome ocean

It is not for another five verses that it becomes unquestionable that it was the woman who asked the opening question, that it is she who is doing the leaving (in more than one sense). You suddenly learn, as if you, too, had received a letter,

> Oh, I got a letter on a lonesome day
> It was from her ship a-sailin'
> Saying I don't know when I'll be comin' back again
> It depends on how I'm a-feelin'

From this point, there will be no more reciprocity, no more alternation. The man, having been wronged, now has the right to speak without heeding the thought of a response. He has heard her out, and anyway it was she who decided that out it is. The last three verses are his. His alone. His, alone.

The final verse, the verse of finality (it is the long-delayed answer to her insistent questioning as to a gift for him), moves on to the offensive, even while being inoffensively couched in the terms not so much of a threat as of a warning, not the terms of any refusal to accept the situation but of finally agreeing – in his way – to accept something to remember her by.

> So take heed, take heed of the western winds
> Take heed of the stormy weather
> And yes, there's something you can send back to me
> Spanish boots of Spanish leather

His earlier "No", positively grateful for her (a much larger thing than being grateful to her), is completed at last by his "yes", negatively grating.

This last verse, the ninth, concludes what had begun as alternating exchanges, no longer happily paired off but with an odd number of verses. A way of getting even. A pair of boots, not the odd boot. She is now (except that she isn't going to do it) asked to give him the boots, having previously given him the boot: "sudden and callous rejection" (*The Oxford English Dictionary*).

With the exception of *sorrow / tomorrow*, to which I'll return, the final rhyme *weather / leather* is the only full rhyme and the only predictable rhyme in the song. But it is predictable only because of the title *Boots of Spanish Leather*, with the teasing complication that, on the one hand, the title of a song is very seldom uttered by its singer, but, on the other, everybody soon comes to know the title of the song and moreover it is given on the album . . . Anyway, the conclusive final line is a pointed modulation of the song's title, which had not spelt out the double Spanish requisition: "Spanish boots of Spanish leather". Spanish boots were an instrument of torture for the Inquisition. They caught on. Germany, Russia . . .[1]

The Spanish leather was perhaps imported from *Gypsy Davey*, a song that Dylan has since recorded.[2] In conversation with Studs Terkel in 1963, Dylan sided with this suggestion for a moment but then sidled away. Is there something I can sing you from across the sea?

---

[1] They give pain in Goethe's *Faust* (Part 1, line 1, 913), as Levi Dalton pointed out to me. Mikhail Bulgakov, *The Master and Margarita*: "'And what is this on her foot?' asked Margarita, tirelessly offering her hand to the guests who had overtaken the hobbling Madame Tofana . . . 'On her foot, Queen, she has a Spanish boot' . . . The Spanish boot interfered with her movement" (tr. Mirra Ginsburg, 1995, p. 282).

[2] As *Blackjack Davey*, on *Good as I Been to You*. "Pull off, pull off them high-heeled shoes / All made of Spanish leather". A present. Hers, not His. Shoes, not boots.

"You wanna hear a love-song?"

Boy meets girl — Bob Dylan, boy meets girl.

"This is girl leaves boy . . . This is called 'Boots of Spanish Leather'"

"Boots of Spanish Leather" — like "Gypsy Davey", a line from it.

"Yeah [plays a few chords and then] — no, not because of that but because I've always wanted a pair of boots of Spanish leather."

A personable personal touch, but not one that we should allow to imperil the impersonality of the song itself. The conjunction of the personal and the impersonal can be heard in Dylan's pronunciation of "leather", itself leathery and subtle and supple.

Clearly, the fact that, upon first hearing, it isn't clear who speaks first — which means that it will not become clear for quite a while exactly how this gendered song was engendered — must imply that later hearings will be different in kind. But this is a commonplace about works of art. If you have seen *Hamlet* before, you know what will happen in the story. (*Dysfunctional family tries to cope with death of father.*) If a story stakes everything on suspense, especially suspense of a tricksy or risky kind, then you may never want to experience it again. At the video store there are thrillers that still thrill and there are those that don't or won't. But it characterizes works of art that to experience them again may be to experience them anew, gaining at least as much as one loses. Suspense may be not abolished but polished.

If we imagine *Boots of Spanish Leather* sung — as it easily could be — by alternate voices (so that the gendresult would be immediately announced), then we find that we are imagining something much *less* lastingly worth while than what we hear while the song is in Dylan's voice throughout. And this, not only because of what Dylan's voice is. A single voice is called upon to tell this story of how the dual partnership of love met duplicity.[1]

This delayed indubitability — as to who is breaking off with whom — has taken up into itself along the way some intimations about these intimacies.

---

[1] These things are the creations of convention, granted, but then conventions are themselves creations: the convention by which a man sings as a woman or vice versa, or the convention that presents an alternation of speakers in one voice throughout. For my part, I am disconcerted or discomposed by the Dylan/Johnny Cash duet in *Girl of the North Country* (on *Nashville Skyline*). Dylan just about saves the day by pushing his voice up so as maximally to distinguish its young love from the male stubble of Cash's voice. True, when Dylan and Cash fool around with *One Too Many Mornings*, as you can hear them doing on bootleg tapes ("You are right from your side, Bob,/And I am right from mine"), it is a different story, a funny story.

These moments are more than tricks; they are to bring out how tricky these things are. Take what happens when two consecutive lines, clearly by alternating speakers, are so phrased as to sound as though they are addressed in the same direction, from him to her. In the second verse, for instance, "Just to carry yourself back to me unspoiled" sounds like – and here is – something that a man says to a woman. For "unspoiled" (not quite the same as "unspoilt") may have a whiff of condescension, and, because of what it is to despoil or violate, may suggest, too, the dangers that women run.[1] But then the reply that at once follows, "Oh, but I just thought you might want something fine", does rather sound as though (again) it is a woman who is being addressed. (Quite wrong of us, of course, to more associate women with wanting something fine, but you know how it is.) What matters is the way in which the uncertainty as to who / whom, a hesitation as to the sex of the speaker, can become part of why it is not a misogynistic song, this and the fact that it never generalizes about women and about men.

The seventh verse, the narrative turn, is divided between the man and the woman, but not as an exchange of two passages of direct speech.

> Oh, I got a letter on a lonesome day
> It was from her ship a–sailin'
> Saying I don't know when I'll be comin' back again
> It depends on how I'm a–feelin'

His two lines directly narrate, but her two are direct speech of calculated indirection: "I don't know when I'll be comin' back again". "It depends on how I'm a-feelin'" – what an unfeeling way of putting it down, of putting him down.

The alternation of feminine and masculine voices, that way round (we find), is something that Dylan rightly makes no effort to dramatize. He doesn't act the song, he sings it, refusing to settle things, unsettlingly. This is in parallel with the alternation of masculine and feminine endings, lines that end with a stressed syllable alternating from the start with lines that end with an unstressed one:

> Oh, I'm sailin' away my own true lóve
> I'm sailin' away in the mórning[2]

---

[1] Dryden's translation of the *Aeneid* (XI, 890–91): "Unspoiled shall be her arms, and unprofaned / Her holy limbs with any human hand".

[2] On feminine and masculine endings, see the commentary on *The Lonesome Death of Hattie Carroll*, p. 222.

In each quatrain, it is lines 2 and 4, only, that rhyme or half-rhyme or off-rhyme.[1] So that the rhymes are all, or all but all, feminine rhymes. For instance:

> Oh, but if I had the stars of the darkest night
> And the diamonds from the deepest ocean
> I'd forsake them all for your sweet kiss
> For that's all I'm wishin' to be ownin'

There Dylan points up the feminine / masculine endings by singing something other than what is printed in *Lyrics 1962–1985*: the lyrics have "There's nothing I wish to be ownin'", but he sings "There's nothing I'm wishing to be ownin'", with the triple -*ing* sounding in our ears, the feminine ending undulating and insistent. Much is offered:

> Oh, but I just thought you might want something fine
> Made of silver or of golden

Or? Choose one? Sorry, you're not going to get something made of silver with a golden inlay . . . That isn't the tone, which is extravagantly (because guiltily already?) eager to bestow:

> Oh, but I just thought you might want something fine
> Made of silver or of golden
> Either from the mountains of Madrid
> Or from the coast of Barcelona

"Made of silver or of golden":[2] this, too, is largesse (*largesse oblige*), luxuriously

---

[1] The rhymes are: verse 1, *morning / landing*. Verse 2, *ownin' / ocean*. Verse 3, *golden / Barcelona*. Verse 4, *ocean / ownin'*. Verse 5, *askin' / passin'*. Verse 6, *sorrow / tomorrow*. Verse 7, *sailin' / feelin'*. Verse 8, *roamin' / goin'*. Verse 9, *weather / leather*. The repetition in verse 4, *ocean / ownin'*, of verse 2, *ownin' / ocean*, a repetition with a reversal, suggests (Jim McCue suggests to me) that things – becalmed – aren't going anywhere, although she is; the plea is repeated, unheeded.

[2] The land of the ballad always welcomes visitors from the land of nursery rhymes.

> I had a little nut tree, nothing would it bear
> But a silver nutmeg and a golden pear;
> The king of Spain's daughter came to visit me,
> And all for the sake of my little nut tree.

Furthermore, "Made of silver or of golden" may be coloured with *ore*, and may be heading for Barcelona, a gold *bar*.

redundant, since we expect either "Made of silver or of gold" or "Made of silver or golden". "Made of silver or *of golden*" overflows to the point of overdoing it, affluently and fluently: is she making too much of this wish to give him something, and giving herself away? At the same time the cadence fulfils the pattern of alternating a stressed and an unstressed final syllable ("fine" / "of gólden") that "of gold" would lack. And rhyming with the line, off-rhyming with it, is the city with the feminine ending, Barcelóna, following upon the previous line and its city with the masculine ending, Madríd.

> Either from the mountains of Madrid
> Or from the coast of Barcelona[1]

It is broadly true, then, that only half of the lines rhyme (the even ones). But only broadly true, for many of the unrhyming words at the ends of the odd lines are gathered up from previous rhymes or rhyme-placings, rhyme-plaitings: so "love" may not be rhymed but it does end two lines, and the same is true of "again" and of "day" and of "me". It is against this interlacing that the rent in the fabric of love is felt.

For the repetitions, which had at first possessed (despite the imminent parting) something light of heart, gain weight:

> If you, my love, must think that-a-way
> I'm sure your mind is roamin'
> I'm sure your thoughts are not with me[2]
> But with the country to where you're goin'
>
> So take heed, take heed of the western winds
> Take heed of the stormy weather
> And yes . . .

Take heed: thrice, like a witch's spell, more like a conjuration than an adjuration.

Nothing could be simpler, in some ways, than the song's movements of mind as it contemplates these movements of the heart. But, yet again, the

---

[1] Something similar is achieved in the lines from *Farewell* quoted on p. 405: "I'm bound off for the bay of Mexico / Or maybe the coast of Californ" – where California, being lopped of its last two letters, becomes a masculine ending: "Californ".

[2] He sings "thoughts are"; as printed in *Lyrics 1962–1985*, "heart is".

simplicity is alive in "that perpetual slight alteration of language" that T. S. Eliot valued.[1]

> Is there something I can send you from across the sea
> From the place that I'll be landing?

Not "From the place that I'll be landing at". It is not that Dylan just had to have "landing" at the end, since he could have done this by singing "From the place where I'll be landing", and it is not that he couldn't fit "landing at" into the line. He can always fit things into lines if need be or even if wish be. No, the point is that the speaker (she, as it turns out) is not imagining merely where she is going to land, or that she is going to land at a place; oh no, she is going to land a place. It makes it sound ominously like some splendid fish or splendid prize, these things that you gleefully land. Too blithe a spirit at parting.

The whole song engages with reciprocity and repetition and these then becoming broken. The first verse, "my own true love", is matched with the second verse, "my own true love", a loving answer it would seem. But by the eighth verse she is not saying any such thing, and he is no longer saying "my own true love" but the milder bleaker "If you, my love, must think that-a-way". No longer my own, no longer my own true love. There is an audible finality. This love is over. Differently over, it is true, from that in *One Too Many Mornings*, with its level dismay ("We're both just one too many mornings / An' a thousand miles behind"). And altogether different from those love songs that really put in one last plea, as does *Don't Think Twice, It's All Right*. *Boots of Spanish Leather* asks for nothing. What gives the finality its high shine is the contrast with all those repetitions along the way, all the hope that used to be invested in "again", a word that embodies the repetitive asking that is an irritant to the lover. "How can, how can you ask me again": deeply felt, the vexation, in that it does itself perpetrate an "again" ("How can, how can . . ."), and then itself has to say "again" again:

> Oh, how can, how can you ask me again
> It only brings me sorrow
> The same thing I would want today
> I would want again tomorrow[2]

---

[1] See p. 382.

[2] What is printed in *Lyrics 1962–1985* has much less sense of an exact fit: "The same thing I want from you today, / I would want again tomorrow".

"The same thing" plays along with all the repetitions within the song, not just words or phrases but whole questions, whole sentiments. But then there comes the final "again", the one that is compounded by an internal rhyme, when word comes from her: "Saying I don't know when I'll be comin' back again".

It is this moment before the letter arrives that warns us that tomorrow will bring sorrow:

> Oh, how can, how can you ask me again
> It only brings me sorrow
> The same thing I would want today
> I would want again tomorrow

Sorrow/tomorrow: this is not just a foreseeable rhyme, but – like the other such one, which closes the song and the relationship – a full true rhyme.[1] All the other rhymes in the song till this point have been imperfect and happy to be so; but the rhyme *sorrow/tomorrow* comes with the predictability of sunrise while dawning on us as a cold sun.

"Take heed, take heed of the western winds".[2] We are to take heed of the unforgettably laconic medieval poem that this sends back to us, sends us back to. Four lines sadly say it all.

> O western wind, when wilt thou blow
> The small rain down can rain;
> Christ that my love were in my arms
> And I in my bed again.

The cry in *Boots of Spanish Leather* is differently poignant: Christ that my love were my love. (But in any case no western wind, being a wind from the west, could bring a ship from Spain to America.) The pressure of "tomorrow" in Dylan's song might send us to another song of his, *Tomorrow*

---

[1] Same rhyme, different reason, at the end of *Oh Sister*: "Oh, sister, when I come to knock at your door/Don't turn away, you'll create sorrow/Time is an ocean but it ends at the shore/You may not see me tomorrow". I for one have the distinct impression that she will see him tomorrow, given how "tomorrow" follows so equably from "sorrow"; does it sound as though there may really be rupture? Time is an ocean but at least it isn't that lonesome ocean.

[2] As printed in *Lyrics 1962–1985*, "wind".

Is a Long Time, and its tribute both to a loved one and to "O western wind", the refrain,

> Only if she was lying by me
> Then I'd lie in my bed once again

In the lost faith or lost fidelity of *Boots of Spanish Leather* this has become a different longing: If only she had lived a truth, and lived it by me.

What Was It You Wanted?

A catechism is a course of instruction that proceeds through a series of questions. The catechism in the Book of Common Prayer ministers to faith, laying out the grounds for the faith that pre-exists you but that is now to prove the grounds of your existence. Since you will in the end confront the Four Last Things,[1] first things first:

Question. What is your name?
Answer. N. or M.
Question. Who gave you this name?

What is your name? Robert or Bob. Dylan or Zimmerman. "You may call me Bobby, or you may call me Zimmy" (*Gotta Serve Somebody*).
    What Was It You Wanted? is a catechism. One with a difference anyway. "Who are you anyway?" Now, I ask you ("exclamatory phr. indicating disgust or asseveration").[2] The questions, though, are designed, not to establish the foundations for faith, but to dig into whether the lover's faith really has any foundation. (Is it groundless?) The song scrutinizes the love or lovelessness of woman (and of man), not the love of God.

Question. What meanest thou by this word Sacrament?
Answer. I mean an outward and visible sign of an inward and spiritual grace.

What Was It You Wanted? inquires not into the meaning of sacrament but into sacrilege, the demeaning of love:

[1] Death, Judgement, Heaven, and Hell. He'll be the Judge of that.
[2] *OED*, "ask", 4c.

> Is it something important?
> Maybe not
> What was it you wanted?
> Tell me again, I forgot

We are to listen for the outward and visible signs of an inward and spiritual disgrace. A frightening crevasse – a cold pause, musical and vocal, of a nature to give you pause – opens between "Is it something important?" and "Maybe not". Far from being a casual fluency, "Maybe" comes out there as rigidly frigid. "Is it something important?" The philosopher J. L. Austin famously remarked, "I am not sure importance is important: truth is."[1]

This song about truth, a song that catechizes and castigates, is a string of questions, coolly plaited into a noose. It takes you back to the good old days when "to go to heaven in a string" was to be hanged.

> Three merry boys, and three merry boys,
>   And three merry boys are we,
> As ever did sing in a hempen string
>   Under the gallow-tree.[2]

It is no merry boys' song, *What Was It You Wanted?* But it does fulfil the educational obligation of a catechism: to be instruction. In faith and in the faith. And in good faith, for it is dedicated to teaching someone a lesson. Two people actually, the woman who is being quizzed and the man who is quizzing her in a tone too monomaniacal to be quizzical. And maybe a third, too, the other man, with whom she may have been faithless. "Someone there in the shadows / Someone that I might have missed". Do I miss you, my darling? Did I miss him, your darling, fail to spot him, or fail to hit him? "Was there a slip of the lip?" A slip of the lip may betray something, may be evidence of betrayal, of unfaith. The sacred world of *I Believe in You* may have been desecrated in the world of earthly love. "Who are you anyway?"

The song launches itself immediately into questioning, with just this one provocative proviso: there is to be no answering, understood?

---

[1] *Philosophical Papers* (1961, 1979 edition), p. 271.
[2] Fletcher, *The Bloody Brother* (1625); both this and "heaven in a string" are in the *OED*, 1a, under "string".

What was it you wanted?
Tell me again so I'll know
What's going on in there
What's going on in your show
What was it you wanted?
Could you say it again?
I'll be back in a minute
You can get it together by then

Good of him to give you a minute to collect yourself, is it not? – but you had better not suppose that in a minute's time, when you *have* got it together, you will get the chance to speak, an opportunity to answer him. Do you have to answer to him? His words are edged. She will not get a word in edge-ways or edge-wise.

The question that glowers darkly through the song is *Get it?* Men just don't get it. Or is she going to be the no-getter? From "You can get it together by then" in the first verse, through "Get it back on the track" in the next verse, arriving in the closing verses, first, at

> Did somebody tell you
> You could get it from me?

– and then at the final question, the one to which you would be well advised not to answer *Yes*: "Am I getting it wrong?" The right answer to that one is not far to seek. How prudent of Latin to build into the language a word of advice as to just where power lies when it comes to these questions: *num*, "introducing a direct question, usually expecting a negative answer". Now there's negative capability for you. Hey *nonne* no. Or rather yes: *nonne*, "in a direct question, *no?* (expecting an affirmative answer)".

Dylan's song *Señor* has its subtitle, or rather, side-title: (*Tales of Yankee Power*). (Those parentheses, those lunulae, or little moons, forecast the eclipse of power.) *Señor* is a song of religious politics, a judgement hymn. *What Was It You Wanted?* is a song of sexual politics, a judgement on him and on her (Señor and Señorita), and its side-title might be "Tales of Man Power". Or should that be "Tales of Woman Power"? For a silent interlocutor (she never does get to reply) is not necessarily the less powerful one. She may, on the contrary, be in the position of strength, holding her fire and letting him question himself out. Buttoned lips, like compressored lips, can emit great force and authority. Men are menacing, but perhaps here the man and the woman, though no love-match, are evenly matched. This, despite his having the first word, the last word, and every word along the way. And perhaps not *despite* but *exactly because he has . . .* He may have the word-power ("It pays to increase your word-power" is how the advertisement words it), but there is such a thing as wordless power, power that is audible in the very wordlessness of the person who is, let us say, among those who are interviewing you. Faced by his or her formidable silence, you want to exclaim, I've had just about enough of your buttoned lip.

The song proliferates its prosecutory questions, and yet it plays this against the disconcerting fact that, as so often in life, it may be not entirely clear whether something really *is* a question.

> What was it you wanted?
> Tell me again so I'll know
> What's happening in there
> What's going on in your show

Is this opening of the song a single-line question, followed by a three-line imperative? You can't tell from the run of the words whether "know" is a transitive or intransitive verb, and you can't tell from Dylan's voicing, either, for it doesn't let on. Perhaps it should go like this:

> What was it you wanted?
> Tell me again so I'll know
> What's happening in there?
> What's going on in your show?

But hang on a moment, it might be better to suspend the sense:

> What was it you wanted?
> Tell me again so I'll know
> What's happening in there
> What's going on in your show

And what would be the point of leaving it dubious, equivocal as to just what is being intimated? To bring out the fact that there is a borderline – between what is a question and what is not – that needs to be policed. *Who do you think you are?* Is that a question? Yes and no. It takes on itself the form or uniform of a question, but it has the function of an arresting accusation.

Dylan's "Who are you anyway?" has this same quasi-question potentiality, potential danger, actual power.

Questions of such a kind that it is in question whether they really are questions: these create a threat that can be felt throughout the song. Coercive, they can pretend to be concessive. (I was only asking.) "Could you say it again?": well, you know that I *could*, but are you genuinely asking me (*please?*) to say it again? "Would you remind me again" (remind me again, not just put me in mind of it again): not a question exactly, a pretence of a courtesy – and the more so because of the pressure (iron hand in velvet glove)[1] of the rhyming, with its silky lining:

> Whatever you wanted
> Slipped out of my mind
> Would you remind me again
> If you'd be so kind

There "my mind" is only too pleased to cooperate with (or is it collude with? or even conspire with?) "remind" – a dry-tongued witticism, since "remind" is "mind" again, with "again" at once following: "remind me again". And so (with these three rhymes working together like three merry boys, hand in glove with one another) on to "so kind", taking the line that can murmur, with a villain's courtesy that could almost be a curtsy, "If you'd be so kind".

The questions have the repetitiveness of yet another turn of the screw, yet another twist of the knife. The title is the opening line, "What was it you wanted?"; this figures twice in both the first verse and the second. Given a break for the next verse (torturers get tired), it comes back (remember "I'm back"?) in the third and fourth verses, though only once each. Back to its full double strength in the fifth verse (with two verses left to go), it is then not allowed to become boring – it is as a drill that it must bore, not as a dullard – so Dylan gives its repetition a new twist at the end of the next verse, the one but last verse: not

> What was it you wanted

returning identically six lines later:

[1] *When He Returns*: "The iron hand it ain't no match for the iron rod" – or for the velvet glove (which is not a matching glove).

What was it you wanted

– but

What was it you wanted

wrested to

Why do you want it

For the man in the song is well aware that repetition is the great penetrator. (You can say that again.) Things come back. "I'll be back in a minute" comes back as "I'm back", and then as "Get it back on the track", and finally as an arsy-versy question in the last verse, "Is the whole thing going backwards?" Ain't no going backwards from the last verse, which completes the execution of the song, the execution that is the song:

Is the scenery changin'?
Am I getting it wrong?
Is the whole thing going backwards?
Are they playing our song?
Where were you when it started?
Do you want it for free?
What was it you wanted?
Are you talking to me?

With every question something or someone is laid low. For this first time that will be the very last time, every singling-out one of the eight lines can be heard – no, must be heard – as a question. For the first time and last time, a verse doesn't start with something related to the two opening words, *What was*:

What was it you wanted?

What was it you wanted?

Was there somebody looking

Whatever you wanted

What was it you wanted?

Whatever you wanted

– and then, from inner space,

Is the scenery changin'?

Don't know about the scenery, but certainly the opening words of the scene are changing. The same goes for other things within this inexorable ending, for instance the rhyme *wrong/song*. It is the only unassisted or unsupported line-ending in the last stanza. For the other rhyme (*free/me*), the one that closes everything, picks itself up from *be/me* in the previous verse.[1] And "changing" is participial (as so much is, within this song that means to go on pounding and needling and nagging);[2] "backwards" picks up the earlier "back"; "started" the earlier "start"; and "wanted" the recurrent ending. So the pairing of "Am I getting it wrong?" with "Are they playing our song?" achieves a unique ache. It is not only the grim thought: "Are they playing our song?" – are you really asking that? For there is the sardonic acuteness of "our". This screed, careful not to be a screech, has been a *you and your/I and me and my* affair. True, it had averred, early on,

We can start it all over
Get it back on the track

But he is only saying that, and what in the end he comes to is this only other invoking of the two of them, seen in a harsh true light: "Are they playing our song?" This, in a song that "we" are hearing, has a moment of De Palma-type bemusement or comic horror. He is playing his song. They are playing his song. They are playing what, thanks to Dylan's creativity, is our song, too.

Exit, with the question that can be heard as not a question exactly (or rather, exactly not a question), although it would be perfectly civil if you

---

[1] The end of *Up to Me* has affinities with this: "And the harmonica around my neck, I blew it for you, free/No one else could play that tune/You know it was up to me". *What Was It You Wanted?* cannot bring itself to offer her the words of responsibility, *Up to You.*

[2] Six participles spread through the first six verses, and then there is the intensification of this insistence with five of them in this last verse.

could bring yourself to take it as sincerely and good-naturedly put: "Are you talking to me?" The question is laced. Is it ever *me*, really, you're talking to? Is it ever *talking*, really, as against verbal tics? Is it ever talking *to* me, really, as against at me?

What Was It You Wanted? is a study of the question as weapon, understanding such aggro ("Abbrev. of AGGR (AVATION or AGGR (ESSION + O"), understanding it and even perhaps forgiving it but aware of the malign form that can be taken by the question that does not ask for or even permit of an answer. Fortunately, there is such a thing as a good form of the self-answering question.

> you ask me questions
> an' i say that every question
> if it's a truthful question
> can be answered by askin' it
> (*Some Other Kinds of Songs*[1])

True, often enough, and truthful. The most famous question ever asked about truth, "What is truth?", came from Pontius Pilate, who notoriously did not stay for an answer. But his question has been recognized for centuries as miraculously containing within itself its answer. For *quid est veritas?* is an anagram of *est vir qui adest*: "It is the man who is here". Christ, one of the three persons of the Trinity, can speak of himself in the third person, creator of the miracle by which a meaning may lurk as a marvel for those who have eyes to see or who have ears to hear. Such, at least, is faith in the divine. Faith in the human is a smaller-minded business. The *catechism* that is *What Was It You Wanted?* has its bitter root in the ancient world: "to instruct orally, originally to resound, sound amiss, 'din one's ears'". Yet how insinuating such a din in one's ears can be, and how right on target, so direct, such sounding amiss. "Someone that I might have missed".

[1] *Lyrics 1962–1985*, p. 154.

Hope

One Too Many Mornings

After one too many maulings, what hopes are left in love? Not many. But not none. *One Too Many Mornings*, firmly declining to decline into flat despair, has a resilience, for all its sombre timbre. Yet what hope, exactly? This, at least: that in escaping one another, the sometime lovers may escape recriminations. That would be something, would offer some hope after all. Not as being reconciled each to each (too late for that), but as reconciled in some measure to the world, to everything that is (sadly) the case.

The situation within *One Too Many Mornings* is plainly hopeless. Plainly yet darkly, for the whys and wherefores, even the rights and wrongs, are responsibly kept private. There is to be no indulging in divulging. How it all came to this: no matter. Decorum is preserved, even though (or if only because) the love itself has proved beyond preservation. The rest of us are not party to (or privy to) what went wrong, there isn't even a hint. Once upon a time my love and I may perhaps have been hopelessly in love, but are now hopelessly out of love. Or out of the reach of love. Too far behind, in both space and time, whether measured in miles or in mornings. Irrecoverably.

One Too Many Mornings is a haunted haunting elegy, simply mysterious. It acknowledges that a transition must take place and may take time. The transitions within the song are then what constitute its unique union of the clear-as-day and the dark-as-night.

> Down the street the dogs are barkin'
> And the day is a-gettin' dark
> As the night comes in a-fallin'
> The dogs 'll lose their bark
> An' the silent night will shatter
> From the sounds inside my mind
> For I'm one too many mornings
> An' a thousand miles behind
>
> From the crossroads of my doorstep
> My eyes they start to fade

As I turn my head back to the room
Where my love and I have laid
An' I gaze back to the street
The sidewalk and the sign
And I'm one too many mornings
An' a thousand miles behind

It's a restless hungry feeling
That don't mean no one no good
When ev'rything I'm a-sayin'
You can say it just as good
You're right from your side
I'm right from mine
We're both just one too many mornings
An' a thousand miles behind

The deserted street has desertion in the air. *The Deserted Village* stayed with the author of *The Waste Land*:

In Goldsmith's poem, the art of transition is exemplified in perfection. If you examine it paragraph by paragraph, you will find always a shift just at the right moment, from the descriptive to the meditative, to the personal, to the meditative again, to the landscape with figures . . .[1]

One Too Many Mornings (a streetscape without figures) happens to have several of the same shifts. From the descriptive to the meditative to the personal: these are the transitions in its opening verse. A description of the immediate present, "Down the street the dogs are barkin'", is followed by a description of the present as it is getting to be the immediate future: "And the day is a-gettin' dark". (Not dark yet, but it's getting there.) Then comes a description-prediction of the next future:

As the night comes in a-fallin'
The dogs 'll lose their bark

Night doesn't do the usual and fall, it comes in (a tide of darkness), and the two phrasings shade into one another, "As the night comes in a-fallin'". "The dogs 'll lose their bark": this is clear to the ear and to the mind, and yet is not – if you think about it – the same as saying that the dogs 'll stop barking. Not a lost dog but a lost bark.

[1] T. S. Eliot, *Johnson as Critic and Poet* (1944); *On Poetry and Poets* (1957), p. 181.

At which moment, the shift (into another stage of the ensuing future) continues still from the descriptive to the meditative to the personal:

> An' the silent night will shatter
> From the sounds inside my mind
> For I'm one too many mornings
> An' a thousand miles behind

City lights: a city twilight of hope was later to drift into Dylan's mind:

That ethereal twilight light, you know. It's the sound of the streets with the sunrays, the sun shining down at a particular time on a particular type of building. A particular type of people walking on a particular type of street. It's an outdoor sound that drifts even into open windows that you can hear.[1]

But the street in *One Too Many Mornings* is without people, is darkened and saddened and late.

The art of transition (Eliot's phrase) may take more than one form, and *One Too Many Mornings* has – as *The Deserted Village* has not – movements or moves that intrigue or puzzle. Each line may be clear, but the line of thought? The song is a conjunction of many feelings, and of its parts of speech it is the small, modest ones such as conjunctions that are the necessary hinges. Sometimes the transition may sound, in the best possible way, slightly unhinged.

The articulated elusiveness that it is good to catch can be felt in a poem by Tennyson, this, too, being a song of lost love, lost, though, not by the death of love, but by the death of a loved one. *Break, break, break* is both a funeral elegy and a love elegy devoted to his friend Arthur Hallam, whom Tennyson believed he would for ever be a thousand miles behind – even in Heaven.[2]

---

[1] *Playboy* (March 1978).

[2] "But evermore a life behind", even in the afterlife. *In Memoriam* XLI:

> A spectral doubt which makes me cold,
> That I shall be thy mate no more,
>
> Though following with an upward mind
> The wonders that have come to thee,
> Through all the secular to-be,
> But evermore a life behind.

In Memoriam, VII, mourning this same lost love, has a few affinities with *One Too Many Mornings*, in the street, the dark, the door, and the morning. Probably coincidences only (though Dylan has mentioned Tennyson), but such analogues can remind us that great upward minds think alike.

Break, break, break opens to sounds from the outside world, and then it moves to the sounds inside my mind ("And the sound of a voice that is still!"), the thoughts that arise in me.

> Break, break, break,
>   On thy cold gray stones, O Sea!
> And I would that my tongue could utter
>   The thoughts that arise in me.
>
> O well for the fisherman's boy,
>   That he shouts with his sister at play!
> O well for the sailor lad,
>   That he sings in his boat on the bay!
>
> And the stately ships go on
>   To their haven under the hill;
> But O for the touch of a vanished hand,
>   And the sound of a voice that is still!
>
> Break, break, break,
>   At the foot of thy crags, O Sea!
> But the tender grace of a day that is dead
>   Will never come back to me.

In *Break, break, break* there is – as in *One Too Many Mornings* – a transparency that is matched with a puzzling obliqueness of reasoning or argument. In a sense, the poem's sense is plain enough; yet it has a riddling quality, too. For it escapes us, the thread of thought by which we are to swing across the gulf from the injunction "Break, break, break" to the "And" of "And I would that my tongue could utter"; from the fisherman's boy and the sailor lad and the stately ships to the "But" of "But O for the touch of a vanished hand"; or from the returning injunction "Break, break, break" to the ultimate "But" of the poignant close:

> But the tender grace of a day that is dead
>   Will never come back to me.

The poem's juxtapositions and conjunctions tantalizingly suggest a progression of thought that yet remains elusive. The heartbreak of which the poem knows (when the poem begins, we do not know what it is that is being urged to "Break, break, break": the heart is heard as a flickering suggestion) is not something of which it can bring itself openly to speak. The dissociative gulf between the outer scene and the inner pain is one that such sturdy words of reason as "And" and "But" can ultimately only pretend to bridge.[1] The same might be said of the scene and the pain in Dylan's song, and of his "An'" and "For":

> The dogs 'll lose their bark
> An' the silent night will shatter
> From the sounds inside my mind
> For I'm one too many mornings
> An' a thousand miles behind

The transition from the dogs' falling silent to the silent night is lastingly perplexing. The sound of the dogs is outdoors ("an outdoor sound", in the words of that vignette by Dylan) and outside the mind, yes. But why "And", as against "But"? And why "For", exactly? Why do the last two lines suppose (*do* they?) that they give the grounds for the previous two, the night lines?

It all has something of a dream's contrariety, a dream's secure unfounded air of reasoning. The vista of the street, with its doorstep, its room, its sidewalk, and its sign, feels dream-lit. Here, as elsewhere, the song (like a painting by Edward Hopper) is at once overt and covert, lucid and opaque. And so is the thought that variously brings each verse to an end, a rephrased refrain:

> For I'm one too many mornings
> An' a thousand miles behind

> And I'm one too many mornings
> An' a thousand miles behind

> We're both just one too many mornings
> An' a thousand miles behind

The Oxford English Dictionary, under *too* ("more than enough"), finds a grim

---

[1] I draw on my book *Tennyson* (second edition 1989), pp. 133–4.

pleasure in displaying all the sad variety of hell to which "too" is happy to minister (as *One Too Many Mornings* is only too aware): "Expressing, sorrowfully or indignantly, regret or disapproval: To a lamentable, reprehensible, painful, or intolerable extent." Moreover, the phrase "*one too many*", with its whitened knuckles and its clenched self-control (*one too many, but who's counting?*), is granted its own entry: "of something not wanted or of something that is repeated to excess".

It cannot be more than a coincidence (but gather from coincidence while ye may?) that the very first *Oxford English Dictionary* citation for *one too many* (it is from Shakespeare) should include, within an exchange of a mere four and a half lines, "down", "the street", "get" [gettin'], "came" [comes], "in", "from", "my", "door", "for", "whence" [where], "walk", "one", "when", and "one too many". Is this, on second thoughts, one too many to be coincidental?

> "Either get thee from the door, or sit down at the hatch.
> Dost thou conjure for wenches, that thou callst for such store,
> When one is one too many? Go, get thee from the door."
> "What patch is made our porter? My master stays in the street."
> "Let him walk from whence he came."
>
> (*The Comedy of Errors*, III, i)

Dylan's tragedy of errors feels nothing remotely like that. Far from conjuring for wenches, the song is abjuring one.

As to being *behind* ("in the rear of anything moving", quoting Dryden, "to lag behind, with truant pace"), this, too, has its own doubling up, for there is a twinge of the other sense, "in reference to the fulfilment of an obligation, *esp.* of paying money due: in arrear". Each of the lovers is behind with the debt of love. The first citation in *The Oxford English Dictionary* for such a sense (the fulfilment of an obligation) happens to be this from a sermon by Wyclif: "So many men in this world ben [be] behind of debt of love."

It may be remembered that Arthur Hallam, to whom Tennyson paid his debt of love in *Break, break, break*, wrote that "Rhyme has been said to contain in itself a constant appeal to Memory and Hope."[1] Hope is abandoned in *One Too Many Mornings*, a song that may be thought to contain in itself a memory of an Australian ballad beginning:

---

[1] See p. 38 on rhyme.

Oh hark the dogs are barking, love,
I can no longer stay.
The men are all gone mustering
And it is nearly day.
And I must off by the morning light
Before the sun doth shine,
To meet the Sydney shearers
On the banks of the Condamine.[1]

It is not only "hark the dogs are barking" and "morning" that suggest Dylan (or that may have suggested something to Dylan), it is the line-ending on -*ing* ("mustering") as well as the strong assonance in *light / shine / Condamine*, an assonance that might be in mind and behind Dylan's *mind / behind*, *sign / behind*, *side / mine / behind*. These, and the thought uttered to his love, a thought more sombre in Dylan, "I can no longer stay".

Dylan's rhyme-scheme is on the face of it both simple and minimal. As in the Australian ballad, the second and fourth lines rhyme, and then, differently, the sixth and eighth. So the first verse proffers *dark / bark* and *mind / behind*. But there are immediate cross-currents, soundwaves:

Down the street the dogs are barkin'
And the day is a-gettin' dark
As the night comes in a-fallin'
The dogs 'll lose their bark
An' the silent night will shatter
From the sounds inside my mind
For I'm one too many mornings
An' a thousand miles behind

For "barkin'" offers something of a rhyme to the next line's "dark", and the -*in'* ending both to this first line and to the third line ("a-fallin'") will not only send an echo down the street of rhyming but will continue half heard in "one too many mornings". So that of the eight line-endings in this first verse, the only one that offers nothing of a rhyme is the fifth: "An' the silent night will shatter".

[1] To be found, for instance, in *The Faber Book of Ballads*, ed. Matthew Hodgart (1965).

> An' the silent night will shatter
> From the sounds inside my mind

Praising "shatter" there as "an interesting example of poetic transference", Michael Gray said: "The prose equivalent, stripped of this transference, would be that the silence (of the night) will be shattered; as Dylan has it, the night will shatter."[1] Gray is right to think that Dylan's phrasing turns upon the commonplace that the silence of the night will be shattered. But what is so well judged in "shatter" is not anything about "poetic transference" (prejudicial and nebulous, any such differentiation of poetry from prose), but that Dylan is seizing from the inside a standard oddity about the verb "shatter": that it can equally and equably mean both "to dash into fragments" and "to be dashed into fragments". The same is true of "break", and of a verb in the next verse, "fade", which would elsewhere be perfectly content to mean either "to lose colour or strength" or "to cause to lose colour or strength".

Hopes shatter. They both break things (hearts, for instance) and are broken. "And the silent night will shatter": the line gets trenchancy from the two-edged "shatter", but it gains its unobtrusive force, which is to be dramatic without being melodramatic, from Dylan's decision simply to have it be the sole unrhyming line.

I want to pass over for a while the second verse (which puzzles me, or has me puzzled as to my own responses), and to feel through the third, the final verse, where there are further turns of the thumbscrew, rhyme-wise.

> It's a restless hungry feeling
> That don't mean no one no good
> When ev'rything I'm a-sayin'
> You can say it just as good
> You're right from your side
> I'm right from mine
> We're both just one too many mornings
> An' a thousand miles behind

The closing rhyme of this final verse, as of the second verse (*sign / behind*), is assonance more than rhyme, *mine / behind*, but this is tightened by the urgencies and exigencies of the assonantal accessaries before the fact:

---

[1] *Song and Dance Man III* (2000), p. 128.

> You're *right* from your *side*
> *I'm right* from *mine*

Oh, this concedes a good deal (unlike the good old condescension of "We are all doing God's work, you in your way, and we in His"), but the fivefold assonance (*right / side / I'm / right / mine*) has its obduracy, with just two chimes in the line that is yours, but with one more (one too many?), three, in the line that just happens to be mine. At least there is an effort at fair play, at landscaping the playing-field (you know, the level one) that is so often invoked these days.[1] At least the effect is not what it would have been, far more one-sidedly, if the lines had gone like this:

> I'm right from my side
> You're right from yours

– where instead of being assonantally three of mine to two of yours, it would have been four to one.

At the start of this last verse it had been its first entire rhyme that created the dead sound, the dead accurate sound, that tolled finality:

> It's a restless hungry feeling
> That don't mean no one no good
> When ev'rything I'm a-sayin'
> You can say it just as good

No good / as good: it feels and is as good as nothing. A rhyme to nullify a state of affairs or a marriage, it is blankness itself.

In *The Lotos-Eaters*, Tennyson's first rhyme was likewise no rhyme at all, offering not the combination of likeness with unlikeness that is a rhyme but an "always" that is eternally the same:

> "Courage!" he said, and pointed toward the land,
> "This mounting wave will roll us shoreward soon."
> In the afternoon they came unto a land
> In which it seemèd always afternoon.

[1] At King Alfred's School, Wantage, in my days (1942–1951), there were hardly any level playing-fields, but we knew that we would be changing ends at half-time. Not to worry. To take into account, though.

Or, One Too Many Afternoons. In the afternoon . . . it seemèd always afternoon: this, from start to finish, or rather, with no way of telling start from finish. Tennyson himself commented on the effect when a "land" comes unto a "land": "'The strand' was, I think, my first reading, but the no rhyme of 'land' and 'land' was lazier."[1] Lazier as being in static sympathy with those who are soon to enjoy the fixity of the drug that is the lotos; for the poet, less lazy than the first-draft rhyme, *strand / land*. It is an apt effect, stagnant the while.

Stagnation is the consequence when the best that "no good" can do turns out to be "as good":

> It's a restless hungry feeling
> That don't mean no one no good
> When ev'rything I'm a-sayin'
> You can say it just as good

This is paralysis. You might think that nothing could be a more perfect rhyme, a more full rhyme, than rhyming a word with itself – but then nothing could be less of a rhyme, either, since there is no plurality, simply a single impasse, no chance to advance. We have the term *rime riche* when rhyme-words sound the same but have a different sense: say, glasses against glasses, with the one being spectacles and the other to drink from. Or the word "well" in *Subterranean Homesick Blues*, where Dylan rhymes "get well" with or against "ink well". An odd kind of rhyme, this, yet with its own nature. But the rhyme-word coming up against the same word in obdurately the same sense? This is not a rich rhyme, but a stricken one in its poverty of spirit, a rhyme that is no good except as conveying that all this is no good. One too many mornings but one too few rhyme-words.

A rhyme can be seen under the aspect of a kiss. Keats has in *Isabella* an exquisite pair of lines, incorporating a rhyme upon "rhyme" that takes up the preceding word "time":

> "And I must taste the blossoms that unfold
>   In its ripe warmth this gracious morning time."
> So said, his erewhile timid lips grew bold,
>   And poesied with hers in dewy rhyme.

[1] *The Poems of Tennyson*, ed. Christopher Ricks (1987), vol. I, p. 468.

But "good" against "good"? Or, worse, "no good" against "as good"? This is like kissing yourself in the mirror, full on the lips, the only place you can kiss yourself in the mirror, and yet somehow not as satisfying as one had hoped, don't you find?

It's a restless hungry feeling, all right, or not at all all right. But one of the things that saves these lines of Dylan from the comforts of despair is their burly refusal to get grammar, to turn King's English evidence, to run any risk of sounding like a prissy sissy. Try this:

> It's a restless hungry feeling
> That means no one any good

– not good. For the song is positively right to feel so negatively about what has come to pass. "That don't mean no one no good": this isn't a double negative, it's a triple whammy. It is true that there are days when "negativity don't pull you through" (*Just Like Tom Thumb's Blues*). But there are mornings when it just might.

Or try this:

> It's a restless hungry feeling
> That's such a living hell
> When ev'rything I'm a-sayin'
> You can say it just as well

– less well said than "You can say it just as good", no? In the particular circumstances, be it said. "A particular type of people walking on a particular type of street".

It is true that those of us who founded the Society for the Protection of Parts of Speech feel very strongly about this particular endangered species, the adverb. But just as Nope does not mean the same as No, so "You can say it just as good" does not mean the same as "You can say it just as well". I still remember the thrill that ran through me in the fifties (I was in my twenties) when I heard that an American poet at Oxford, Donald Hall, fully five years my senior, had said of poetry that "You gotta fake it but you gotta fake it good". True, the well-educated young Don was kinda faking it, but he knew who he was talking to (to whom he was talking?): even-younger Englishmen and Englishwomen who would all but swoon at the uncowed manliness that knew better than to say "fake it well" when it was so much more democratic, so much less truckling, to say "fake it good". Agreed, there is truckling and truckling. For an artist to unload his head, he needs *not* to truckle. Which is why "You can say it just as good" succeeds in splicing two things to say: You can say it just as well / You can say something just as good.

> When ev'rything I'm a-sayin'
> You can say it just as good

This is the moment in the song, late in the song, when there arrives a real *you* at last, someone addressed, not respectably dressed as in the "my love and I" of the middle verse. *Just as good*: the word "just", with its low-key cold charity, comes twice in this last verse, and just in this verse.

> We're both just one too many mornings
> An' a thousand miles behind

We're both just hopeless. We're both a great way behind, and so neither of us has fallen behind the other – which is how it had sounded when it was just a matter of saying

> And I'm one too many mornings
> An' a thousand miles behind

The first verse of *One Too Many Mornings* had left unrhymed a single line. The hopes in the mind of the last verse are even more shattered. There is an appeal to Hope that is launched by rhyme and assonance, but it falls on deaf ears: *no good / as good, side / mine / behind, feeling / a-sayin' / mornings.* That all eight lines, not just the founding four, are held together: this might have been heartening. But not here. Held together: here it feels like a vice, thanks (no thanks) to the metal plates aligned as *no good / as good*.

Which leaves the verse that I left behind, the middle verse.

> From the crossroads of my doorstep
> My eyes they start to fade
> As I turn my head back to the room
> Where my love and I have laid
> An' I gaze back to the street

> The sidewalk and the sign
> And I'm one too many mornings
> An' a thousand miles behind

I have vacillated about this verse, and still do. In the days when I was brief and stern, the principle invoked was the one so imaginatively marked by Gerard M. Hopkins:

Great men, poets I mean, have each their own dialect as it were of Parnassian, formed generally as they go on writing, and at last, – this is the point to be marked, – they can see things in this Parnassian way and describe them in this Parnassian tongue, without further effort of inspiration. In a poet's particular kind of Parnassian lies most of his style, of his manner, of his mannerism if you like . . . Now it is a mark of Parnassian that one could conceive oneself writing it if one were the poet. Do not say that *if* you were Shakespeare you can conceive yourself writing Hamlet, because that is just what I think you can*not* conceive.[1]

Hopkins's principle is itself an inspiration,[2] and I hold to it. But I have become more than uneasy about holding it to this particular moment in *One Too Many Mornings*. Not that it would be possible for Dylan to have escaped Parnassian – one of the best things about the way in which Hopkins puts his point is his understanding of the naturalness, the inevitability, the commonalty of it all ("Great men, poets I mean", all of them), along with the sincere admiration that the poetry of Tennyson excited in him. *Enoch Arden*, published the previous month in 1864, was what prompted Hopkins in this letter of his.

[1] 10 September 1864, to A. W. M. Baillie; *Further Letters of Gerard Manley Hopkins*, ed. C. C. Abbott (1956 edition), pp. 215–19.
[2] Dylan's report of what it is like to fall short of inspiration is attached to *Caribbean Wind* (which was previously unreleased) on *Biograph*:

"That one I couldn't quite grasp what it was about after I finished it," said Dylan. "Some times you'll write something to be very inspired, and you won't quite finish it for one reason or another. Then you'll go back and try and pick it up, and the inspiration is just gone. Either you get it all, and you can leave a few little pieces to fill in, or you're trying always to finish it off. Then it's a struggle. The inspiration's gone and you can't remember why you started it in the first place. Frustration sets in. I think there's four different sets of lyrics to this, maybe I got it right, I don't know. I had to leave it. I just dropped it. Sometimes that happens."

I think one had got into the way of thinking, or had not got out of the way of thinking, that Tennyson was always new, *touching* beyond other poets, not pressed with human ailments, never using Parnassian. So at least I used to think. Now one sees he uses Parnassian; he is, one must see it, what we used to call Tennysonian. But the discovery of this must not make too much difference. When puzzled by one's doubts it is well to turn to a passage like this. Surely your maturest judgment will never be fooled out of saying that this is divine, terribly beautiful – the stanza of *In Memoriam* beginning with the quatrain

> O Hesper o'er the buried sun,
>   And ready thou to die with him,
>   Thou watchest all things ever dim
> And dimmer, and a glory done.

I think one had got into the way of thinking, or had not got out of the way of thinking, that Dylan was always new, touching beyond other poets. Now one sees he uses Parnassian. But the discovery of this must not make too much difference. When puzzled by one's doubts it is well to turn to a passage like this. Surely your maturest judgement will never be fooled out of saying that this is beautiful:

> Down the street the dogs are barkin'
> And the day is a-gettin' dark
> As the night comes in a-fallin'
> The dogs 'll lose their bark

But as to my judgement that the second verse of *One Too Many Mornings* is Parnassian: I am no longer sure that I was right, even from my side.

> From the crossroads of my doorstep
> My eyes they start to fade

This, unlike the first and last verses which are inspired, is Parnassian, and – like most Parnassian – it is, in its complaisance, vulnerable to humour, such a worse than unwanted suggestion as "From the crossroads of my doorstep / My eyes they start to cross". I can conceive myself writing "the crossroads of my doorstep" if I were Dylan – and I do not say to myself that if I were Dylan I can imagine myself writing the inspired no-rhyme of "good" and "good" in the song's last stanza . . . This, in its pained numbness, is something quite other than "From the crossroads of my doorstep", which I can conceive myself writing if I were the artist who wrote, elsewhere, "through the smoke rings of my mind". Do not say that *if* you were Shakespeare you can imagine yourself writing *Hamlet*; come to that, do not say that *if* you were Dylan you can imagine yourself writing "Ophelia, she's 'neath the window, / For her I feel so afraid".[1]

It used to go like that. Now it goes like this, or might go on like this.

Just a minute, you're using the phrase "through the smoke rings of my mind" as a smokescreen. It is really nothing like "From the crossroads of my doorstep". The line from *Mr. Tambourine Man* (or rather, half-line) floats free, and knows it: "Then take me disappearin' through the smoke rings of my mind". It is up and away. The line – full line, this one – from *One Too Many Mornings* is quite a different story, and it tells a different story. For one thing, it is two things.

"The smoke rings of my mind" is a figure of speech that makes amiable relaxed sense by an airy movement of mind. (The impassive smoking might have been a vaporous lounging in a brown study.) The figure is evanescent, a bright exhalation. The prepositional movement ("of my mind") conjures up a settled inwardness altogether different from "the sounds inside my mind" that mount the untoward pressure within *One Too Many Mornings*. By contrast with those drifting smoke rings, the line "From the crossroads of my doorstep" is not airy at all. It is a stumbling block, blocked and blockish, scowling as though set to thwart any attempt to make sense, relaxed or otherwise. A doorstep, yes, and a crossroads, yes, especially in the figurative application that *The Oxford English Dictionary* defines as "a point at which two or more courses of action diverge; a critical turning-point". But "the crossroads of my doorstep"? Can a doorstep be a crossroads?

Yes it can, when you put your mind (that smoke-free zone) to it, given the dictionary's "a critical turning-point".

> As I turn my head back to the room
> Where my love and I have laid

You can set off from the doorstep to left, or to right, or straight ahead. From the T-junction of my doorstep? But don't forget the fourth dimension, for there may be nothing to stop you from turning not only your head but your

[1] *Literary principles as against theory* (1985); *Essays in Appreciation* (1996), pp. 330–31.

whole self back to the room where your love and you have laid (or lain, if you prefer) – and where perhaps she lies still wondering whether you will come back. The word "back" comes back again in two lines' time, its simple longing unappeased:

> From the crossroads of my doorstep
> My eyes they start to fade
> As I turn my head back to the room
> Where my love and I have laid
> An' I gaze back to the street
> The sidewalk and the sign
> And I'm one too many mornings
> An' a thousand miles behind

Just how unpredictable, how free from Parnassian mannerism, is the line "From the crossroads of my doorstep" may be seen from a differently pained Dylan song that brings together the crossroads and my mind, *Mama, You Been on My Mind*:

> Perhaps it's the color of the sun cut flat
> An' cov'rin' the crossroads I'm standing at
> Or maybe it's the weather or something like that
> But mama, you been on my mind

No risk of stumbling at those crossroads, straightforward even if the decision may now have to be to go other than straight forward. The impassive calm of mind in "the crossroads I'm standing at" is completely different from the impasse "From the crossroads of my doorstep".

> From the crossroads of my doorstep
> My eyes they start to fade

Light fades, and has been felt to do so at the start of the song. Memories will fade, not only precious memories but bankrupt ones too – this being a hope glimpsed off the end of the song. "My eyes they start to fade". Though a sight may fade from one's eyes, one doesn't usually think of eyes as fading, but there is a sad scene in Keats ("As when, upon a trancèd summer-night . . .") that arrives at a glimpse of something divine, terribly beautiful:

> Until at length old Saturn lifted up
> His faded eyes, and saw his kingdom gone,
> And all the gloom and sorrow of the place
> > (*Hyperion*, I, 89–91)

One aspect of the gloom and sorrow of *One Too Many Mornings* is the
self-saturation of this middle verse. The crux is this: that whereas the first
verse speaks only twice in such terms ("my", "I'm"), and the final verse
three times ("I'm", "I'm", "mine"), this middle verse eight times fixes its
I's upon itself: "my doorstep", "My eyes", "I", "my head", "my love",
"I", "I", "I'm".

Is this a self-absorption succumbed to by the song? So I used to think (or
feel). But why should it not be a succumbing that is dramatized, "placed",
within the song?[1] The lapse would then be not a lapse by the song but one
within the song's setting, a sinking into self, moreover, that recovers its better
self as the song moves on. One hesitates to say *move on* these days, so often
have the words been glibbed. But the voice, the consciousness within the
song, does move its attention, so as to do right not only by the word "I"
but by "you" and "we":

> You're right from your side
> I'm right from mine
> We're both just one too many mornings
> An' a thousand miles behind

If I am right in having come to believe that in due course *One Too Many
Mornings* rescinds the state of mind that dominated the middle verse, then
I need to rescind my adverse judgement on what I took to be a lack of
judgement. The same may go for my having taken against the interplay of
"crossroads" and "my eyes":

> From the crossroads of my doorstep
> My eyes they start to fade

My eyes they start to cross? I still see the sequence as inviting this
grotesque squinny, but does this disconcerting glimpse of crossed eyes

---

[1] This critical term, to *place* (to set within a context that makes such judgements possible),
is from Henry James, himself a master of love-lorn streetscapes and of the sadly human
propensity to self-absorption.

have to be a "worse than unwanted suggestion"? Couldn't it be an insight at a tangent? For what is so hoped for is a brave gaze at their plight, but this falters:

> An' I gaze back to the street
> The sidewalk and the sign
> And I'm one too many mornings
> An' a thousand miles behind

Things are crossed, thwarted, must be seen simultaneously from two angles, two sides (your side and mine). His head is on straight, but in the circumstances he can't always see straight. He may be forced to squint. Of love, it was said long ago that it is a mistake to draw Cupid as a blind boy, "for his real character is a little thief that squints".[1]

And it looks as though I may have been squinting at (glancing at with dislike or disapproval)[2] the rhyming in the middle verse. Just as this verse is different from the others in the matter of "I", so it is in its rhyming. My restless hungry feeling went like this: something slips out of Dylan's hands here, instead of escaping from his lips. The rhyme-scheme is no more than the rhyme-skeleton, *fade / laid*, *sign / behind*. Unimaginative: "fade" against "laid" has nothing wrong with it, but nothing particularly right, either, and the other words at the line-endings, setting aside the refrain (with which the others have no contact, whereas in the first and third verses there are tendrils twining from the refrain), are nothing more than the topography of the song: *doorstep / room / street*. Painfully faithful, perhaps, but sadly flat.

But what if the painful, the faithful, the sad and the flat, are the truth that is levelled? The lines, then, would be an evocation of a flattened emotional world, in which an "I" does this and does that and does the other, all as though mechanically, ineffectually, and affectlessly.

> From the crossroads of my doorstep
> My eyes they start to fade
> As I turn my head back to the room
> Where my love and I have laid
> An' I gaze back to the street

---

[1] Richard Steele, *The Tatler*, No. 5 (1709).
[2] *OED*, 2c.

> The sidewalk and the sign
> And I'm one too many mornings
> An' a thousand miles behind

That there is at the line-endings *no* "constant appeal to Memory and Hope", only the flattened hopelessness of the locations, *doorstep / room / street*: such is one of the uses of adversity. Adversity is not simply triumphed over in the final verse, not put in its place. But it is placed, and held in place:

> You're right from your side
> I'm right from mine
> We're both just one too many mornings
> An' a thousand miles behind

I am not the only one, and you are not the only one. Come to that, we are not the only ones. For this song of memory rings a bell with thousands.

Moonlight

Never send to know for whom the bell tolls. "For whom does the bell toll for, love? It tolls for you and me". It is a mercy that, long after *One Too Many Mornings*, there proves to be a world elsewhere, in which *Moonlight* is attuned in love to an air so light.

"Won't you meet me out in the moonlight alone?"

One answer to this pleaful refrain, especially once its plea has been entered six times, might be a counter-question: Are you, for your part, ever going to refrain? How long are you going to go on asking me this? Hope springs eternal in the human breast, yes, but songs, or lovers' wishful wistfulnesses, do not have all the eternity in the world.

A nineteenth-century song along the same lines, by Joseph Augustine Wade, gained an entry in *The Oxford Dictionary of Quotations*: *Meet me by moonlight, alone.* But this reiterated request was cast as an enjoining, not as a question.

How much longer? Dylan has always been fascinated with the question of how you may intimate that something is, or soon will be, all over, or how you bring something to an end: a song or a song-book, an interview or an album, a concert or the first half of a concert or even the pretend-conclusion of a concert, when a staged pause (for a wile), a finale known to be unfinal, is calculated to prompt our imploring an encore, beseeching "bis bis!"

There is a moment near the beginning of the unapologetically extensive film *Renaldo and Clara* when the man on the radio warns drivers about the wet road: "Hydroplaning can seriously impair your stopping-ability." At which moment, something unseriously impairs the music in the background. Dylan has always been on the *qui vive* when it comes to stopping-ability. Ninety miles an hour (down a dead end street). Brake, brake, brake.

How long can you go on saying the same thing? Say, assuring some-one:

> All I really want to do
> Is, baby, be friends with you

You can issue this assurance a few times, but there's a point at which it wears out or thin. How long can you go on urging, "Don't think twice, it's all right"? More than twice, agreed, but seventy-times-seven? Or there is pretending to urge:

> But if you gotta go, go now
> Or else you gotta stay all night

How much longer, the shuddering in *Desolation Row*. The needling, in *Ballad of a Thin Man*. The exulting, in *Like a Rolling Stone*. The steeling, in *Positively 4th Street*. The consoling, in *To Ramona*. The shaking the dust off – off of – your feet (don't look back), in *My Back Pages*. The jeering, in *Down in the Flood*. The prosecuting, in *Hurricane*. The avenging, in *Can You Please Crawl Out Your Window?* The begging: "Please, Missus Henry, Missus Henry, please! / I'm down on my knees". (Till you have calluses?) The quidding pro quo, in *Cry A While*: "Well, I cried for you, now it's your turn, you can cry awhile". Or the nagging about being nagged, in *Rainy Day Women # 12 & 35*.

"I keep asking myself how long it can go on like this" (*Million Miles*). "And I don't know how much longer I can wait" (*Can't Wait*).

Then there is *Silvio*, up and away, "I gotta go" – but just hear how reluctant the song is to end, repeating over and over again that it's gotta go, a tearaway song that just can't tear itself away. "Looks like tomorrow is a-comin' on fast" – brisk, at risk. "One of these days and it won't be long".

Days aren't. And the last prophecy before the last chorus? "Going down to the valley and sing my song". And? "Let the echo decide if I was right or wrong". Just like that, right or wrong. Listen to the difference between the last lines of *Silvio* and those of *Ring Them Bells*:

> Oh the lines are long
> And the fighting is strong
> And they're breaking down the distance
> Between right and wrong

Breaking down the distance, not (as you might have expected) the *difference* between right and wrong. This makes all the difference in the world and in the other world. Observe the distance that Dylan puts here, in the singing, between right and wrong, by his clasping his breath for part of a second, a second that is split between the two words.

There are some words of his that don't get printed in the lyrics, when the women in *New Pony* sing in chorus, many a time, "How much longer?" This may be mostly a question about how much longer you will be satisfied with your new pony-woman and not have to shoot her to put her out of her misery so that you can get some other new pony, but soon the words do come to mean, as well, how much longer is the song itself going to go on.

"Won't you meet me out in the moonlight alone?"

Either she will accede, or the moon will set and in due course the day will dawn, truth then dawning.

MOONLIGHT

The seasons they are turnin' and my sad heart is yearnin'
To hear again the songbird's sweet melodious tone
Won't you meet me out in the moonlight alone?

The dusky light, the day is losing, orchids, poppies, black-eyed Susan
The earth and sky that melts with flesh and bone
Won't you meet me out in the moonlight alone?

The air is thick and heavy all along the levee
Where the geese into the countryside have flown
Won't you meet me out in the moonlight alone?

Well, I'm preachin' peace and harmony
The blessings of tranquility
Yet I know when the time is right to strike
I'll take you 'cross the river dear
You've no need to linger here
I know the kinds of things you like

The clouds are turnin' crimson – the leaves fall from the limbs an'
The branches cast their shadows over stone
Won't you meet me out in the moonlight alone?

The boulevards of cypress trees, the masquerade of birds and bees
The petals, pink and white, the wind has blown
Won't you meet me out in the moonlight alone?

The trailing moss and mystic glow
The purple blossoms soft as snow
My tears keep flowing to the sea
Doctor, lawyer, Indian chief
It takes a thief to catch a thief
For whom does the bell toll for, love? It tolls for you and me

My pulse is runnin' through my palm – the sharp hills are rising from
The yellow fields with twisted oaks that groan
Won't you meet me out in the moonlight alone?

There can be no doubting the melodious buoyancy of *Moonlight*, but how is it that this buoyancy comes out to play? For the song, on the face of it, makes much of things that suggest, as against levity, gravity. A groan, and tears, and a funeral bell, for a start. But then the song achieves its sense of relief and release by incorporating within itself reminders of all those things in life that cast shadows, those weights that make us seek relief and release in the first place and in the last place. *Moonlight* achieves light-heartedness not in spite of but because of the many intimations of mortality, of sadness and loss, that it touches upon or that touch it.

The opening words may be, in their manner and movement, altogether unafflicted, but they do speak – with whatever stylization – of affliction. "The seasons they are turnin' and my sad heart is yearnin'". True, the yearning – as soon as Dylan turns the corner of the line – turns out not to be the deepest kind of heartache (not actually, or not yet, yearning to meet *you*, my dear):

> The seasons they are turnin' and my sad heart is yearnin'
> To hear again the songbird's sweet melodious tone

– for it is the songbird, the cooperative little competitor, for whom my heart is yearning and whose tone I want to hear and to emulate. But anyway, there is an endearing continuity, in the melodious slide from "sweet" to "meet", of the one hope into the other:

> To hear again the songbird's sweet melodious tone
> Won't you meet me out in the moonlight alone?

But you won't BE *alone* if I meet you. True, but you know what I mean, and one of the things that I most mean is that "alone" is at its best when it means just you and me.[1] Added to which, there is the comic effect of a refrain that keeps on ending with a rhyme on the word "alone". Which cannot leave it alone.

What happens is that a loss is spoken of, while exactly not being felt, even as an apocalyptic vision is then spoken of, but exactly not felt. We are being relieved of these.

> The dusky light, the day is losing, orchids, poppies, black-eyed Susan
> The earth and sky that melts with flesh and bone
> Won't you meet me out in the moonlight alone?

Simple yet cryptic wording, "the day is losing": does it mean *the dusky light [that] the day is losing*? This would be a retrospective touch. Or is the word-order prospective? *The day is losing [sight of] the orchids, poppies, black-eyed Susan.*[2] Or is the thought more final than that, destined for the melting of earth and sky?[3] *The day is losing*: losing the fight; losing, *period*.

What the song seizes is the indispensable truth that a light-hearted song will end up being light to the point of weightlessness or emptiness unless

[1] *One More Weekend*: "We'll go someplace unknown / Leave all the children home / Honey, why not go alone / Just you and me".

[2] Keats, *Ode to a Nightingale* (songbird par excellence): "I cannot see what flowers are at my feet, / Nor what soft incense hangs upon the boughs, / But in embalmèd darkness, guess each sweet / Wherewith the seasonable month endows / The grass".

[3] Amos 9:5: "And the Lord God of hosts is he that toucheth the land, and it shall melt." 2 Peter 3:10: "But the day of the Lord will come as a thief in the night; in the which the heavens shall pass away with a great noise, and the elements shall melt with fervent heat, the earth also."

it calls to mind – but in such a way as not to call mournfully to heart –
the dark heavy aspects of life. "Black-eyed", as the dictionary knows, is
amenable to romantic feelings, but not to those feelings alone. So although
it would be morbid to yield to the thought of a bruise in the black-eyed
Susan, or to wince from the knowledge that a black-eyed Susan is slang
for a revolver,[1] we shouldn't avert our eyes, whether black or blue or
brown, from the presence throughout the song of these darker possibilities,
possibilities that are certainly not meant to be actualized into painful realities
but are not meant to be naively inconceivable, either; are meant, rather, to
be glimpsed as everything that the song so blessedly floats free of.

Floats free of, or ushers us free of. It had been in *I Shall Be Free* that
Dylan first played with and worked with the rhyme *heavy / levee*:

> Oh, there ain't no use in me workin' so heavy
> I got a woman who works on the levee

What raises a smile is the way in which "levee", of all words, gravitates to
the heavy, instead of levitating.

> The air is thick and heavy all along the levee
> Where the geese into the countryside have flown
> Won't you meet me out in the moonlight alone?

The air is thick and heavy? Not this musical air. It flies, lighter than those
geese, even – as light as goose feathers. And yet this very effect depends
upon the light-hearted feeling that issues from the thought of the thick and
heavy having been raised only to be dissolved, solved.

It is the bridge of the song that is then, naturally, the perfect place for
the assurance "I'll take you 'cross the river dear".

> Well, I'm preachin' peace and harmony
> The blessings of tranquility

– and, rest assured, I practise what I'm preaching. But peace and harmony
and blessings and tranquillity are meaningless in the absence, not so much of

[1] *OED*, 2b: *U.S. slang* with American English (1869), "Among names of revolvers I
remember . . . Black-eyed Susan", and *Americanisms* (1888), "Texan for a revolver".

war and cacophony and curses and rage in themselves, as of any conceiving even of such ugly realities. Which is why those two reassuring lines about peace and tranquillity are immediately succeeded by a kindly thought that would need only the slightest turn to become threatening:

> Well, I'm preachin' peace and harmony
> The blessings of tranquility
> Yet I know when the time is right to strike

We feel no danger from that last line, but then that's what's so sweetly secure about it. The tone is right to strike. Likewise, there is melting and melting: that of earth and sky in the day of the Lord, as against that of music-making in our day or in the good old days – as when Herrick played melodiously *Upon Julia's Voice*:

> So smooth, so sweet, so silv'ry is thy voice . . .
> Melting melodious words, to lutes of amber.

To hear again his songbird's sweet melodious tone.

What befalls is happily casual, a casualness without fear of casualty. The rhyme is free to fall where it feels like.

> The clouds are turnin' crimson – the leaves fall from the limbs an'
> The branches cast their shadows over stone
> Won't you meet me out in the moonlight alone?

How relaxed, *crimson / limbs an'*. And how relaxing, this confidence that the phrase "cast their shadows" won't cast any shadow over the scene, and that "cast" won't fix things with "stone" to harden the heart as though it's all cast in stone.

> The boulevards of cypress trees, the masquerade of birds and bees
> The petals, pink and white, the wind has blown
> Won't you meet me out in the moonlight alone?

It is an exclamatory scene of delight, and the more delightful because cypress is usually associated not with gaiety but with funerals, with mourning.[1]

---

[1] And, elsewhere in Dylan, with seasonal change that is sadder than in *Moonlight* (where "The seasons they are turnin'"). *Idiot Wind*: "I waited for you on the running boards, near the cypress trees, while the springtime turned / Slowly into autumn".

Wordsworth steered clear of the cypress when he wanted a heartening scene (with many of the same properties: the birds, the trees, the wind and water, the moon and all). But Wordsworth's settling so securely into the scene then conveys less of authentic freedom because his lines have only a narrowly social sense of what such a night is freed from:

> The sun has long been set,
>   The stars are out by twos and threes,
> The little birds are piping yet
>   Among the bushes and trees;
> There's a cuckoo, and one or two thrushes,
> And a far-off wind that rushes,
> And a sound of water that gushes,
> And the cuckoo's sovereign cry
> Fills all the hollow of the sky.
>   Who would go "parading"
> In London, and "masquerading",
> On such a night of June
> With that beautiful half-moon,
> And all these innocent blisses?
> On such a night as this is!

On a night like this . . .

The bliss in *Moonlight*, with its anticipated further bliss (do meet me on this), is never shattered but it is suddenly pierced with the entirely unexpected welling of tears:

> The trailing moss and mystic glow
> The purple blossoms soft as snow
> My tears keep flowing to the sea
> Doctor, lawyer, Indian chief
> It takes a thief to catch a thief
> For whom does the bell toll for, love? It tolls for you and me

Suddenly, from nowhere, "My tears . . .". They are flowing to the sea, but where are they flowing *from*? They don't sound like tears of joy; rather, as if they might be mildly luxuriating in their love-lorn grief. Inexplicable. In Tennyson's terms:

> Tears, idle tears, I know not what they mean,
> Tears from the depth of some divine despair
> Rise in the heart, and gather to the eyes,
> In looking on the happy Autumn-fields,
> And thinking of the days that are no more.

Tennyson's poem – which is moved to puzzle its head and its heart, "So sad, so fresh", "Ah, sad and strange" – evokes a consciousness that loves to stay with its mysterious grief; Dylan's song, a consciousness that at once pulls itself together, flowing on to something quite other: "Doctor, lawyer, Indian chief". Out you go. But who's counting?

Anyway, just accept the rueful realities, such as "It takes a thief to catch a thief", especially if you are yourself in the light-fingered business – here within *"Love And Theft"* – of snatching up an unconsidered trifle here (from a nursery rhyme, or a book about a Japanese gangster), and a trifle there, from Donne and Hemingway. "For whom does the bell toll for, love? It tolls for you and me". For whom does it toll for? For sure, it doesn't toll only for thee (Donne: "Any man's death diminishes me, because I am involved in mankind; and therefore never send to know for whom the bell tolls; it tolls for thee"), so we might as well have a "for" each. It was a funeral bell, no doubt about that, but how unfuneral it all feels on this occasion, how much more like marriage bells for you and me. A bit like those cypress trees, freed from their dark associations. And then the same goes for – goes from – the song's last lines, where the pulse is healthy (as it might not always be), and where what is sharp is not going to hurt anybody, and where what is twisted is given to us straight, and where a groan doesn't sound remotely like a groan, given how blithely it is all sung:

> My pulse is runnin' through my palm – the sharp hills are rising from
> The yellow fields with twisted oaks that groan
> Won't you meet me out in the moonlight alone?

Nothing is here for groans. The words that are dark find themselves lightened, and the heavy words lightened. Dylan, like Shakespeare,[1] loves

---

[1] Of some punning lines in *The Merchant of Venice* (V, i), Dr Johnson wrote: "There is scarcely any word with which Shakespeare so much delights to trifle as with 'light', in its various significations." Again, of *Antony and Cleopatra* (I, iv), "The word 'light' is one of Shakespeare's favourite play-things."

the range that the word "light" can command in English, from an effect of the light, the moonlight, to an effect of not being weighted upon by anything heavy.

How long, still, will the question persist, "Won't you meet me out in the moonlight alone?"? At what point might even the most hopeful of lovers yield to hopelessness? There was a moment of ominous jealousy in *A Midsummer Night's Dream* (II, i):

Enter the King of Fairies at one door with his train, and the Queen at another with hers

OBERON: Ill met by Moonlight, proud Titania.

But the song lives in hope: Well met by Moonlight.

Forever Young

First things first. The First Cause is the Creator of the Universe. So: "May God bless and keep you always". In the beginning was the Word, and the Word was with God, and the Word was God. At once, in the first words of a song that constitutes a prayer, the Word is of God. "May God bless and keep you always". The Lord bless thee and keep thee.[1] The Father comes to the mind of a father. "I wrote it thinking about one of my boys" (*Biograph*).

> May God bless and keep you always
> May your wishes all come true
> May you always do for others
> And let others do for you
> May you build a ladder to the stars
> And climb on every rung
> And may you stay forever young
> Forever young, forever young
> May you stay forever young

The entrance is all the more forceful for its being gentle. This, and the way in which the initiating *May* . . . is set to distinguish itself from

[1] Numbers 6:24.

one distinctive opening to a Dylan song: an injunction crouched in the imperative. Imperious, sometimes, whether in dismissal, "Go 'way from my window", or in enrolment: "Look out your window, baby, there's a scene you'd like to catch". But often inviting: "Come gather 'round people".[1]

Such imperative openings are admittedly only one of the instantly embroiled ways in which a Dylan song may hit the fan running,[2] but they are assuredly characteristic, from "Lay down your weary tune" and "Hey! Mr. Tambourine Man, play a song for me", to "Don't ya tell Henry" and "Look out across the fields, see me returning". But *Forever Young* is in no position to command (it kneels and it bows its head), and anyway God is not to be commanded, and so the opening is rightly a prayer's hope: "May God bless and keep you always".

God, first, then, and then there is an intermediate step that has to be taken before the prayer can arrive at what it most or mostly calls upon as its ritual wording (*May you . . .*). The song has passed at once from God to you ("May God bless and keep you always"), but now it moves on to a stepping stone that it never leaves behind: *your wishes*, which are not you exactly, or are exactly not you. "May your wishes all come true". The singer puts those first, or all but first, but he lets it be understood that the hope is not only that your wishes may all come true but that so may all his wishes for you. Your wishes are granted pride of place, but it is clear that this rests upon a further act of trust: that your wishes are and will be wise ones. Just think of all the wish-stories where the wish-fulfilment is the worst thing that could have happened, issuing in farce or tragedy. Be careful what you wish for, lest your wish be granted. But as to *your* wishes, may they all come true, for I trust your judgement, as I trust in God's. "Trust ye in the Lord for ever".

So now the prayer can return to *you* – but be patient just a moment longer, for its first thought, now that it has returned, is of others. "May you always do for others". Put others first, within this veritable series of things that are to come first. And, first and last, may you be granted an understanding of human reciprocities:

> May you always do for others
> And let others do for you

---

[1] Absolutely imperative (given the absence of a comma before "people"), the apostrophe in "'round". [Square people, stay right where you are.]

[2] Dylan: "'Repent, the Kingdom of God is at hand.' That scares the shit out of people" (*Biograph*).

A mistaken pride might have put yourself before others. We have put that behind us, and yet an equally mistaken pride may sometimes stand between us and being ministered to by others. It may be no less blessèd to receive than to give. So there is a pressure, mild but firm, given to the word upon which this ensuing thought turns, the word "And":

> May you always do for others
> And let others do for you

And – no less important – let others do for you.

The prepositional phrase "do for", in this positive sense,[1] does well: "to act for or in behalf of; to manage or provide for". *The Oxford English Dictionary* brings home the age-old association of "do for" with what Providence provides, with God's wishes on our behalf. "God did for them" (1523). "When God does for man, he expects that man should do for God" (1658). "If ye do for them which do for you, what thank are ye worthy of?": a question asked by the Son of God (Luke 6:33).[2] The turn of phrase that we might expect at this moment in *Forever Young* is not "do for others" but "do unto others", and this not just because it is more often heard but because Dylan later has it within the refrain of *Do Right to Me Baby (Do Unto Others)*:

> But if you do right to me, baby
> I'll do right to you, too
> Ya got to do unto others
> Like you'd have them, like you'd have them, do unto you

The archaic joins the demotic in "Ya got to do unto others / Like you'd have them do unto you" (Do unto others *as* . . ., right?) to establish a jaunty jocularity, whereas *Forever Young* needed something at once more simple and less familiar:

> May you always do for others
> And let others do for you

Anyway, the usual way of putting it can open a whole other can of worms

---

[1] As against, and perhaps actively against, the other sense of *do for*. "To ruin, damage, or injure fatally, destroy, wear out entirely".

[2] Tindale's translation (1526). In the King James Bible: "And if ye do good to them which do good to you, what thank have ye?"

that turn. George Bernard Shaw: "Do not do unto others as you would they should do unto you. Their tastes may not be the same."

Meanwhile, as the song makes its way – at once pressing on and circling back for ever – there can be heard the forward movement of mind and of voice from "for others" through "for you" to "forever", itself then repeated for what must seem ever.

True, the song is of the simplest. But then these effects are themselves of the simplest. Inspired, they are a matter of order, of ordering things aright, as is true of every ritual and perhaps of every prayer.

"*Forever Young*, I wrote in Tucson," Dylan remembered. "I wrote it thinking about one of my boys and not wanting to be too sentimental. The lines came to me, they were done in a minute. I don't know. Sometimes that's what you're given. You're given something like that. You don't know what it is exactly that you want but this is what comes. That's how that song came out. I certainly didn't intend to write it – I was going for something else, the song wrote itself – naw, you never know what you're going to write. You never even know if you're going to make another record, really."[1]

"May you always know the truth": including this truth about such creations, that I don't know, you don't know, you never know, you never even know. The simple repetitiveness of all those hovering remarks, their easy brooding and giving ("Sometimes that's what you're given. You're given something like that"), are very endearing and truthful in relation to this song that is likewise so happy to repeat itself forever as it unfolds its wishes ("You don't know what it is exactly that you want") for another's well-being.

In *Ode on a Grecian Urn*, Keats had been explicit not only with "for ever" but with "happy":

> And, happy melodist, unwearièd,
>   For ever piping songs for ever new;
> More happy love! more happy, happy love!

Ah, "happy" recurs so often as to feel immitigably sad: four times in those three lines, and this after the sigh "Ah, happy, happy boughs!"

Forever Young may wish "May you be happy", but this is the wish that is

---

[1] *Biograph*. "Tucson" / "one of my boys". (Not that he has only two sons.) Like God, words and pronunciation move in a mysterious way. "I certainly didn't intend . . ."

unheard. (Heard wishes are sweet, but those unheard are sweeter?) This is the more telling in that the song lives within a society that knows the truth to be self-evident, that among our inalienable rights are life, liberty, and the pursuit of happiness. The song silently declares its independence of any such claims for, or to, happiness. "May your heart always be joyful": joy is something else, as is clear if you try thinking of utilitarianism as committed to the greatest joy of the greatest number. Although *Forever Young* may breathe the wish that its beneficiary be happy, it doesn't voice this. For the direct pursuit of happiness has a way of leading you astray, away from happiness proper as well as away from all the allegiances owed to values other than happiness. The song settles for the larger hopes:

> May you grow up to be righteous
> May you grow up to be true
> May you always know the truth
> And see the lights surrounding you
> May you always be courageous
> Stand upright and be strong
> And may you stay forever young
> Forever young, forever young
> May you stay forever young

"Forever": Keats had rung the changes on the word, or rather, words (in his better day, usually two words, *for ever*):[1]

[1] C. S. Calverley mockingly apprehended what had happened when "for ever" became "forever":

> Forever; 'tis a single word!
>   Our rude forefathers deemed it two:
> Can you imagine so absurd
>   A view?
>
> Forever! What abysms of woe
>   The word reveals, what frenzy, what
> Despair! For ever (printed so)
>   Did not.

Calverley lauds the innovator:

> But in men's hearts shall be thy throne,
>   While the great pulse of England beats.
> Thou coiner of a word unknown
>   To Keats!

For ever wilt thou love, and she be fair!

For ever piping songs for ever new;

For ever warm and still to be enjoyed,
      For ever panting, and for ever young –

There is poignancy in Keats's so ordering things that "for ever young" is the sixth and last "for ever" of his sequence. In Dylan, it is "young" that forever succeeds "forever", four times in each verse. Its brother, "always", sounds as though it is always going to lag behind (for ever panting?): "always" only twice in the first verse, and only twice in the second verse . . . But in the end it catches up and matches up: it, too, comes four times in the last verse. The sibling synonyms are finally all-square.

Dylan had at once known the truth about where the danger lay: "too sentimental". Poets have long been alert to the need to ward off sentimentality in such prayers. Yeats, for instance, in *A Prayer for my Daughter*, immediately follows his "May . . ." ("May she be granted beauty") with "and yet", in a thorough and prompt prophylaxis against being too sentimental:

> May she be granted beauty and yet not
> Beauty to make a stranger's eye distraught,
> Or hers before a looking-glass, for such,
> Being made beautiful overmuch,
> Consider beauty a sufficient end,
> Lose natural kindness and maybe
> The heart-revealing intimacy
> That chooses right, and never find a friend.

Then there is Philip Larkin, no less wary of "the usual stuff / About being beautiful", who seeks to escape sentimentality in his poem for Sally Amis, first by means of a rueful pun in the title, *Born Yesterday* (I wasn't born yesterday, even if she was), and then by jeering relaxedly at the . . . – well, wishers:

> Tightly folded bud,
> I have wished you something
> None of the others would:

> Not the usual stuff
> About being beautiful,
> Or running off a spring
> Of innocence and love –
> They will all wish you that,
> And should it prove possible,
> Well, you're a lucky girl.
>
> But if it shouldn't, then
> May you be ordinary

– at which point Larkin, sensing that this way of putting it was in danger of overestimating how much understatement he could count on, has to spend eight lines getting out from under just about everything that we mean by *ordinary*, and then has to end his poem by wishing ditchwater on her – only to have to hasten immediately into explaining away this even blunter word of his:

> In fact, may you be dull –
> If that is what a skilled,
> Vigilant, flexible,
> Unemphasised, enthralled
> Catching of happiness is called.

This is as sentimental as they come, given the fact that by no stretch even of Larkin's imagination is *dull* what a skilled, vigilant, flexible, unemphasized, enthralled catching of happiness is called. Larkin's sally fails, lapsing into what is just one more form that sentimentality may take: a miscalculated risk taken mistakenly and then rescinded.

In *Forever Young*, on the other hand, Dylan does catch what you might call a skilled, vigilant, flexible, unemphasized, enthralled catching of happiness. And of values other than happiness. His prayer (that he not be too sentimental) is among those answered.

There is a special grace in the song's resisting the temptations of senti-mentality. Sometimes the vigilance is a matter of sensing something dark that is in the air.

> May you build a ladder to the stars
> And climb on every rung

Dylan's knowing at least something of the work of Blake[1] might mean that this wish (for a child, too) could be seen in contrast to *For Children: The Gates of Paradise*, where Blake – in a famous caricature – projects a demented demandingness. The shrilling thrilling insistence is both a title and a claim to entitlement: *"I want! I want!"*[2] "A tiny man mounts a ladder propped against a quarter moon, while two others watch him. In the background are seven stars in a dark, cloudless sky."[3] Anything but that, please. May you – in quite the opposite spirit – build a ladder to the stars and climb on every rung.

Forever Young is a dedication to hope. Among the poems that Dylan values is one by Rudyard Kipling, and it came to his mind, he says, in the wake of the terrorism of September 11th, 2001. "My mind would go to young people at a time like this."[4] *Gentlemen-Rankers* imagines hopelessness, so it needs to speak of Hope, and – like *Forever Young* – it speaks of Truth (rhyming it with "youth"), and it prays for the young – a word that the poem rhymes, as Dylan's song does, with "rung". Dylan is in hopes.

> May you build a ladder to the stars
> And climb on every rung
> And may you stay forever young

Kipling, in the four lines that Dylan was later to quote, imagines what it must be to have done with Hope and Honour, and to be lost to Love and Truth:

> We have done with Hope and Honour, we are lost to Love and Truth,
>   We are dropping down the ladder rung by rung,
> And the measure of our torment is the measure of our youth,
>   God help us, for we knew the worst too young!

"And climb on every rung": but "down the ladder rung by rung", and not

---

[1] *11 Outlined Epitaphs*: "above the bells of William Blake" (*Lyrics 1962–1985*, 1985, p. 115).

[2] In our world, this would need to be "I need! I need!", as in the child's cry "Need candy!"

[3] *William Blake's Writings*, ed. G. E. Bentley, Jr (1978), vol. I, p. 167.

[4] *Rolling Stone* (22 November 2001).

even climbing down, dropping down. "God help us". "May God bless and keep you always".

> May you grow up to be righteous
> May you grow up to be true
> May you always know the truth
> And see the lights surrounding you
> May you always be courageous

Plainly it is a simple positive sense that commands this occasion on which "true" and "truth" can calmly succeed one another as the due process for consummating their consecutive lines. It is the occasion for "true" and "you" to rhyme again, as they had done in the first verse. (The final verse, with something of surprise, is to move on from this rhyme *true / you*, reaching forward with a different movement in the rhyme *swift / shift* and its meaning.)

> May you always know the truth
> And see the lights surrounding you

May you always see the lights surrounding you. (Some hear "light" in the singular. As printed in *Lyrics 1962–1985*, it is "lights", which avails himself of the sibilant succession in "lights surrounding". More than one light is more generous, less likely to harden into a one-thing-necessary.) First, may such lights always be there. Next, may you always perceive that there are such lights that benignly surround you – and that are close at hand, not distant like the stars. And may you always see to it that there be such lights. Perhaps, without overdoing things and issuing a halo, the lights surrounding you may be lights that you bring with you, no less than those that life may bring to you. To see the lights surrounding you, especially when you know the truth (which is often not a bright thing to be seen with delight), is never to lose sight of hope.

> Cease, every joy, to glimmer on my mind,
> But leave, oh! leave the light of Hope behind!
> (Thomas Campbell, *The Pleasures of Hope*)

"And see the lights surrounding you": this breathes a larger air. But there is a touch, too, of something salutarily unsentimental about the sequence in which the line figures. For when the phrase "surrounding you" is at once followed by "May you always be courageous", we may be reminded that what surrounds us in this life, all too often, is not light but darkness. (So the word "lights" would be touched with an emphasis.) The word "surround" often has its dark side. Dylan has elsewhere "Surrounded by fakery" and "controversy surrounds him"; danger lurks in the line, "Well, he's surrounded by pacifists who all want peace", and what might have seemed to be a benign surrounding, "He's surrounded by God's angels", turns to be dark:

> Now her vengeance has been satisfied and her possessions have been sold
> He's surrounded by God's angels and she's wearin' a blindfold[1]

Which leaves "And see the lights surrounding you" as the only unshadowed use of "surround" in Dylan's songs, so there may be at least the possibility that "surrounding you" contains – or rather, might ill have contained – a threat, such a threat as would make sense of an immediate move to "May you always be courageous".

The final verse, too, may have a glimpse of a faint threat to our hopes, in the knowledge that such a conceivable shadow may do something to make unsentimentally real the benevolence that is being prayed for.

> May your hands always be busy
> May your feet always be swift
> May you have a strong foundation
> When the winds of changes shift

A good wish, that your hands may always be busy, and yet possibly hinting at what it is that goodness may be up against:

> In works of labour, or of skill,
>   I would be busy too;
> For Satan finds some mischief still
>   For idle hands to do.
>   (Isaac Watts, *Against Idleness and Mischief*)

---

[1] *Angelina*. The previous instances are from *Sign Language*, *Handy Dandy*, and *Neighborhood Bully*.

It is likewise a high hope, that your feet may always be swift, one that might be associated not only with hope ("True hope is swift"[1]) but with love: "Love is swift of foot".[2] And yet this again is possibly a wish that acknowledges the existence of dark alternatives. Of the six things that the Lord hates (Proverbs 6:18), one is "feet that be swift *in running to mischief*" (mischief again), and when feet are swift in the Epistle to the Romans (3:15), it is that "their feet are swift *to shed blood*".

But last things last, the lasting things.

> May your heart always be joyful
> May your song always be sung
> And may you stay forever young
> Forever young, forever young
> May you stay forever young

The song's last wish remains what it has been throughout. And the one-but-last wish? "May your song always be sung". You have a song of your own, you know (sings this unique singer to a child of his, and to us, and to himself), *your* song. Your song, as the one that you will have as your own, everybody having his or her song, even those of us who don't write songs or can't sing. Your song, as this one of yours, this one for you, this one – *Forever Young* – in which I do for you. (May I always do so.) Always be sung, as continue to be sung (may it always find itself sung). Always be sung, there being – as earnest of this hope – two versions of this song on this one album.

A prayer is not an end in itself. Those of us who are old enough (though forever youthful) to remember the sweet startlement with which in 1974 we first heard *Forever Young* will never forget what it was like to turn *Planet Waves* over (something that is lost in the single-sidedness of a CD) and discover that the first track on the second side was a discovery, an utterly – no, an utterredly – different version of the song we had just heard as the last track on the first side. Forever indeed. The reprise was a feat of modesty and pride. Modesty, in acknowledging that even Dylan himself couldn't sing one of his songs so that *everything* about it was

---

[1] *Richard III*, V, ii.
[2] George Herbert, *Discipline*.

realized in one performance.¹ Pride, in this same fact, that he could create a work of art that greatly escapes even the artist's power over it (like a child, really), pride that here was to be heard the living witness of what it is for a work of art to be forever young – and forever new.

> And, happy melodist, unwearièd,
>> For ever piping songs for ever new . . .

   To hear the song is to realize how much Dylan, the happy melodist, unwearied, can realize. There is the staying power that waits so patiently after the word "stay", so that the line is not

> And may you stay forever young

but

> And may you stay   forever young

– with "stay" extending its stay. And there is what we hear in the close of the refrain, which is not what we might read ("Forever young, forever young / May you stay forever young") but something audibly true, something that the eye cannot fathom, something in the timing that cannot be rendered by placing and spacing, however much we exercise our liberties:

> Forever y o u n g forever y o u n g
> May you s t a y forever y o u n g

Even as the nymph Melisma stays forever young . . .² The longing is in the

---

¹ Wilfred Mellers reviewed *Planet Waves* (*New Statesman*, 8 March 1974):

The first version is as guileless as a white gospel song, though its "gift to be simple" doesn't preclude subtlety: consider the reverberation of Dylan's voice at the end of the stanzas, or his unexpected *speaking* of the words about the surrounding light. The second version of the song apparently debunks the first, banishing hymnic innocence with fast, parodistic country rock; yet even the parody is heart-felt, the first version is not discredited.

² For melisma, see p. 403.

elongations, as well as in the complementary rhyme ("May you stay . . ."),
even as the shift "When the winds of changes shift" is a shift in how a
word is voiced by the wind that is breath, and thereby changed.

When young, or when even younger than he was when he wrote *Forever
Young*, Dylan had set down *Bob Dylan's Dream*, a dream that had gone but
had left a memory at once happy and sad:

> By the old wooden stove where our hats was hung
> Our words was told, our songs was sung
>
> With hungry hearts through the heat and cold
> We never much thought we could get very old
> We thought we could sit forever in fun

Our songs were sung: May your song always be sung. We never much
thought we could get very old . . . forever in fun: forever young. And
behind *Forever Young* there may be a deep memory not only of the memory
that is *Bob Dylan's Dream* but of Isaiah 26:1–4:

In that day shall this song be sung in the land of Judah; We have a strong city;
salvation will God appoint for walls and bulwarks. Open ye the gates, that the
righteous nation which keepeth the truth may enter in. Thou wilt keep him in
perfect peace, whose mind is stayed on thee: because he trusteth in thee. Trust
ye in the Lord for ever. Trust ye in the Lord for ever.[1]

"May God bless and keep you always".

---

[1] "Whose mind is stayed on thee". Whose mind? There are moments when the
two are of one mind: "song be sung" / "song always be sung"; "have a strong city;
salvation" / "have a strong foundation"; "the truth may" / "May you always know the
truth"; "stayed" / "stay". These, and *God, righteous, keep, for ever.*

Charity

Watered-Down Love

At Stanford University in California, the Memorial Church is decked with allegorical figures: Faith, Hope, Charity, and Love. Designed by the great architect Maximus Crassus Ignoramus (of Soloi, birthplace of the solecism), the Memorial Church is certainly a memorial to something. A memorial to the railroad millionaire Leland Stanford's wish to railroad St Paul by erecting not just the Christian trinity of graces, Faith, Hope, and Charity, but a quadrangle that can then grace university expansion. Fourfold! Billfold! A memorial to institutional indifference towards the English language as well as towards history, including the history that it purports to honour. For charity *is* love, or certainly was so (and therefore is so, if you respect the enduring life of the tradition that you are invoking), within the supreme sequence voiced in St Paul's First Epistle to the Corinthians, chapter 13: "And now abideth faith, hope, charity, these three; but the greatest of these is charity."

But now abideth in an educational establishment not just these three but these four. And once Love is to be granted a separate spot, what is left for Charity to undertake? Up there on the façade of the Memorial Church, she is apparently doling out soup to the unfortunate. Well worth doing, and the great virtue that is Charity does not disdain such compassionate doing of good. But this is not because she is distinct from Love, it is because she incorporates such love within the many kinds and kindnesses of her patient love. "Charity suffereth long, and is kind." Charity is pure love.

> Love that's pure hopes all things
> Believes all things

The opening words of *Watered-Down Love* are themselves an act of hope and of belief: in the simplest way, the hope that those who hear the song will recognize (in both senses of recognize) what is being alluded to, together with the belief that St Paul is to be believed when (in the words of that glory of the language, the King James translation) the saint speaks with such divine eloquence of this the highest form of Love, the form that the English language then called Charity so as to distinguish it from, for instance, the love that is erotic love. (Love that's pure "Won't sneak up into your room, tall, dark and handsome".[1]) Charity gives way to none of the sins, least of all pride.

Charity suffereth long, and is kind; charity envieth not; charity vaunteth not itself, is not puffed up, doth not behave itself unseemly, seeketh not her own, is not easily provoked, thinketh no evil; rejoiceth not in iniquity, but rejoiceth in the truth; beareth all things, believeth all things, hopeth all things, endureth all things.

Those closing clauses constitute one of the most noble progressions ever realized. Dylan's song does nothing to demean this but does have the courage to play mischievously with it (as against competing with it) when calling it into play. Instead of "endures" and "bears" along with "believes" and "hopes", there is this at the very start:

> Love that's pure hopes all things
> Believes all things, won't pull no strings

Allusion always pulls strings. And the more so when there may be a stringed instrument (contributing to the medium) in the immediate vicinity. One shouldn't harp on this, but allusion may itself be thought of as a stringed instrument. Love that's pure "won't pull no strings": this strings us along by means of the plain-spun double negative, the grammatical solecism ("Won't pull *any* strings, Master Dylan") that then strings together "to pull strings" ("to exert influence privately") and "no strings attached": *string*, "a limitation, condition, or restriction attached to something. *Freq.* in phr. *no strings attached*."

Charity "beareth all things" and "endureth all things" – including bearing and enduring this sort of thing, this taking of a liberty to the point of

---

[1] Rhyming with "Capture your soul and hold it for ransom". The *handsome / ransom* rhyme had tickled Byron (*Don Juan*, II, v, st. 9), but closer by is Bruce Springsteen: "So you fell for some jerk who was tall, dark and handsome, / Then he kidnapped your heart and now he's holding it for ransom. / Well, like a mission impossible I'm gonna go and get it back. / You know I would'a taken better care of it, baby, than that" (*I'm a Rocker*). The printed version in *Lyrics 1962–1985* (1985) had been, not "Capture your soul", but "Capture your heart". At first he gave us "your heart" but he wanted "your soul".

blasphemy. But then religious art has to be willing to risk the accusation of blasphemy.[1]

> The bells of the evening have rung
> There's blasphemy on every tongue
> (*'Cross the Green Mountain*)[2]

Every tongue, not just as deploring blasphemers but as including all who ever venture to speak of religion, even the bells (for a bell has a tongue).[3] If the charge of blasphemy were never even to arise, that could only be because the art were playing safe, and in art nothing is more dangerous than playing safe. What saves the song from being blasély blasphemous or shallowly sacrilegious is its conviction that these are strings that can be plucked in plangent comedy. This, which is implicit in the song, is explicit in an interview. Dylan is considerate of God: "He's got enough people asking Him to pull strings. I'll pull my own strings, you know." An assurance that sounds a different note when it comes from a guitar-player.

Are there any heroes or saints these days?
"A saint is a person who gives of himself totally and freely, without strings. He is neither deaf nor blind."[4]

What strings of saintliness, within a Christian song, might connect "deaf" to "strings"? The miracle in Mark 7:30–35:

Be opened. And straightway his ears were opened, and the string of his tongue was loosed, and he spake plain. And he charged them that they should tell no man: but the more he charged them, so much the more a great deal they published it; and were beyond measure astonished, saying, He hath done all things well: he maketh both the deaf to hear, and the dumb to speak.[5]

---

[1] See p. 378, on faith.

[2] Dylan's song on the soundtrack of *Gods and Generals* (2003).

[3] Emily Dickinson: "It was not Death, for I stood up, / And all the Dead, lie down – / It was not Night, for all the Bells / Put out their Tongues, for Noon". A. E. Housman: "When the bells justle in the tower / The hollow night amid, / Then on my tongue the taste is sour / Of all I ever did".

[4] *Playboy* (March 1978).

[5] If this miracle is in the hinterland of Dylan's words there, the link might be that the verses of 1 Corinthians immediately preceding the great chapter 13 on charity ask: "are all workers of miracles? Have all the gifts of healing? do all speak with tongues?"

And in this as in so many miraculous Dylan songs, straightway our ears are opened. So much, pure love can do, charity, or loving kindness, or "love that's pure". The song sets itself to rescue the idea and the ideal of charity from the slightly archaic colouring of that word, a colouring that has come to make people mistake its largest meaning.

"Love that's pure, it don't make no false claims". What kind of false claim might charity ever be accused of making? Admittedly, there is the dangerous pasture "Where charity is supposed to cover up a multitude of sins". But *Something's Burning, Baby* knows the difference between covering up and covering. St Peter's First Epistle does not speak of covering up when it promises that "charity shall cover the multitude of sins". (To cover, as benignly to protect, to clothe, and so – by extension – to forgive.) Psalms 32:1: "Blessed is he whose transgression is forgiven, whose sin is covered". Proverbs 10:12: "Hatred stirreth up strifes: but love covereth all sins". Charity is the opposite of any covering up.

Charity firmly sets its gentle face against sin, the sin of envy, for one. Charity envieth not. Charity thinketh no evil. Love that's pure

> Won't pervert you, corrupt you with foolish wishes[1]
> Will not make you envious, won't make you suspicious

But the song is not content either to update or to endorse St Paul, for those would be presumptuous as well as needless. *Watered-Down Love* takes up its own enterprise when it sets "love that's pure" against love that isn't.

Such a contrast was no part of St Paul's undertaking in chapter 13 of the First Epistle to the Corinthians. Plainly, one enemy of the charitable is the uncharitable. Less plainly, another enemy of the love that is charity is the love that falls short because it is diluted or impure. Love that's pure is to be contrasted with love that's watered-down.

> You don't want a love that's pure
> You wanna drown love
> You wanna watered-down love

"You wanna drown love" – which does not then form, as you might have

---

[1] As printed in *Lyrics 1962–1985*, "stupid", which is uncharitable in comparison with "foolish". 1 Corinthians 1:20: "hath not God made foolish the wisdom of this world?"

expected, an exact parallel with "You wanna watered-down love", for then it would have had to be "You wanna drowned love". And "wanna" is compact in more than one way: "you want a . . ." (which is how the previous line spelt it out) plus "you want to . . ." But circulating throughout the song is this contrast of the pure with the watered-down, the strong drink with the drowning of the drink. Too much tonic. Love that's pure might even have been love's that neat, if it weren't that this would have been too neat by half. Love that's proof (against temptation)?

But love that's pure doesn't have to insist on purism, on pure English. The song has as usual the unusual feats that characterize the true claims of Dylan's words.

> Love that's pure, it don't make no false claims[1]
> Intercedes for you 'stead of casting you blame

– 'stead of casting it as you might have expected, namely "'stead of casting the blame on you". Or might it have been "'stead of casting you as the one to be blamed"? Either way, I'd like to intercede on behalf of "casting you blame". Or there is the *transgression / confession* rhyme, grilling you (at the police station or through the confessional's grill) about the transgression without which you wouldn't have to be coming to confession:

> Will not deceive you, lead you into transgression
> Won't write it up and make you sign a false confession

– an ugly conjunction of the police and the priest.

"Will not" do this, "Won't" do that: these are all among the negative things that are positively negated by "love that's pure", and this way of establishing the positive power of love by setting it against the negatives that it defies and defeats is itself fully in the spirit of St Paul, however different its idiom may be. Has the small inexorable word "not" ever been called upon to do more sterling positive work than in St Paul's celebration of this, the most positive virtue of all?

---

[1] As printed in *Lyrics 1962–1985*, "no claims"; he sings "no false claims".

Charity envieth not; charity vaunteth not itself, is not puffed up, doth not behave itself unseemly, seeketh not her own, is not easily provoked, thinketh no evil; rejoiceth not in iniquity . . .

There is a cascade of heartening negatives throughout the Dylan song, too:

> Love that's pure won't lead you astray
> Won't hold you back, won't get in your way[1]

It is the pressure of all the negatives, some of them working positively ("Won't hold you back") and some of them negatively (alas, "You don't want a love that's pure" – would that you did), that explains why such force attaches in the song to the utter simplicity of the greatest praise that Dylan gives to love that's pure: "It knows that it knows". Now there's something entirely positive for you, for you not against you, as against the repudiation of all those ways of being bad. A positive good: "It knows that it knows".

> Love that's pure, no accident[2]
> It knows that it knows, is always content

The words as printed in *Lyrics 1962–1985* had been "Always on time, is always content" – a good thing to be, certainly, for punctuality is the politeness of princes, and to speak in a song of being "Always on time" is to be alert to the musical humour of putting it like that. But "Always on time" didn't attain the utterly unmisgiving rightness, the repudiation of all misguided sophistication, that is the justified confidence of "It knows that it knows". With, behind it, the authority of this same chapter of St Paul on charity: "For we know in part . . . now I know in part; but then shall I know even as also I am known." We know in part, and I know in part, but "It knows that it knows". With consummate assurance. And yet

[1] As printed in *Lyrics 1962–1985*, "won't mess up your day", which was too close to the condescending sarcasm of the bumper-sticker that told people (other people, natch) that one nuclear bomb could ruin your whole day. The smug bares its gums.

[2] As printed in *Lyrics 1962–1985*, "ain't no accident". The secure swiftness, rhythmical and syntactical, that cuts from the one to the other, not needing even the verb "to be", "Love's that pure, no accident", is paralleled elsewhere in the song, when Dylan – who had printed "Will not deceive you or lead you to transgression" – sings "Will not deceive you, lead you into transgression". Confident at the wheel.

– so that the whole thing not repose in complacency – this, too, is set against the warning with which the song comes to an end, the warning that you (by which the song means all of us, the speaker included) are always going to be tempted by the lesser love, the watered-down love. A more insidious temptation than anger, say, for watered-down love isn't one of the sins, after all. The song ends, not with the words as printed, but with the addition of something newly admonitory, the reminder over and over again of the human propensity to lapse, to settle for the diluted or the polluted:

> Watered-down love
> You wanna watered-down love
> Watered-down love
> You wanna watered-down love
> *Yes you do, you know you do . . .*

– this repetition itself being then repeated. From "It knows that it knows" to "Yes you do, you know you do".

The song doesn't sermonize or speechify, choosing instead to avail itself of the angled accents of speech. One discreet skill here is the song's ways with parts of speech, and with one part of speech in particular: the adverb. Deftly, unobtrusively. The enterprising song is, as you would expect, happy to accommodate a wide range of different parts of speech: verbs as tonally different as "sneak up" and "intercede", nouns as different as "strings" and "transgression", adjectives as different as "foolish" and "eternal" . . . The other members of the family are there, too: prepositions ("up" and "down"), conjunctions ("and" and/or "or"), interjections (that undulating "ooh-ooh-ooh" near the end), pronouns ("Yes you do, you know you do"). But one part of speech does take some time to arrive. You don't want adverbs? Despite all the verbs (seven in the first verse alone) that might enjoy the company of an adverb? After a while, I find myself starting to feel hungry for an adverb – granted, the other linguistic dishes are fine in their way, but not in *its* way. What is keeping it? So there is gratification for me, halfway through the song, when "astray" strays into the song: "Love that's pure won't lead you astray". But not fully satisfying, this, since a fully satisfactory adverb has a way of ending, as "fully" does, with *-ly*. Patience will be rewarded, though, for the last verse of the song (before it enters its final refrain and coda) is rife with adverbs: first, "always", and then two adverbs that are manifest*ly* such:

> Love that's pure, no accident
> It knows that it knows, is always content
> An eternal flame, quietly burning
> Never needs to be proud, loud or restlessly yearning[1]

Quietly, never restlessly. And then it is the very last word, "yearning" (the last asseveration of the song proper), that Dylan sings less in exhortation, than in exaltation and exultation. His voice ripples the word out so that it does itself become an eternal flame.

The effect is thrillingly contrarious, for in the very moment when it is being insisted that love that's pure "Never needs to be proud, loud or restlessly yearning", there is to be heard in the very word this unassuageable yearning. Do you understand this? "Yes, you do, you know you do". For although we may aspire to being beyond such yearning, we cannot fully achieve this (any more than we can entirely extirpate the deadly sin that is pride). Moreover, what is to be heard in the yearning with which "yearning" is voiced is not the false claim that charity suffers from yearning (for it "Never needs to be proud, loud or restlessly yearning"), but our yearning for it.

The album *Shot of Love* was unlovingly shot down by the reviewers. And *Watered-Down Love* (which is not a watered-down song at all, being a variant on the thought of a shot of love, "I need a shot of love") was among the targets. Which is where the vexatious question of what a song actually sounds like must become central. "Be opened. And straightway his ears were opened". Stoning the album in *Rolling Stone*,[2] Paul Nelson managed to hear its Christianity as seething with "hate" (his word, and not just word), and then had no difficulty in hating it:

Dullards that we are, we can't understand God. We don't understand Dylan. Our love is no damn good (*Watered-Down Love*) . . . Therefore, each and every one of us can go to hell.

In *Watered-Down Love* . . . the singer's so mad that he can barely manage his splutters of spite.

For my part, I don't think that *Watered-Down Love* says anything like "Our

---

[1] As printed in *Lyrics 1962–1985*, "Never needs to be proud, restlessly yearning". The praise of "love that's pure" in "Never needs to be proud, loud" recalls St Paul: "charity vaunteth not itself, is not puffed up, doth not behave itself unseemly".
[2] *Rolling Stone* (15 October 1981).

love is no damn good" or that "each and every one of us can go to hell", but more crucially I don't think that the song *sounds* anything like those damning sentiments. From its opening notes and its opening words, it moves more jauntily than jouncily, a series of acts of serious jesting, not a solemn commination. This song recital is no recital of divine vengeance against sinners. "Splutters of spite"? But Nelson, blind in at least one eye: I see no spite. I hear no evil. And I don't think that I am the one who has his hands to his ears. If there should be love that's pure, so there should be hate that's pure, too, unpolluted by injustice and inattention. Nelson sounds as though it is he who needed a shot of hate.

A shot of scepticism, fine. "And now abideth faith, hope, charity, these three; but the greatest of these is charity." "Doubt, Despair and Scrounging, shall I hitch my bath-chair to the greatest of these?" The question is pondered by one of Samuel Beckett's delinquents.[1]

Yet there is a moral, hereabouts, in a vital change that Dylan made to the song. The change brings home how hideously easy it can be to lapse from charity, from a love that's pure, and to fall into what does sound all too like spluttering and spite. The studio out-take (which is the performance that was released but with a final verse that was edited out when released) ends its assurances not with the rising delight felt in the confidence that love that's pure "Never needs to be proud, loud or restlessly yearning", but with a further verse that would have demeaned the song into the self-serving, the self-pitying, and the self-praising:

> Love that's pure is not what you teach me
> I've got to go where it can reach me
> I've got to flee towards patience and meekness
> You miscalculate me, mistake my kindness for weakness

I don't mean that we would have had to take this as autobiographical; not that it would save the artistic situation to make the claim (false or not) that Dylan is imagining and dramatizing another's betrayal in love. For the move out from the large love that is charity to a love-affair about which one of the parties now feels uncharitable, this move is in itself a false move artistically. Whereas the song as released, and as blessedly released from its final verse, does not have even once any of the words "I", "me", or "my" (and not because Dylan is exempting himself from the need to give and to

---

[1] Belacqua, in *A Wet Night* (*More Pricks than Kicks*, 1934).

receive such love as is charity), this misjudged verse that so enjoys passing judgement has in its four lines *me / I / me / I / me / my*.

> I've got to flee towards patience and meekness
> You miscalculate me, mistake my kindness for weakness

This was itself a miscalculation, a mistake, mistaking unkindness for strength. Its excision proved to be one of Dylan's best revisions. For "charity vaunteth not itself".

Centuries ago, a preacher named Hill was not allowed to become a priest because he was an itinerant preacher. But he won a place in dictionaries of quotations for these good words: "He did not see why the devil should have all the good tunes." Dylan is an itinerant non-preacher. *Watered-Down Love* doesn't preach. It has a good tune, thanks be not to the devil but to God, and it is aware that "Though I speak with the tongues of men and of angels, and have not charity, I am become as sounding brass, or a tinkling cymbal."

If Not For You

Charity is love, Christian love in the main, whether as God's love to man, or man's love of God and of his neighbour. But a love not restricted to the Christian. *The Oxford English Dictionary* extends such love: "Without any specially Christian associations: Love, kindness, affection, natural affection: now esp. with some notion of generous or spontaneous goodness." In short, such a love as might come esp. with some notion of *If not for you . . .*

If charity be love, can there be a love song that is a charity song? If so, it would be characterized by its shaping spirit, not by any shapely body, and it would move with and be moved by affection, natural affection, and by loving-kindness, the lovely compound that Coverdale in the sixteenth century, in praise of his Creator, created from the two words "loving" and "kindness". Coverdale translated Psalms 25:6 as "Call to remembrance, O Lord, thy tender mercies and thy loving kindnesses, which have been ever of old." So the dictionary, thanking Coverdale, promotes *loving-kindness*: "Affectionate tenderness and consideration; kindness arising from a deep personal love, as the active love of God for his creatures." God, to whom a believer would most wish to say *If Not For You.* "Without your love I'd be nowhere at all". Those words of Dylan's are addressed to one of God's creatures, such a one as the "lady of unbounded loving-kindness" whom Washington Irving praised in the America of his day. Just such a lady or woman is praised in *If Not For You*, an unbounded love song of which the kind of love is loving-kindness, affectionate tenderness and consideration received with thanks and reciprocated with thankfulness.

The spirit of *If Not For You*, in so very far as its words are concerned, is realized in rhyme. From the start it sets itself to make a good end. For dear life.

> If not for you
> My sky would fall

The song will have to come to an end, but there must not be the feeling that the affection of gratitude has come to an end, or been switched off or faded out. "If not for you": if your heart sings this to someone, and then immediately starts listing things –

> If not for you
> Babe, I couldn't find the door
> Couldn't even see the floor

– there's no reason why you shouldn't end up having no end of a list, giving an inventory of the universe. If she really is the *sine qua non*, makes possible everything for you, then without her you wouldn't be able to find not only the door and the floor, but the stairs, and the fridge; and if not for her, you wouldn't be able to hear not only the robin sing, but the lark, the windhover, the cassowary . . .

How does the end of *If Not For You* succeed in ringing true? The inescapable acknowledgement that even gratitude cannot be expressed for ever is brought home by Dylan's decision to depart from the song with the words "If not for you" repeated and repeated – in their beautiful simplicity – as if they, though they have got to go, could go on ad infinitum. But this simple device (not signing off but singing off) succeeds only because it is confirmed and happily compounded by Dylan's recourse to a different rhyming at the end.

So evenly does the singing move, like the music, that it sounds as though each verse has the same rhyme-scheme. But not so. And this confirms the sense that to be truly grateful is to feel something that is the good old story and yet is ever new, ever so slightly different. Here is the first verse:

If not for you	*a*
Babe, I couldn't find the door	*b*
Couldn't even see the floor	*b*
I'd be sad and blue	*a*
If not for you	*a*

The rhyme-scheme, then, is *abbaa*, beginning and ending with the refrain "If not for you".

The second verse sounds as though it is set to do the same, with the new rhyme *c* replacing *b*, and it too begins and ends with the refrain "If not for you" – but it goes *accaaa*:

If not for you	*a*
Babe, I'd lie awake all night	*c*
Wait for the mornin' light	*c*
To shine in through	*a*
But it would not be new	*a*
If not for you	*a*

Three times now, the *a* rhyme, not twice, and this is something new. It is, as it happens, the line "But it would not be new".

The third verse starts as though it is going to follow the pattern, since it begins *ad*, but then it reverts immediately to *a* (not *add*, but *ada*, as though it can't tear itself away from the rhyme that is due to "you"); so the rhyme-scheme has now become *adadaa*.

If not for you	*a*
My sky would fall	*d*
Rain would gather too	*a*
Without your love I'd be nowhere at all	*d*
I'd be lost if not for you	*a*
And you know it's true	*a*

And with this verse – unlike those that precede it, and that had apparently established the refrain as the right opening and closing of each verse – now having "If not for you" not as the last line but as the one but last:

I'd be lost if not for you
And you know it's true

Easily said, this knows, but this time, come on, you know it's true, with this insistence spilling over the edge of the rhyme-scheme, or rather, the refrain-scheme.

The next verse might seem to be only a reprise of this one, since it, too, has the scheme *adadaa* and mostly the same words:

If not for you	*a*
My sky would fall	*d*
Rain would gather too	*a*
Without your love I'd be nowhere at all	*d*
Oh! what would I do	*a*
If not for you	*a*

But it isn't the same, for now the refrain-scheme has reasserted its rights, restoring its claim to have the verse end as it begins:

Oh! what would I do
If not for you

As it begins, and yet not altogether so, for that "Oh!" could make all the difference in the world.

And then to the fifth and final verse, which again might seem to be identical with an earlier one (the second verse), since it, too, has the scheme *aeeaaa*: "you", "spring", "sing", "clue", "true", "you".

If not for you	*a*
Winter would have no spring	*e*
Couldn't hear the robin sing	*e*
I just wouldn't have a clue	*a*
Anyway it wouldn't ring true	*a*
If not for you	*a*

But just a moment, is that it exactly? For the one but last line, the one that leads into that very last "If not for you" (the refrain that will then be repeated as if for ever), ends not with the one word "true" but with the two words "ring true", and the word "ring" picks up the verse's other rhyme, *spring / sing*. So the scheme is *a e e a ea a* —

Anyway it wouldn't ring true   *ea*

– and the words "ring true" plait together the verse's two rhymes, there at the end as a love-knot, a ribbon that ties up the gift of gratitude that is the song. Or, to slip the metaphor on to the finger of the words, as itself a ring, a pledge, an emblem of true love, endless, a virtuous circle.

If the song is to end, and it must, you know, then in some way it must itself "ring true" that this is an ending, not a stopping. And this word "true" is the only rhyme-word that has returned, other than that of the refrain. "And you know it's true" returns now as "Anyway it wouldn't ring true" – and this with a reminder about the challenge to which all art has to rise. For the earlier rhyme on "new" ("But it would not be new") asks to be taken in conjunction with "true", to remind us that the challenge to the poet is to say something at once new and true. (Love, too, always new and true. With rhyme as a relationship.) It's not difficult to say something new if it doesn't matter whether it's true, or to say something true if it doesn't matter whether it's new. Dylan's song rings new and true. And it does so by courtesy of rhyme, including that dual rhyme with which it enters upon its ending:

> If not for you
> Winter would have no spring
> Couldn't hear the robin sing
> I just wouldn't have a clue
> Anyway it wouldn't ring true
> If not for you

But once again it matters that a device, a technique, will always be not a direction, but an axis. In the case of *If Not For You*, the penultimate line's dual rhyme, "ring true", is in both senses a happy effect. Elsewhere exactly the same device can be used to be moving in the opposite direction, with the poignancy of a love-knot that is yearned for and is never to be secured. I'm thinking of the end of a poem by William Barnes. A woman speaks, in Dorset English.[1]

LWONESOMENESS

> As I do zew, wi' nimble hand,
>   In here avore the window's light,

---

[1] I draw on an essay of mine on *Loneliness and Poetry* (*Allusion to the Poets*, 2002).

How still do all the housegear stand
   Around my lwonesome zight.
How still do all the housegear stand
Since Willie now 've a-left the land.

The rwose-tree's window-sheädèn bow
   Do hang in leaf, an' win'-blow'd flow'rs,
Avore my lwonesome eyes do show
   Theäse bright November hours.
Avore my lwonesome eyes do show
Wi' nwone but I to zee em blow.

The sheädes o' leafy buds, avore
   The peänes, do sheäke upon the glass,
An' stir in light upon the vloor,
   Where now vew veet do pass.
An' stir in light upon the vloor,
Where there's a-stirrèn nothèn mwore.

This win' mid dreve upon the maïn,
   My brother's ship, a-plowèn foam,
But not bring mother, cwold, nor raïn,
   At her now happy hwome.
But not bring mother, cwold, nor raïn,
Where she is out o' païn.

Zoo now that I'm a-mwopèn dumb,
   A-keepèn father's house, do you
Come of'en wi' your work vrom hwome,
   Vor company. Now do.
Come of'en wi' your work vrom hwome,
Up here a-while. Do come.

Notice – again, we register it even if we don't consciously remark it – the truncated final line in both the last two stanzas. Earlier the last line has always, like the other lines of the stanza, had eight syllables ("Where there's a-stirrèn nothèn mwore"), but now it is reduced, bleakly, to six syllables: "Where she is out o' païn". And again: "Up here a-while. Do come". But it is the plea, the hushed but insistent plea, of those last two words of the poem, "Do come", that consummates its sympathy and ours. For the word "come" comes in the poem, first in a sentence of twenty words, then in one of ten words, and then, finally, in one of two words: "Do come", where not only does "come" rhyme, but "do" is the other rhyme-word of this concluding stanza: at the line-endings, "do you", into "Now do", and at last into "Do come". What in the Dylan song was the happy gratitude of "ring true", both words being rhyme-words in his last verse, is in the Barnes poem the sorrowing wish – *need* – for somebody to be grateful to: "Do come". And for something to be grateful for: that is, such charity as is free from the grudgingness that *The Oxford English Dictionary* sadly recognizes in the end as lurking within one of the forms that charity may take.

A disposition to judge leniently and hopefully of the character, aims, and destinies of others, to make allowance for their apparent faults and shortcomings; large-heartedness. (But often it amounts barely to fair-mindedness towards people disapproved of or disliked, this being appraised as a magnanimous virtue.)

This, with an air of mild surprise, itself a strict appraisal (ensconced within its parentheses). Loving-kindness is more open.

> If not for you
> Babe, I couldn't find the door

There at the song's opening, an open door.

Eternal Circle

Dylan's love songs both evoke and evince a true surprise of love: they are individual, intensely idiosyncratic, and yet ripplingly everybody's. So that to know Dylan personally is disabling when it leaves Joan Baez saying that "everybody in the world thinks Bobby's written songs about them, and I consider myself in the same bag".[1] She doesn't mean everybody in the world, she just means Dylan's entourage, and she just means songs with her in mind. What matters, rather, is what the songs mean to those who cannot be under the illusion that Dylan had them in mind but who feel ominously divined.

---

[1] Anthony Scaduto, *Bob Dylan* (1971, revised edition 1973), p. 201.

"You know, I like Robert Graves, the poet. Do you?" (Dylan).[1] Graves was the twentieth-century love poet who particularly commanded this combination of love's individuality and love's commonalty. It is a source of deep relief, with Graves and with Dylan, that my strongest feelings should turn out to be so like everyone else's. Everyone's else.

> But if you want me to
> I can be just like you

This is sardonic in the song – *I Don't Believe You (She Acts Like We Never Have Met)* – but it can be taken appreciatively elsewhere. Since we can easily, and wrongly, be afraid of ordinariness, can feel it as a threat to our uniqueness and not as a stabilizing complement to it, we feel gratitude to the songs and poems that put such heart in us, helping us not to take it amiss that we are like a lot of people. Of *Don't Think Twice, It's All Right*, Dylan wrote: "A lot of people make it sort of a love song – slow and easy-going. But it isn't a love song. It's a statement that maybe you can say to make yourself feel better."[2] No, it's something even better: the dissolving of any such distinction. Even gratitude can be oppressive, but *If Not For You* makes gratitude seem – or rather, shows it to be – simply a delight.

A love song imagines someone in love, someone to love and be loved by. Or, admittedly, someone to have loved or been loved by. Perhaps someone to grieve the loss of, since love songs are often many too many mournings. Such a loved one can be real, and occasionally is so (sometimes fortunately), but she or he still has to be imagined, for imagination is no less necessary when the engagement is with a figure who is far from imaginary. Being imaginative is always the thing that is called for, even though the imagination's responsibilities are bound to be different when devoted to someone existent – take *Sara* – as against the newly called into being.

Added to which, to multiply the matter, the love song has a further responsibility: not just to imagine love but to love singing. Love song? Yes, he does. He loves it in itself and for itself. Over and over and above.

Eternal Circle is an entrancing dance of shadows in which there are three pairs of partners. One pair is a man and a woman; another is the love of a woman and the love of singing; the third is the song that we are hearing

---

[1] Quoted in Scaduto, *Bob Dylan*, p. 68.
[2] The sleeve-notes to *The Freewheelin' Bob Dylan*.

and the song that we are hearing about. Each pair weaves its ways, and all are interwoven.

The woman happens to be a total stranger, but then this turns out to be by no means totally unsatisfactory. For one's love-life, whether on-stage or off-stage, is often intimate with fantasy-life. Whereas people known to you have a way of thwarting your fantasy-life (or even taking it), you can't beat a stranger as a person about whom to fantasize.

The singer may be no stranger in the eyes – the "dark eyes" and "A million faces at my feet", in *Dark Eyes* – of all those out there in the auditorium, but the hearers (setting aside an underwhelming minority of them) are strangers to the singer. Probably the performing artist would never be able to carry the whole thing off if he or she weren't half carried away by postulating the pulsation out there of some particular endeared stranger, unknown (as yet?) though not simply unbeknownst.

Then again, this whole indulging is not just a fantasy, since there really are people out there who are in love with the performer, whether it be the over-laureated poet who is reading, the long-legged Principal Boy in the pantomime, or the bootlegendary singer who is there before their very eyes and ears. This singer especially. "We love you Bob" (without even a comma before "Bob"), you can hear them exclaim at the concert, in concert with him and with one another.

But it so happens that those who trumpet their love are always going to find themselves trumped by the performer's thought of one attent and silent gazer.

> I sung the song slowly
> As she stood in the shadows
> She stepped to the light
> As my silver strings spun
> She called with her eyes
> To the tune I's a-playin'
> But the song it was long
> And I'd only begun
>
> Through a bullet of light
> Her face was reflectin'
> The fast fading words
> That rolled from my tongue
> With a long-distance look

Her eyes was on fire
But the song it was long
And there was more to be sung

My eyes danced a circle
Across her clear outline
With her head tilted sideways
She called me again
As the tune drifted out
She breathed hard through the echo
But the song it was long
And it was far to the end

I glanced at my guitar
And played it pretendin'
That of all the eyes out there
I could see none
As her thoughts pounded hard
Like the pierce of an arrow
But the song it was long
And it had to get done

As the tune finally folded
I laid down the guitar
Then looked for the girl
Who'd stayed for so long
But her shadow was missin'
For all of my searchin'
So I picked up my guitar
And began the next song

Eternal Circle is a song the resilient sadness of which springs in part from the exquisite twining of the two kinds of love upon which it reflects. For even apart from the shadow that was missing (the only shadow on the scene missing), there cannot but be a shadowed side to the whole performing world. There is something sacrificial to it, something that can be heard in the very moment when Dylan in an interview speaks candidly about what brings him happiness: "The stage is the only place where I'm happy."[1] The

---

[1] Interview with Dave Fanning, *Irish Times Magazine* (29 September 2001).

only place? This is a claim so bright and so dark. "It's the only place you can be what you want to be." Those words, "the only place", are said there not only once but twice, in a succession that acknowledges the price that may have to be paid for all such success.

What the song brings itself to imagine is someone out there whose responsive presence can take the dark out of the shadow-time:

> I sung the song slowly[1]
> As she stood in the shadows
> She stepped to the light
> As my silver strings spun

One of the shadows is consciousness that there may be impurity in the air, the suspicion that may overshadow – even though it need not smutch – all these great exhibitions in performance. Again this is something about which Dylan has been open. "When you're up there and you look at the audience and they look back then you have the feeling of being in a burlesque." The thought, one that then thickens into a feeling, that even in this moment of unique happiness you are by way of being a stripper (for such is the kind of burlesque that Dylan is glimpsing): come to think of it, there is a thought to be going on with, or a thought that might make you want to be off. To be off-stage, even. Dylan spells it out, sings out, in *Gotta Serve Somebody*: "You might be a rock 'n' roll addict prancing on the stage". Not dancing but prancing.

The diction of addiction is there again, in his own person, as the next thing that needed to be said in the interview:

When you're up there and you look at the audience and they look back then you have the feeling of being in a burlesque. But there's a certain part of you that becomes addicted to a live audience.[2]

Some days I get up and it just makes me sick that I'm doing what I'm doing. Because basically – I mean, you're one cut above a pimp. That's what everybody who's a performer is.[3]

---

[1] As printed in *Lyrics 1962–1985*, "sang", but he sings "sung". See T. S. Eliot on Tennyson, p. 196.
[2] *Irish Times Magazine* (29 September 2001).
[3] *Newsweek* (6 October 1997).

This was seized on:

Years ago you said that sometimes it feels only one better than being a pimp.
"Well, unfortunately there is a nature of that. Yeah, I do feel that way. Performing's all the same. When you're up on stage and you're looking at a crowd and you see them looking back at you, you can't help but feel like you're in a burlesque show. I don't care who you are. Pavarotti might feel the same way, I don't know. I would think that part of him sincerely does."[1]

What is it that's only "one cut above a pimp"? Prostituting oneself? And yet if there were no erotic charge (however suspect) to these occasions, would they ever be able to surge as they do?

I hope that Dylan actually said "Well, unfortunately there is a nature of that", for it dextrously combines "Well, unfortunately there is a touch of that" and "Well, unfortunately that is the nature of it." Anyway he had been aware of this exposure – aware of needing to beware of something that lurks within it – back then in *11 Outlined Epitaphs*.[2] Of what reporters write, he wrote:

> they can build me up
> accordin' t' their own terms
> so that they are able
> t' bust me down
> an' "expose" me
> in their own terms
> givin' blind advice
> t' unknown eyes
> who have no way of knowin'
> that I "expose" myself
> every time I step out
> on the stage

Immediately following *11 Outlined Epitaphs* in *Lyrics 1962–1985* there comes *Eternal Circle*, a song that sees unknown eyes, that understands what it is to expose one's self (not just expose oneself) as a performing artist, and that sets the thought of "every time I step out / on the stage" to the tune of

---

[1] Interview with Serge Kaganski, *Mojo* (February 1998).
[2] Liner-notes to *The Times They Are A-Changin'* (1964); *Lyrics 1962–1985*, p. 113.

"She stepped to the light / As my silver strings spun". There is surprise but also justice in *Eternal Circle*'s being available to us only (so far as I know) in the one studio out-take that Dylan finally released in *the bootleg series*: she stepped to the light, he has not stepped to the lights.

"Spun" is fine for the strings, when what they bring into existence is felt as in touch with how one kind of string might come into existence. I and my strings call to her (with silver sounds), and she calls back. And this without uttering a sound. For the line "She stepped to the light" soon steps with perfect poise to "She called with her eyes". ("Light" into "eyes" as though the eyes light up.) The singer will heed this call of hers, only to find in the end that she is no longer to be found. Meanwhile, the transition from the strings to the eyes is one that calls to – and may call upon – an ancient love-thought, of lovers' reciprocated gazings as a cat's cradle perfect for purring in.

> Our eye-beams twisted, and did thread
> Our eyes, upon one double string.
> > (Donne, *The Ecstasy*)

The song's wording is itself a tremulously sensitive stringing of it all together, and this without ever stringing anyone along.

> She called with her eyes
> To the tune I's a-playin'

– this plays not only with *eyes / I's* but with the delighted duplicity of "To", which pivots from "called to" into "to the tune of". How he hopes to be able to take the opportunity to take up with her. And how fitting it is that she has her importunity, not being too proud to call again, though this time with a different angle:

> My eyes danced a circle
> Across her clear outline
> With her head tilted sideways
> She called me again

"She called with her eyes" is recalled as "She called me again", and that tilt of her head is enough to tilt everything in her favour. But then the song breathes a suggestive spirit, with the singer either being sweetly solicited or letting his thoughts run away – no, drift away – with him.

> As the tune drifted out
> She breathed hard through the echo

– you get the drift, for sure, but although it would be hard to paraphrase this ("through" being a word that teases again elsewhere in the song, in the run "Through a bullet of light"), it is not hard to feel, in "She breathed hard through the echo", the breath of desire. Hers or his or his yearning for hers.

Unlike *Fourth Time Around*, which – for all its "Around" – is scant of breath in its linear weariness, *Eternal Circle* dances to the word "circle":

> My eyes danced a circle
> Across her clear outline

"Eternal" is clear enough, and goes without singing. For this is an eternal circle in that it is a song about having sung a song, the present song folding the past one.

Yet although the narrative may be straightforward, to end it is no straightforward matter. Fortunately, the rhyme – the paradoxical rhyme – of "again" and "end" is happy once more to be of service. The central verse employs it as the only rhyme: "She called me again" / "And it was far to the end". Or rather, as the only one at the line-ending, since there is an internal rhyme within the one-but-last line that is heard in four verses out of the five: "But the song it was long".

Until the song duly arrives at its end (such an end as a circle can't even begin to think of), this line, "But the song it was long", has performed the office of a rhyming refrain. It had not itself been one of the rhyming lines, of which there had only ever been two, the fourth and eighth lines in each verse. These were always responsible for submitting a report on the progress of the song that is being sung about (with its intriguing relation to the song that is being sung here and now). These two lines, the only rhymed ones, stage the stages of the past song – as yet uncompleted – that is being recalled within this song. So in the verse that begins the song, the rhyming lines move from "As my silver strings spun" to end with "And I'd only begun". In the second verse, "That rolled from my tongue" to "And there was more to be sung". In the third verse, "She called me again" to "And it was far to the end". And in the fourth verse, "I could see none" to "And it had to get done".

But this insinuating insistent shape, this report on the work that (back then) had been in progress, has to cease when the present song (framing the past one) braces itself to cease. For, like the old song, the present song does have to get done, and would not feel done if it were still doing the same old thing with rhymes and all. So at this final point, the line that till then had always been the penultimate line, "But the song it was long", is ultimately sundered, so that it can furnish instead the rhyming that now at last can round off the eternal circle: "Who'd stayed for so long"/"And began the next song".

The ten lines that rhyme are set to preserve community and continuity, for their sound is this: *spun/begun*; *tongue/sung*; *again/end*; *none/done*; *long/song*. Essentially they all intone an *n*. They even resound to the nth, being drawn out by all those other line-endings: a-playin', reflectin', outline, pretendin', missin', searchin'. . . Dylan knows how much the nose can effect through the mouth, and what all those *n*'s and their endings enhance is the sung song's tone, its sinew and sinuous drone.

"But the song it was long": yet this present song, as against that past one, is not long (a mere five verses of eight short lines), and it has now fulfilled its reminiscential arc. "But the song it was long": the internal rhymes of this are at last brought to external life, are reversed, and are finally folded. And this, with the words "so long" hovering around the thought of saying goodbye (too good a word), and with "the next song" saying goodbye to this one:

> As the tune finally folded
> I laid down the guitar
> Then looked for the girl
> Who'd stayed for so long[1]
> But her shadow was missin'
> For all of my searchin'
> So I picked up my guitar
> And began the next song

---

[1] As printed in *Lyrics 1962–1985*, "stayed"; some of us think that he sings at least a suggestion of "stared", which would go with everything that we hear about eyes in the song, including "She called with her eyes/To the tune I's a-playin'" and "That of all the eyes out there/I could see none". The first four verses each mention eyes, hers and his and others'; if we look for "eyes" in the last verse, we find "Then looked for the girl/Who'd stayed for so long", which picks up – at some distance – "With a long-distance look/Her eyes was on fire". Like all those eyes, she did not stay till the final end.

This final verse is different, first, because "guitar" rhymes with itself: "I laid down the guitar" lays down the word, and then "So I picked up my guitar" picks it up. Then "long" rhymes with "song", and "missin'" is in the vicinity of "searchin'" (something for which it is searching, which is missing?). Although this last pair is not the verse's rhyme (which is *long/song*), "But her shadow was missin'/For all of my searchin'" touches upon a rhyme. The strings are plaited here.

"As the tune finally folded": finely folded, too, given how much the word "fold" may enfold. Came to an end, came to its end. Did so by means of a spiral or sinuous form, coiled and wound. Did so with a particular arrangement, where one thing lies reversed over or alongside another, doubled or bent over upon itself. Reversed: as the rhymes in "But the song it was long" came to be, happily – for if this is a reversal, it isn't one in the sense of a defeat, just as the thought that "the tune finally folded" is not an admission of defeat, since – and this is the point – it is not that the tune (which has finished its unfolding) folded in the sense that it gave way, collapsed, failed, or faltered.[1] But (sadly, this time) likewise not *folded* in the sense of an erotic glimpse of being folded in someone's arms, embraced. For "her shadow was missin'/For all of my searchin'". Nor was it only her shadow that was missing. She, too. Not that you can take in your arms a shadow anyway.

And not that he then immediately "began the next song".

When in the end he released *Eternal Circle* from the studio demo tape, he ended with a few chords. This performance is the only one we've got, apparently, and there is something at once endearing and eerie about having only one performance of a song about performing. On the illegitimate bootleg that was out before his *bootleg series*, he was heard to play more than those few final chords, leading into them with the whole tune again instrumentally. Whether with that fullness or as officially released and reduced, there is no equivalent to such effects when a poem ends. The words of *Eternal Circle* come to an end, but its music does not at that moment, or does not altogether. But since a poem consists of nothing but words and their punctuation, a poem can end with something that is both like and unlike "And began the next song". Take John Berryman's *Dream Song* number 168, *The Old Poor*, which ends:

---

[1] Spenser, *Hymn to Heavenly Beauty*: "I feel my wits to fail, and tongue to fold". Dylan: "The fast fading words/That rolled from my tongue", "As the tune finally folded".

> I have a story to tell you which is the worst
> story to tell that ever once I heard.
> What thickens my tongue?
> and has me by the throat? I gasp accursed
> even for the thought of uttering that word.
> I pass to the next Song:

Berryman's colon at the very end presses you to presume that the next Song is the one that follows, number 169. But you will never really know for sure. Yet how different it is at the end of a page to write and read

> I pass to the next Song:

turning the page to the words of a next song. For the next sound after Dylan's concluding line "And began the next song" is not words but music, the guitar and at least a snatch of the past tune.

There are many moments when Berryman and Dylan are akin. Berryman: "He stared at ruin. Ruin stared straight back". Dylan: "i accept chaos. i am not sure it accepts me".[1] But much more than a moment is constituted by Berryman's *Dream Song* number 118. The scene is a poetry reading, not a concert, but there stands a performing artist: Henry, who both is and is not Berryman, rather as the singer, past and present, in *Eternal Circle* both is and is not Dylan. (The Dylan "I", while it holds certain things in safe-keeping, is less evasive, more accountable, than the bluff "he" of Berryman.) The performer is likewise involved in – involved with? – a stranger out there imagined or imaginary.

> He wondered: Do I love? all this applause,
> young beauties sitting at my feet & all,
> and all.
> It tires me out, he pondered: I'm tempted to break laws
> and love myself, or the stupid questions asked me
> move me to homicide –
>
> so many beauties, one on either side,
> the wall's behind me, into which I crawl
> out of my repeating voice –

[1] Berryman, *Dream Song* number 45. Dylan, *Bringing It All Back Home*, jacket-notes; *Lyrics 1962–1985*, p. 180.

the mike folds down, the foolish askers fall
over theirselves in an audience of ashes
and Henry returns to rejoice

in dark & still, and one sole beauty only
who never walked near Henry while the mob
was at him like a club:
she saw through things, she saw that he was lonely
and waited while he hid behind the wall
and all.

Like *Eternal Circle*, this poem has to risk self-pity. Berryman may even court it, but neither of them is wedded to it. D. H. Lawrence thought that human beings should be ashamed of this mawkish weakness of theirs:

SELF–PITY

I never saw a wild thing
sorry for itself.
A small bird will drop frozen dead from a bough
without ever having felt sorry for itself.

Both Berryman's poem and Dylan's song are about self-pity, as against merely manifesting it, but Berryman − even if we acknowledge that he knows he is fantasizing − does rather enjoy his concluding plangency:

she saw through things, she saw that he was lonely
and waited while he hid behind the wall
and all.

The American turn with the phrase "and all" differs from British English, which often has an air of strong impatience ("and so on and so forth") or of specificity ("Old Uncle Tom Cobbleigh and all" − all of them available to be named). These lack the sidling sliding sidelong movement of the American "and all". In *Visions of Johanna*, Dylan can turn the acquiescent helplessness and uselessness of "and all" into the far-from-hopeless or -useless energies of aggression and baffled anger:

> Now, little boy lost, he takes himself so seriously
> He brags of his misery, he likes to live dangerously
> And when bringing her name up
> He speaks of a farewell kiss to me
> He's sure got a lotta gall to be so useless and all
> Muttering small talk at the wall while I'm in the hall

– where "and all" is itself a kind of muttering but is not small talk; threateningly, it is talking big.[1]

Berryman proffered himself as little boy lost, and he liked to live dangerously, and he sure had a lotta gall. In *Dream Song* number 118, does he brag of his misery? We might set the tone of his scene against the candidly healthy word "pretendin'" in *Eternal Circle*:

> I glanced at my guitar
> And played it pretendin'
> That of all the eyes out there
> I could see none

One impulse that, when not resisting self-pity, may endorse self-pity is aggression. The *Dream Song* is explicit about such feelings both towards the listeners ("the stupid questions asked me / move me to homicide") and from them: "while the mob / was at him like a club". Just because it is a fan club doesn't mean that it won't beat you to death. (A reader of the *Dream Song* may think of Berryman's friend Dylan Thomas.) But in *Eternal Circle* the possibility of aggression is entertained but rescinded. It is felt, for instance, in "the pierce of an arrow" (the guitar string vibrating to the bow-string):

> As her thoughts pounded hard
> Like the pierce of an arrow

There is a feeling that "her thoughts" may be not her thinking about him but his thinking about her (the performer may be tempted to flatter himself), the thought of her, with the thought of an arrow certainly having been prompted by the existence of his silver strings. This, and the effect, tilted

---

[1] I draw on an essay of mine on *American English and the inherently transitory* (*The Force of Poetry*, 1984).

sideways, of "the pierce of an arrow": first, the penetration that comes from having "pierce" be a noun as against a verb (a piercing effect that is unusual but not unprecedented[1]), and second the coincidence that would advertise "the pierce of an arrow" compacted as the car that is called a Pierce Arrow.[2]

As so often with the company of strangers, danger may be glimpsed in a cryptic turn of phrase:

> Through a bullet of light
> Her face was reflectin'
> The fast fading words
> That rolled from my tongue

"Through"? Danger, then, perhaps. Or danger as the thing that might have been expected to arise but then is not permitted to. For the equanimity of the song is such as to suggest that the hope within it, or the fantasy if you wish, is proof against any such bullet or any such arrow or any such accidental automobile. The final resignation in the song is felt as endorsing the all-too-human wish that, for the two of them, this intense way of being together without being alone together, this meeting at a public distance (a long distance, looking to be bridged by the communion of song), might somehow have been succeeded by a meeting that would have been deeply private, not only personal but individual. And not at all to be grouped with groupies.

No such meeting was to be. And yet not just eyes had met, or mouths and ears, but hearts, too? You can hear a related hope in the words with which Dylan entered upon *Oh Sister* on the *John Hammond Show* (10 September 1975): "I want to dedicate this to – er – someone out there watching tonight I know – she knows who she is."

When paying tribute to another singer (Dave Van Ronk), Dylan was able to imagine an enamoured stranger most tenderly:

---

[1] *OED* has the noun "pierce" as *rare*, from 1613, with Keats, *Isabella*, XXXIV: "Like a lance, / Waking an Indian from his cloudy hall / With cruel pierce".

[2] The car is heard in Robert Lowell's poem *Grandparents*, in *Life Studies* (1959): "the Pierce Arrow clears its throat in a horse-stall". Lowell, with whose art Dylan's has affinities (including these contrarious puns or anti-puns), said in conversation: "Dylan is alloy; he is true folk and fake folk, and has the Caruso voice. He has lines, but I doubt if he has written whole poems. He leans on the crutch of his guitar" (to Gabriel Pearson, *the Review*, summer 1971).

And Dave singin' "House a the Rising Sun" with his back leaned against the bricks an words runnin out in a lonesome hungry growlin whisper that any girl with her face hid in the dark could understand —[1]

For his own part, he sometimes needs to keep both feet on the ground, not drifting (however hauntingly) into any such fantasy: "When I'm up there, I just see faces. A face is a face, they are all the same."[2] On another occasion, when he needed to give vent to his vexation with the reviewers of *Renaldo and Clara*, he leapt to these terms:

Look, just one time I'd like to see any one of those assholes try and do what I do. Just once let one of them write a song to show how they feel and sing it in front of 10, let alone 10,000 or 100,000 people. I'd like to see them just try that one time.[3]

His thoughts pounded hard there, as you can tell from the likeness not only to *Eternal Circle* and *Dark Eyes* but to *Positively 4th Street*: "just one time", "for just one time" (more than one time), with its compacted repeated impact.

The eternal triangle is as nothing compared to the eternal circle. "The stage is the only place where I'm happy." But this has its own sadnesses, like so much love. He is the one person who has to be at a Dylan concert and the one person who can't go to a Dylan concert.

---

[1] Sleeve-notes to Peter, Paul and Mary, *In the Wind* (1963); *Bob Dylan in His Own Write*, compiled by John Tuttle, p. 23.

[2] Interview, London (4 October 1997); *Isis* (October 1997).

[3] *Rolling Stone* (16 November 1978).

Acknowledgements

Jeff Rosen could not have been more generous in granting permission to quote the songs and writings of Bob Dylan; the freedom that he made possible has no precedent for me in any such professional dealings. Others, too, have been good friends to the book. For criticisms large and small, for apt advice and sheer information, and for not only giving ear but lending ears, I am thankful for Jim McCue, as well as for many others: Tim Dee, Roger Ford, Mark Halliday, Kenneth Haynes, Steven Isenberg, Marcia Karp, Michael Madden, Julie Nemrow, Lisa Rodensky, Frances Whistler, Glenn Wrigley, and Bret Wunderli. My further indebtedness to Lisa Nemrow incorporates not only her reading these pages with sympathetic stringency, but her imaginative promptings as to a good many Dylan songs where I had despaired of ever noticing enough; sometimes, then, I managed to surprise myself, though never as much as the songs surprise me. Tony Lacey, as publisher, and Donna Poppy, as copy-editor, cooperated entirely; my thanks to them, to Zelda Turner for her handling of permissions, and to Steven King for the thorough skill of his index.

The Publishers wish to thank the following copyright holders for permission to quote copyrighted material:

Reprinted by permission of A. P. Watt Ltd on behalf of Michael B. Yeats.

William Empson: excerpts from *Seven Types of Ambiguity* and *Argufying*. Reprinted by permission of Curtis Brown Ltd, London, on behalf of the Estate of William Empson. Copyright © William Empson. Excerpts from *Seven Types of Ambiguity* published by the Hogarth Press. Used by permission of Lady Empson and the Random House Group Ltd. Excerpts from *The Complete Poems* edited by John Haffenden (Allen Lane, The Penguin Press, 2000) copyright © Estate of William Empson, 2000.

T. S. Eliot: excerpts from *The Waste Land, Sweeney Among the Nightingales, Gerontion, Little Gidding, Ash-Wednesday, Selected Essays, The Use of Poetry and the Use of Criticism* (1964), *Letters*, Volume 1, *On Poetry and Poets* (1957), *A Guide to the Selected Poems of T. S. Eliot, Nightwood* (Introduction) and *The Sacred Wood*. Reproduced by permission of Faber and Faber.

Wallace Stevens: excerpts from *The Emperor of Ice-Cream* and *The Plot Against the Giant* from *Collected Poems of Wallace Stevens*. Reprinted by permission of Faber and Faber.

Philip Larkin: *Love Songs in Age, Home is so Sad*; excerpts from *The Life with a Hole in it*, from *Collected Poems by Philip Larkin, All What Jazz* and *Required Writing*. Reprinted by permission of Faber and Faber.

Dream Song 118, excerpts from *Dream Song 45, 168*, from *The Dream Songs* by John Berryman. Reprinted by permission of Faber and Faber.

Bob Dylan: the following excerpts reproduced by permission of Special Rider Music. All rights reserved. International copyright secured. Reprinted by permission.

Abandoned Love. *Copyright © 1975, 1976 by Ram's Horn Music*

Advice for Geraldine on Her Miscellaneous Birthday. *Copyright © 1964 by Special Rider Music*

Ain't No Man Righteous, No Not One. *Copyright © 1981 by Special Rider Music*

All Along the Watchtower. *Copyright © 1968 by Dwarf Music*

All I Really Want to Do. *Copyright © 1964 by Warner Bros Inc.*

All the Tired Horses. *Copyright © 1970 Big Sky Music*

Angelina. *Copyright © 1981 Special Rider Music*

Are You Ready? *Copyright © 1980 by Special Rider Music*

Baby, I'm in the Mood for You. *Copyright © 1963, 1966 by Warner Bros Inc.; renewed 1991 Special Rider Music*

General Index

Index of Dylan's Songs and Writings

Which Album a Song is on

Abandoned Love: *Biograph*
Ain't No Man Righteous, No Not One: not on an official album
All Along the Watchtower: *John Wesley Harding*
All I Really Want to Do: *Another Side of Bob Dylan*
All the Tired Horses: *Self Portrait*
Angelina: *the bootleg series*, volume 3
Apple Suckling Tree: *The Basement Tapes*
Are You Ready?: *Saved*

Baby, I'm in the Mood for You: *Biograph*
Baby, Let Me Follow You Down: *Bob Dylan*
Baby, Stop Crying: *Street-Legal*
Ballad in Plain D: *Another Side of Bob Dylan*
Ballad of a Thin Man: *Highway 61 Revisited*
Blind Willie McTell: *the bootleg series*, volume 3, and *The Essential Bob Dylan*
   (UK issue only, which has six more songs than the US)
Blowin' in the Wind: *The Freewheelin' Bob Dylan*
Bob Dylan's Dream: *The Freewheelin' Bob Dylan*
Bob Dylan's New Orleans Rag: not on an official album
Boots of Spanish Leather: *The Times They Are A-Changin'*
Brownsville Girl: *Knocked Out Loaded*
Bye and Bye: *"Love And Theft"*

Can You Please Crawl Out Your Window?: *Biograph*, and *The Essential
   Bob Dylan* (UK issue only)
Cat's in the Well: *Under the Red Sky*
Catfish: *the bootleg series*, volume 3
City of Gold: *Masked and Anonymous*, soundtrack
Clean-Cut Kid: *Empire Burlesque*
Clothes Line Saga: *The Basement Tapes*
Country Pie: *Nashville Skyline*
'Cross the Green Mountain: *Gods and Generals*, soundtrack
Cry A While: *"Love And Theft"*

Dark Eyes: *Empire Burlesque*
Day of the Locusts: *New Morning*
Dead Man, Dead Man: *Shot of Love*
Dear Landlord: *John Wesley Harding*
Death is Not the End: *Down in the Groove*
Desolation Row: *Highway 61 Revisited*
Dirge: *Planet Waves*
Disease of Conceit: *Oh Mercy*
Do Right to Me Baby (Do Unto Others): *Slow Train Coming*
Don't Fall Apart on Me Tonight: *Infidels*
Don't Think Twice, It's All Right: *The Freewheelin' Bob Dylan*

Emotionally Yours: *Empire Burlesque*
Eternal Circle: *the bootleg series*, volume 2

Farewell: not on an official album
Farewell, Angelina: *the bootleg series*, volume 2
Foot of Pride: *the bootleg series*, volume 3
Forever Young: *Planet Waves*
Fourth Time Around: *Blonde on Blonde*
From a Buick 6: *Highway 61 Revisited*

Gates of Eden: *Bringing It All Back Home*
Girl of the North Country: *The Freewheelin' Bob Dylan*
Goin' to Acapulco: *The Basement Tapes*
Going, Going, Gone: *Planet Waves*
Gotta Serve Somebody: *Slow Train Coming*

Handy Dandy: *Under the Red Sky*
A Hard Rain's A-Gonna Fall: *The Freewheelin' Bob Dylan*
Hero Blues: not on an official album
Highlands: *Time Out of Mind*
Highway 61 Revisited: *Highway 61 Revisited*
Hurricane: *Desire*

I and I: *Infidels*
I Believe in You: *Slow Train Coming*
I Don't Believe You (She Acts Like We Never Have Met): *Another Side
 of Bob Dylan*

I Dreamed I Saw St. Augustine: *John Wesley Harding*
I Shall Be Free: *The Freewheelin' Bob Dylan*
I Shall Be Free No. 10: *Another Side of Bob Dylan*
I Shall Be Released: *the bootleg series*, volume 2
I Wanna Be Your Lover: *Biograph*
I Want You: *Blonde on Blonde*
Idiot Wind: *Blood on the Tracks*
If Dogs Run Free: *New Morning*
If Not For You: *New Morning*
If You Gotta Go, Go Now: *the bootleg series*, volume 2
I'll Keep It with Mine: *Biograph*
In the Summertime: *Shot of Love*
Isis: *Desire*
It's All Over Now, Baby Blue: *Bringing It All Back Home*

Jokerman: *Infidels*
Just Like Tom Thumb's Blues: *Highway 61 Revisited*

Lay Down Your Weary Tune: *Biograph*
Lay, Lady, Lay: *Nashville Skyline*
Let's Keep It Between Us: not on an official album
License to Kill: *Infidels*
Like a Rolling Stone: *Highway 61 Revisited*
The Lonesome Death of Hattie Carroll: *The Times They Are A-Changin'*
Long Ago, Far Away: not on an official album
Love Minus Zero/No Limit: *Bringing It All Back Home*

Maggie's Farm: *Bringing It All Back Home*
Mama, You Been on My Mind: *the bootleg series*, volume 2
Masters of War: *The Freewheelin' Bob Dylan*
Maybe Someday: *Knocked Out Loaded*
Million Dollar Bash: *The Basement Tapes*
Mr. Tambourine Man: *Bringing It All Back Home*
Moonlight: *"Love And Theft"*
Most of the Time: *Oh Mercy*
Mozambique: *Desire*
My Back Pages: *Another Side of Bob Dylan*

Neighborhood Bully: *Infidels*
New Pony: *Street-Legal*

No Time to Think: *Street-Legal*
North Country Blues: *The Times They Are A-Changin'*
Not Dark Yet: *Time Out of Mind*

Odds and Ends: *The Basement Tapes*
On a Night Like This: *Planet Waves*
On the Road Again: *Bringing It All Back Home*
One More Weekend: *New Morning*
One Too Many Mornings: *The Times They Are A-Changin'*
Only a Pawn in Their Game: *The Times They Are A-Changin'*
Oxford Town: *The Freewheelin' Bob Dylan*

Percy's Song: *Biograph*
Please, Mrs. Henry: *The Basement Tapes*
Pledging My Time: *Blonde on Blonde*
Positively 4th Street: *Greatest Hits* [1], *Biograph*, and *The Essential Bob Dylan*
Precious Angel: *Slow Train Coming*
Pressing On: *Saved*

Quit Your Low Down Ways: *the bootleg series*, volume 1

Ring Them Bells: *Oh Mercy*
Rita May: single (A-side), and *Masterpieces*

Sad-Eyed Lady of the Lowlands: *Blonde on Blonde*
Sara: *Desire*
Saved: *Saved*
Saving Grace: *Saved*
Señor (Tales of Yankee Power): *Street-Legal*
Seven Curses: *the bootleg series*, volume 2
7 Deadly Sins: *Traveling Wilburys*, volume 3
Shooting Star: *Oh Mercy*
Shot of Love: *Shot of Love*
Sign Language: duet with Eric Clapton on his *No Reason to Cry*
Sign on the Window: *New Morning*
Silvio: *Down in the Groove*
Simple Twist of Fate: *Blood on the Tracks*
Slow Train: *Slow Train Coming*

Solid Rock: *Saved*
Someone's Got a Hold of My Heart: *the bootleg series*, volume 3
Something's Burning, Baby: *Empire Burlesque*
Song to Woody: *Bob Dylan*
Stuck Inside of Mobile with the Memphis Blues Again: *Blonde on Blonde*
Subterranean Homesick Blues: *Bringing It All Back Home*
Sugar Baby: *"Love And Theft"*

T. V. Talkin' Song: *Under the Red Sky*
Talkin' John Birch Paranoid Blues: *the bootleg series*, volume 1
Talkin' World War III Blues: *The Freewheelin' Bob Dylan*
Talking New York: *Bob Dylan*
Temporary Like Achilles: *Blonde on Blonde*
Things Have Changed: *The Essential Bob Dylan*
Tight Connection to My Heart (Has Anybody Seen My Love): *Empire Burlesque*
Time Passes Slowly: *New Morning*
The Times They Are A-Changin': *The Times They Are A-Changin'*
Tomorrow Is a Long Time: *More Greatest Hits*
Tonight I'll be Staying Here with You: *Nashville Skyline*
Trouble in Mind: single (B-side)
True Love Tends to Forget: *Street-Legal*
Trust Yourself: *Empire Burlesque*

Under the Red Sky: *Under the Red Sky*
Union Sundown: *Infidels*
Up to Me: *Biograph*

Visions of Johanna: *Blonde on Blonde*

Waitin' for You: *Divine Secrets of the Ya-Ya Sisterhood*, soundtrack
Walkin' Down the Line: *the bootleg series*, volume 1
Watching the River Flow: *More Greatest Hits*
Watered-Down Love: *Shot of Love*
We Better Talk This Over: *Street-Legal*
Went to See the Gypsy: *New Morning*
What Can I Do For You?: *Saved*
What Was It You Wanted?: *Oh Mercy*
When He Returns: *Slow Train Coming*

When I Paint My Masterpiece: *More Greatest Hits*
When the Night Comes Falling from the Sky: *Empire Burlesque*
When the Ship Comes In: *The Times They Are A-Changin'*
When You Gonna Wake Up?: *Slow Train Coming*
Where Are You Tonight? (Journey Through Dark Heat): *Street-Legal*
Who Killed Davey Moore?: *the bootleg series*, volume 1
Winterlude: *New Morning*

Yonder Comes Sin: not on an official album
You Angel You: *Planet Waves*
You're a Big Girl Now: *Blood on the Tracks*
You're Gonna Make Me Lonesome When You Go: *Blood on the Tracks*